# Succeeding with Your Masters Dissertation

## A step-by-step handbook

# Succeeding with Your Masters Dissertation

**A step-by-step handbook**

Fourth edition

*John Biggam*

 Open University Press

Open University Press
McGraw-Hill Education
8th Floor, 338 Euston Road
London
England
NW1 3BH

email: enquiries@openup.co.uk
world wide web: www.openup.co.uk

and Two Penn Plaza, New York, NY 10121-2289, USA

First published 2008
Second edition published 2011
Third edition published 2015
First published in this fourth edition 2017

A catalogue record of this book is available from the British Library

ISBN-13: 978-0-335-24321-1
ISBN-10: 0-33-524321-5
eISBN-978-0-335-24322-8

Library of Congress Cataloging-in-Publication Data
CIP data applied for

Typeset by Transforma Pvt. Ltd., Chennai, India

# Praise Page

"This book is a really excellent and friendly guide through the Master's dissertation process. It is clearly and engagingly written and easily understandable to a student. It also guides students gently from a general understanding in the first chapter, down to a significant level of detail in each subsequent chapter with worked examples and relevant practical tips. It also usefully highlights common mistakes. The book presents a realistic view of undertaking a Master's degree, presenting the generic skills needed for success and acknowledging that life outside the dissertation is complex, messy, and can sometimes get in the way!

It is particularly useful and relevant to my students as, unlike many other books on this topic, it does not ignore practice-based forms of research, in fact the book includes a substantial chapter on practice-as-research in the creative disciplines. This chapter includes software alongside creative arts and is therefore particularly suitable for inter- or multi-disciplinary postgraduates using technology to enhance their existing understanding of a subject (or their practice) through research.

I also really like the fact that the chapter on Abstracts is at the end (where it belongs!) and that students are explicitly told to write it last – no matter how many times I tell my students this, it is a common and recurring mistake!"

*Daisy Abbott, School of Simulation and Visualisation,*
*The Glasgow School of Art, UK*

"The dissertation component of a Master's programme can be very daunting for students. In this book John Biggam demystifies both the concept, and process of a dissertation. Biggam clearly explains the different parts of a dissertation, and offers a pragmatic structure which can be used by students to help frame their ideas. Also, the guidance given in the book is written in a reassuring tone which is never patronising. The summary on good practise in dissertation writing should be particularly useful during the planning stage, and as a final check for students."

*Dr Donna Murray SFHEA, Head of Taught Student*
*Development, Institute for Academic Development,*
*The University of Edinburgh, UK*

# Dedication

This book is dedicated to:

The memory of Hugh Higgins. Shug taught trade union studies at Stow College, Glasgow and, above all else, he knew the value of education.

# Contents

x Contents

# Acknowledgements

The author once again touches his hat in recognition of the part played by students in the creation of this book.

# Chapter  1

# Introduction

> • A Master's dissertation: what is it? • So, what skills do you need to succeed? • Developing your i-skills • Using social media in research • Watch your words! • How to use this book • Further reading • Summary of key points

This chapter fleshes out the meaning of a Master's dissertation, including the generic and specific skills required to complete one (i-skills, in particular, are explored), provides examples of how to exploit social media for research purposes, and underlines the need to keep to your university's prescribed word-limit. How the book is structured is also explained.

## A Master's dissertation: what is it?

A professor was approached by one of her students, who enquired: 'Is it all right to put bullet points in an essay?' Another student queried: 'When you say you want journal articles, how many?' The academic was disappointed that her students required their assessment criteria to be explained in such minutiae (Wojtas, 2006, p. 2). What may appear trivial to a dissertation supervisor can be a source of concern to you, the student. A Master's dissertation traditionally consists of the production of a substantial piece of written work of about 15,000 words. On the other hand, practice-based dissertations, favoured by Art and Drama Schools, normally involve the submission of a created art form such as, for example, a ceramic piece, a musical score or a dance performance, alongside critical commentary of roughly 7,500 words. Irrespective of the type of dissertation you will be submitting – traditional or practice-based – it is likely that this is the first time you have encountered such a task. Therefore, it is important that you understand fully what is required of a Master's dissertation student and, equally, how to manoeuvre safely through the dissertation journey, from grasping an overview of the main phases of writing a dissertation (submitting your dissertation proposal, clarifying your research objectives, writing the Literature Review, etc.) to the finer detail of composing the content for each of these phases. This book provides in-depth guidance on how to complete your dissertation, thus meeting the needs of students eager for practical assistance in this commonplace, but challenging, mode of assessment.

Dissertations have always been a problematic area for students. Students registered for a *taught* Master's programme not only have to cope with their core subject areas, but they are also required, largely through independent study, and within tight time constraints, to complete a substantial dissertation project. Students registered for a Master's by *research*, although they have no taught element to contend with, often find the dissertation process equally stressful. For many Master's students, their venture into the world of the dissertation becomes nothing short of a guessing-game, where the tasks to be completed are difficult to comprehend, and where the final mark awarded for their efforts can be even trickier to fathom. Students are aware that they have to write an *Introduction*, but they are not really sure how to go about it; they sort of know that they have to complete something called a *Literature Review*, but they are at a loss where to start or what it ought to contain, or what will get them good marks; the section on *Research Methods* (necessary if students are implementing their own practical research work to complement their Literature Review) seems so abstract to them, and concepts such as 'positivism' and 'phenomenology', so revered by some supervisors, do not help matters; and so on.

There are many different types of Master's dissertations: some focus on a review of literature relevant to a topic of study; others also require the implementation of practical research; some involve a presentation of the dissertation findings; others, still, oblige you to attend an oral examination. At the heart of each of these types of dissertations is the study of a particular subject, usually selected by you, the student.

How does a Master's qualification differ from an undergraduate qualification? The traditional view of a graduate degree qualification – such as a Bachelor of Arts (B.A.) in Business Studies – is that it is evidence that the holder of the degree has attained a level of *general* knowledge related to the subject area(s) named in the award (Hart, 2006). For instance, a B.A. in History indicates that the holder has a general knowledge, at university level, of history, or certain aspects of history; similarly, a B.A. in Hospitality Management indicates that the holder has a general knowledge of hospitality management. A *Master's* qualification, by contrast, signifies that the holder has reached beyond the acquisition of general knowledge and has *advanced* knowledge of a subject. Master's programmes come in various guises; the more traditional and well-known Master's titles – MSc., MA, MLitt., and MPhil. – are shown in Table 1.1.

This is by no means an exhaustive list of Master's titles found in university programmes. For example, Newcastle University in the UK offers a Master of Music (MMus), while the University of Wollongong in Australia lists a Master of Nursing International (MNurseInt) within its postgraduate portfolio, and the

**Table 1.1** Traditional *Master's* programmes

| Postgraduate title | Latin name | Abbreviation |
| --- | --- | --- |
| Master of Science | *Magister Scientiae* | MSc. |
| Master of Arts | *Magister Artium* | MA |
| Master of Laws | *Legum Magister* | LL.M. |
| Master of Letters | *Magister Litterarum* | MLitt. |
| Master of Philosophy | *Magister Philosophiae* | MPhil. |

University of Nevada in the USA advertises a Master of Education (M.Ed.). The form of the title abbreviation is left to individual institutions, with some institutions using upper case (e.g. MANP), some placing a period after abbreviations (e.g. M.Ed.), while others use a mix of upper and lower case and ignore periods altogether (e.g. MSc).

Confusingly, an MSc. – Master of Science – does not necessarily indicate that the topics studied are science-based, as many business schools within universities now offer MSc. programmes (e.g. MSc. in International Business). Equally confusing is the fact that not all Master's programmes are postgraduate programmes, where a related degree is the usual entrance qualification. For instance, the MA is traditionally viewed as an undergraduate degree in the UK, yet when offered in the USA it is usually offered as a postgraduate qualification. It is also worth noting that universities in the UK and the USA sometimes use different terminology to refer to postgraduate programmes – UK universities stick to the term 'postgraduate' while universities in the USA commonly use the term 'graduate'.

A critical element of most Master's programmes is the requirement to complete a *dissertation*. So, what is a dissertation? *The Concise Oxford Dictionary* (1998, p. 391) defines a dissertation as 'a detailed discourse on a subject, esp. one submitted in partial fulfilment of the requirements of a degree or diploma'. In effect, it appears to be a very long essay. A dissertation is more than an extended essay, however: it is an independent piece of work to be completed (by you, the student) in such a way as to satisfy the examiner(s) that you are a *competent researcher* with advanced knowledge on a specific topic, normally chosen by you, which relates to your Master's programme.

A *Master's* dissertation, as with Master's titles and programmes, can come in many shapes and sizes, varying from university to university, and even within different departments in the same university. The types of Master's dissertations available can include the straightforward Literature Review; or a work-based report wherein you explore a particular problem in an organisation, making practical recommendations based on your findings; or a laboratory-based dissertation, where you carry out experiments and then report on your results; or a dissertation which encompasses both a Literature Review and the collection and analysis of your own primary research data, providing you with the opportunity to compare theory (from your Literature Review) with practice (from your collected primary data, e.g. from interviews or question-naires); or the creation of an art or performance piece (e.g. a sculpture or a dance or a musical piece) which you then evaluate.

Your university should provide you with a Master's handbook containing information on aspects of your dissertation. The handbook will normally clar-ify the maximum length of your dissertation, required format (line spacing, text type and size, style of referencing, page numbering, dissertation structure, etc.), expected minimum content for each major section of your dissertation (e.g. main areas to be covered in your chapter on Research Methods), the department's marking scheme, and details of your role and responsibilities.

Successful completion of a Master's dissertation, however, is more than adhering to technical submission requirements: you need competence in specific *dissertation-related skills* and a certain street savvy about the *rules of the game.*

## So, what skills do you need to succeed?

To pass a Master's dissertation, you need to show that you are a *competent researcher*. On the face of it, this might appear a daunting task, mainly because it is probably the first time that you have attempted an independent piece of research work of this magnitude. A competent researcher is someone who can, in the context of a Master's dissertation, exhibit proficiency in tackling the various phases normally found in the *Dissertation Life Cycle* (DLC) illustrated in Figure 1.1.

Note that the DLC shown in Figure 1.1 represents the traditional approach to completing a dissertation, where students are required to review literature on their topic and then carry out their own survey or case study, etc., but this approach may vary from one institution to another. For instance, some stu-dents may be asked to submit a Contextual Review (see Chapter 5) or a Sys-tematic Review (see Chapter 6) rather than a Literature Review. Also, where Art and Drama Schools allow their students the option of creating an 'artefact' as part of their Master's, two boxes in Figure 1.1 would change:

- 'Empirical Data to be collected?' would be replaced by 'Artefact to be created?'
- 'Design Method(s) for Collection of Empirical Data' in box 3 would be replaced by 'Design *Artefact and* Method(s) for Collection of Empirical Data'

To complete the DLC successfully, you are required to show proficiency in skills specific to each stage of the cycle, i.e. you need to be able to do the following:

- Put forward a credible research proposal (Stage 1).
- Evaluate literature, citing a variety of sources, pertinent to your research objectives (Stage 2).

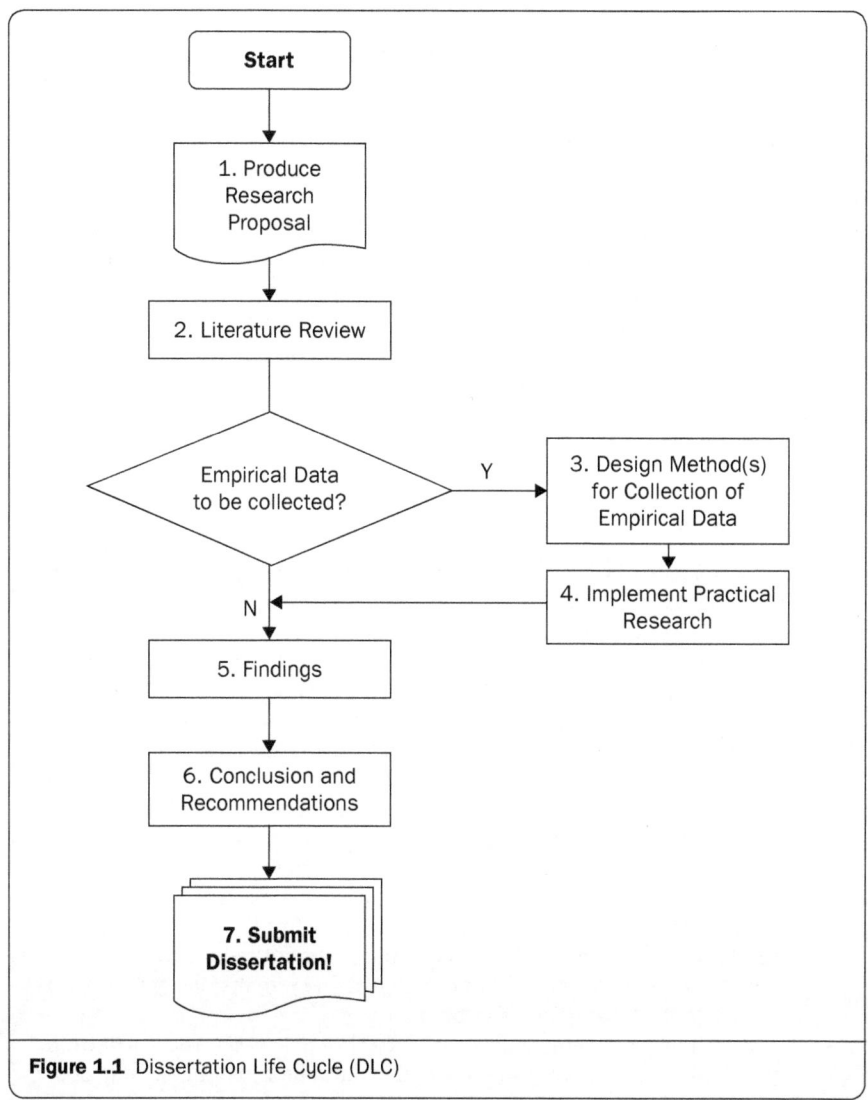

**Figure 1.1** Dissertation Life Cycle (DLC)

- If implementing a traditional dissertation: explain how you will collect and analyse your own research data (Stage 3).
- If implementing practice-based research: explain how you will create your artefact, collect data about your artefact, and analyse the artefact (alternative Stage 3).
- Implement your own empirical research (Stage 4).
- Discuss and analyse your findings (Stage 5).
- Wrap up your research work (Stage 6).

Be aware that the DLC is rarely a straightforward linear process, where the journey from Stage 1 to Stage 7 is smooth and untroubled. The DLC is an iterative process, so get used to the idea that you will be looking over your shoulder to review and improve earlier parts of your dissertation, perhaps as a result of advice from your supervisor or because you have come across additional material that enhances aspects of your dissertation. There are other elements to a dissertation that are not listed as main phases of the DLC but which nonetheless will be included in your final submission, such as an Abstract (sometimes referred to as the Synopsis), an Introduction, and a section listing your References, all of which are discussed in detail later.

As well as skills pertinent to particular stages of the DLC – producing a credible research proposal, critically evaluating literature, etc. – you will also need to acquire *generic* skills, i.e. skills that are useful regardless of the stage of the DLC in which you find yourself:

---

### Generic skills

- *Time-management skills*. You need to be able to manage your time effectively. You do this by adopting two types of time-management perspectives: macro-management and micro-management. *Macro-management* requires that you manage your time in terms of the bigger dissertation picture, guessing intelligently how long you think it will take you to complete each chapter in your dissertation, dovetailing nicely into the required submission date. Whereas macro-management is about the outline, *micro-management* is about the detail, working out the time it will take you to do the sub-sections that go to make up a particular chapter. For example, as a result of a macro approach to managing your time, you might decide that it will take you three weeks to write the introductory chapter to your dissertation and that, switching to micro mode, this chapter will have three parts to it and that you intend allocating one week to each part. Apportioning time slots, in both macro- and micro-management mode, will give you a sense of awareness about what lies ahead, and with that insight comes a sense of control over your dissertation.
- Linked to time-management skills are *organisational skills*. You will have to organise a variety of dissertation-related activities: meetings with your supervisor, the overall structure of your dissertation, sub-sections within each chapter, your ideas and arguments, visits to the library, internet-based activities, reading material, recording sources, meetings with research subjects (e.g. people you might want to interview), and so on.
- *Self-discipline skills*. Keeping to your own timetable of activities will not prove easy. You will have other demands on your time, some predictable (e.g. parties, holidays, other assessments, part-time work, family commitments, etc.), others unpredictable (illness, relationship problems, family issues, etc.). Supervisors are realistic and accept that most students stray from their dissertation work from time to time, but the key to avoiding derailment is self-discipline, and that requires focus and an inner strength to keep going when things are getting on top of you. Time-management

▶

▶ and sound organisation will help you achieve a disciplined approach to your dissertation.

- *Communication skills*, both verbal and written. Communicating your ideas, arguments, rationale for choices made, whether at meetings with your supervisor or in your submitted work, requires clarity of thought and expression. If you cannot say or write what you mean, your work will suffer. When communicating, in whatever form, keep it *simple*, keep it *clear*, and keep it *relevant*. Waffle helps no one, least of all you.
- Effective communication also requires good *listening skills*. It is important that you learn to listen to your supervisor when advice is given – supervisors do not offer advice for the sake of their own health. When your supervisor suggests that perhaps you should alter an aspect of your work in some way, you are being told politely that it is deficient in some respect and that corrective action is required. If you listen carefully, your supervisor is telling you how to gain marks and, equally important, how to avoid losing marks.
- *Presentational skills*. You may be required to present your work to examiners, in which case you ought to be aware of how to produce a skilful presentation, including use of appropriate technologies, voice projection techniques, audience engagement tricks, etc. Presenting your work periodically to friends, and your supervisor, will provide you with invaluable experience in finding out what works and does not work *for you*.
- *Social skills*. Getting on well with people – your supervisor, fellow students, research subjects, departmental secretary, etc. – will ease your dissertation journey.
- *Technical skills*. Internet searching skills, library skills, email and word-processing skills are all essential aspects of dissertation work. Learn to regularly back up your work!
- *Independent learner skills*. The shift from *directed* learning to *independent* learning is the main difference between undergraduate degree work and Master's level work. Most dissertation handbooks highlight the importance of this requirement by including a separate section on your responsibilities, emphasising that it is *your* responsibility to identify a research topic, to put forward a research proposal, to plan and implement *your* dissertation activities, and to be proactive in contacting your supervisor, i.e. to produce an independent piece of research. If you are a final-year undergraduate student considering applying to 'do' a Master's programme, then you need to appreciate that Master's work is very different from undergraduate work. Essentially, the difference is that at undergraduate level the learning primarily takes place through the lecturer (in the form of lectures, seminars, tutorials, laboratories, etc.), whereas at Master's level the learning is mainly student-centred, i.e. there is a major switch of responsibility from the tutor to you, the student; your supervisor acts as an adviser, albeit an important one, but you take the lead. Taking responsibility for your own work can be quite liberating but it requires the development of new skills as well as confidence in your own abilities. By covering the Master's dissertation process in detail, from start to finish, this book provides the practical skills necessary to allow you to approach each stage of your dissertation with confidence.

Dissertation work can be a lonely process, so it is no bad thing to lessen any sense of isolation by sharing your ideas about your work with your fellow students. This can be done more formally and constructively through something called *learner circles* (Biggam, 2007a). This is where a group of students – a learner circle – get together (e.g. over coffee) to discuss their work-in-progress at regular intervals. They can also formally present their work to one other, using modern technology such as a data projector to display PowerPoint presentations, in which case a data projector will be required as well as access to a room at the university. Learner circles are generally led by a supervisor – in effect, enacting group supervision – but they can be set up by students themselves without the participation of a supervisor. Akister *et al.* (2006) produced evidenced-based research showing that students who were supervised in groups were more positive when undertaking their dissertation and had a higher completion rate than students dependent on the more traditional one-to-one supervision model.

Finally, in addition to the aforementioned skills – specific and generic – there are certain personal *qualities* that are necessary prerequisites for the completion of a successful dissertation: *self-motivation, self-confidence*, and *self-centredness*. A lack of motivation will greatly reduce the chances of you completing your dissertation. A Master's dissertation is the type of assessment that demands your time, concentration, and enthusiasm over a lengthy period. A serious lack of genuine interest on your part will cause you to view every task as a tiresome activity, with the first real difficulty encountered probably resulting in the abandonment of your dissertation. On the other hand, if your motivation is strong, and you adopt a positive outlook, you can face every stage with enthusiastic curiosity, making the whole experience enjoyable and, ultimately, fruitful.

Have confidence in your own abilities. Occasional self-doubt is natural – everyone, staff and students, suffers from bouts of self-doubt. It is a natural human condition. In a Master's dissertation, you are required to judge the work of other researchers (for example, within your review of literature). Critiquing the work of respected academics demands a level of self-confidence to allow you to express your views on what these people are saying. One supervisor recalls a student lamenting, 'Who am I to criticise this author when I am just a student and he has such an international reputation?' Your views are as valid as anyone else's, providing, of course, you back them up with supporting evidence! You are on a Master's programme because the admissions tutor has confidence that you will complete your studies. All supervisors start from the default position that their students will produce a solid piece of research, with the proviso that advice given is followed. Nothing pleases supervisors more to see their students pass, and with flying colours at that! Others have faith in your abilities, so have faith in yourself.

There will be occasions during your dissertation journey when those close to you – friends, family members, boyfriends/girlfriends, partners, spouses, etc. – will make demands upon your time. You need to focus on your dissertation. Self-centredness is a quality that will serve you well during your dissertation. From the outset, inform those close to you that you are serious about completing

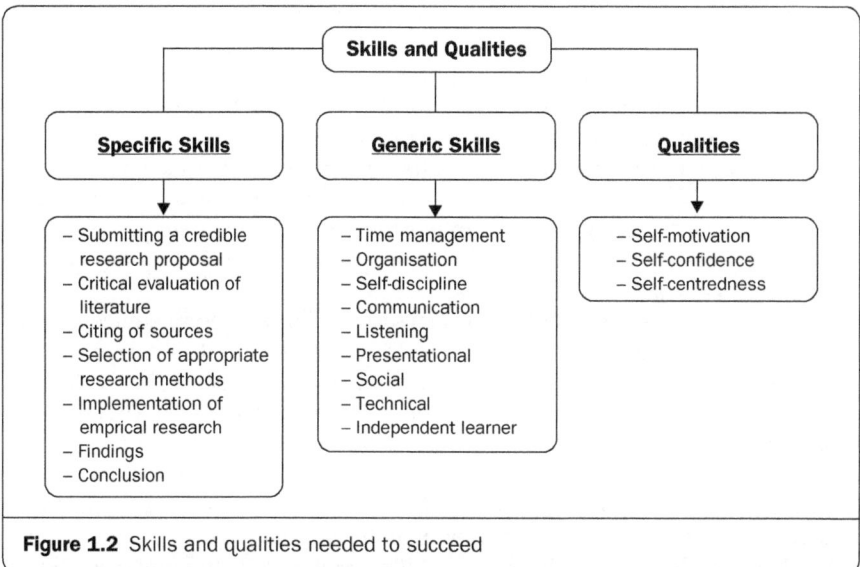

**Figure 1.2** Skills and qualities needed to succeed

your dissertation, that it is a priority for you, and that you will require their understanding and patience as you devote time and energies to give of your best.

Figure 1.2 summarises the combined skills – specific and generic – and personal qualities that you need to complete a winning dissertation.

What of the *rules of the game*? Although this is your first time attempting a Master's dissertation, your supervisor has probably marked hundreds of dissertations. Through experience, supervisors learn how to assess the type of student they are supervising. With each meeting, email communication, telephone conversation, and work-in-progress submitted, your supervisor will form an accumulative picture of your abilities. The rules of the game refer not only to the university's *formal* rules and regulations in terms of your submitted dissertation (word count, page format, style of referencing, etc.) but also to the *informal*, unwritten processes and behaviour that constitute your dissertation journey, such as how you conduct yourself at meetings with your supervisor, the impression you give when you email your supervisor, the quality of your work-in-progress, and so on. For example, if you ask no questions at meetings with your supervisor or spend your time complaining that you cannot find any material on your subject area (a common student complaint!), then you are ignoring the informal rules of the game: if you want to be viewed as a 'good' student, then behave like one. Engage in meaningful discussion, seek clarification, probe perceived wisdom, meet your deadlines. In short, show enthusiasm.

## Developing your i-skills

Information is key to any academic study. Paradoxically, there is so much information available to today's students that the business of collecting and analysing what you need under tight timescales can present something of a headache, leading to *information anxiety*: 'not understanding information; feeling overwhelmed by the amount of information to be understood; not knowing if certain information exists; not knowing where to find it; and knowing where to find it but not having the key to access it' (Girard and Allison, 2008, p. 125). The way to reduce information anxiety is to develop your *information skills* (Figure 1.3). Some of these skills have already been mentioned but they are so important that they are worth exploring in some detail (*literature search skills* and *critiquing skills* are more appropriately covered in Chapter 5: 'The Literature Review').

Information skills are usually associated with literacy competences – the ability to find literature, evaluate it, and communicate it – together with the proficiency to understand your overall information needs. The USA and Australia tend to use the term *information literacy*, while the UK favours the phrase *information skills*, although the terms are interchangeable without any loss of meaning. *Information skills* are often shortened to the more fashionable *i-skills*. Abbreviations are trendy in this modern digital age, particularly ones preceded by 'i-' or 'e-'. Unfortunately, this may cause casual readers to conflate i-skills solely with Internet skills; i-skills do include Internet skills but not exclusively so. JISC (2005, p. 3) defines i-skills as the ability to 'identify, assess, retrieve, evaluate, adapt, organise and communicate information within an iterative context of review and reflection'. Let's look at how to fine-tune your i-skills.

### Determining your information needs

Identifying your information needs is a fundamental skill. To do this you need to reflect on two related questions:

Q1. What information do you require to complete your dissertation?; and
Q2. Where will you get that information?

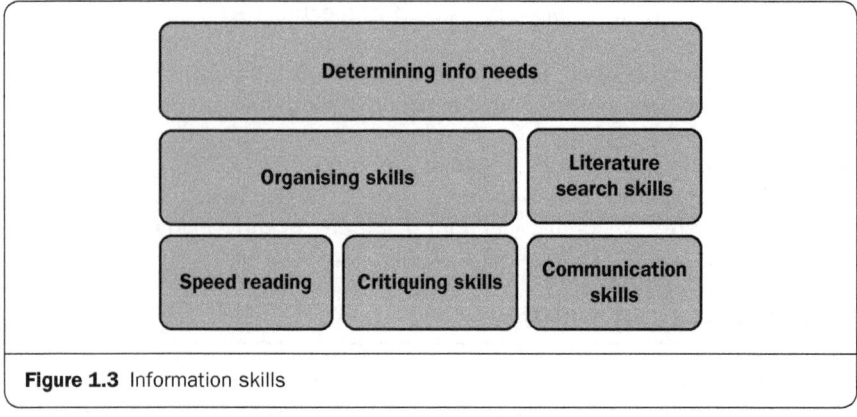

**Figure 1.3** Information skills

The answers to each of these questions will provide helpful signposts to the various roads that you will need to travel in order to complete your dissertation journey.

*Question 1: What information do you need to complete your dissertation?*

It is more useful to answer this question in stages depending on where you are in your dissertation. Before you start your dissertation, you should know the following:

- The maximum length of your dissertation, including margins of error. Dissertation length is normally expressed in words not pages. For example, if the dissertation length is stated as '12,000 words ± 10%', then this means that you can submit a dissertation of length between 10,800 and 13,200 words.
- The submission date, including penalties for late submission (and any requirement to submit a draft).
- Structure and formatting requirements. It is normal practice for institutions to stipulate both the basic structure of your dissertation (Title Page, Abstract, Contents Page, Introduction, etc.) and acceptable formatting (font size, font type, line spacing, etc.).
- Where you can obtain access to past dissertations (university library, departmental office?).
- Supervisor contact details (name, telephone number, room number, email address).
- Your research topic and specific research objectives.

As you progress through your dissertation, your information needs will alter accordingly. Below is a list of some of the information required for each of the chapters/sections in a typical student dissertation:

- Abstract: summary information on your completed dissertation.
- Introduction: background information; research topic and objectives; outline research plan; value of your research.
- Literature Review: *who-is-writing-what* in relation to your research area(s).
- Research Methods: information about your research strategy, data collection techniques, how you intend to analyse your collected data, and limitations of your research.
- Findings: information about the data you collected and how it compares against your Literature Review findings.
- Conclusion: summary conclusions and recommendations.
- References: information on sources used.
- Appendices: supplementary material, e.g. interview questions.

If your dissertation does not involve your own empirical study, then your research information requirements will focus on a literature study.

*Question 2: Where will you get that information?*

The information that you need to complete your dissertation will come from a variety of sources (Figure 1.4):

- University regulations (e.g. information on plagiarism).
- Dissertation handbook (information on structure of dissertation, word count, submission date, responsibilities of supervisor and student, etc.).
- Supervisor (e.g. feedback on your progress).
- Fellow students (e.g. sharing ideas, contacts, etc.).
- Past dissertations (normally to be found in departmental/university library).
- University website (e.g. university regulations).
- Library, Internet, books, articles, reports, lecture notes/handouts.
- University support services (e.g. for courses/leaflets on academic writing skills).
- Research subjects (i.e. those you intend to interview/question/observe, etc.).

Having an awareness of the type of information that you need to complete your dissertation and the knowledge of where to get that information will give you an excellent platform from which to attempt the different chapters in your dissertation with confidence.

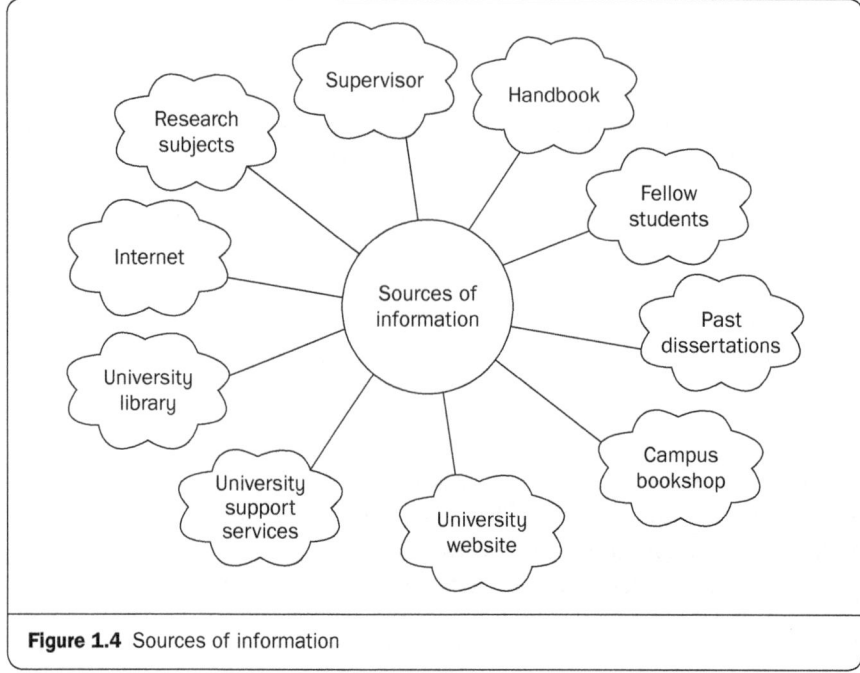

**Figure 1.4** Sources of information

## Organising skills

Your dissertation will not happen by chance. Success in your dissertation will depend, *inter alia*, on the orderly and disciplined approach that you bring to bear on your dissertation. You should be organised on two levels: at a *strategic* level and at an *operational* level. For the former – the strategic level – you should be mindful of the timescales and deadlines you have to meet and have a feel for the general direction your dissertation ought to be heading in. To do that you need to have a plan, however basic or approximate, that plots activities against timescales. Some of these timescales will be dependent on your institution (e.g. final submission date), while others may be self-imposed (e.g. completion of individual dissertation chapters). Having an overall plan allows you to compare your actual progress against your initial timescale of activities and to take corrective action to keep things on track.

Organising your dissertation work at an operational level requires discipline and dedication. Here is a list of techniques and activities to help you organise your work:

- Decide *where* you will do most of your dissertation work. Having a regular place of study will force your brain to associate your study area with dissertation work and make it easier for you to relax and focus quickly on your work. It may be a public library, some favourite corner of your university, a coffee shop or a quiet spot that you have set aside in your student flat. Sitting with your laptop and books in front of the television is not conducive to studying. It has to be some place where you feel comfortable and can achieve a level of peace and privacy to allow you to concentrate.
- Decide *when* you will study. Doing a bit every day, or most days, however little, is a better strategy than leaving your dissertation to some unspecified time in the future ('after the exams' or 'during the holiday period' are common self-delusions). Viewing your dissertation as a normal, everyday activity will keep your research work alive and make it easier to progress. Small, regular incremental steps are more achievable – and will strengthen your confidence – than the alternative of last-minute all-night cramming sessions. Do not be fooled into thinking that you can leave major dissertation activities to some distant period – if you do not have the will-power, motivation or self-discipline to start your dissertation now, then how will that change in the future? One of the reasons students fail their dissertation, or fail to achieve their potential, is a lack of self-discipline, not ability.
- Focus on *specific activities* within *defined timeframes*. For instance: 'Today I will write down my research objectives'. Wandering about in a library or browsing the Internet without any particular purpose, for example, will prove a waste of your time; whereas 'This week I shall visit the university library to see what I can find on Porter's Five Forces' makes much more sense because it is focused on a specific activity within a set timeframe.
- *To-do* lists. Use simple Post-it® notes to indicate your next list of activities. Once an activity is completed, just place a tick (✔) against it. A To-do list will

reinforce a sense of focus, remind you of what you have to do, and give you a picture of the tasks that you have completed and the ones that you have still to complete. You might have a weekly To-do list pinned on your bedroom wall or stuck on the fridge door, e.g.:

Things to do:

1. Write out research objectives!
(Look at other dissertations)
2. Meet with supervisor
(Agree on research objectives)

- *Read* then *write*. Once you have read a sizeable chunk of literature on a particular topic, write it up. Suppose that your dissertation topic is 'The Impact of Outsourcing on Organisations' and that you have agreed with your supervisor that you will review: (i) definitions and types of outsourcing; (ii) positive impacts of outsourcing; (iii) negative impacts of outsourcing; and (iv) models of good practice. Once you have read about the definitions and types of outsourcing, write up what you have found out. Similarly, when you have finished reading about the positive impacts of outsourcing, write that up as well; and so on. That way you will have a record of what you have read and you will gain confidence from seeing your dissertation build up incrementally.
- *Record references.* Creating a reference list is a tedious, but necessary, task. You can make life easier for yourself if you record your references as you go along. If you are quoting an author or summarising their views, then, at the same time, insert the source details in a reference or bibliography list. It is not unknown for students to write about an article, fail to record the source information (e.g. author name, date of publication, article title, etc.), misplace the article, then struggle to find the source details at a later date. You might find it helpful to make up a collection of cards – physical or digital – and keep them close at hand so that you can quickly jot down referencing details: one type for a book source, another for a journal article, a third for web sources, a fourth for newspaper articles, and so on (Figure 1.5 (a), (b), (c) and (d)). As you read an article, for instance, you can use the relevant card to note down details of the source from which you can then, at a more convenient time, add to your reference or bibliography list in your dissertation using the correct referencing format (Harvard, APA, MLA, or whatever).
- *Diary/notebook.* A diary or notebook is useful for noting supervisor appointments, highlighting deadlines, recording activities, and generally scribbling down ideas. It is also evidence that your dissertation is your own work, in the unfortunate event that you are accused of cheating.
- *Keep everything!* Keep a copy of everything that you write, preferably in a separate media recording device. There are good reasons for doing so. You will regularly edit your work and, inevitably, there will be occasions where,

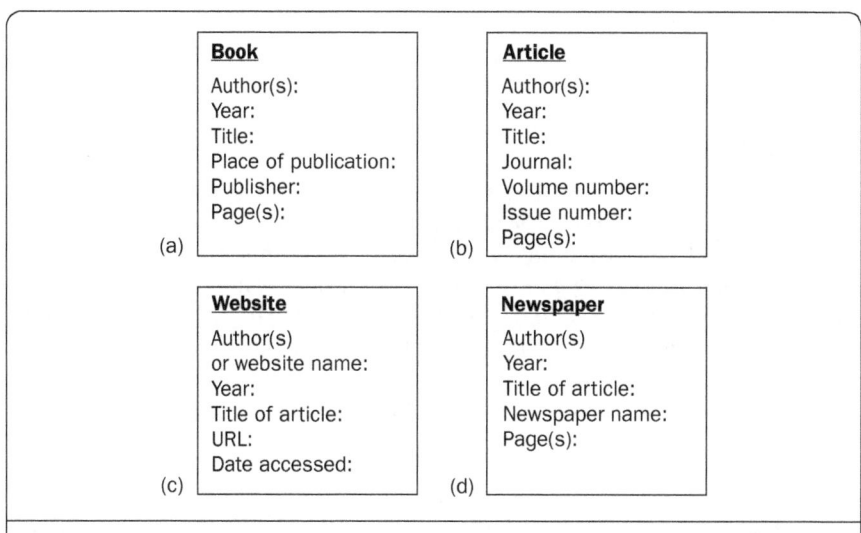

**Figure 1.5** (a) Book template, (b) article template, (c) website template, (d) newspaper template

on reflection, you prefer an earlier version of a sentence or paragraph or section or chapter. If you save your work as you go along – e.g. 'Dissertation' – and make a duplicate copy of specific parts at meaningful intervals – e.g. 'Intro Copy 1', 'Intro Copy 2', 'Intro Final', 'Lit Rev Copy 1', 'Lit Rev Copy 2', 'Lit Rev Copy 3', etc. – then you will have the flexibility to dip in and out of previous versions as you see fit. In the event of a catastrophic failure (e.g. computer malfunction/corrupt media), you will be in a position to recover a recent version of your work. As you progress through your dissertation, these copies will also provide a chronological map of your dissertation journey and, not least, your intellectual development.

Orna and Stevens (2009) recommend having a filing system to manage your research documents. This is a sound idea. In the context of your dissertation, this would involve having folders for each of the following: your institution's dissertation regulations; correspondence with your institution, including emails and feedback from your supervisor; your research proposal; your mind-maps (discussed later in this chapter); your dissertation schedules; external communications (e.g. with research subjects); and a research diary. You would also have a folder to store your dissertation thesis itself, either electronically or physically (or both).

Lastly, as far as is reasonable, set down the *ground rules* for your family and friends. Let them know of your study plans, where and when you are likely to study, emphasising that this time is your time. By doing so you are making them aware of the importance you attach to your dissertation.

## Literature search skills

This is covered in Chapter 5: 'The Literature Review'.

## Speed reading

This might seem a trivial skill but it is one that, once learned, will prove invaluable beyond the life of your dissertation. Speed reading is the ability to read – *and understand* – information quickly. Reading without comprehension is a complete waste of time. Speed reading is not a question of reading so many words per minute: speed reading is relative, i.e. relative to *your* normal reading speed. If you can quicken the rate at which you read, while maintaining a consistent level of comprehension, then you will have improved your reading speed. There are a number of simple techniques that you can use to improve your reading speed:

- As you read a sentence, avoid reading each word aloud in your head. This is called *silent reading* or, in technical jargon, *sub-vocalisation*. Silent reading will slow you down and should be avoided. People who sub-vocalise Read. Each. Word. Or. Small Blocks. Of words. Like This.
- Use your finger! If you quickly move your finger under the sentence that you are reading, from left to right, your reading speed will immediately improve (Figure 1.6). Why? This is because:
  - Your eye and brain, in trying to catch up with your finger, force you to read faster;
  - You no longer read each word separately but see a fluid line of words strung together; and
  - *Skip-back* is reduced, i.e. there is less opportunity for your eyes to wander back over previous words.

  Using your finger to read might feel awkward, even embarrassing, but the more practised you become, the better your ability to speed read. You are in effect asking your brain to fast-forward, a task it is very capable of performing. Students who download audio podcasts of lectures onto their iPods or mobile phones often listen to them at a faster than normal speed. Although the accelerated podcast sounds odd to listen to, it is nonetheless perfectly comprehensible to those students familiar with the technique. The human brain can cope with speed listening and it can also cope with speed reading.
- Skim passages. Skimming is used when you are trying to determine if the article, paper, etc., is relevant to your studies. It involves quickly scanning for words or phrases that suggest that the document, or parts of it at least, are worth reading. This is not speed reading, as that involves actual reading – albeit at an increased rate – and comprehension. There are two types of skimming: headline skimming and passage skimming (see below). You should view skimming as a precursor to speed reading.

- Combine each of the above techniques to form an overall reading strategy. Suppose that you have downloaded a scholarly article from the Internet. An intelligent reading strategy would be to do the following:
  - Skim the title, headings, and sub-headings (this is called headline skimming).
  - Read the abstract (a sort of summary that appears at the start of many academic papers). This is important because you will get a quick understanding of the article's content and, at this early stage, you might discover that the paper is not relevant to your research and so dismiss it without any further ado.
  - If the article is of interest, then start speed reading.
  - If, however, after reading the title, abstract/summary, and main headings, you are still not sure if the article relates to your dissertation topic, then skim passages searching for words or phrases that might suggest otherwise (e.g. 'Picasso', 'Blue Period', 'Causes/Origins').

Reading the title, abstract, and all the headings will allow your brain to adjust to the subject matter and to make quick associations when you apply your speed reading technique.

**Figure 1.6** Student using her finger to speed read!

## Critiquing skills

This is covered in Chapter 5: 'The Literature Review'.

## Communication skills

The ability to communicate your ideas is central to your whole dissertation. Successful communication requires that you clarify your thoughts and present them in a clearly expressed manner. It is difficult to find a simpler and more effective communication technique than *mind-mapping*. Mind-mapping is an easy way to collect and communicate your thoughts and ideas. It is a useful tool to crystallise your own thoughts and as a means of imparting those ideas to your supervisor as you progress through your dissertation. The main tools are a pen and a piece of paper. What is mind-mapping? It is a visual way of arranging information, created by Buzan (1974) in his popular book *Use Your Head*. The general structure of a mind-map is shown in Figure 1.7 (idea taken from Chik *et al.*, 2007).

You create a mind-map by first drawing your *topic circle* in the middle of a piece of paper. In this circle you jot down the topic that you would like to reflect upon or communicate to others, e.g. Picasso's Blue Period (Figure 1.8). Next, you scribble down the issues that you want to express or investigate in relation to your central topic, in this case Picasso's Blue Period. These ideas radiate from the central circle, giving a spidery feel to your drawing (Figure 1.9). Then, to reveal further connecting relationships, you can break down sub-topics as shown in Figure 1.10.

A mind-map is a communication tool that will serve you well throughout your dissertation. It allows you to view a concept, problem, topic, etc., in both overview and detail at the same time while capturing associations or *relatedness* between ideas. In short, it helps to clarify your thinking. It is also a creative tool that can be used to express just about anything in your dissertation: your overall research aim, together with the objectives required to

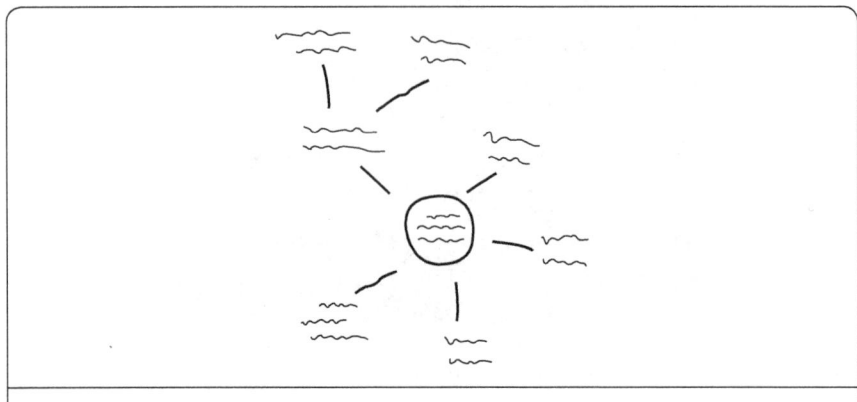

**Figure 1.7** Generic mind-map structure

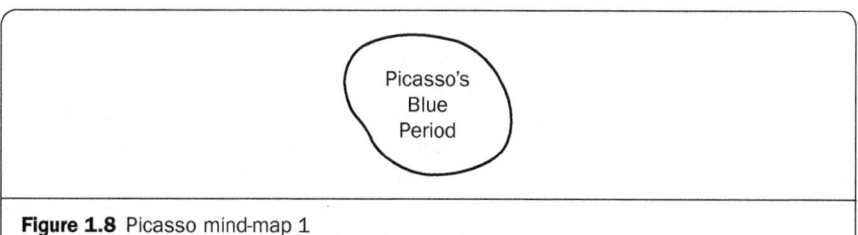

**Figure 1.8** Picasso mind-map 1

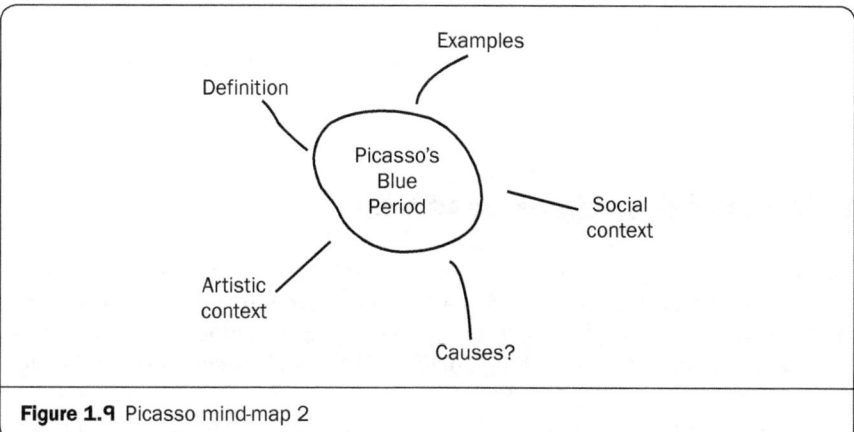

**Figure 1.9** Picasso mind-map 2

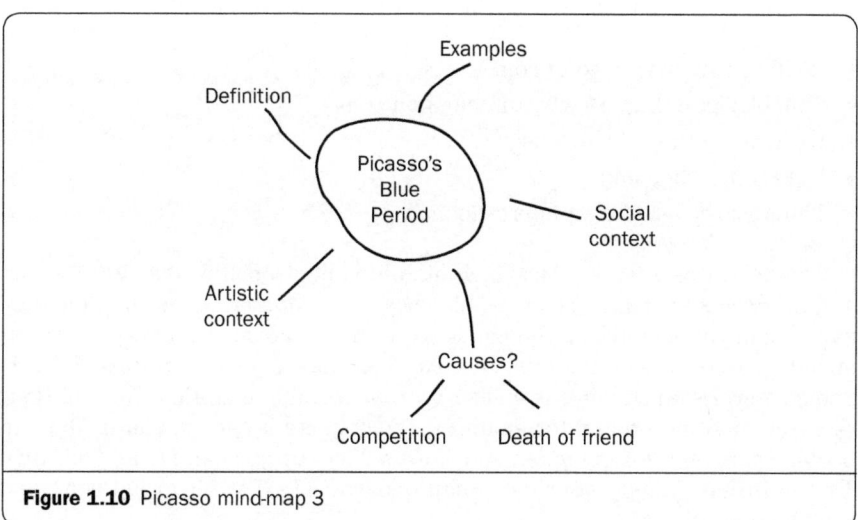

**Figure 1.10** Picasso mind-map 3

meet that aim; the key activities facing you; a breakdown of your Literature Review; your views on a particular author's theory; your chosen research strategy and related data collection techniques; your summary findings, and so on. One student was so taken by the benefits of mind-mapping that, as she progressed through the different stages of her dissertation, she created a one-page mind-map and stuck it up on one wall of her flat, eventually covering the whole wall with a collection of mind-maps, providing a rich visual record of her dissertation journey. She could see the big picture and discuss in detail the various strands of her dissertation. She passed with flying colours.

A mind-map is a sketch, not a work of art. There is no need to use your best handwriting. Draw a rough circle in the centre of a blank page, note down your central concept and away you go! You can use mind-mapping software tools if you want but they cost money, take time to learn, require a computer to use, and can slow down your thought processes. Pen, paper, thinking cap on – that is all you need.

## Using social media in research

Internet search engines, such as Google, and university research databases, both external and internal, are invaluable sources of information. Social media sites are also useful tools. Social media, as the name suggests, allow users to share experiences, views, and information. How could social media sites help you advance your dissertation work?

An obvious place to begin is *bookmarking*. During the course of your dissertation you will gather a great deal of information from all sorts of sources. Bookmarking sites allow you to at least keep track of (i.e. *bookmark*) your web sources. These saved links might access articles, book summaries, comments, photographs or even videos. Popular bookmarking sites include:

- Reddit (http://www.reddit.com/)
- StumbleUpon (http://www.stumbleupon.com/)
- Delicious (https://del.icio.us/)
- Digg (http://digg.com/)
- Pinterest (https://www.pinterest.com/).

Twitter (https://twitter.com/) is a microblogging social media site. You can 'follow' tweets from particular people, even eminent academics: anytime they tweet, you will be notified. You can ask questions and share views on Twitter, including web links to material that can help direct your Literature Review. Some enterprising students even use Twitter to obtain empirical data for their research, inviting others, for example, to complete a questionnaire. You can become part of a group in your specialist subject or you can create your own Twitter group. Joining your university department's Twitter group is a good starting point.

Blogging is another interesting tool for students. A blog typically consists of diary-type articles and a facility for group discussion. You can either access a blog that someone else has created or create your own blog. WordPress (http://wordpress.com/) is a common blogging tool and, importantly, it is free and easy to use. Students have been known to create a blog to report on their trials and tribulations as they progress through their dissertation journey.

Video linkups can be accessed through mobile technologies on the web. Skype (http://www.skype.com/en/) and FaceTime (http://www.apple.com/uk/mac/face-time/) are two such social media tools. The person you wish to communicate with must have the same technology as you. These tools can be used to augment discussions with your supervisor or fellow students or research subjects, particularly if geographical location is an issue.

MeetUp (http://uk.meetup.com/) can be used to form a group of dissertation students from your own university or a neighbouring university who might wish to meet up on a regular basis to discuss common issues.

GoogleDocs (http://docs.google.com/) is a web social media tool that can be used to improve communication between student and supervisor. You can store your dissertation work on GoogleDocs and share it with your supervisor. His or her comments will appear highlighted. Your supervisor can see your dissertation as it builds up and can use it as an on-going focal point before, during, and after supervisory meetings. Office Web Apps (http://office.microsoft.com/en-GB/web-apps/) is an alternative document-sharing tool.

A word of caution about social media sites: be careful what you write and to whom. Everything you write will be forever stored on the web for the whole world to see. Furthermore, be careful about disclosing personal information or confidential data related to your research. Millions of people on social media sites behave in a perfectly responsible manner but try and avoid being one of the few that hits the headlines for the wrong reason!

# Watch your words!

Word-limit has been mentioned before but it is important. Your dissertation handbook will stipulate the maximum number of words that your submitted dissertation must not exceed. For example, it might state that 'The word limit for your dissertation must not exceed 15,000 words.' Or your dissertation guidelines may include a word limit with a leeway of ±10%, meaning that you can be 10% over or under the recommended word limit without suffering any penalty.

It is important that you adhere to the stated dissertation word-length for your Master's dissertation, for a number of reasons. The first, and obvious one, is that you may lose marks for ignoring your institution's guidelines. If your dissertation is to be no more than, say, 10,000 words, and you write 14,000 words, then you may be penalised before your marker actually starts to read your dissertation! The actual penalty incurred depends on your institution's rules and regulations, but it is not uncommon to lose 5–10% of your overall mark.

On the other hand, your institution may ignore your transgression, provided the extra words add value to your dissertation. One supervisor in a university was known to stop reading (and marking!) a dissertation after the allocated words had been reached! Incidentally, if you have exceeded the recommended number of words but your institution's handbook makes no mention of a possible penalty for such a breach, then you may be in a position to argue that you should not be penalised because the lack of a stated penalty implied that none would be given or that the 'recommended' word-length was not to be taken too seriously.

When you start your dissertation, you will have no idea whether or not you will exceed your allocated dissertation word-length. It is only when you are knee-deep in the write-up that you will begin to have an inkling of how quickly you might be eating up your available words. For instance, suppose that you have just finished writing your Literature Review and that it took you 8,000 words to do so. However, from sample dissertations borrowed from the university library, you notice that the number of words used for that particular section was typically in the region of 3,500. As a result of this comparison, you might reasonably conclude that you are in danger of exceeding your overall word-limit. This issue reflects how well you have *macro-managed* and *micro-managed* your activities: the tasks that you have to do (e.g. write your dissertation Introduction, Literature Review, Research Methods chapter, collect data, etc.), the time you expect each of these tasks to take (e.g. one week for the Introduction, six weeks to write the Literature Review, etc.), the outline content for each of these chapters, as well as the number of words that you anticipate each chapter to use up (e.g. 800 words for the Introduction, 3,500 words for the Literature Review, etc.).

Another reason why exceeding the recommended word-length might be unwise is that you may be guilty of *padding*. Sticking to an expected word-length is evidence that you can say something in a given number of words. If you go over the limit, then you may be indicating an inability to write succinctly. Padding occurs when you include irrelevant material just for the sake of 'beefing up' your dissertation. It is easy to spot and will not gain you extra marks. More often than not it will lose you marks because it is an unnecessary distraction interfering with the focus and substance of your dissertation. It is a great temptation to include material that you have read, even if it is not *really* relevant, just because you have gone to the trouble of finding and reading it! Have the courage to reject what is not *really* relevant to your stated research objectives.

What do you do if you suspect that you are going over the recommended dissertation word-length? First of all, remove any padding. If you still consider that you need extra words to play with, then ask permission to exceed the word-length. Write to your supervisor, giving the following information:

A. Your request to exceed the recommended word-length.
B. The (new) word-length that you need to complete your dissertation.
C. The reason(s) for needing the extra words.

Point C above is important. It is insufficient to write, for example, that you need an extra 3,000 words over and above the recommended limit because that is how many words it has taken you, or will take you, to complete your dissertation. It is likely that your supervisor will inform you that you are in the same boat as other students and that you need to reduce your word-length accordingly. On the other hand, if you were to explain, for example, that your data collection was extensive and that to do it justice and capture the richness of the empirical work requires the extra words, then you would be better placed to secure permission to exceed the word-length without penalty. You need to think about the position of your supervisor when you make a request to go over the word-length: if your supervisor allows one student, *without good reason*, to exceed the word-length, then the same opportunity must be made available to all other students on the same programme/course, which makes the idea of a word-length meaningless – hence the need for a valid reason to go beyond the declared limit.

Finally, it is good practice when you have finished your dissertation to include the word-count near the start of your dissertation, somewhere between the cover page and your introductory chapter (check your dissertation handbook for guidance). All word-processing software has a facility for a word-count. Remember to exclude appendices from your word-count, as well as your reference list, as these are not normally included in the word-count.

# How to use this book

Writing a Master's dissertation is not easy: if it were, then it would not be worth doing. Fortunately, there are things that you can do to improve the opportunities to secure impressive marks. This book takes you patiently through the stages of a dissertation – the Dissertation Life Cycle – explaining how to gain (and lose!) marks at each stage of the marking scheme, as well as exploring a worrying feature in many dissertations: plagiarism (Biggam, 2007b). The topics to be covered include: how to reference; preparing for your dissertation (including submitting a research proposal); structuring your dissertation; clarifying your research objectives; writing the introductory chapter; how to write a Literature Review (and an alternative review, called a Contextual Review); how to complete a Systematic Review; describing and justifying your research methods; developing a framework for analysing your empirical research; producing a solid conclusion to your work; writing a competent abstract; preparing for a viva; and the importance of paying attention to the marking scheme. Detailed sample answers, together with relevant practical examples, will be used throughout to illustrate good and bad practice. As you approach each stage of your dissertation, use this book for comprehensive guidance on good and bad practice.

Traditionally, students complete a review of literature and then implement their own empirical study (a case study or survey, etc.). This is reflected in two core chapters within their dissertation (after Chapter 1: Introduction):

Chapter 2: Literature Review
Chapter 3: Research Methods

However, some students are required to review literature and non-literature sources (e.g. drawings, sculptures, musical performances, plays, etc.) as well as create something themselves. These students might prefer to rename the above core chapters to reflect the practical nature of their research:

Chapter 2: Contextual Review
Chapter 3: Research Methods: Practice-based Research

Contextual Reviews are covered in Chapter 5: 'The Literature Review', as they are a variation of a Literature Review. Practice-based research is covered in Chapter 8: 'Research Methods 2: Artist as researcher'.

Also, some other students, particularly those in the health professions, might be asked to complete a Systematic Review instead of a Literature Review. Although a Contextual Review is not a million miles away from a Literature Review, a Systematic Review is a very different beast with clearly defined protocols and procedures. Systematic Reviews are covered in this book in Chapter 6: 'Systematic Reviews'.

Regardless of the type of dissertation you are required to complete, read every chapter in this book. You will then get a more rounded understanding of a Master's dissertation and be better placed to include good practice and advice from a variety of perspectives in your own dissertation.

> **!  A common mistake by students**
>
> In each chapter of this book, common mistakes made by students with regard to dissertation writing will be highlighted. For instance, if it is necessary to warn you about bad practice related to referencing literature, then this book will go on to indicate errors that are commonly made by students when they try and reference works that they have read. For example, a common mistake by students is to ignore the advice of their dissertation supervisor, although one student, after listening attentively to a supervisor explaining the technique of writing a Literature Review, and ending with the words 'blah blah blah', took his supervisor's advice too literally. When the student submitted his Literature Review, it contained only the words 'blah blah blah'! True story.

To get a good start on your dissertation, it is necessary to be well prepared for what lies ahead, otherwise 'a great deal of time can be wasted and goodwill dissipated by inadequate preparation' (Bell, 1993, p. 1). To prepare properly, you will need to appreciate the phases that your work will go through, from outlining your research objectives to concluding your dissertation, and know how to address each of these phases. This book will take you through each phase in detail. By the end of this book, you should fully comprehend the parts that form a dissertation, what makes a good dissertation and, of equal importance, why students often fail to secure easy marks. Writing a dissertation need not be a guessing-game. Writing a dissertation that will achieve pass marks or – even better – excellent marks is as much a science as it is an art. The aim of this book is to lay bare the techniques that you need to undertake a dissertation – in effect, to equip you with the knowledge and skills to produce a highly competent piece of work. There is truth in the old adage *knowledge is power*; in your case, knowledge = marks.

# Further reading

Buzan, T. (2011) *Buzan's study skills: memory maps, memory techniques, speed reading.* Harlow: Pearson Education.

Cottrell, S. (2013) *The study skills handbook.* 4th edn. Basingstoke: Palgrave Macmillan.

Moore, C., Neville, C., Murphy, M. and Connolly, C. (2010) *The ultimate study skills handbook.* Maidenhead: Open University Press.

Ó Dochartaigh, N. (2012) *Internet research skills.* 3rd edn. London: Sage.

Orna, L. and Stevens, G. (2009) *Managing information for research.* 2nd edn. Maidenhead: Open University Press.

Roberts, B. (2007) *Getting the most out of the research experience.* London: Sage.

Rumsey, S. (2008) *How to find information: a guide for researchers.* 2nd edn. Maidenhead: Open University Press.

## Summary of key points

- An undergraduate degree is evidence that the holder has a *general knowledge* of the named subject area; a Master's degree is normally a postgraduate qualification, indicating that the holder has *advanced knowledge* of the named subject area.
- Master's programmes come in many guises (*taught* Master's, Master's by *research*, with a variety of titles – MLitt., MSc., MPhil., MMus., etc. – and different assessment requirements).
- The Master's dissertation is a long research-based essay, typically 10,000–15,000 words in length, though practice-based dissertations are shorter in length.
- The Dissertation Life Cycle (DLC) highlights the conventional stages of the dissertation journey: produce a research proposal, write a Literature Review (or equivalent), design appropriate research methods, implement empirical research, analyse the findings, conclude the research, and submit the completed work.
- To complete a Master's dissertation, you require a combination of generic skills (time-management, organisational, self-discipline, communication, listening, presentational, social, technical, independent learner skills) and personal qualities (self-motivation, self-confidence, and self-centredness), as well as skills specific to dissertation writing (submitting a realistic research proposal, writing a Literature Review/Contextual Review, proper citing of sources, etc.).
- Information skills – or *i-skills* – consist of a number of key skills: the ability to determine your information needs, organising skills, literature search skills, speed reading, critiquing skills, and communication skills.
- *Mind-mapping* is a visual way to clarify and communicate information. Using only a pen and a blank piece of paper, it is easy to display interconnecting relationships between concepts and views.
- Social media tools can be used to access, store, and share information.
- Take cognisance of the maximum word-length for your dissertation. If you anticipate exceeding the word-limit, then request permission from your supervisor, giving your reason(s).

# Chapter  2

# Referencing and plagiarism

> • What is referencing? • In-text referencing • Using Latin abbreviations
> and terms • Creating a reference list • Plagiarism • Further reading
> • Summary of key points

This chapter defines referencing, explains why, where, and how to reference, illustrates the use of Latin abbreviations and terms when referencing, and discusses the thorny issue of plagiarism.

## What is referencing?

Referencing is an essential skill that you need to get to grips with early on. A dissertation is an academic body of work. This means that you will have to show that you are well read in your subject area. To do that, you will be expected to refer to relevant sources. You reference these sources in two places in your dissertation: in the body of your dissertation and at the end of your dissertation. When you cite sources in the body of your dissertation, this is called *in-text citation* or *in-text referencing*. You must also inform the reader where to find these sources and you do so in a reference list at the end of your dissertation.

Referencing – both in-text and in a reference list – is important for a number of reasons: it is evidence that you have read widely; it shows others where your own ideas come from; it lends support for your ideas; it is a way for you to credit the contribution of others; it tells those reading your work where to find the sources you cite; and it keeps you at arm's length from plagiarism. In short, it is a record of your reading.

As a matter of fact, referencing is not limited to work that you have 'read'. Although referencing is normally associated with written material – books, articles, reports, etc. – it also encompasses other sources of information, such as videos, photographs, works of art, exhibitions, software programs, theatrical performances, and so on. When this book refers to 'authors', it therefore takes a wider view of what constitutes an author. 'Author' means whoever wrote or created the work you cite in the body of your dissertation, whether that is a book, an article, a painting, a photograph, etc.

There are many established referencing styles. Table 2.1 lists the main referencing styles used in academia. The Harvard style is one of the more commonly used styles, particularly in the UK, primarily because it is clear and concise and easy to follow. Accordingly, it is the one that will be used for demonstration purposes throughout this book.

The Harvard style is often referred to as the author–date style because author name(s) and year of publication are the two main elements used to identify a source in your in-text narrative. When you cite authors in the body of your work, you need to remember that you are also required to record the details of your sources (author's name, date of publication, title of publication, etc.) in a References section at the back of your dissertation.

Too many students neglect to compile their References section as they go along and as a result get into an unnecessary panic at the end when they cannot locate a source for an in-text reference. When you cite a source (book, journal, website article, etc.), get into the habit of simultaneously updating your References section with full source details (author's name, date of publication, page numbers, etc.).

The obvious chapter where you cite sources is in your Literature Review. There are variations of a Literature Review chapter that serve the same purpose. One is called a Contextual Review (see Chapter 5) and the other is called a Systematic Review (see Chapter 6).

**Table 2.1** Referencing styles

| Referencing style | Usage |
| --- | --- |
| APA (American Psychological Association) | Social Sciences (Economics, Political Science, Geography, Sociology, etc.) |
| Chicago | English, History, and Fine Arts |
| Harvard | A generic style used across most discipline areas |
| IEEE (Institute of Electrical and Electronic Engineers) | Computer Science and Electronics |
| MHRA (Modern Humanities Research Association) MLA (Modern Language Association) | Humanities (Languages, Literature, History, Philosophy, Religion, the Arts, etc.) |
| OSCOLA | Law |
| Vancouver | Medicine and Science |

Every other chapter in your dissertation, though, will, to a lesser extent, make use of literature sources: your dissertation Introduction (to set the scene and justify your research); your chapter on Research Methods (to show that you understand the theory of Research Methods and can justify your chosen research methods); the write-up of your findings (when you compare theory with practice); and in your Conclusion (mainly to remind the reader of core theory).

You really ought to get full marks for your referencing because it is not difficult. Remember, if you are not sure how to reference sources, either in the corpus of your dissertation or in your list of references, then you will lose silly marks. Let us deal first of all with the art of citing sources in the body of your dissertation.

# In-text referencing

In-text referencing is the way you cite sources in the body of your dissertation. There are two ways that you can cite a source: you can either paraphrase your source or quote your source. *Paraphrase* is a word that originates from Greek: *para* means 'beside' or 'side by side', while *phrase* comes from *phrazein*, meaning 'to tell'. Therefore, paraphrase means 'to tell in other words'. If you are reading a newspaper and someone asks you to tell them what is in the news and you tell them in your own words, then you are said to be paraphrasing. When you paraphrase a source in your dissertation, you are expressing someone else's views in your own words. Here is an example of paraphrasing, using Harvard referencing:

Dixon (2017) reminds us that pacifists oppose all forms of warfare.

Note that the author has been identified in two ways: first, by name; and secondly, by giving the year of the source publication (that is why the Harvard style is referred to as the author–date system). This is an example of **direct referencing**, i.e. when you explicitly refer to an author in a sentence.

If an author expresses the same view in more than one publication and you want to record this fact explicitly, then you do so as follows, separating the different years with a semi-colon:

Reardon (2010; 2015) is in favour of capital punishment.

If an author has more than one publication in the same year, then refer to the first one as 'a' and the second one as 'b', and so on, as in:

Thomson (2003a; 2003b) holds consistently to the view that referencing is a dying art.

If an author has more than one publication in one year and a publication in another year, then separate the publications with semi-colons:

Deacon (2006a; 2006b; 2014) complains about political apathy in modern Britain.

**Indirect referencing** occurs when an author cited is enclosed within parentheses. For example:

Twitter is fast replacing the art of face-to-face discourse (Arden, 2016).

Indirect referencing uses a comma to separate the author's surname from year of publication, e.g. *(Arden, 2016)*. Whether you wish to cite a single source directly – by explicitly referring to an author by name – or wish to cite an author indirectly within parentheses, is a matter of personal choice. Here is the same source cited directly then indirectly:

Dixon (2017) reminds us that pacifists oppose all forms of warfare.

Pacifists oppose all forms of warfare (Dixon, 2017).

Indirect referencing, where the author's name is placed in parentheses, can be conveniently used when referring to two or more authors who hold the same view. When two or more authors are grouped together, their works are separated chronologically using semi-colons. For example:

Ryanair changed the face of air travel (Boulder, 2014; Appleston, 2015; Ripley, 2017).

Note that when listing two or more works in parentheses, the works appear in chronological order, i.e. the earliest one first.

To cite a webpage is easy. Here is the general format: (URL, year). For example:

The Scottish government provides ample online advice on how to use technology to enhance teaching (http://www.gov.scot/Topics/Education/Schools/ICTinLearning, 2017).

There will be times when you are reading a source (book, journal article, etc.) and the author of the book/journal/article that you are reading cites another source, a source that you yourself want to cite. For example, suppose that you have in front of you a book written in 2007 by someone called Barlow. Suppose further that Barlow refers to a journal article written in 2004 by someone called MacFarlane and that you also wish to refer to MacFarlane. You do so as follows:

Example (using direct referencing):
MacFarlane (2004, cited in Barlow, 2007) holds the view that . . .

Example (using indirect referencing):
One view expressed forcefully holds that . . . (MacFarlane, 2004 cited in Barlow, 2007) . . .

As well as paraphrasing a source – directly or indirectly – you can also *quote a source*. If the quotation is not too long, you can embed it in a sentence, as follows:

Ryan (2001, p. 10) warns that universities 'must provide professional development to support the academic development of their staff'.

The page number where the quotation is to be found is indicated opposite the year of publication, e.g. *Ryan (2001, p. 10)*. You can use single or double quotation marks – the choice is yours. If the quotation is long, and by that one means it is three or more lines in length, then you ought to place it in a paragraph in its own right and indent it to show that it is a quotation and not just another paragraph. Here is an example of in-text referencing where the quotation requires a separate, indented, paragraph:

This point is made by the Australian National Training Authority (2003, p. 16) when, in a report for their Flexible Learning Framework, they try and identify what they mean by e-Learning (in their case, in relation to vocational training):

> *'e-Learning is a broader concept (than online learning), encompassing a wide set of applications and processes which use all available electronic media to deliver vocational education and training more flexibly. The term 'e-Learning' is now used in the Framework to capture the general intent to support a broad range of electronic media: Internet, intranets, extranets, satellite broadcast, audio/video tape, interactive TV and CD-ROM.'*

You could, if you prefer, cite the source at the end of the quotation as follows. Also, it is not necessary to use quotation marks or *italicise* the text, or even reduce the text size (all optional):

> *'e-Learning is a broader concept (than online learning), encompassing a wide set of applications and processes which use all available electronic media to deliver vocational education and training more flexibly. The term 'e-Learning' is now used in the Framework to capture the general intent to support a broad range of electronic media: Internet, intranets, extranets, satellite broadcast, audio/video tape, interactive TV and CD-ROM'* (Australian National Training Authority, 2003, p. 16).

So, with a long quotation you place it as a paragraph in its own right, indent it, surround it with quotation marks (optional), *italicise* it (optional), and reduce the font size (optional). This makes it easier for your reader to recognise these paragraphs as large quotations and not confuse them with 'normal' paragraphs. It also makes the text stand out – one assumes that if you are inserting a large quotation, then you do so because you consider the quotation to be of some importance.

Sometimes when citing sources, you can include page numbers in the body of your document *and* in your References section at the back of your dissertation. For example, suppose that in your Literature Review you have introduced a quotation and decide to follow common practice by citing the page number beside the author's name, as in:

> Peeke (1984, p. 24) asserts that 'to be a successful researcher can demand a lessening commitment to the task of teaching'.

If the source for this quotation is a journal, then when you are completing your References section you need to record where the whole article (not just the quotation) appears in the journal, as follows:

> Peeke, G. (1984) 'Teacher as researcher', *Educational Research*, 26(1), pp. 24–26.

Similarly, if citing a printed newspaper article, then the page number(s) of the article should appear in the reference list entry. Incidentally, a single 'p.' is used to refer to a specific page (e.g. p. 24), whereas 'pp.' indicates a range of pages (e.g. pp. 24–26). So, pp. 24–26 means the range of pages from page 24 to page 26 inclusive. Interpret 'pp.' to mean 'plural pages', from an old English habit of doubling a letter to indicate the plural of something, itself a derivation of a Latin custom.

You do not need to quote every source you cite. In fact, if you do so, you are in danger of boring the reader and, ironically, lessening the impact of your quotations. If you want your quotations to stand out, be selective in their use. Furthermore, too many quotations eat into your word count, thus reducing the opportunity for your own 'voice' to shine through.

## Using Latin abbreviations and terms

There may be occasions when the source that you are citing in the body of your dissertation has more than one author. If the source has two authors, refer to them in the following way, either directly or indirectly:

> Beatty and Jefferson (2006) . . .
>
> or
>
> . . . (Beatty and Jefferson, 2006).

If there are three or more authors, it is convention to cite the first author and refer to the others using the Latin abbreviation '*et al.*', which means 'and others'. For example:

Hogarth *et al.* (2004) . . .

or

. . . (Hogarth *et al.*, 2004).

The *et al.* indicates that there are at least three authors responsible for this source. The '*et al.*' is actually an abbreviation of '*et alii, et alia*, etc.', hence the period after '*al*' to indicate that the Latin phrase is itself an abbreviation.

However, when you list all your references at the end of your dissertation (in your References section), make sure that you replace the '*et al.*' part of your citations with author names. It is not a crime if you forget, but it does show your supervisor that you are careful about recording all your sources. Your supervisor may not be bothered either way but it is good academic practice; besides, if you were one of the authors who had contributed to a publication but found that in the References section (or Index) your identity was hidden by the Latin abbreviation *et al.*, you would not be a happy bunny.

Some universities ask that you use *et al.* when referring to four or more authors, not three. Thus, in the previous example, Hogarth *et al.* (2004) would indicate at least four authors. Following this advice would mean that you are required to cite up to three authors before using *et al.* You would cite three authors as follows:

Broon, Cunningham and Sands (2017) . . .

or

. . . (Broon, Cunningham and Sands, 2017).

Universities following the advice given by Pears and Shields (2016) in their publication *Cite Them Right* use *et al.* when citing four or more authors.

*Ibid.* is another useful Latin term. To avoid citing the same source, again and again, you can use the Latin word *ibid.* (= *ibidem*), which stands for 'in the same place', to indicate that you are referring to the *previously* cited source, as shown in the text below:

Barlow and Hogarth (2007) argue that mobile technologies are detrimental to the educational development of university students. Perceptions of the advantages of interconnectivity are often exaggerated. Even the simple skill of handwriting has been replaced by ungrammatical abbreviations (*ibid.*).

Yet another Latin term you can exploit is *op. cit.* (= *opere citato*), which means 'from the work cited'. You use *op. cit.* to indicate that you are referring to a source that you have already cited (somewhere) in your dissertation. *Op. cit.* is different from *ibid.* in that *ibid.* refers only to the last source cited (as in the above example) whereas *op. cit.* refers to a source cited *somewhere* previously in your dissertation, i.e. it need not be the last source cited in your discussion. For example:

> Biggam and Murphy (2007) recommend a strategic approach to tackling plagiarism in universities. Other academics adopt a similar position (Thomson, 2003; Edwards, 2005; Smith, 2006). Differences of opinion surface, however, when it comes to deciding upon appropriate levels of punishment for transgressors. Some researchers argue for leniency, claiming that students are victims themselves. Biggam and Murphy (*op. cit.*) refute this line of argument.

*Viz.* and *inter alia*. *Viz.* is an abbreviation of the Latin word *videlicet* (itself a combination of two Latin words, *videre* 'to see' + *licet* 'it is permissible') and its meaning is captured in the terms 'in other words', 'that is to say', and 'namely'. It is used to introduce examples and lists ('namely') or to interpret meaning ('in other words', 'that is to say'). Examples of usage include:

> Robert had a number of complaints that he wished to raise with his boss, *viz.*: his lack of promotion; his unreasonable working hours; and his workload.

> Stevenson (2007) underlined the importance of education, *viz.* that a learned society is better placed to cope with life's challenges.

> Fotheringham's main point, *viz.* that good teachers were born and not made, was much disputed.

Annoyingly, students often use the term viz-a-viz, through comical ignorance, as a synonym for viz. Viz-a-viz is not a valid term, in any language, and has no meaning. *Vis-à-vis* (pronounced vee-a-vee, not veez-a-veez), on the other hand, is a valid term: it is French and means 'face-to-face' and is used when comparing two things (facing each other). The term, therefore, is translated to mean 'compared with' or 'with respect to' or 'in relation to', as in 'Eastern Philosophy *vis-à-vis* Western Philosophy' or 'Boys *vis-à-vis* Girls are a troublesome lot'. A looser interpretation of 'with respect to' allows the term *vis-à-vis* to be linked closely with the word 'namely' as used in the Latin abbreviation *viz.*, for example: 'Questions about the human condition *vis-à-vis* love, jealousy, anger, pity, etc. remain as yet unanswered.'

*Inter alia* is a Latin term meaning 'among other things'. Examples of its use are:

> The supervisor advised his dissertation students, *inter alia*, to improve their grammar.

> Thomson (2004) believed that personal fulfilment depended on, *inter alia*, financial security.

The judge said, *inter alia*, that the time to bring the case to court had elapsed.

Occasionally you will come across a source you wish to quote but you spot a grammatical error or spelling mistake in the source text. It is not your place to correct the use of language but what you can do is quote verbatim and place *sic* in square brackets (i.e. [*sic*]) to indicate that you are aware of the error and that it is not your error. '*Sic*' is Latin (surprise, surprise!) and stands for 'thus, so, as it stands'. It always appears in square brackets, is normally italicised, and has no full stop because it is a proper word in its own right. For example, suppose that you wish to quote the following sentence, written in 1982 by someone called Grearson:

The age of consumerism is well and trully integrated into today's society.

You notice that the word 'trully' is a mis-spelling and should instead read 'truly'. Rather than correct the mistake you can place [*sic*] after the mis-spelling to show that you are aware of the error and that it is not your error:

Grearson (1982, p. 10) captured the essence of Thatcher's Britain when he observed that the 'age of consumerism is well and trully [*sic*] integrated into today's society'.

You would adopt the same approach if you noticed a *grammatical* error in a sentence that you wished to repeat. Suppose someone called Thomson (1996) wrote that 'To have the opportunity to carefully observe people at work is a fruitful activity.' There is a grammatical error in the sentence, occurring in the text 'to carefully observe', where an infinitive has been split (*to* and *observe* should not be separated). A grammatically correct, if somewhat inelegant, version would be: 'To have the opportunity *to observe carefully* people at work is a fruitful activity.' Remember, it is not your job to repair grammatically challenged sources: just quote the source and place '[*sic*]' where the error appears. For example:

Thomson (1996, p. 21) recognises the importance of observation as a research activity: 'To have the opportunity to carefully observe [*sic*] people at work is a fruitful activity.'

It is permissible to use square brackets to insert a word or phrase that makes it clear to the reader what something is referring to, as in:

Stevenson claims that sexism is rife in the modern world: 'too often they [women] are treated as second class citizens'.

You are not altering the source text in any way: all you are doing is attempting to clarify meaning. Be careful, though, that you do not abuse this facility, as it can be very irritating to the reader, particularly if the missing information is trivial and probably known to the intended audience. For example:

> The manager was impressed with his team [Celtic], commenting that '[Henrik] Larsson was brilliant again. The way he tackled [players] and ran back [to aid his team-mates] was awesome. We can't wait for the new [football] season to start again!'

Other Latin abbreviations include *i.e.*, which is Latin for *id est* and means 'that is'. Think of i.e. to mean 'in other words' and so use i.e. when you want to clarify something. Example:

> Casey was wholly prejudiced against women, i.e. he considered them to be physically, intellectually and morally inferior to men.

*e.g.* is Latin for *exempli gratia*, and means 'for the sake of an example', and is used when you want to provide an example, or examples, of something:

> Many literary geniuses hold politically liberal views (e.g. D. H. Lawrence).

> Exercise has undoubted advantages (e.g. keeping fit, weight loss).

*etc.* is Latin for *et cetera*, and means 'and other things', 'and so forth'. Use etc. to indicate continuation of a list that does not need to be fully itemised. For example:

> Romans used many types of weapons: spears, short swords, slings, etc.

(i.e., e.g., and etc. are now so integrated into the English language that we no longer italicise them to indicate their Latin origins.)

*v.i.* is Latin for *vide infra* and means 'see below'. For example:

> Criticisms of capitalism are numerous (*v.i.*, Table 6).

And *v.s.* is Latin for *vide supra* and means 'see above'. For example:

> The history of Ireland has been one of turmoil (*v.s.*) but the future is one of optimism.

Some Latin abbreviations are falling out of favour. *Ibid.* and *op. cit.* are seen less and less in student dissertations. Similarly, *v.i.* and *v.s.* are becoming rare, even in academic publications. More's the pity. Latin has always been viewed as the language of scholars. Anything that helps maintain the fabric of scholarship is worth the effort.

## Creating a reference list

When you cite sources in the body of your dissertation, you are not obliged to identify the type of source (book, newspaper article, etc.) – you are only required to identify the author(s), year of publication and, if quoting a source, the page number. It is at the end of your dissertation – normally after your concluding chapter and before any appendices – where you are required to list all your in-text references and write down the full details for each source. You create a list of references for two main reasons: (1) it is evidence that your sources exist; and (2) it allows others to locate those sources for their own use. You can include a Bibliography instead of a References chapter but it does not make sense to do both. A References chapter is a list of all the sources that you have cited explicitly in the body of your dissertation, whereas a Bibliography lists all the sources that you have referred to explicitly in the body of your text *plus* sources that you have read but not included in the body of your text. It is much simpler to stick with a References chapter but check with your supervisor.

Your References chapter, which tends to appear after your Conclusion chapter and before any Appendices, is, under the Harvard system, an alphabetical list of all your in-text sources including books, journal articles, websites, etc. Typically, your list will start to look something like this:

### References

Alstyne, V., Brynjolfsson, E. and Madnick, S. (1995) 'Why not one big database? Principles of data ownership', *Decision Support Systems*, 15, pp. 267–284.

Anderson, L. W. and Krathwohl, D. R. (2001) *A taxonomy for learning, teaching and assessment: a revision of Bloom's taxonomy of educational objectives.* New York: Longman.

Azouzi, R., Beauregard, R. and D'Amours, S. (2009) 'Exploratory case studies on manufacturing agility in the furniture industry', *Management Research News*, 32(5), pp. 424–39.

Barrett, E. and Bolt, B. (2010) *Practice as research: approaches to creative arts enquiry.* London: Routledge.

Bates, A. (2000) *Managing technological change: strategies for colleges and university leaders.* San Francisco, CA: Jossey-Bass.

Bell, J. (2014) *Doing your research project: a guide for first-time researchers,* 6th edn. Maidenhead: Open University Press.

You need to be aware that there is no definitive approach to recording entries in a reference list, even using the straightforward Harvard system. To illustrate this point, imagine that you have a printed book in front of you and its source details are as follows:

**Author:** Tierney, J.
**Title:** Criminology
**Year published:** 2009
**Publisher:** Longman
**Place of publication:** London

To reference in-text is pretty standard from university to university. An example of in-text referencing (or in-text citation, if you prefer) is as follows:

> Tierney (2009) highlights the legal words and themes required to succeed in the world of criminology.

However, recording the source information for Tierney's book in a reference list can differ slightly depending on where you seek advice. Table 2.2 shows you how Tierney's book would be recorded at the end of your dissertation if you were using Harvard at either the Open University or Anglia Ruskin University, or sought advice from the referencing site Cite This For Me (previously called RefME) or read the book *Cite Them Right* by Pears and Shields (2016).

None of the referencing formats in Table 2.2 are wrong, even though no two are completely identical. Can you spot the differences? Most have the author's initial ending with a period, one doesn't; most have the year of publication enclosed within parentheses, one doesn't; two have a period before the book title, two don't; all have the book title *italicised*; three have a period after the book title, one has a comma; three separate the place of publication and the publisher with a colon, one has a comma.

This lack of a common approach to creating a reference list using Harvard is reflected in wider academia. Nonetheless, the advice in Pears and Shields' book *Cite Them Right* is understandably proving to be very popular in universities, evidenced by the fact that many departments have adopted it as a referencing guide for their students. The Harvard formatting advice given in this book adheres to that found in *Cite Them Right*. Where any differences occur, an explanation is provided.

**Table 2.2** Referencing a book using Harvard style – different advice, different formats

| Institution | Book |
| --- | --- |
| Open University (http://www.open.ac.uk/libraryservices/ documents/Harvard_citation_hlp.pdf) | Tierney, J. (2009) *Criminology*, London, Longman. |
| Anglia Ruskin University (http://libweb.anglia.ac.uk/referencing/ harvard.htm) | Tierney, J., 2009. *Criminology*. London: Longman. |
| Cite This For Me (http://www.citethisforme.com/guides/ harvard/how-to-cite-a-book) | Tierney, J. (2009). *Criminology*. London: Longman. |
| Pears, R. and Shields, G. (2016) *Cite them right: the essential referencing guide*, 10th edn. Basingstoke: Palgrave Macmillan. | Tierney, J. (2009) *Criminology*. London: Longman. |

To give you an idea of how to create entries in your reference list, formatting templates for the more common sources, with completed examples, are given below. A quick-access summary formatting template is given in Appendix A, 'Harvard referencing formats (with examples)'.

## Book

Author's surname, initials (year) *Title of book*. Edition if not first. Place of publication: Publisher.

Examples:

I. Dreyfus, H.L. (2001) *On the internet.* London: Routledge.
II. Neville, C. (2016) *The complete guide to referencing and avoiding plagiarism.* 3rd edn. London: Open University Press.
III. Pears, R. and Shields, G. (2016) *Cite them right: the essential referencing guide.* 10th edn. Basingstoke: Palgrave Macmillan.
IV. Boland, A., Cherry, M. G., and Dickson, R. (2013) *Doing a systematic review.* London: Sage.
V. Hoaglin, D. C. *et al.* (1982) *Data for decisions: information strategies for policymakers.* Cambridge, MA: Abt Books.
VI. *The Concise Oxford Dictionary* (1988) 9th edn. London: BCA.

Note that example V above includes *et al.* Cite Them Right advises that where there are four or more authors, then list the first author – in this case, Hoaglin – and use the Latin term *et al.* (meaning 'and others') to cover the other authors. This is perfectly acceptable. However, if you are one of the 'and others', then you would not be best pleased: contributing authors understandably like to see their work credited. There is nothing wrong with replacing example V with an expanded reference entry to include all contributing authors:

Hoaglin, D. C., Light, R. J., McPeak, B., Mosteller, F. and Stotos, M. A. (1982) *Data for decisions: information strategies for policymakers.* Cambridge, MA: Abt Books.

In the body of your dissertation you would be expected to cite this as Hoaglin *et al.* (1982) but it makes sense to give credit to all authors when you create your reference list.

Note that example VI shows you how to write a reference entry where there is no author – in which case, the title of the book, *italicised*, appears in place of an author.

## E-book

Author's surname, initials (year) *Title of book*. Available at: URL (Downloaded: date).

Taylor, M. and Mayled, J. (2009) *OCR Philosophy of Religion.* Available at: https://www.amazon.co.uk/OCR-Philosophy-Religion-AS-A2/dp/0415468248 (Downloaded: 18 March 2017).

## Conference paper

Author's surname, initials (year) 'Title of paper', *Title of conference*, location, dates of conference. Place of publication: publisher, page(s).

Bloom, J. (2017) 'Picasso turns blue', *Straight from the artist's mouth*, Art Institute, Falkirk, 2–3 March 2015. London: Artbooks, pp. 36–40.

If viewed online:

Author's surname, initials (year) 'Title of paper', *Title of conference*, location, dates of conference, page(s) if available. Available at: URL (Accessed: date).

Conole, G., Oliver, M., Isroff, K. and Ravenscroft, A. (2004) 'Addressing methodological issues in e-learning research', *Proceedings of the Networked Learning Conference*, Lancaster University, UK, 5–7 April. Available at: www.sef.ac.uk/nlc/Proceedings/Symposa4.htm (Accessed: 2 October 2004).

Or (using *et al.*):

Conole, G. *et al.* (2004) 'Addressing methodological issues in e-learning research', *Proceedings of the Networked Learning Conference*, Lancaster University, UK, 5–7 April. Available at: www.sef.ac.uk/nlc/Proceedings/Symposa4.htm (Accessed: 2 October 2004).

*Note 1*: For conference papers you include what information you have. If it is published, give the publishing details; if it is viewed online, give the URL details; if it is not available (or no longer available) online, then give the conference details.

*Note 2*: In the above example, '*Proceedings of*' means from a collection of conference papers.

## Government publication

When governments, or departments, outsource research (normally to universities), then author name(s) will be credited in the government publication and so should be included in your reference.

Author's surname, initials (year) *Title of publication*, Place of publication: Publisher.

Goulding, A. and Cavanagh, B. (2013) *Charges reported under the Offensive Behaviour at Football and Threatening Communications (Scotland) Act in 2012–2013*, Edinburgh: Scottish Government Social Research.

If viewed online:

Author's surname, initials (year) *Title of publication*, Place of publication: Publisher. Available at: URL (Accessed: date).

Sosenko, F., Livingstone, N. and Fitzpatrick, S. (2013) *Overview of food aid provision in Scotland*, Edinburgh: Scottish Government Social Research. Available at: http://www.gov.scot/Resource/0044/00440458.pdf (Accessed: 23 July 2016).

However, many government publications are written internally by government departments and therefore author names are often unavailable, in which case you should give the name of the source department (Health Department) or service (e.g. Justice Analytical Services) or, failing that, the government (e.g. Government of Canada) in place of author name(s):

Department/service/government name (year) *Title of publication*, Place of publication: Publisher.

Justice Analytical Services (2013) *An examination of the evidence of sectarianism in Scotland*, Edinburgh: Scottish Government Social Research.

If viewed online:

Department/service/govt name (year) *Title of publication*, Place of publication: Publisher. Available at: URL (Accessed: date).

Animal Health and Welfare Division (2013) *Promoting responsible dog ownership in Scotland: microchipping and other measures*, Edinburgh: APS Group Scotland. Available at: http://www.gov.scot/Resource/0044/00441549.pdf (Accessed: 14 March 2014).

### Journal paper

Author's surname, initials (year) 'Title of article', *Name of Journal*, volume number (issue number), page(s).

Burns, E. (1994) 'Information assets, technology and organisation', *Management Science*, 40(12), pp. 645–662.

Tearle, P., Dillon, P. and Davies, N. (1999) 'Use of information technology by English university teachers. Developments and trends at the time of the National Inquiry into Higher Education', *Journal of Further and Higher Education*, 23(1), pp. 5–15.

*Note*: interpret 'pp.' to mean plural pages. So, pp. 5–15 means pages 5 to 15 inclusive.

If viewed online:

Author's surname, initials (year) 'Title of article', *Name of Journal*, volume number (issue number), page(s) if available. Available at: URL (Accessed: date).

Gwatipeda, J. and Barbier, E. B. (2013) 'Environmental regulation of a global pollution externality in a bilateral trade environment: the case of global warming, China and the US', *Economics*, 2013 (60), pp. 1–43. Available at: http://www.economics-ejournal.org/economics/discussionpapers/2013-60 (Accessed: 18 August 2014).

### Newspaper article

Author's surname, initials (year) 'Title of article', *Name of Newspaper*, day and month of publication, page(s).

Riddell, P. and Webster, P. (2006) 'Support for Labour at lowest level since 1992', *The Times*, 9 May, p. 2.

Where the author is not known, then use the name of the newspaper instead:

*Name of newspaper* (year) 'Title of article', day and month of publication, page(s).

*The Indian Agra News* (2007) 'Carbon footprints and economic globalisation', 18 April, p. 4.

If viewed online:

Author's surname, initials (year) 'Title of article', *Name of Newspaper*, day and month of publication. Available at: URL (Accessed: date).

McArdle, H. (2013) 'Officials say new Forth bridge on schedule', *The Herald*, 30 December. Available at: http://www.heraldscotland.com/news/13138238.Officials_say_new_Forth_bridge_on_schedule/ (Accessed: 30 December 2013).

Where the author is not known, then use the name of the newspaper instead:

*Name of newspaper* (year) 'Title of article', day and month of publication. Available at: URL (Accessed: date).

*The Herald* (2013) 'Officials say new Forth bridge on schedule', 30 December. Available at: http://www.heraldscotland.com/news/13138238.Officials_say_new_Forth_bridge_on_schedule/ (Accessed: 30 December 2013).

### Theses and dissertations

Author's name, initials (year) *Title of thesis/dissertation*. Level of award. Institution.

Aitken, R. (2008) *Exploring the role of laughter in the workplace*. PhD thesis. Inverclyde University.

Denison, F. (2013) *Poetry and sedition*. Undergraduate dissertation. Inverclyde University.

If viewed online:

Author's name, initials (year) *Title of thesis/dissertation*. Level of award. Institution. Available at: URL (Accessed: date).

Bancroft, T.D. (2016) *Scalar short-term memory*. PhD thesis. Wilfrid Laurier University. Available at: http://scholars.wlu.ca/cgi/viewcontent. cgi?article=2927&context=etd (Accessed: 24 March 2017).

### Website

Author's name, initials (year) *Title of web page*. Available at: URL (Accessed: date).

Brender, A. (2004) *Speakers promote distance education to audiences in Asia*. Available at: www.chronicle.com (Accessed: 12 November 2015).

You might find that you have little information to write down, or that the content you once read on a website is no longer there. Do not worry: write down as much as you can at the time the link was available. If there is no author for the web article/source, then record the name of the website or organisation instead. For example:

The eLearning Centre (2005) *eLearning is taking giant steps*, etc.

The next example is about recording a source that is referred to in another source, such as when you read in a book about a journal article and you want to cite the journal article. To record the example where Barlow, on page 634 of her book written in 2007, cites a journal article written by MacFarlane in 2004, and where you have also referred to MacFarlane in the body of your text, then you can note this information in your References section by first of all citing MacFarlane's journal article – because that is the source that most interests you – to which you add the phrase 'cited in', followed by Barlow's book in the normal way, as follows:

MacFarlane, K. (2004) 'Alternative approach to cognitive learning', *Organisational Learning*, 10(2), pp. 23–45, cited in Barlow, A. (2007) *Learning Again*. Buckingham: Open University Press, p. 634.

Suppose that you have read a book entitled *Classic and Cavalier: Essays on Jonson and the Sons of Ben*. This book consists of chapters written by different authors and you want to record the reference details for the chapter that was written by Martin Elsky, which appears from page 31 to page 44 in the book. You reference the chapter first, then indicate the general book details, as follows (this time just use *in* rather than *cited in* because the article appears *in* a book):

> Elsky, M. (1982) 'Words, things, and names: Jonson's poetry and philosophical grammar', in Summers, C. J. and Pebworth, T. L. (eds) *Classic and cavalier: essays on Jonson and the sons of Ben.* Pittsburgh, PA: University of Pittsburgh Press, pp. 31–44.

All the above formatting examples relate to common sources of information regularly sought out by students. However, those students who want to cite and reference 'things', such as art works, exhibitions, photographs, computer programs, software apps, etc., also need advice. In Chapter 5, 'The Literature Review', advice is given on how to cite these *things* in the body of a dissertation and how to include their full source details in a reference list.

Citing and referencing sources is a laborious, mechanical process but it is a necessary part of being viewed as a competent researcher. The upside is that there are easy marks up for grabs. Appendix A contains common Harvard referencing templates, with examples, largely based on the approach advanced in the book *Cite Them Right* by Pears and Shields (2016).

# Plagiarism

In the world of education, technology is ubiquitous. Understandably, student use of the Internet in support of their academic studies is common in universities; indeed, it is to be encouraged. A student interested in Renaissance Art can be transported, with a few clicks of the keyboard, to a virtual gallery depicting works by Michelangelo, Leonardo Da Vinci, and Raphael. The same student can also access expert opinion on these artists. However, with a similar paucity of keyboard clicks, students can effortlessly cut and paste material found on the Internet, insert it into their assignments, and submit it as their own work. Herein lies the danger with coursework and easy access to the Internet: avenues and opportunities exist that may tempt you to cheat.

Plagiarism is a problem in the world of education. School pupils reared on the Internet, and the move to continuous assessment, have contributed towards a 'cut and paste' generation. Another important factor is the rise of bespoke essay-writing websites. Mostrous and Kenber (2016), in an article for *The Times*, reported that nearly 50,000 students in Britain's universities had been caught cheating over a three-year period. Given the seriousness of this issue, this is a topic that needs to be addressed.

In the first instance, what counts as plagiarism? It needs to be emphasised that it is your institution's view of what counts as plagiarism that matters most, not the one that is given in this book. Marshall and Garry (2006) raise the point that many students themselves appear to be unaware of what constitutes plagiarism. Find out what your institution has to say on the issue of plagiarism, including the consequences of such cheating if you are caught. If you are not sure what counts as plagiarism, then be proactive and ask your dissertation supervisor to give you examples of what constitutes plagiarism and how to avoid it.

Defining plagiarism is not an abstract, academic exercise: how an institution views what counts and does not count as plagiarism can impact not only on a student's future career – your future – but also on an institution's reputation. A simple definition of plagiarism is given by Northwestern University (http://www.northwestern.edu/provost/policies/academic-integrity/how-to-avoid-plagiarism.html, 2017): 'submitting material that in part or whole is not entirely one's own work without attributing those same portions to their correct source'. An obvious example of plagiarism that would meet this definition is where a student takes a complete chapter from a book, changes the authorship, and then submits it as his or her own work.

What if a student 'stole' a paragraph (not a whole chapter) from another source, copied it into their essay, word for word, and failed to cite the source. Is that plagiarism? For example:

*Cryptography may seem to be a black art requiring extremely complex mathematics and access to supercomputers. This may be the case for professional cryptanalysts (codebreakers). But for ordinary people who need to protect data, cryptography can be a strong, often simple to use, and sometimes freely available tool.*

The actual source of the text can be found on the web, but the source is not acknowledged; nor is the verbatim text placed in quotation marks. The absence of source information and quotation marks implies personal authorship. Even though it may only form a small part of an essay, it is still plagiarism ('submitting material . . . in part . . .'). By the same logic, even if a student copies one sentence verbatim without acknowledgement, that is still plagiarism. It is a simple fact: taking someone else's text, word for word, without due acknowledgement, is a straightforward act of plagiarism.

The types of plagiarism that students get up to include:

- Copying whole paragraphs verbatim, e.g.:
  *There is no easy or perfect solution, no silver bullet to eliminate the security risks involved in operating online. Threats and vulnerabilities are constantly evolving. Moreover, a network is as weak as its weakest point: if one component is compromised, whether deliberately or by accident, everyone connected to the network is potentially exposed.*
- Copying whole sentences verbatim, e.g.:
  *Cryptography, when used properly, should increase security in a computing environment.*
- Copying part of a sentence verbatim, e.g.:
  Conflicting goals appear to be in operation too: *security is based on limiting access, while collaborative computing requires that access to certain information be shared.*

- Copying text verbatim – paragraph/sentence/part sentence – and citing the author, but failing to use quotation marks (thereby giving the false impression that you are paraphrasing), e.g.:

  *Digital signatures can be a significant tool in reducing online fraud and can thereby increase consumer confidence in online transactions (Kontogeorgou and Alexiou, 2002). Digital signatures should enable enforceable online transactions since any specific transaction is tightly if not irrevocably tied to a specific person. Businesses utilising digital signatures should be more efficient – since online transaction processes will be streamlined – and consequently highly competitive again thereby increasing their appeal to consumers.*

So there you have it: copying text verbatim without sufficient acknowledgement of the actual source(s) is plagiarism, irrespective of whether it occurs in part of a sentence, a complete sentence or a full paragraph.

Plagiarism also occurs when you use someone else's ideas without sufficiently acknowledging the source. *Sufficient acknowledgement* means that when you are using someone else's ideas, you have to cite the author, and that when you are using another author's words, you do two things: cite the author and place the verbatim text in quotation marks.

If someone retorts that 'surely copying part of a sentence, or even a complete sentence, can't be treated as plagiarism?', then they are confusing an act of plagiarism with how a university intends to respond to such an act. If an institution chooses to ignore it, then that is an institution's choice but the institution's action cannot be justified on the basis that there is no plagiarism (unless the institution defines plagiarism differently). Such a decision could only then be based on the grounds that the institution does not take that level of plagiarism seriously. If verbatim text has been copied and is insufficiently acknowledged, then plagiarism has occurred, pure and simple. That is different from deciding how an institution reacts to such incidences, and that depends on the extent of the plagiarism unearthed in a student's assessment.

When institutions define plagiarism as occurring if '*substantial* unacknowledged incorporation . . .' has taken place, they are in fact implying that a certain level of plagiarism is acceptable. In one sense this is understandable: do you instigate formal proceedings against a student for plagiarising a sentence? Clearly not, but you ought to educate the student that this is careless and bad academic practice. It does, however, beg the question as to what is an acceptable or unacceptable level of plagiarism.

One must accept, though, that it can sometimes be difficult to rewrite sentences, particularly short sentences, and to paraphrase in a way that does not lose the gist of what the original text is saying and at the same time does not cross the boundary into plagiarism. This is the problem with paraphrasing: you can unknowingly wander across the divide between receiving praise for skilful interpretation of an author's work and finding yourself accused of plagiarism. Nonetheless, lazy paraphrasing can result in plagiarism and ought not to be encouraged.

Plagiarism can still occur even where there is good paraphrasing of wording and sentence structure but the author's original ideas are not cited. Bone (2003, p. 1) emphasises that students 'need a very clear understanding of . . . where to draw the line between copying and paraphrasing'.

Another facet of plagiarism that needs to be confronted is the notion that only *deliberate* plagiarism counts as plagiarism, for reasons that will be made clear. *The Concise Oxford Dictionary* (1998) records that the word *plagiarise* has its roots in the Latin word *plagiarius*, meaning 'kidnapper', and goes on to define the verb plagiarise as the attempt to 'take and use (the thoughts, writings, inventions, etc. of another person) as one's own'. Given that you cannot kidnap someone accidentally, this definition, in effect, implies that when a student commits plagiarism, they are engaging in a *deliberate* attempt to kidnap the work of another and pass it off as their own. The Council of Writing Program Administrators (Bone, 2003, p. 2) concurs with this interpretation when it defines plagiarism as occurring when 'a writer deliberately uses someone else's language, ideas, or other original (not common-knowledge) material without acknowledgement'.

However, to include student intentions in a definition of plagiarism is to conflate the act of plagiarism with student motivation. If a student copies pages of text verbatim and neither cites the author(s) nor uses quotation marks, then plagiarism has occurred regardless of the student's intentions. When determining incidents of plagiarism, universities need to separate a student's intentions from the act of plagiarism. Student intent should only come in to play when determining punishment, not when making the initial judgement. A work is either plagiarised or it is not: in coming to that decision the motivation of the student is irrelevant. The UK Centre for Legal Education (Bone, 2003, p. 1) supports this position when it concludes that the 'general view, however, is that intention is irrelevant – and that leniency should relate to the penalty and not to the definition', warning that 'otherwise serious cases of plagiarism in the final year may be defended by statements such as *I didn't know* or *I must have accidentally pasted those three pages across*'.

If a university decides that intention should be an important factor in deciding whether to accuse a student of plagiarism, then there is the potential for staff to be influenced by whether or not they like the student or perceive the student to be a 'good' student, or consider it unlikely that such a student could behave in this manner. Such extraneous influences may expose universities to the criticism that students are being treated differently based on staff perceptions of student personality traits rather than on evidence of plagiarism.

The Council of Writing Program Administrators (*op. cit.*, p. 2) makes the valid point that one should distinguish between plagiarism and a student's incompetent attempt at citation, and that the latter is not plagiarism:

> A student who attempts (even if clumsily) to identify and credit his or her source, but who misuses a specific citation format or incorrectly

*uses quotation marks, or other forms of identifying material taken from other sources, has not plagiarized. Instead such a student should be considered to have failed to cite and document sources appropriately.*

Students who mix and match in-text referencing styles or who slightly misplace quotation marks or, when collating sources in a References section, italicise the wrong part of a journal reference or fail to record a Web source properly, are guilty of incompetence, not plagiarism.

On the other hand, if you decide to 'cut and paste' work from the Internet but stop short of crediting your sources, then you are inviting the charge of plagiarism, as illustrated in the top half of Figure 2.1. It is an easy matter, and good academic practice, to go that bit further and quote or paraphrase your borrowed text, formally identify your source, and update your list of references (the bottom half of Figure 2.1).

Identifying what counts as plagiarism is not as daunting as it may appear. Although there are degrees of plagiarism, essentially copying text verbatim without sufficient acknowledgement is plagiarism. What is more problematic is determining when inadequate paraphrasing has occurred. Although it should be discouraged, it is a lesser form of plagiarism, particularly when the original source is cited; and in this case the remedy lies in education rather than punishment.

Plagiarism is easy to do, and it is also easy to detect. You should be aware that many universities are now turning to the use of plagiarism-catching software such as Turnitin (www.turnitin.com). Staff submit a student's essay to

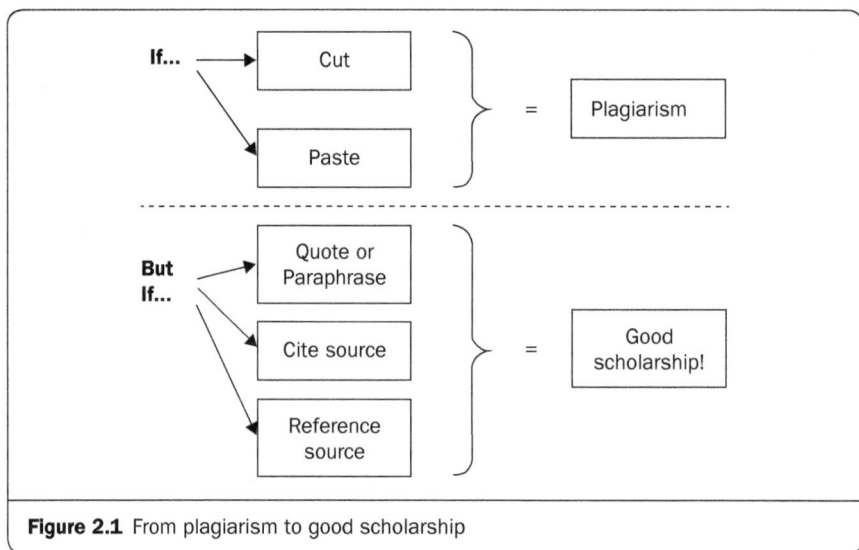

**Figure 2.1** From plagiarism to good scholarship

the Turnitin facility and within minutes an Originality Report is produced, providing a 'similarity index' of matching text (e.g. 80%), with colour-coding of text that was found elsewhere. The software does not accuse the student of plagiarising. That is left to the institution. Turnitin is proving a useful resource in the efficient detection of incidences of plagiarism.

Biggam and McCann (2010) also used Turnitin as a broader educational tool, allowing students, throughout the duration of their dissertation, to submit their individual dissertation chapters and to learn from the Turnitin feedback without fear of punishment from university authorities. Staff also had access to the student submissions and results and took the opportunity to discuss specific examples of suspected plagiarism, including consultation on wider academic issues: dissertation development, evidence of critical evaluation, referencing, grammar, and so on. This approach allowed staff and students to iron out suspected incidents of plagiarism without fear of punishment prior to submission of the final dissertation. The company supplying Turnitin has adopted a similar educational approach – their online site is now given the softer heading 'Feedback Studio'.

That is not to argue that technology is the solution to the thorny matter of plagiarism – the problem is far more complex than that, involving student education, ethics, cultural issues, law, staff training, what it means to learn, concepts of ownership, and so on. Supervisors are key players in reducing any student tendency to sleep-walk into plagiarism: your supervisor can inform you of the university rules on plagiarism, what is allowed and what is not allowed, guidance on how to paraphrase, as well as emphasising the importance of full and proper referencing. Staff can also set up the Turnitin system to allow students to submit their own work for self-checking, encouraging students to view such software as a useful facility rather than an attempt by their university to 'catch them at it'. Turnitin's database is impressive: over 600 million student papers and 60 billion indexed Web pages.

What if you are accused of plagiarism?

(a) Obtain a copy of your institution's plagiarism procedures.
(b) Ascertain how your institution defines plagiarism.
(c) If there are mitigating circumstances, then they must be considered (e.g. bereavement, ill health, disability, plagiarism not explained to you, cultural issues, financial problems, computer failure).
(d) Your hearing must be fair and in line with natural justice (Jones, 2006); and
(e) Any penalties applied must be consistent and not arbitrary (Deech, 2006).
(f) As a last resort – when all internal avenues have been exhausted – there is normally an independent body you can complain to if you are not happy about how you have been treated by your university (see Table 2.3 for examples of such bodies).

**Table 2.3** External independent adjudicators

| Country | Body | Website |
|---|---|---|
| England and Wales | The Office of the Independent Adjudicator (OIA) | http://www.oiahe.org.uk |
| Scotland | The Scottish Public Services Ombudsman (SPSO) | http://www.spso.org.uk/college-or-university-complaints |
| Northern Ireland | The Northern Ireland Public Services Ombudsman (NIPSO) | https://nipso.org.uk |
| Ireland | Office of the Ombudsman | http://www.ombudsman.gov.ie/en/ |
| Australia | State or Territory Ombudsman | E.g. NSW Ombudsman: https://www.ombo.nsw.gov.au |
| New Zealand | Ombudsman | http://www.ombudsman.parliament.nz |
| Canada | Province Ombudsman | E.g. Ombudsman Ontario: https://www.ombudsman.on.ca/Home.aspx |

Hopefully, this discussion has added to your understanding of plagiarism, at different levels. At the root of all this is the simple fact that you need to give credit where credit is due! To do that, you need to reference your sources.

# Further reading

McMillan, K. and Weyers, J. (2013) *How to cite, reference & avoid plagiarism.* Harlow: Pearson Education.

Neville, C. (2016) *The complete guide to referencing and avoiding plagiarism.* 3rd edn. Maidenhead: Open University Press.

Pears, R. and Shields, G. (2016) *Cite them right: the essential referencing guide.* 10th edn. Basingstoke: Palgrave Macmillan.

Pecorari, D. (2013) *Teaching to avoid plagiarism: how to promote good source use.* Maidenhead: Open University Press.

Williams, K. and Carroll, J. (2009) *Referencing and understanding plagiarism.* Basingstoke: Palgrave Macmillan.

## Summary of key points

- The art of *referencing* is an important part of writing an accomplished dissertation. Referencing is good scholarship because it is transparent evidence of knowledge rooted in verifiable sources.
- Different types of referencing systems are used in academia but one of the most popular is the *Harvard System*, referred to more commonly as the *author–date* system.
- *Reference your sources in two places*: within the body of your dissertation where you summarily *cite your sources* (e.g. using the author–date system) and in a References section at the end of your dissertation where you provide the full *source details*.
- The use of Latin terms can add an intellectual flavour to your dissertation, provided they are applied correctly. In the context of a dissertation, useful Latin terms include: *et al.*, *ibid.*, *op. cit.*, *viz.*, *inter alia*, [*sic*], *i.e.*, *e.g.*, *etc.*, *v.i.*, and *v.s.*
- *Plagiarism is to be avoided*. Essentially, it occurs when someone else's words and/or ideas are used without due acknowledgement.
- *To avoid plagiarism, cite your sources* in the body of your dissertation – using paraphrasing or direct quotations – and record the *full reference details* in your References section (or Bibliography) at the back of your dissertation.
- Students who have been accused of plagiarism and are unhappy about how their case has been dealt with by their institution can seek redress, *as a last resort*, through an ombudsman.

# Chapter  3

# Preparing for your dissertation

• *Putting together your research proposal* • *Producing a dissertation template* • *Supervision: roles, responsibilities, and meetings* • *An emotional journey* • *Further reading* • *Summary of key points*

This chapter tells you how to put together a research proposal, introduces the usefulness of a dissertation template, clarifies the nature of the relationship between supervisor and student and how to get the best out of supervision meetings, and concludes by openly highlighting the ups and downs experienced by all dissertation students at one time or another, with the message that it is an emotional journey as well as an academic one – so be prepared for the ride!

## Putting together your research proposal

The first thing you need to do is to put together a research proposal. A good research proposal will:

- Have a **working title**.
- Sketch some **background information** on the general area that interests you, including the rationale behind why you want to focus on a particular aspect of this subject.
- Identify the **overall aim** of your research (i.e. what you are trying to achieve). Some institutions prefer this to be in the form of a research question.
- Specify the **individual objectives** required to help you achieve your overall research aim. Once again, some institutions prefer these individual research objectives to be in the form of questions.

- Outline how you will carry out your research (this is called your **research methods**), including a **timetable** to complete these activities.
- State the **value** of your intended research (you need to convince your supervisor that this is an area worthy of study).
- Indicate whether or not **ethical issues** arise from the proposal (e.g. research on vulnerable citizens) and, if so, how these issues will be addressed to meet the institution's ethical standards in research. Some institutions prefer that a separate form on ethics is completed and submitted alongside the dissertation proposal form; other institutions include a question on ethics in the dissertation proposal form itself.
- List **key literature** that you have referred to in producing your proposal, either in the form of a Reference list (i.e. a list of all the literature explicitly cited in the body of your research proposal) or a Bibliography list (i.e. a list of all the literature explicitly referred to in the body of your proposal and other literature that has impacted on your thinking).

Note the words 'sketch', 'identify', 'specify', 'outline', 'estimate', 'state', 'indicate', and 'list': they emphasise that your proposal is a brief document, normally consisting of one or two pages in length, three at most. Nearly all universities provide their dissertation students with a formal dissertation proposal form to complete. The format of the form may differ from institution to institution but the elements to be completed will generally reflect the checklist above. Some institutions will ask you to complete and submit the dissertation proposal online, in which case they will normally provide a template; others may ask you to submit a structured two- or three-page essay explaining your research proposal; others, still, may provide something in-between, such as an online template to complete, print out, sign, and submit to a specific office. Appendix B contains an example of a typical dissertation proposal form.

From the perspective of your institution, the submitted research proposal serves a number of functions: (a) it allows the department to determine if your research proposal meets the institution's academic standards; (b) it facilitates the allocation of supervisors; and (c) it reassures the department that any ethical issues arising from the proposal are addressed to the institution's satisfaction.

### Research proposal: working title

The main task in your research proposal is to clarify whatever it is that you propose to research. That is not as easy as it sounds. First of all, you need to pick a subject that grabs your attention; then you have to focus on some aspect of that subject which you think is worth researching (though you should be aware that some institutions will decide your topic and focus of research, particularly in the hard sciences); and finally, you need to communicate those ideas in writing.

Suppose that you are a Master's student interested in choosing e-Learning as the subject of your dissertation. However, you cannot do a dissertation on the general subject of e-Learning: your proposal must be *focused* on a particular aspect of e-Learning. If you were keen to investigate how academic staff are being prepared to cope with the challenge of e-Learning in the university environment, then that would qualify as an example of a focused project. On the other hand, if you were interested in 'studying computer security', then that would be too vague for a research proposal; changing that to 'a study of online banking breaches and their impact on customer confidence' would form a much more focused area of study.

The trick to achieving 'research focus' is, first of all, to think of a subject area in general terms (e-Learning, computer security, drugs, domestic abuse, absence management, etc.) and then to home in on a particular aspect of that subject. Even then, you cannot simply pluck your research focus out of thin air. You need to do some background reading to determine if it is a topic worthy of study. For example, published reports and articles may highlight the need for more research in your chosen field, thereby providing evidence in support of your research proposal.

Your working title should succinctly capture the essence of what you want to research for your dissertation. Remember, think of your dissertation topic in general terms (e.g. greenhouse gases) and then identify the aspect of that general topic you want to research (e.g. cost of prevention to UK agriculture and forestry). Join both together to form a title (e.g. *The Cost of Greenhouse Gas Mitigation to UK Agriculture and Forestry*). You can, if you wish, convert your title into a question (e.g. *What is the Cost of Greenhouse Gas Mitigation to UK Agriculture and Forestry?*). It is very common, although not obligatory, for students to state in their title where they will get their empirical data (e.g. *The Impact of a Management Bonus Culture on the General Public: A Case Study of The Royal Bank of Scotland*).

To give you an idea of the sort of titles that students produce, below are some example titles:

1  *Accommodation for the Homeless: Analysis and Design Criteria*
2  *Testing for European Equivalence: An Evaluation of Budget Deficits and Economic Growth*
3  *Perceptions of Community Policing in the Rural Areas*
4  *First Time Fathers' Experiences of Parenthood.*

It is easy to work out how each of these titles was formed from the general (research area) to the specific (research focus). Let's take the first example: *Accommodation for the Homeless: Analysis and Design Criteria*. The formation of the title is clever in its simplicity. The general area is on the left-hand side of the colon (*Accommodation for the Homeless*) and the specific focus is on the right-hand side of the colon (*Analysis and Design Criteria*). You could adopt that technique yourself.

Example 2, *Testing for European Equivalence: An Evaluation of Budget Deficits and Economic Growth*, follows the exact same pattern as the first: the general subject area is on the left-hand side of the colon (*Testing for European*

*Equivalence*) and the specific research focus is on the right-hand side (*An Evaluation of Budget Deficits and Economic Growth*).

Example 3 also moves from the general to the specific but dispenses with the colon. This example – *Perceptions of Community Policing in the Rural Areas* – could easily have been rewritten with a colon without loss of meaning (*Perceptions of Community Policing: The Rural Areas*).

Example 4, *First Time Fathers' Experiences of Parenthood*, also contains the general and the specific (but with the specific focus mentioned first in the title – *First Time Fathers' Experiences*) and could have been rewritten with the general topic first, followed by the specific, with a colon separating one from the other, as in *Parenthood: First Time Fathers' Experiences*.

Table 3.1 breaks down the development of each of these titles. It is a matter of personal choice whether you start with the general topic and move to the specific focus (as in examples 1, 2, and 3) or emphasise the specific focus of your research first and then the general topic (as in example 4), or use colons to separate one from the other (as in examples 1 and 2) or dispense with colons altogether (as in examples 3 and 4). However, what you must do somewhere in your title is state your general research topic and the specific research focus.

Let's look at one more title:

*External Branding in the Public Sector: A Case Study in the NHS.*

In this case, the general topic (*External Branding*) and the specific focus (*in the Public Sector*) appear before the colon. However, the student has decided to highlight the empirical research strategy (*A Case Study in the NHS*). Broken down into its component parts, this title format is:

general + specific: example of specific.

**Table 3.1**  Developing a dissertation title

| Example | General topic area | Specific topic focus | Title |
|---|---|---|---|
| 1 | Accommodation for the Homeless | Analysis and Design Criteria | Accommodation for the Homeless: Analysis and Design Criteria |
| 2 | Testing for European Equivalence | An Evaluation of Budget Deficits and Economic Growth | Testing for European Equivalence: An Evaluation of Budget Deficits and Economic Growth |
| 3 | Perceptions of Community Policing | in the Rural Areas | Perceptions of Community Policing in the Rural Areas |
| 4 | Parenthood | First Time Fathers' Experiences | First Time Fathers' Experiences of Parenthood |

If you follow any one of the approaches outlined above, it should not take you long to produce a title for your dissertation.

### Research proposal: background information

One of the questions that your supervisor will ask is, 'Why do you want to study this area?' or 'What evidence is there that it is an area worthy of study?' This is where your background reading comes into play: you show your supervisor that you have done some initial reading by explaining the rationale behind your proposal. For instance – staying with the e-Learning example (how academic staff are coping with the challenge of e-Learning) – it could be that there are conflicting reports on the progress of e-Learning in universities, with some literature enthusiastically predicting exponential growth in e-Learning as a means of teaching students and staff embracing e-Learning with open arms; while other literature casts doubt on such views, complaining that evidence of staff opinions and experiences of e-Learning are anecdotal in nature (perhaps universities are blowing their own trumpets!) and that proper research needs to be carried out to find out how staff are indeed being prepared to meet this technological challenge.

Do not get carried away with your background information. This is not the place for a comprehensive review of literature on your dissertation topic. There will be plenty of opportunity in your dissertation to implement such a review. Instead, be brief and be focused. All that you need do at this stage is to provide some basic contextual information, supported by relevant literature, to justify your proposal. It is only once you start your dissertation proper – that is, after your proposal has been accepted – that you will be required to complete a substantial review of literature. Nonetheless, this background work will cite appropriate literature sources. Your completed dissertation proposal – from title to list of key references – may stretch from one to three pages, or more depending on your institution's requirements, and your background information will form part of that submission.

To recap: your background information (1) sets the scene by briefly explaining the general topic area (e.g. e-Learning in universities), (2) introduces the focus of that area that interests you (e.g. preparing staff to deliver e-Learning to students), and (3) emphasises why that specific area is important to research (e.g. growth in digital learning, implications if staff are unprepared, need for in-depth study to ascertain staff views, etc.).

### Research proposal: overall research aim

Next, after completing your background information, you will need to clarify your *overall research aim* and the *specific objectives* that you intend to meet in order to achieve your overall research aim. For now, let us concentrate on your overall research aim. Your overall research aim will be a general statement. It tends to derive from your focus of study. In the e-Learning example, where the research focus is to investigate how academic staff are being prepared to cope with the challenge of e-Learning in the university environment, the research aim could be expressed as follows:

Research Focus: To investigate issues surrounding the preparation of university academic staff for e-Learning.

Research Aim: The overall aim of this research is to advance an understanding of the issues surrounding the preparation of university academic staff to support student e-Learning.

An easy way to arrive at your overall research aim is to break the process down into simple steps (Figure 3.1), starting with Step 1 where you think up one word to identify your research area of interest (e.g. 'e-security'). Then, in Step 2, you include other words to give a clearer idea of your research focus (e.g. 'e-security', 'breaches', 'customer confidence', 'online banking'). Finally, in Step 3, you connect these words to form a sentence (e.g. 'This is a study of e-security breaches and their impact on customer confidence in the area of online banking'). It is then an easy matter to go one step further and incorporate the phrase 'overall aim' (abbreviated to 'aim' if you want) to produce your formal research aim:

> The overall aim of this research is to explore the impact of e-security breaches on customer confidence related to online banking.

Suppose that you change your mind and opt instead to write a dissertation on how to achieve a top mark in employment aptitude tests in the banking industry (somewhere in your dissertation you will need to define what you mean by a 'top mark'). To arrive at your overall research aim, you repeat the same process as before, this time concentrating on your new topic (Figure 3.2).

Once again, think of your research area in terms of one word or label (e.g. 'Employment aptitude tests'); add other words to help clarify your research focus (e.g. 'Top marks', 'What it takes'; 'Banking industry'); and then write this as a sentence (e.g. 'This is a study of what it takes to achieve a top mark in employment aptitude tests in the banking industry'). Finally, convert this into a formal research statement:

> The overall aim of this research is to elucidate the elements that determine a top mark in employment aptitude tests set by the banking industry.

**Figure 3.1** Writing your overall research aim

If you follow this process, it will allow you to arrive with confidence at your overall research aim. For easy reference it is summarised below:

Step 1:   Think of your research area in terms of *one* word or label
Step 2:   *Add* other words to help clarify the context/focus of your research
Step 3:   *Connect* these words to form a sentence
Step 4:   *Convert* this sentence into a formal research statement, 'The overall aim of this research . . .'

Professional researchers often prefer to formulate their overall research aim as a *research question*. Rather than writing that your overall research aim

**Figure 3.2** Another example of how to arrive at your research aim

is 'to elucidate the elements that determine a top mark in employment aptitude tests set by the banking industry', you could instead articulate your
research task in the following terms: 'Central to this research is the need to
answer the question, *what are the elements that determine a top mark in
employment aptitude tests set by the banking industry?*' In this way, you
may find your research task to be more focused and driven in the pursuit of
an answer.

The next sub-section will explain how to achieve your (overall) research aim
by breaking it down into specific, achievable *research objectives*.

## Research proposal: specific research objectives

You now have to decide what it is you need to do to fulfil your overall research aim. This means that you have to list your individual objectives, or mini aims. Listed below are objectives for the aforementioned e-Learning dissertation (which we will develop and use for reference throughout this book):

Specifically, within the context of higher education, the objectives of this research are to:

1 *Identify* the forces driving e-Learning and the barriers to the successful delivery of e-Learning programmes
2 *Evaluate critically* models and frameworks relevant to supporting academic staff in coping with e-Learning
3 *Explore* staff stakeholder views and practices related to e-Learning preparation, including drivers and barriers to e-Learning
4 *Formulate* recommendations on staff preparation issues.

(An obvious title for the dissertation on e-Learning would be: 'Preparing University Academic Staff for e-Learning: A Study of Drivers, Barriers and Preparation Models/Frameworks'.)

The words in italics – *Identify, Evaluate, Explore*, and *Formulate* – are called *keywords*. There are a whole host of keywords that are available for student use, such as *analyse, assess, classify, discuss, establish, evaluate, explore, identify, investigate, outline*, etc. They indicate the type of research activity to be carried out for each objective. For instance, *identify* normally suggests a straightforward academic undertaking, one not requiring much in the way of intellectual discussion and debate. In the above example, the student would use the first objective to set the scene by ascertaining the forces driving e-Learning and the barriers to the successful delivery of e-Learning (even then, the student would link the drivers and barriers to the focus of the research study, i.e. staff preparation for e-Learning).

It is important that for your big objectives you incorporate keywords that indicate in-depth academic study. Keywords such as *evaluate critically, assess critically, explore, investigate, examine*, all imply an appropriate level of intellectual activity suitable for a Master's dissertation. Hence, Objectives 2 and 3 use the keywords *evaluate critically* and *explore* to indicate to the supervisor that these objectives will form the main part of the student's research. Objective 4 uses quite a neutral keyword – *formulate* – implying that as a result of the research, the student will make certain recommendations.

Students tend to have difficulty expressing their overall research aim and related individual objectives. It is not unknown for students to be still grappling with their objectives long after their dissertation has started. At a first supervisor meeting, one student presented her objectives in the following general format:

1 Identify . . .
2 Identify . . .
3 Identify . . .
4 Identify . . .
5 Identify . . .
6 Identify . . .
7 Identify . . .

By including the keyword *identify* for each objective, she was suggesting that her work would be superficial in nature throughout and so lacking in depth. Normally, using *identify* is acceptable for an early, straightforward objective (e.g. to provide background information) but try and steer clear of using such a keyword in other objectives, although there are exceptions. For example, it may be that you wish to identify the causes of a particular military conflict and that such a task is widely recognised as a significant achievement in itself; in which case the use of *identify* would be an acceptable keyword.

The above student also had far too many individual objectives (seven in total). This would have had the effect of either making her work appear piecemeal or unnecessarily increasing her workload. Four or five objectives are typical. Another student did not specifically list his research objectives, but instead, in a woolly and long-winded paragraph, vaguely referred to about ten general things he wanted to do. He was trying to cover too many issues; in any case, he ought to have clearly itemised his individual research objectives.

If your objectives are not in a convenient format (e.g. in the form of a numbered list), then you are making the reader work hard to understand what your research is all about and, furthermore, you are not making it easier for your marker, or yourself for that matter, to ascertain if, at the end of your dissertation, you have completed your stated objectives. In addition, if you do not enumerate and clarify your research objectives, then, at a later stage in your dissertation, you may find yourself straying from what you think you set out to study. Play safe and make life easy for everybody: by all means explain your research objectives but write them down in a numbered list.

Students who are unaware of how to list their research objectives tend to use vague terms (such as 'do' or 'study' or 'look at' or 'learn about') that shed inadequate light on the level or type of research study to be undertaken. Using fuzzy terms will make it difficult for you – and your marker – to determine if, at the final submission of your work, you have met your initial research objectives (e.g. how does your supervisor assess whether or not you have 'looked at' your area of study?).

In general, a good approach to listing objectives is to:

• Use a simple keyword for the first objective (such as *identify, define, outline,* etc.) to provide the background to your subject area.

- For the other objectives (excluding the last one) use keywords that suggest in-depth research work (such as *explore, evaluate critically, assess critically, examine, analyse, determine,* etc.).
- And for the final objective use a keyword that links easily to a concluding activity (such as *formulate, produce, develop, recommend, propose, advance,* etc.).

If you have converted your overall aim into a specific research question to which you seek an answer, then you may also decide to similarly reshape your individual research objectives into sub-questions, the answers to which will help you meet your main research question.

Appendix C contains a list of keywords to use with your research objectives.

## Research proposal: research methods

As well as containing background information, your overall research aim, and your individual research objectives, your research proposal should also include information on how you intend to do your research. The latter is referred to as your *research method(s)*. For your research proposal, it is only necessary to provide an outline of how you will conduct your research. Two ways in which Master's dissertation students are normally expected to implement their research work are as follows:

1 Through a Literature Review.
2 By collecting empirical data.

The Literature Review forms one of the main activities in your formal dissertation and is where you seek out literature from a number of sources (journals, books, conference proceedings, etc.) with a view to showing that you are well read in your topic area and that you can describe and evaluate sources germane to your research. However, within your research proposal, in terms of identifying your research methods, all that is required is that you indicate the types of literature you will be sourcing in your full study. You do this in two ways: by referring to general kinds of literature sources, such as books, journals, conference proceedings, reports, etc., and by giving some examples of the literature that you will use in your research. You should also indicate the library databases that you will need access to in order to support your research. Thus, if your research area was in the area of computer security, you might make the following statement:

> This study will make use of a number of literature sources, including reference to pertinent books, journals, reports, conference proceedings and Government publications. Examples of these include: periodical surveys such as the DTI Information Security Breaches Survey and the CSI/FBI Computer Security Breaches Survey; the *Journal of Information Warfare*; and proceedings of the European Conference on Information Warfare. Importantly, the following library databases will, in particular, be utilised to support this research: Web of Science, ACM Digital Library, and Computer and Information Systems Abstracts (ProQuest).

If your research does not depend solely on a Literature Review (i.e. it is not based purely on theory) and you intend collecting your own data to supplement your Literature Review findings – which is the normal position for a Master's dissertation – then you must state the research approach you intend adopting to accomplish your empirical (i.e. practical) work. For example, if you know that you will be implementing an experiment of some sort, then say so. Similarly, if you expect to explore a specific type of organisation (e.g. a university), then once again state this. You also ought to articulate how you expect to collect your data (questionnaires, interviews, etc.). For example:

> The primary data (i.e. empirical data) will be collected through a case study. A case study is a study of a single unit (Cohen *et al.*, 2005), allowing exploratory research in depth (Yin, 2003). The case unit will consist of an academic department within Inverclyde University.

> The means of collecting primary data will be based on an initial questionnaire from which a subset of the target population will be subject to a detailed follow-up interview. In addition, a number of elite staff – those responsible for the success of e-Learning and staff training – will be interviewed. The combination of a literature review and empirical research will allow theory and practice to be compared, from which a rich picture of academic staff preparation should emerge.

> This research does not aim to generalise the status of staff preparation in e-Learning but, instead, seeks an in-depth understanding of the elements that constitute e-Learning preparation, including drivers and barriers. Hence the use of a case study to support an extensive literature review.

Chapters 7 and 8 of this book explore different research strategies and methods of data collection in depth. Chapter 7 – 'Research Methods 1: Traditional approaches' – deals with traditional research methods, while Chapter 8 – 'Research Methods 2: Artist as researcher' – is intended for those students who are required to create something (typically art and drama students), such as a piece of software, a work of art, a musical score, a play, etc., and are then required to write about their creation.

## Research proposal: setting a timescale

It is standard practice to include an estimate of how long you expect each stage of your research work to take. To work this out, write down the distinct phases of your dissertation and opposite each phase enter the number of weeks or months you expect the corresponding activity to last. For example, a Master's dissertation to be completed over a four-month period between June and September might have the timescale shown in Table 3.2. This is assuming that you are writing up your dissertation as you go along. Your timings may differ because your dissertation may be longer or shorter in duration; nevertheless, the principle is the same.

**Table 3.2** Project timescales (four-month Master's dissertation)

| Dissertation activity | Duration (weeks) | Month |
|---|---|---|
| Clarify Aim/Objectives | 2 | June |
| Literature Review | 4 | June–July |
| Research Methods | 2 | July |
| Data Collection | 3 | August |
| Findings | 3 | August–September |
| Conclusion | 2 | September |

Some of the dissertation activities will overlap and so the picture is not as straightforward as depicted in Table 3.2. For example, it appears that the Literature Review chapter is expected to be completed in four straight weeks (if you have the timescale as shown in Table 3.2) but the reality is that you will be reading and using literature sources at other times outwith this period. The four-week block is simply signalling to your supervisor where in your dissertation journey you expect to complete the bulk of your Literature Review and how long you expect that activity to last.

Also, Table 3.2 does not take into account variations in holiday periods and this has to be borne in mind when you develop your own timescales. Furthermore, it is rare that you will adhere rigidly to your initial projected timescales. It is not a fault; it is just that life rarely follows our intentions to the letter. Incorporate free weeks to accommodate the unexpected (such as flu, tiredness, other project deadlines, domestic situations, etc.) when you plan your activities.

Nonetheless, listing dissertation activities against rough timescales will help you gain an overview of what lies ahead and provide you with an appreciation of how much time you have to play with for each of your dissertation elements (clarifying your research objectives, writing your Literature Review, etc.).

If you use a chart, such as a bar chart, to display your timescale, then this will add a professional look to your presentation. Figure 3.3 shows the projected timescales for another Master's dissertation, but in the form of a bar chart.

Other charts could be used with similar success. For example, a Gantt chart is a good way to display your research tasks graphically. A Gantt chart is a special type of bar chart, where the bars represent the duration of each task and are placed in the chart to show the sequence of tasks as well as potential overlap. Figure 3.4 is an example of a Gantt chart for a dissertation to be undertaken between September and April.

If you are an art student or a drama student and you are also expected to create a piece of art or drama, as well as write about it, then your activities and timescales will differ accordingly, with perhaps more weight given to the creation process.

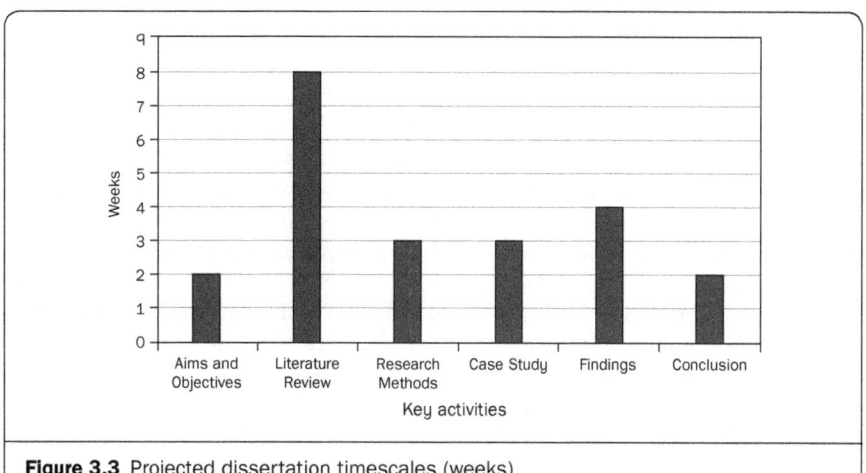

**Figure 3.3** Projected dissertation timescales (weeks)

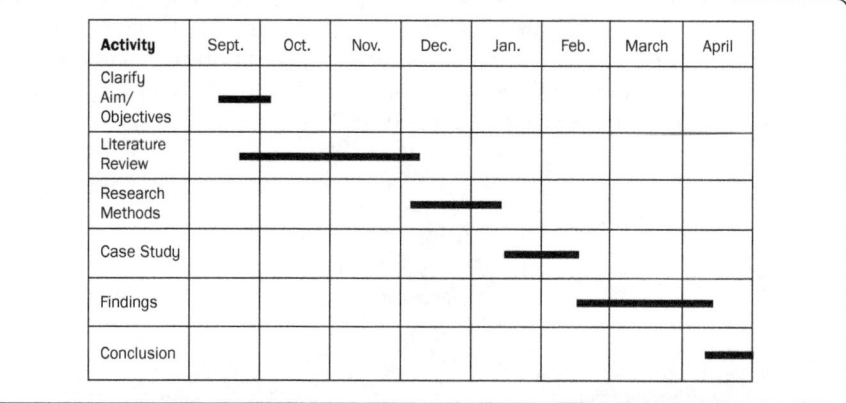

**Figure 3.4** Gantt chart showing dissertation timescales

You must take every opportunity, however small, to show your work in the best possible light. Using tables and charts to display information is one way to make your work look good and gain easy marks. Your supervisor will appreciate your efforts and will already begin to see you as a 'good' student.

Appendix D contains an example of a completed dissertation proposal where the student has been required to submit in the shape of a structured essay. If an institution instead required all research proposals to be submitted using a standard research proposal form, then the various parts that go to make up the structured essay would simply slot into the research proposal form. The advantage of writing the research proposal in the shape of a short, structured essay is that the essay itself can then form the basis of the introductory chapter to the dissertation.

## Research proposal: ethics

When we are young, our parents teach us how to behave. As we grow older, our conduct becomes shaped by other influences: friends, religion, the law of the land, colleagues, sporting allegiances, etc. When we adopt a *moral stance* on how we think we, and others, ought to behave, we are entering the world of *ethics*. Ethics is essentially a code of conduct on how we ought to lead our lives. Sometimes it can appear in written form – as reflected in the laws of the land – but it can also be present in unwritten philosophical and social beliefs that manifest themselves in everyday behaviour. Ethics is not a science – that is, it is not absolute – people can, and often do, disagree on what is acceptable and unacceptable conduct. For example, one country's citizens may believe that hanging is unethical whereas those in another country may hold a different point of view; similarly, one student may consider that cheating is an efficient use of his or her time while another student might argue that such behaviour is wholly unethical. Ethics is now a popular concept that impacts on many diverse strands of our lives, from banking to shopping to environmental issues.

*Research ethics* refers to the application of a moral code of conduct when human participants are the focus of empirical research. As you design your approach to carrying out your own empirical research (e.g. focus groups of employees in a particular company), you need to give serious consideration to the matter of research ethics. There are a number of core ethical principles that your research should meet (captured in Figure 3.5):

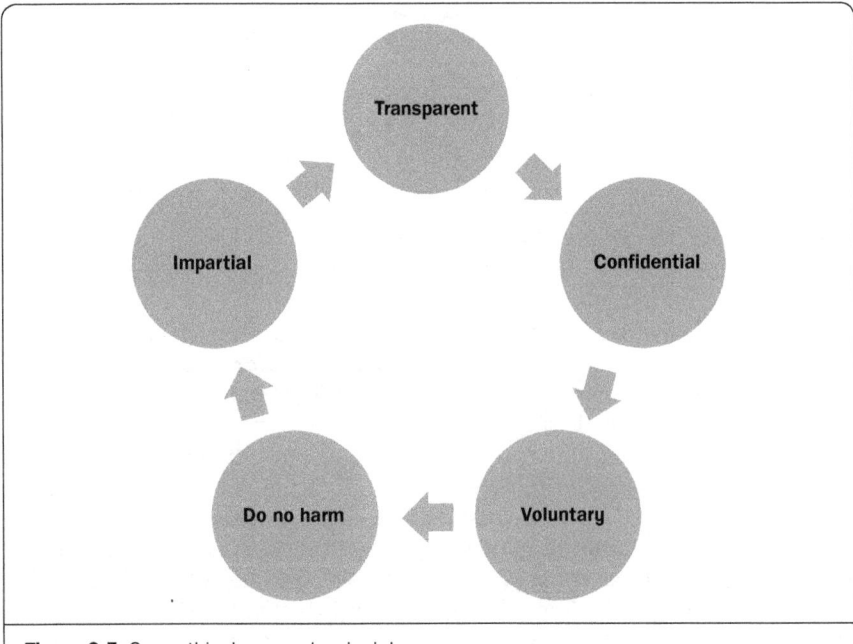

**Figure 3.5** Core ethical research principles

---

**Participant Information Sheet and Consent Form**

---

**Research title:**

**Research method(s) (e.g. interviews):**

**Purpose of this research:**

**Researcher (including contact details):**

**Participant statement:**
*The purpose of this research work has been explained to me,
including the use to which this research will be put and my part
in this research project. I also understand that my details will
remain confidential and that my anonymity will be respected.*

**Signed:**
**Date:**

**Figure 3.6** Participant Information Sheet and Consent Form

---

- *Transparency*: The purpose of your research should be explained clearly to your research participants (e.g. 'to ascertain employee views on *whistleblowing*'), as should how you will conduct the primary research (e.g. interviews) together with the intended use of your findings (e.g. as part fulfilment of a Master's dissertation). Providing participants with a Participant Information Sheet is good practice, showing a professional approach to your dissertation. The Participation Information Sheet can also double up as a consent form (Figure 3.6). Participants should only give consent after they have been fully informed of the purpose of your research, how they will be involved, together with any health/risk implications: this is called *informed consent*.
- *Confidentiality*: You must respect the confidentiality and anonymity of participants. If you fail to do so, you may be in breach of your country's Data Protection Act. By revealing details that can identify individuals, you may also be placing participants at risk.
- *Voluntary*: Participants must not be coerced to become part of your research work and should be free to withdraw at any time.
- *Do no harm*: Your research work should not place your participants in any danger. Equally important, you should not put yourself at risk (if you intend to interview, for example, drug addicts or criminals, then you need to seek professional advice on safety precautions).
- *Impartiality*: If you are connected to the research participants in any way (e.g. fellow students or relatives) or it might be perceived that you could be

biased (e.g. you do a case study of an organisation where you work part-time), you need to declare the nature of the relationship.

It is normal practice for dissertation students to complete a Research Ethics Approval Form before commencing their primary research. Depending on the ethical issues, approval can be granted at supervisory/departmental level or may require scrutiny by the university's research committee or call for approval from an external body such as the National Health Service (NHS). The answers to the questions on the Research Ethics Approval Form will dictate at what level approval is needed.

If your research entails human participation and the ethical issues are straightforward matters where the core ethical principles of *transparency, confidentiality, voluntary* input, *(no) harm*, and *impartiality* are not transgressed, then it is normal for approval to be granted at supervisory/departmental level.

If your research necessitates working with 'vulnerable populations' or is likely, for whatever reason, to breach any of the core ethical research principles (e.g. you require to hide the nature of your research from the research participants so as not to influence their conduct or there is some physical risk to yourself or to the participants), you should seek guidance and approval from your university's research ethics committee. Figure 3.7 highlights groups that are commonly seen as 'vulnerable populations' in the context of research: children, people with learning/communication difficulties, those in custody or on probation, or engaged in dubious/illegal activities.

Lastly, if your research participants are working for, or are patients of, the NHS (or the equivalent in whichever country the research is conducted), you will need to submit an application for ethical approval to the NHS National Research Ethics Service (NRES). Useful information can be obtained from the Centre of Research: Ethical Campaign (http://healthpartner.co.uk/welcome-to-centre-of-research-ethical-campaign/). Table 3.3 lists links to a selection of national and international bodies dealing with ethical codes of practice in research.

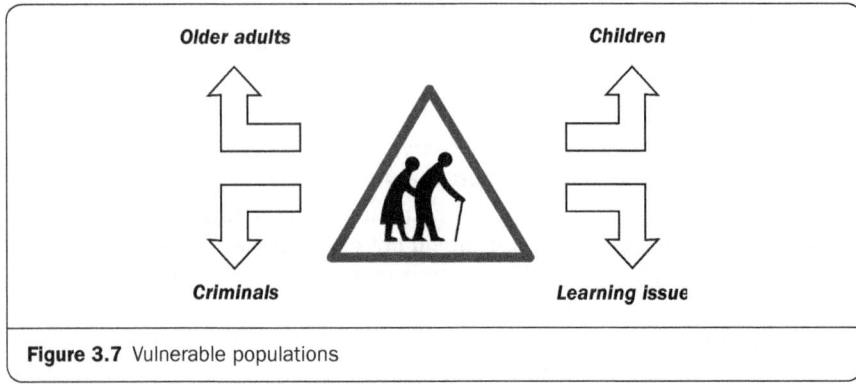

**Figure 3.7** Vulnerable populations

**Table 3.3** Ethical codes of practice

| Committee | Website |
|---|---|
| NHS National Research Ethics Service (NRES) | http://www.hra.nhs.uk/about-the-hra/our-committees/hra-approval/ |
| American Anthropological Association (AAA) | http://www.aaanet.org/committees/ethics/ethcode.htm |
| American Medical Association (AMA) | https://www.ama-assn.org |
| Health Professions Council of South Africa (HPCSA) | http://www.hpcsa.co.za/# |
| National Health and Medical Research Council (NHMRC) Australia | http://www.nhmrc.gov.au/publications/synopses/r39syn.htm |
| British Psychological Society (BPS) | http://www.bps.org.uk/what-we-do/bps/ethics-standards/ethics-standards |
| British Sociological Association (BSA) | https://www.britsoc.co.uk |
| Economic & Social Research Council (ESRC): Research Ethics Framework (REF) | http://www.esrc.ac.uk |
| Human Sciences Research Council (HSRC) South Africa | http://www.hsrc.ac.za/en |
| Council for International Organizations of Medical Sciences (CIOMS) | http://www.cioms.ch/ |
| World Medical Association (WMA) | http://www.wma.net/en/30publications/30ethicsmanual/index.html |

# Producing a dissertation template

Once your research proposal has been approved, create the cover pages for each of the main sections/chapters that you expect to appear in your final submission. Collectively this is called a *dissertation template*. It will typically include the cover pages shown in Figure 3.8, although the headings and arrangement of sections may change depending on the guidelines set out in your dissertation handbook.

To begin with, most of the pages will be empty pages (i.e. they will contain just a heading or two). Importantly, though, they will give you a sense of direction and discipline. Indeed, depending on your project, and if you want to divide the pages further, you might create as many as twenty 'empty' pages in the first day of your dissertation! Psychologically, this should give you a boost. Put these pages inside a folder labelled 'Dissertation'. As you advance through your dissertation journey, complete each section in detail. On a practical level, it will make it easier for you and your supervisor to appreciate, at a few glances, how your dissertation is progressing.

# Supervision: roles, responsibilities, and meetings

### Roles and responsibilities

From the outset, let us clarify the difference between a *role* and a *responsibility*. A role refers to an expected function. For example, the role of a teacher is to educate while the role of a student is to learn. With roles, or functions, come responsibilities. In the context of your dissertation, your supervisor will have a specific role (or roles) and related responsibilities, as will you.

In a study of supervisor experiences and perceptions (Todd *et al.*, 2006, p. 166), one lecturer neatly summed up his role: 'I think my role is essentially to try and help make their project realisable, rather than impose something on them.' To help you *realise* your dissertation, your supervisor will act as your expert guide and 'critical friend'. As such, it is probably more helpful to view your supervisor as having a twin role: someone who will be both inquisitor – in the nicest possible sense – and adviser. When your supervisor asks questions about your work, it is not an attempt to 'catch you out' but to engage you in discussion with a view to offering advice in line with your intentions.

It is normal practice for universities to provide supervisors with a list of supervision responsibilities. Experienced supervisors are well aware of their supervisory duties but it is a gentle reminder of what their university and students expect of them. These expectations form the ground rules upon which the supervision function is based and usually include the following responsibilities:

- To offer advice on your proposed research topic, specific research objectives and timetable of activities to allow you to complete your dissertation in time.
- To give guidance on the standard of work necessary to pass a dissertation.

- To meet with you regularly to discuss your work-in-progress.
- To provide constructive criticism.
- To respond timeously to your queries.
- To warn you if you are in danger of failing.
- To treat you fairly and with respect.

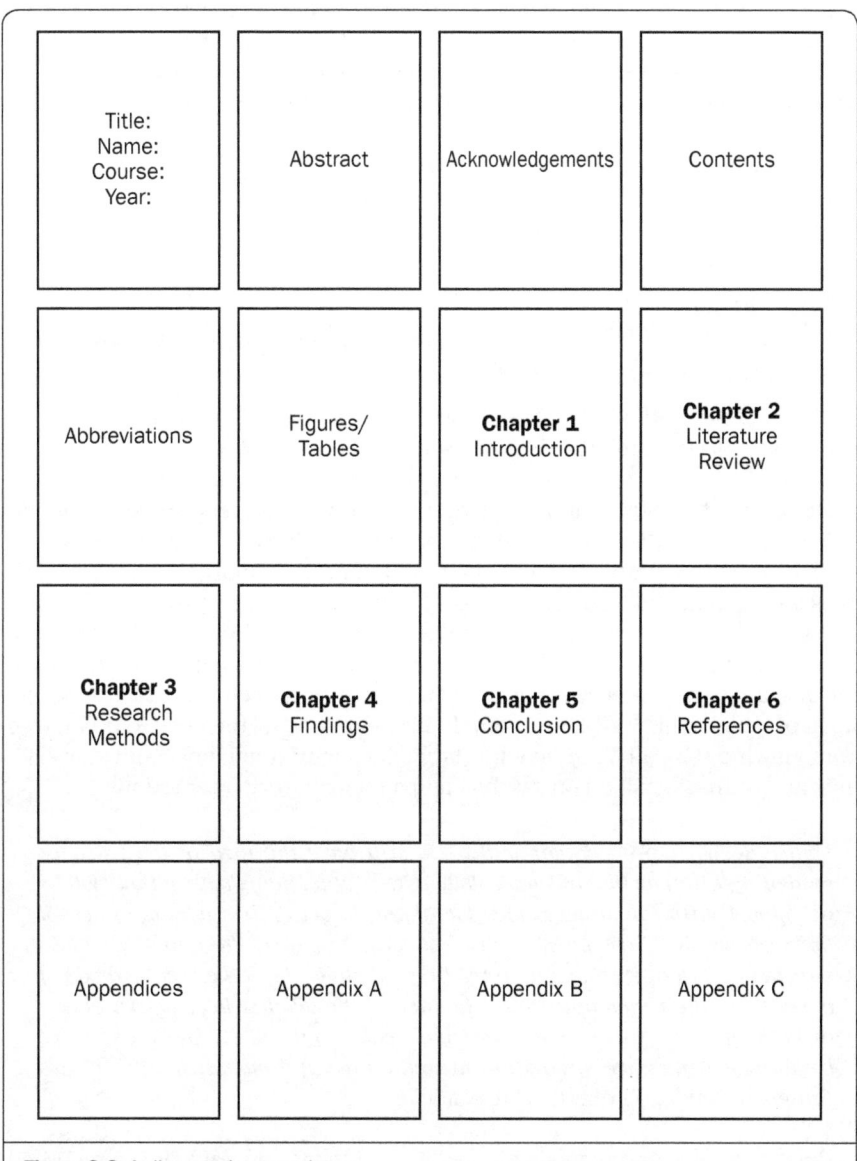

**Figure 3.8** A dissertation template

What part do you – the student – play in the supervisor–student relationship? It is your dissertation, so you take the lead role. Your role is to do the dissertation. This does not mean that you have complete freedom to do what you want when you like. Rather than *complete freedom*, what you have is *positive freedom*. Complete freedom is an abnegation of your supervisor's responsibilities and your responsibilities; positive freedom is a reaffirmation of your lead position within an agreed framework: 'No man and no mind was ever emancipated merely by being left alone. Removal of formal limitations is but a negative condition; positive freedom is not a state but an act which involves methods and instrumentalities for control of conditions' (Dewey, 1927, p. 168). With freedom comes responsibility. It is your responsibility to do the following:

- Familiarise yourself with the dissertation guidelines.
- Agree on a suitable research topic with your supervisor, including timetable of activities to complete your dissertation on time.
- Arrange a schedule of meetings with your supervisor.
- Meet with your supervisor regularly.
- Participate in supervision meetings (discuss, ask questions, give views, etc.).
- Submit work regularly for review.
- Submit your final dissertation on time.
- Submit a dissertation that is your own work.

Dissertation supervision is a partnership between supervisor and student. The supervisor–student relationship is based on reciprocity: for it to work, you need to cooperate mutually and to do that you need to appreciate each other's roles and responsibilities. Mary Parker Follett, in an address to the University of Boston in 1927, gave a speech entitled 'The Teacher–Student Relation'. The speech was believed to have been burnt with many other papers on her death but was later discovered and published in 1970. Her speech was full of wisdom, much of which still holds true today. In it, she reiterated the need to break free from viewing the teacher–student relation as one of dominance and subservience and to focus instead on establishing a contributory interaction:

> *I have deeply regretted that many … still have the idea of the teacher–student relation as that of leader–follower. That is, they think of their job as an opportunity for propaganda, for trying to get their students to accept their opinions … In most of our colleges, however, the effort is not to spread certain opinions, but to try to train students in the best methods of arriving at their own opinions. The task of the teacher here again is one of making the relation such that both contribute to it. Here, as in all human relations, we are abandoning the idea of domination, of Freud's father-authority.* (Follett, 1970, p. 150)

When the roles and responsibilities of supervisor and student are recorded in the student handbook, they form a contract between the institution and the student. Some universities may create a formal dissertation contract, requiring the signatures of student, supervisor, and director of studies. Dissertation supervision contracts can differ in size and detail. They will at least contain the names of the supervisor(s) and student, a working title, focus of study, time plan, date supervision begins, confidentiality clauses, and signatures of student and supervisor. They may also include details of any training you require to complete your dissertation. The roles and responsibilities of supervisor and student may appear in the formal contract. Figure 3.9 shows an example Dissertation Supervision Contract.

| DISSERTATION SUPERVISION CONTRACT | |
|---|---|
| Student Name: | Supervisor Name: |
| Programme: | Other Supervisor(s): |
| Working Title: | Focus of Study: |
| Timescale: | Skills Training Required: |
| Responsibilities of supervisor:<br>• To offer advice on proposed research topic, specific research objectives and timetable of activities<br>• To give guidence on expected standard of work<br>• To meet with the student regularly to discuss work-in-progress and provide constructive criticism<br>• To respond timeously to student queries<br>• To warn student if in danger of failing<br>• To treat the student fairly and with respect | Responsibilities of student:<br>• To be familiar with the dissertation guidelines<br>• To agree on a suitable research topic with the main supervisor, including timetable of activities<br>• To arrange a schedule of meetings with supervisor(s)<br>• To meet with supervisor(s) regularly<br>• To participate in supervision meetings (discuss, ask questions, give view, etc.)<br>• To submit work regularly for review<br>• To submit final dissertation on time |
| Signature of student: | Date: |
| Signature of supervisor: | Date: |
| Signature of Director of Studies: | Date: |

**Figure 3.9** Example Dissertation Supervision Contract

## Meetings

Too often students arrive at their first supervision meeting with no clear idea of what they want to study. This sets a bad first impression. Although your supervisor can help shape your initial ideas, it is not for your supervisor to think up your ideas in the first place or to produce your detailed research objectives. If you leave your supervisor to develop your research ideas, you may end up with a research proposal that fails to fire you with enthusiasm. Students who actually enjoy their work, and take pride in what they are doing, are more likely to gain good marks. You need to take control of your own research proposal and engage in a project (a) that you understand and (b) which interests you – two elements that will form a solid basis for your dissertation journey. For those reasons, most staff tend to leave the initial topic selection entirely up to the student. Of course, that does not mean that you can pick any topic and expect it to be worthy of study.

You will be better placed to advance your dissertation if you understand how to take advantage of meetings with your supervisor. When you arrive for your first meeting with your supervisor, *come prepared* and *armed with questions*. Be able to state quite clearly your area of study, overall aim and related objectives, including a rationale for your chosen topic. Also, present your supervisor with a working title for your dissertation (this can change as your work progresses):

> The title of my dissertation is xxxx and my overall aim is to study . . . with a view to getting a deeper understanding of . . . The reason I want to study this area is because preliminary literature review findings indicate . . . For example, Burns in his report published in 2007, titled . . . argues that there is a need . . .

> Example:

> The title of my dissertation is 'A Study of Algorithms to Facilitate Software Testing in a Mobile Environment' and my overall aim is to study the appropriateness and effectiveness of current software-testing paradigms in such environments, with a view to identifying deficiencies and developing an improved algorithm to meet the needs of mobile computing software developers. The reason I want to study this area is because new technologies are being produced at an alarming rate, becoming smaller and personalised (e.g. iPads, notebooks, advanced mobile phones, etc.), and as this is taking place there is an increasing need to ensure that those who are developing new mobile technologies do so using relevant and effective testing algorithms, otherwise the security of the products may be compromised. A number of researchers have expressed concern about this very issue . . .

Your supervisor will be looking at your initial proposal in terms of: does the intended research have focus?, are the objectives clear?, and are the objectives achievable in the timescale? Ask for your supervisor's opinion of your dissertation topic (after all, your supervisor may also be marking your submitted dissertation): 'Is my research topic worthy of study?'; 'Are my objectives clear to you?'; 'Do you think I will be able to do them in the time available?' In other words, 'is my proposal realistic?'

Prior to each meeting, email your work-in-progress to your supervisor. If you do not do so, then much of your supervision meeting might be a very silent affair, with you waiting patiently until your supervisor has finished reading your work. Avoid sending irritatingly mysterious emails, where you do not identify who you are, or emails that assume a casual level of intimacy that is inappropriate. Keep your emails friendly but professional, informative but brief. Your supervisor will have many students to deal with, so always identify who you are, together with your dissertation title. If you have a particular issue that you would like addressed before – or discussed during – your supervision meeting, then state this in your email. By emailing your ideas, work-in-progress, specific problem areas, etc., your supervisor is given time to prepare for your meetings.

At each meeting summarise your latest work and seek specific feedback (e.g. request advice on issues that concern you). Stay clear of this howler, however: 'I can't find anything on this subject!' Every year there is one student who arrives at a first meeting and complains: 'I can't find anything on this subject!' Declaring 'I can't find anything on this subject!' just shows laziness on your part and a lack of serious intent about your dissertation. If you really are struggling to find information on your dissertation topic, then at least tell your supervisor the type of information you sought and where you looked for this information. Establishing a working relationship with your supervisor requires an honest attempt to engage with the dissertation process.

For future meetings with your supervisor, adopt a similar approach: *show your work-to-date* and *ask questions*. If you have created a dissertation template (as described in the previous sub-section), then you can incrementally build up your work, permitting your supervisor to quickly and conveniently assess your progress. Unfortunately, there are students who will arrive at meetings with no work to show, ask no questions, and wait for their supervisor to tell them what to do.

These meetings are not interviews, so don't view them as such. Your supervisor is not trying to interrogate you. He or she genuinely wants to know how your work is progressing in order to pinpoint areas where you might need help, and this requires both parties to communicate with one another. Phillips and Pugh (2007, p. 15) emphasise that 'good communication and rapport between students and their supervisors are the most important elements of supervision'. The only way you can start to achieve a decent rapport with your supervisor, and communicate dissertation issues, is if you arrive at meetings prepared.

Meetings with your supervisor should be looked upon as an opportunity to gauge your supervisor's opinion about your work and to seek corrective action when things are going wrong. Every meeting with your supervisor, if handled properly, could be saving you marks that you would otherwise have lost. And remember this – students who rarely turn up for meetings, rarely pass.

One other thing – if you cannot make a meeting with your supervisor, send an email as early as possible (not five minutes before the meeting) explaining the reason for your non-attendance. That is only good manners; and you should expect the same courtesy from your supervisor.

## An emotional journey

Doing a dissertation is an emotional rollercoaster of a ride. Some days you will be on a deserved high. On other days you will feel down: it might be comments from your supervisor that upset you; or perhaps a library book that you are after is never available when you want it; or an agreed interview with a research subject has fallen through at the last minute; or you are panicking because your friends seem so far ahead in their dissertation. Sometimes the reasons for your emotional disposition might not even have anything to do with your dissertation. Domestic problems, personal relationships, family concerns, health, future employment prospects, all are examples of external issues that can knock your studies temporarily off course.

Here is something you need to understand from the very beginning: ALL dissertation students experience ups and downs in their dissertation journey. John Biggam became Dr John Biggam only after surviving the same dissertation (mis)adventures as other students, first during his maiden undergraduate dissertation, followed by his Master's (MPhil.) and then, finally, his doctorate thesis (PhD). Recognising that other students are encountering similar problems, and have done so since the dissertation was first invented, is comforting because that means that the problems are inherent in the dissertation journey, not you. If the Master's dissertation was easy and problem-free, it would not have the academic credence that it currently merits.

Although stressful situations will pop up here and there during your dissertation journey, if that stress becomes excessive you need to seek professional help immediately. In which case, your doctor will be your first port of call but every university has a counsellor trained to offer advice, so make use of these professional services. There are practical benefits to keeping your university informed of any issues that are having a negative impact on your dissertation work: as well as directing you to specialist help, the university will liaise with your supervisor in an attempt to keep you on track and, importantly, will treat any future request for an extension to your submission date sympathetically. Your personal health is more important than your dissertation: you can always defer your dissertation; the same cannot be said for your health.

Below are typical issues that can upset students, predominately dissertation-related. Included is helpful commentary.

### 'I didn't get the supervisor I wanted'

Supervisors are allocated on the basis of best fit and availability, not favouritism. This is a fairer system than allowing students to select their supervisor or, for that matter, permitting supervisors to cherry-pick their dissertation students. There have been occasions when students have felt disappointed or apprehensive about their allocated supervisor, only to appreciate further down the line the deliberate thought gone into supervision selection. The student–supervisor relationship requires both parties to be enthusiastic and engaging from the outset, so you need to set aside any initial disappointment and buckle down to make the partnership work. Think positively and trust in your supervisor's experience.

### 'I want to change my supervisor'

Think very carefully before making a request for a change of supervisor. Not liking your supervisor is not a valid reason; nor is preference for another supervisor. The main reasons that normally justify a change of supervisor are: (1) incompetence on the part of the supervisor or (2) a complete breakdown in the student–supervisor relationship. For incompetence you need to argue that either the supervisor is not knowledgeable in your subject area or lacks ability to supervise a dissertation (e.g. is confused about the dissertation process). For an irretrievable breakdown in relations you need to provide evidence, in the form of a timeline of accumulative incidents, where issues raised were not addressed to your satisfaction and, collectively, are to your serious disadvantage. If either of (1) or (2) arises, then you are perfectly entitled to request a change of supervisor.

However, if you are thinking about changing your supervisor, be sensible and adopt the following staged process. Speak informally to your supervisor in an attempt to reach an amicable resolution (it may be the case that friction has been created as a result of a mutual misunderstanding). If that fails, speak informally to whoever is in charge of the postgraduate dissertations for your programme (i.e. do not rush into a premature formal complaint). If that fails, then make a formal appointment to speak to the Head of Department and/or a student academic advisor to progress your concerns. On each occasion, do not resort to petty, personal accusations – be polite and professional but firm. Remember, you are entitled to a competent and supportive supervisor.

### 'I don't know where to start'

Creating a dissertation template is a sensible place to start (see 'Producing a dissertation template' above). Construct a word-processed document for your dissertation and enter all the headings for your main sections onto separate blank pages: Abstract, Acknowledgements, Contents Page, Introduction, Literature Review, etc. Print out this digital document and carry it with you in a folder. That should immediately give you a sense of structure and direction and, therefore, a degree of confidence. Next, work out when and where you will do your main studying/writing. Then pin a timetable of dissertation activities, as a chart, up on the wall. Place beside it a numbered list of your research objectives/questions. You have already started! Now learn how to write your introductory chapter (see Chapter 4, 'The Dissertation Introduction'). Make an early appointment to see your supervisor to discuss your research objectives/ questions, your planned schedule of activities, and joint expectations. As you complete the content under each of your dissertation template headings, supported by supervisory meetings, your dissertation will increase in size, as will your confidence.

### 'I can't find anything on my dissertation topic'

You have been looking for a book with the name 'Your Dissertation' writ large on the front cover. Such a book does not exist. Do not type in your dissertation title to Google and expect to be inundated with perfectly formed information on your complete dissertation topic. You may need to think tangentially. If you are unable to acquire literature sources on, for example, the *barriers* to e-Learning in universities, then look up sources on e-Learning in universities and from there you may come across an author discussing the barriers. From that source you may get leads to other sources, and so on. You will need to explore the possible places where this information might reside: other student dissertations, departmental library, internal university library databases, external university library databases, books, conference proceedings, lecture notes, etc.

Write and reference as you go along. You will soon build up a healthy collection of material. Initially, you will make slow progress but you will soon become adept at recognising what to search for and where to search.

### 'I've got too much information'

You need to be brave and only retain material that is relevant to your specific research objectives (or research questions). If you have picked up a book or a journal paper or an internet article that is interesting but irrelevant, then ditch it. You do not have time to be distracted. Get into the habit of skim reading literature to determine relevance, ruthlessly binning anything that does not obviously align with any of your numbered objectives. Literature that repeats what you already have (e.g. barriers to e-Learning) can be used to emphasise agreement/disagreement between authors but at some stage you need to start writing! When you have collated enough information to write meaningfully on one aspect of a chapter within your dissertation template, then that is when you begin. For example, if there is a chapter in your dissertation entitled 'Drivers and Barriers to e-Learning', then once you have collected material on the drivers, start writing.

### 'I don't know how long this chapter should be'

Think sensibly. The bulk of the marks tends to be distributed between the Literature Review, Research Methods, and Discussion/Analysis of any empirical work, with the Introduction and Conclusion securing less marks. If there is a formal written marking scheme, detailing the marks allocated to the separate parts of the dissertation, then get hold of it. That will confirm the weighting of the marks, and hence give you a good guide to the weighting of your word allocation. If your Literature Review is worth, for example, 25 per cent of the marks, then devote roughly 25 per cent of your overall word-count to your Literature Review, and so on. Check your dissertation handbook for your university's guidelines and confirm your strategy with your supervisor. Also, have a look at past dissertations to get a measure of word distribution.

### 'I'm not sending my work-in-progress until it is perfect'

Your supervisor is looking for your work-in-progress, not perfection. You can tidy up aspects of your language later. As long as the work that you show your supervisor reflects agreed expectations and allows for meaningful discussion, you will be making progress. If you delay showing your supervisor your work until it is 'complete', then by the time that you realise perfection is an illusion, you will have missed crucial opportunities for early feedback. The benefit of timely feedback far outweighs any pleasure you take from producing a more polished chapter. Besides, you can always tidy up your written work after your meetings with your supervisor; more so, given feedback on the substance of your work-in-progress.

### 'I'm writing in a language that is not my mother tongue'

Do not fret. Your university has deemed your language skills to be good enough for you to embark on a Master's course. Thousands of non-native speakers obtain Master's degrees every year. Ability in English (or whatever language is native to the country in which your university resides) is rarely a predominant reason for failing a Master's dissertation – in some marking schemes, 'skill in language' may only form 5 per cent of the overall mark. Furthermore, supervisors do make allowances for those who are not native speakers. Nevertheless, if you, or your supervisor, are concerned about your language skills, then get hold of past dissertations to gauge expected standards and speak to your academic counsellor about acquiring additional support.

### 'My supervisor keeps criticising my work'

That is your supervisor's job! Do not take it personally. You would be more upset if your supervisor offered no criticism and then, without warning, failed your final submission. There are two reasons why your supervisor will 'criticise' your work: (1) it is an attempt to get you to defend your work and so start an intellectual debate, and (2) to highlight a defect in your work and allow you to take corrective action. Respond enthusiastically to the first type of 'criticism' and for the second, more serious type, be glad that your supervisor is keen to point out how to improve your dissertation. Criticism has negative connotations – try instead to view comments by your supervisor as 'helpful interjections'.

*'Other students are so far ahead with their dissertation'*

No they are not. Students are not the best judge of their own progress; even less are they best placed to comment authoritatively on the progress of other students. Go at the pace that you have agreed with your supervisor and which suits your temperament and needs. If your supervisor is happy with your progress, then you should be happy too. Remember the tale of the slow but steady tortoise and the bragging hare.

*'My friend's supervisor is giving different advice from my supervisor'*

Your friend would then be able to make the same comment about your supervisor! Neither you nor your friend needs to panic. Your friend's dissertation is different from your dissertation, so the advice will be different. Your friend's supervisor is not marking your dissertation. Ignore the advice given to your friend and listen to your own supervisor.

*'I lack confidence and have low self-esteem'*

You are as good as any student on your course. It is a strange phenomenon, but it is commonplace for highly educated students on a postgraduate course – the top strata of educated citizens in society – to lack confidence in their ability to complete a dissertation. The author of this book recalls a mature student, constantly predicting dissertation doom. Another student would regularly leave the dissertation meeting upset at the merest hint of perceived negative feedback. Both students were incredibly hard working but lacked confidence in their own abilities for long spells (even when receiving praise). Both students received a distinction and deservedly so. The huge smiles on their faces at graduation reflected a wonderful personal triumph for both of them, from nervous students to proud researchers. You are travelling a path that many have gone before. They succeeded and so should you.

*'This evening job is exhausting me'*

There are many positive benefits to part-time student employment, not least of which is money in your pocket. If, however, your work is affecting your studies, then consider leaving your part-time work. Your student job is temporary while your qualification is for life. If you need your student job to make ends meet, or you consider the benefits far outweigh the disadvantages, then try to come to an arrangement with your employer in terms of a more favourable work–study balance. Alternatively, look for another part-time job that better accommodates your studies. For example, most universities offer part-time work to their own students (students' union, academic departments, international office, sport, web team, business development, conference, widening access, finance office, and so on). Your students' union will give you excellent advice.

*'My boyfriend/girlfriend is so demanding of my time'*

Perhaps your boyfriend/girlfriend is not aware of the effort required to complete a Master's dissertation. Make it clear to your partner from the outset that your Master's is important to you, and your career prospects, and that to succeed with your Master's dissertation, you will need to devote time and space to your studies on a regular basis. If this fails to elicit a sympathetic response, and you can't come to a sensible compromise, then you may have a simple choice to make: your studies or your partner?

*'I have a disability. How can my university ensure that I am not disadvantaged?'*

Universities are particularly keen to ensure that no student is disadvantaged in their studies and will make every effort to accommodate those with a physical disability, long-term health or mental condition, or learning difficulty. You may be able to apply for financial assistance, in the form of a disabled student's allowance, dependent upon your disability (not your income). This could help you acquire, for example, specialist software, a note-taker or reader, the cost of braille paper, and extra travelling costs. You need to make your university aware of your disability so that you can receive the help you need.

*'I'm not sure how to carry out my own empirical research'*

First of all, understand the main research strategies (case study, survey, experiment, action research, historical research, etc.) available to you, including data collection methods (interviews, questionnaires, observation, etc.). Then, decide what strategy and data collection method(s) best fit with your research. Discuss the options openly, in a relaxed way, with your supervisor. Check out past dissertations in your subject area to see the choices made by other students (importantly, note how the students justify their choices). See Chapter 7, 'Research Methods 1: Traditional approaches' and Chapter 8, 'Research Methods 2: Artist as researcher' for details.

*'Oh no, I can't find anyone to interview for my empirical research'*

That is probably because you have left the practicalities of data collection to the last minute and expect others to compensate for your lack of forethought. Once you have chosen your research methods, you need to start making solid arrangements to collect your data. Calling senior staff up one week before you want to interview them is unlikely to meet with much success. Agree a date, time, duration, and purpose well in advance of your proposed data collection periods. Every so often remind your research participants of their agreed contribution to your empirical research, just in case they can no longer be available (e.g. leaving job, pressures of work, change to holiday periods, sudden family commitments, etc.) and you need to make alternative arrangements.

*'My supervisor knows that I am knowledgeable, so in my final submission I don't need to write down all my main arguments/ideas in any great detail'*

Yes, you do. You get marks for what you write, not for what you said in some past conversation. The marker – very often your supervisor – allocates marks, not from memory or hearsay, but from the written evidence presented in the shape of your final submission. Gaps in your submitted arguments/ideas mean gaps in your marks.

*'This dissertation work is draining me. I'm so tired'*

The dissertation journey is a long haul and the constant effort can take its toll if you are not careful. Fatigue lowers the power of your faculties and can make you susceptible to illness. Take a break! Sit in a coffee shop and watch the world go by, visit a gallery, go for a walk in the park, even take a short holiday. Do something different. Join the boxing club – that will waken you up! If you are tired, then you need to recharge your batteries.

*'I'm glad this dissertation is coming to an end. I'll just bash off a quick conclusion'*

No! A hasty conclusion will diminish the worth of your dissertation and reduce your overall mark. Put in as much effort and enthusiasm into your conclusion as you did for your introduction. A hitherto meritorious cinema movie with a rushed, discarded ending is such a disappointment: do not make the same mistake. Start your dissertation with a bright flourish and end it in a victorious parade. See Chapter 10, 'Concluding Your Dissertation'.

*'I'm running out of time to complete my dissertation'*

At the start, most students think they have all the time in the world to complete their dissertation. In that respect, you will probably be no different, but before you know it the days become weeks, the weeks become months, and the final submission date will be staring you in the face! Even the top students are taken aback by how quickly the end-date changes from a distant deadline to sudden reality.

To minimise the risk of delaying key milestone activities until it is too late to do yourself justice, set down a timetable of activities at the beginning of your dissertation journey. Supervisors can always spot a hurried dissertation: the introduction is usually well written, the Literature Review is inconsistent in depth and theme, the research methods chapter is skeletal and unconvincing, the write-up is superficial and lacking detailed analysis (partly because the empirical research was minimal), and the conclusion ends abruptly with little attempt to tie everything together.

*'I've got all the time in the world to do my dissertation'*

See 'I'm running out of time to complete my dissertation'.

*'I won't be able to complete my dissertation in time, so I'll just hand it in late'*

Be careful. An unauthorised late submission will incur a penalty. Some universities may even award a mark of zero. An authorised late submission may still result in a penalty unless the reason for the request is the result of a factor beyond your control, such as ill health. Under such circumstances, make your request timely and provide supporting documentation. Bad time management is not a valid reason for a penalty-free late submission; if it were otherwise, then the concept of a formal submission cut-off date would be entirely meaningless and unfair on those students who stick to the rules.

The emotional issues listed above are not there to scare you or place a negative slant on the dissertation journey; rather, they are highlighted to present a realistic picture of the feelings that you might experience as you progress through your dissertation, with the key message that you are not alone. Supervisors recognise this and are there to help you – and not just academically. They can be a great source of emotional support and if they can't help you, then they know people who can. Producing a Master's dissertation is an intellectually enriching experience, but you ought to recognise that there may be times when you need emotional as well as academic support.

# Further reading

Bell, J. (2014) *Doing your research project: a guide for first-time researchers*, 6th edn. Maidenhead: Open University Press.

Denicolo, P. and Becker, L. (2012) *Developing research proposals*. London: Sage.

Denscombe, M. (2012) *Research proposals: a practical guide*. Maidenhead: Open University Press.

Oliver, P. (2010) *The student's guide to research ethics*. 2nd edn. Maidenhead: Open University Press.

Thomas, G. (2013) *How to do your research project: a guide for students in education and applied social sciences*. 2nd edn. London: Sage.

## Summary of key points

- A dissertation research proposal contains a *working title*, *background information*, your *overall research aim*, the *individual research objectives* deemed necessary to achieve your main research aim, an outline of the *research methods* needed to implement your research, expected *timescales*, potential *ethical issues* (including how they will be addressed), and a list of sources used.
- To write your overall research aim, think of your research subject in terms of one word, add other words to clarify your research focus, connect them to form a sentence, and convert the sentence into a formal research aim. You can, if you wish, rewrite your formal research aim as a research question.
- In addition to your overall research aim, you must list the individual research objectives that you believe will, when added together, fulfil your overall research aim. Start each of your research objectives using a keyword (*identify*, *assess*, *explore*, etc.), i.e. a verb to suggest type and depth of study related to each research objective. You can, as with your main research aim, formulate your individual research objectives as research questions.
- You will also need to outline in your research proposal your research methods, i.e. how you will carry out your research (e.g. review of relevant literature and/or collection and analysis of empirical data).
- Include in your research proposal a timescale indicating how long you expect each research task to take. You can illustrate your timescale using a simple table or, more interestingly, a chart (e.g. a bar chart or a Gantt chart).
- Where you are implementing your own practical research, you should behave ethically towards your research participants. You should adhere to the five core ethical principles of *transparency*, *confidentiality*, have *voluntary* (research participants), *do no harm*, be *impartial*; and meet any additional code of practice set down by your university.
- A dissertation template is a useful way of structuring your dissertation, gaining a quick overview of your progress, and providing a sense of direction and discipline. Create a folder to house your dissertation template and complete it accumulatively, bringing it with you to meetings with your dissertation supervisor.
- Meetings with your supervisor should be constructive and that, in turn, requires you to come prepared with ideas and a draft version of your work. Ask questions!
- The role of the student is to do the dissertation and the role of the supervisor is to support the student in completing that task.
- The student–supervisor relationship is based on mutual cooperation and respect to allow each other to fulfil their respective roles and responsibilities.
- A Dissertation Supervision Contract is a legally binding contract between the university and the student on how the supervision will be conducted.
- Completing a dissertation is as much an emotional journey as it is an academic one. Be prepared to experience emotional peaks and troughs as you traverse the dissertation landscape. It is a well-worn path. You need to pace yourself, stay focused, show resilience, and not panic in the face of adversity, but recognise when to rest and know where to seek additional support.

# Chapter  **4**

# The dissertation Introduction

> • *The general structure of the Introduction • Background • Research focus (revisited) • Overall research aim and individual research objectives • Outline research methods and timescales • Value of your research • A further suggestion • Summary of key points*

This chapter shows you how to write the introductory chapter to your dissertation.

## The general structure of the Introduction

The introductory chapter to your dissertation is typically labelled 'Chapter 1 Introduction'. Your Introduction ought to do a number of things:

- Provide preliminary background information to place your study in context.
- Clarify your focus of study.
- Specify your overall research aim and individual objectives.
- Outline your research methods and timescale of activities.
- Point out the value of your research.

Accordingly, you could structure your introductory chapter as follows:

**1 Introduction**
1.1 Background
1.2 Research Focus
1.3 Overall Research Aim and Individual Research Objectives
1.4 Outline Research Methods and Timescales
1.5 Value of this Research

There is a sort of stepwise refinement taking place from 1.1 down to 1.5, starting with general background information, then homing into the focus of the research, identifying the specific research objectives, outlining the research methods and timescales, and concluding with a comment on the value of the research.

If you find it more convenient, it is perfectly acceptable to merge subsections as you see fit. It is also your choice whether or not to number the sub-headings or, indeed, to have sub-headings at all, as long as the expected content is covered. This chapter will now go through and explain each of the above elements of the dissertation Introduction. Much of what is written in Chapter 3, 'Preparing for Your Dissertation' applies to this chapter and, consequently, students often take the bulk of their initial research proposal, tweak it after feedback from their supervisor, and re-use it for their dissertation Introduction. It is no coincidence that the structure of a research proposal and the introductory chapter of a dissertation are similar – because they perform a similar job, i.e. revealing the area of research. Nevertheless, this chapter will take you carefully through each component of a dissertation Introduction, showing examples of good (and bad) practice to illustrate salient points. At the end of this chapter, you should be in an excellent position to write the introduction to your own dissertation.

## Background

It is generally bad practice to jump in and immediately identify the focus of your study. Why? Because your supervisor (and external marker) will want to know what led you to study your specific research area. This usually means identifying a gap in existing research or revealing a problem that needs addressing. Perhaps you are looking at a topic from a different angle or maybe recent reports indicate that there is a call for research in your particular area of interest. It is not enough to write that you have decided upon your field of study because you find it interesting: you need to go further and explain the rationale in terms of either a *need* or a *benefit* or both.

> **!  A common mistake by students**
>
> A common mistake by students is to pay scant attention to background reading. As mentioned earlier, students at the start of their dissertation can sometimes be seen shaking their head while exclaiming to their supervisor that they 'cannot find anything' on their dissertation topic, e-Learning, for example, or e-security. The conversation usually goes something like this:
>
> 'Hi, Dr Biggam.'
> 'John, call me John.'

'Well, eh, John, it's just that I can't find anything on e-security.'

'OK, if I remember correctly, Bob, you are supposed to be looking at e-security and Spam. Specifically why, despite technological advances in e-security, computer users are still getting inundated with Spam. Is that correct?'

'Yes.'

'And you say you cannot find anything on e-security and spam? Ziltch, nada, nothing?'

At this point Dr Biggam turns to his computer, accesses the university library database, and types the words 'E-security and Spam' and, lo and behold, before their very eyes the screen magically fills up with a multitude of sources. 'Isn't technology wonderful!' announces the supervisor.

Do not depend on your supervisor finding your background reading for you, because you may end up adopting this lazy approach throughout the duration of your dissertation. You might think it is a great idea to find such a 'helpful' supervisor, but there is a potential problem with this approach. When you finally submit your work, you will lose marks for showing a lack of independence. Therefore, if you are interested in not just passing your dissertation but gaining good marks, then avoid over-dependence on your supervisor for material and instruction. That is not to say that your supervisor cannot advise you on the relevance of your material or attempt to guide you in the right direction by, on occasion, referring you to pertinent articles/reports, etc., but there is a line between guidance and spoon-feeding that, if repeatedly crossed, undermines the claim that your dissertation is an 'independent piece of research'. Detailed feedback is a different matter altogether: it is providing commentary on your work, not presenting solutions.

You need to show some preliminary reading in your Introduction that has influenced your proposed research. Get into the habit of using your university's library system to access internal and external subject databases (see section 'University library databases' in Chapter 5, 'The Literature Review'). A structured approach to using a simple search facility such as Google or Google Scholar should also yield profitable results (see section 'Literature search techniques' in Chapter 5, 'The Literature Review'). For example, if your research focus was on e-security and Spam, and you wanted access to Spam statistics, then type in 'Spam Statistics'; to access Spam reports, type in 'Spam Reports'. You can put the year after your request to help find up-to-date material, for example 'E-security and Spam reports 2017'. Similarly, you can endeavour to understand why Spam is on the increase by typing in 'Spam failings' or 'Spam failures' or some variation on the same theme. Unfortunately, public search engines, although enormously useful, can produce too much information, much of which may not be relevant. If you want to confine your search to complete documents, then type 'pdf' at the end of your query, for example 'E-security and Spam 2017 pdf'. PDF stands for Portable Document Format, i.e. a document that is read by Adobe Acrobat. PDF documents in your subject area have the advantage that they are usually complete documents and so tend to be well written and can contain references to other literature/websites that will further aid your research.

*Emerald Insight* is another online facility used by academics (http://www. emeraldinsight.com/), a source that you may find useful. You will require a username and password to access the articles stored in Emerald Insight. Most academic institutions have access to Emerald Insight; ask your supervisor about your institution's username/password.

The Internet is a great place to get a quick feel for your subject area, and to acquire otherwise expensive reports for free, but it is important that you access other sources: visit your university library and check out respected academic journals relevant to your work; use your department's resources; exploit your supervisor's knowledge of articles/books appropriate to your dissertation topic; learn to utilise your university's library database systems; have a coffee in your local bookstore and browse the bookshelves. In other words, the Internet is all fine and dandy, but good research involves using a variety of sources to acquire a balanced and credible picture of whatever it is you are studying.

Once you get a feel for your subject, and you know what you specifically want to research and why, you can then start to write the *Background* part of your Introduction. You do this first of all by gently introducing the reader to your general research area. That is to say, if your research focus was on, for example, the need to study the type of people who spread viruses on the Web, you do not start your Introduction by stating: 'There is a need to study the type of people who spread viruses on the Internet. This dissertation will do that by . . .'. Instead, it is better to begin by smoothly introducing the reader to the idea of e-security threats: 'E-security is of growing concern for those who use the Internet (DTI, 2016). These threats can range from Denial of Service (DOS) attacks, Web vandalism, Spam, viruses to fraudulent use of emails . . .'. Note that the first sentence contains a reference to literature (in this case, the Department of Trade and Industry, i.e. DTI). Let the reader know, as early as possible, that you are well read in the area; and there is no better time to do that than in the first paragraph of your dissertation.

Let us now return to the e-Learning example identified in Chapter 3, 'Preparing for Your Dissertation'. The overall aim of that dissertation topic was to 'advance an understanding of the impact of e-Learning in the university environment in relation to academic staff training preparation'. A sample Introduction is included in Appendix E. This sample Introduction has taken the Research Proposal in Appendix D and altered it, adding parts here and there, to fit into the sub-headings above. The length of the sample Introduction could easily be condensed if word-length were an issue. For now we will concentrate on the sample Background. Read this section now.

Note also the structure of this Background: the specific focus of the research is not identified in the Background (that is done in the sub-section 'Research focus').

Instead, the reader is eased into the chosen subject area – academic staff and e-Learning in the university environment – through a general discussion of traditional teaching and learning, followed by reference to the drive for e-Learning in the university environment, leading to a changing role for academic staff, and ending with the need for staff to be prepared to cope with this change. By quickly setting the scene and placing the research in context, the reader should begin to appreciate the dissertation's research focus.

> ## !  A common mistake by students
>
> If students do not write *too little* on their background section, then paradoxi-cally another common mistake by students is to go to the other extreme and spend *too much* time on background information. Normally, one or two pages should suffice. You want to arrive at your research focus quite quickly, but not before you provide some basic information that places your research in context and allows the reader to appreciate your (soon to be identified) research focus. You need to remember that this is a basic Introduction you are talking about here, so you do not want to spend too much time on back-ground information, otherwise the reader will start to wonder what your research is supposed to be about. Aim for simple clarity. The time for in-depth discussion will come later. The length of your Background will depend on the number of words that you have to play with in your dissertation.

The sample Background in Appendix E has some good points that need empha-sising. In the very first paragraph there is a reference to other literature:

> *Aristotle's lectures, preserved in the writings of Plato, are examples of such an approach, where the student is educated on particular topics through the mechanism of illuminating conversations – dialogues – between tutor and student* (Taylor, 1955).

By doing so, you are letting the reader know that you understand good aca-demic practice: you are supporting your ideas with reference to other authors and you are showing that you know how to cite sources (in this case, using the Harvard author–date system of referencing; see Chapter 2, 'Referencing and Plagiarism' for details on how to reference). Secondly, in the sample Back-ground there is a mix of in-text references. Examples of these different ways to present information are extracted from the sample Background and illustrated below:

1. *Indirect referencing*:
Aristotle's lectures, preserved in the writings of Plato . . . between tutor and student (Taylor, 1955).

2. *Direct referencing:*
Haywood *et al.* (2004) believe that most students . . .

3. *Direct referencing with quotation embedded in sentence:*
There is also much interest from universities to exploit ICT in distance learning, with Moe and Blodget (2000, p. 104) emphasising that 'the next big killer application for the Internet is going to be education'.

4. *Direct referencing with separate indented quotation:*
As early as 1997, the Dearing Report foresaw benefits of using ICT in higher education:

> . . . *we believe that the innovative application of . . . C&IT holds out much promise for improving the quality, flexibility and effectiveness of higher education. The potential benefits will extend to, and affect the practice of, learning and teaching and research* (Dearing, 1997, 13.1).

5. *Multiple indirect referencing:*
Online learning, networked learning, distributed learning, flexible learning, virtual learning, are some of the terms used to describe learning that uses technology as a vehicle for educational delivery (Salmon, 1998; Jung, 2000; Rosenberg, 2001; Collis and Moonen, 2001).

Also note that the sources might appear dated: 1998, 2000, 2001, etc. However, when this work was submitted, the in-text references were recent and relevant.

It is in the next sub-section – 'Research focus' in the sample Introduction – where you reveal the actual focus of your research, which includes the rationale for your research together with the specifics of what you intend doing. At this stage, you have made your job easier by framing your research in a wider context.

# Research focus (revisited)

Two things your supervisor will want to know are: (1) the focus of your research, and (2) the rationale for your study. It is important that you clarify the areas you intend researching and that you also explain why you want to research these areas (there will be more than one area you will want to research because you will have more than one research objective).

Reference will be made to the sub-section 'Research focus' in the sample Introduction (in Appendix E) to make some pertinent points on how to elucidate the focus of your research, so read it now. The sample 'Research focus' sub-section in Appendix E starts by linking back to the Background sub-section ('There is some confusion about the benefits of e-Learning'). Try and imitate this approach because it lets your discussion flow and keeps the reader on track (as well as yourself!).

> **!** **A common mistake by students**
>
> A common mistake by students is to begin each sub-section as if it were unrelated to the previous sub-section: this can disrupt the flow of your dissertation and, more importantly, cause you to stray from your main thesis. When supervisors read a new part of a chapter, and it begins with no apparent link to the previous part, they will begin to ask themselves one or two questions, such as 'What does this have to do with the previous bit?' or 'Is the student going off at a tangent?'

As stated, the sample 'Research focus' sub-section starts by linking back to the Background sub-section ('There is some confusion about the benefits of e-Learning'). The same paragraph then goes on to provide some examples of this confusion about the benefits of e-Learning by citing literature sources, thereby convincing the supervisor and marker (they may well be the same person) that the writer is a well-read researcher, and not someone who makes statements without providing supporting evidence.

> **!** **A common mistake by students**
>
> A common mistake by students when first introducing their chosen field of study, is to provide one or two sentences on their dissertation topic and think that they have provided enough justification on why their topic is worthy of study. No! You must convince the reader that you have a 'worthy area of study' by (1) referring to other literature, and (2) persuading the reader of the need for your study. While completing (1) and (2), you also tailor your examples and discussion to reflect the individual objectives that are of interest to you.

The second paragraph in the sample 'Research focus' sub-section – 'In particular, e-Learning commentators are warning that academic staff in universities need to be prepared to cope with e-Learning, to make the shift from *sage on the stage* to *guide on the side*' – introduces what will be the main focus of study for the student's dissertation (i.e. preparing university staff for e-Learning). Once again, the writer has taken the opportunity to refer to other authors, either through direct quotations or via simple author–date in-text referencing.

Once you have justified your general area of study – in this case, staff e-Learning preparation – you can then discuss the rationale behind what will become your individual research objectives. It is your general area of study that is eventually moulded into your overall research aim (e.g. 'The overall aim of this research is to advance an understanding of the impact of e-Learning in the university environment in relation to academic staff training preparation').

The main argument behind your individual research objectives, whatever they are, tends to be that by achieving them you will achieve your overall research aim. To remind you, the sample research objectives are:

Specifically, within the context of higher education, the objectives of this research are to:

1 *Identify* the forces driving e-Learning and the barriers to the successful delivery of e-Learning programmes.
2 *Evaluate critically* models and frameworks relevant to supporting academic staff in coping with e-Learning.
3 *Explore* staff stakeholder views and practices related to e-Learning preparation, including drivers and barriers to e-Learning.
4 *Formulate* recommendations on staff preparation issues.

However, these objectives need to be revealed gradually, in an evolutionary way. Thus, you do not start your 'Research focus' sub-section by blatantly stating your overall research aim and your associated individual objectives: that is too crude an approach. It is much better to allow your overall aim and specific objectives to appear as a result of academic discussion. The second paragraph in the sample Introduction introduced the focus of the overall aim and the remaining paragraphs break down the overall research aim into individual objectives, while also justifying the need for these specific areas of study.

The third and fourth paragraphs in the sample Introduction – 'Critical to this study is an understanding of the type of support that is required . . .' and 'The importance of research in this field of e-Learning becomes even more apparent . . .') – focus on the need to assess staff e-Learning preparation models and frameworks and the need to ascertain staff views on their experiences.

The fifth paragraph – 'If academic staff do not accept the educational benefits of e-Learning . . .' – justifies the need to clarify the drivers and barriers to e-Learning.

And the last paragraph neatly summarises, in one sentence, the aforementioned focus of the research: 'To gain a deeper understanding of these issues related to academic staff preparation, two main activities will need to be tackled: a review of relevant literature to ascertain current research findings on e-Learning preparation issues, including drivers and potential barriers; and empirical data collection on academic staff experiences of preparing for e-Learning.'

Note that the terms 'overall research aim' and 'specific research objectives' are not actually used in the sample 'Research focus' sub-section: this is a matter of choice. If you wish, you can use the 'Research focus' sub-section to clarify your overall research area, justify it, and identify the specific research areas that you will be studying, and not worry too much about labels. It is in the next sub-section of the Introductory chapter – 'Overall research aim and individual research objectives' – where you finally nail down for the reader your specific research focus using the terms 'research aim' and 'individual research objectives'.

# Overall research aim and individual research objectives

This sub-section should be relatively easy for students. It is in the previous sub-section of your introductory chapter (i.e. 'Research focus') where you ought to have explained to your supervisor what you intend to study and why. This sub-section is important because it is where you take your research focus and shape it into clearly stated tasks that you are asking your marker to judge your work against. So think carefully about the tasks that you set yourself!

The sample sub-section begins by re-stating the overall aim of the student's research ('The overall aim of this research is to advance an understanding of the issues surrounding the preparation of university academic staff to support student e-Learning'). Try and adopt this practice.

In this part of your Introduction you must state unequivocally, using simple terse statements, the specific research objectives that you intend meeting in order to achieve your overall research aim, as in the sample chapter:

---

Specifically, within the context of higher education, the objectives of this research are to:

1 *Identify* the forces driving e-Learning and the barriers to the successful delivery of e-Learning programmes.
2 *Evaluate critically* models and frameworks relevant to supporting academic staff in coping with e-Learning.
3 *Explore* staff stakeholder views and practices related to e-Learning preparation, including drivers and barriers to e-Learning.
4 *Formulate* recommendations on staff preparation issues.

---

If you want to lose marks, then make sure that your objectives are inappropriate, unfocused, vague, and unrealistic. You can do this by ensuring that you include objectives that have little to do with your stated aim, are too general in nature, include fuzzy keywords (such as 'look at'), and are unrealistic (i.e. are overambitious). On the other hand, to achieve good marks in this area you need to list objectives that are:

- Appropriate (i.e. clearly related to what you want to study);
- Focused (i.e. each objective is distinct and incrementally aids in achieving your overall research aim);

- Clear (i.e. avoids ambiguity and includes snappy, meaningful keywords); and
- Achievable (i.e. is realistic, given the timescale available to complete the dissertation).

Initially, you will be marked on the appropriateness of these objectives and perceived focus (or lack thereof), including how realistic they are. When you finally submit your dissertation, you will also be marked on whether or not you have achieved your research objectives. So think carefully about your individual research objectives. In effect, when you list your specific research objectives, you are really saying to your supervisor: 'This is what I am going to do in this dissertation, so mark me on these objectives. If I write about other, unidentified, objectives, then mark me down.'

---

**Some advice**

- Start each objective with a key word ('Identify', 'Assess', 'Evaluate', 'Explore', 'Examine', 'Investigate', 'Determine', 'Review', etc.). This will help you focus. Appendix C contains a list of keywords that you may find useful.
- The first individual objective tends to be a simple one, such as 'Identify' or 'Clarify', to help set the scene in your research study ('identify security issues', 'clarify the causes of smoking', etc.) prior to in-depth research in the main body of your work.
- The other keywords ought to indicate depth of study ('Evaluate critically', 'Explore', etc.) because the associated objectives will form the main part of your research. In the above example, 'evaluate critically' and 'explore' are used in objectives 2 and 3 respectively, where objective 2 will involve an extensive review of relevant literature, while objective 3 refers to the collection of empirical data.
- Do not have too many objectives: one or two is too few; six tends to be too many. Have one objective that sets the scene (e.g. to define a subject under study), another that will form the bulk of the Literature Review, another still that will refer to the empirical study (i.e. collection of raw data, e.g. interviews), and a final objective related to making recommendations. That makes four objectives. If you feel it necessary to include an additional objective, this tends to occur in objective 2, where you have the opportunity to indicate two major areas of study in the Literature Review (e.g. 'review the e-learning initiatives *and* their effectiveness in the workplace', 'assessing e-security threats *and* countermeasures', etc.). There is no definitive rule to the number of objectives allowed, but having too few is just as problematic as having too many, with the former leading to vagueness and the latter resulting in piecemeal work.

What follows is a fine example of a crisply written research aim and associated research objectives:

> The aim of this dissertation is to gain an understanding of how Cybercrime is affecting the online business community, with a view to offering guidance on the way forward. The following objectives have been identified of paramount importance in helping to achieve the aforementioned aim:
>
> - *Clarification* of what is meant by the term *Cybercrime*.
> - *Exploration* of the vulnerability of business organisations to Cybercrime.
> - *Critical assessment* of the effectiveness of current preventative measures.
> - *Implementation* of a case study of Cybercrime on an online business.
> - *Recommendations* to the business community, through a generic online security framework, on how to combat Cybercrime.

The above objectives are clear and logical and there is a developmental flow to the student's proposed research. The student could go on to justify the need for each of the objectives and offer some insight into each area: 'The first objective is necessary because the term Cybercrime can be misleading . . . Objectives 2 and 3 will form the core of the Literature Review and will involve the study of areas such as . . . Objective 4, the collection and analysis of empirical data, will allow the researcher the opportunity to study, in depth, one organisation . . . Finally, as a result of the Literature Review findings and an analysis of the case study, recommendations . . .'.

Your supervisor may request that you pose your research in the form of specific research questions. This is easy to do. First of all write down your overall research aim, then the individual objectives you think you need in order to satisfy this overall aim (as suggested above). Next, convert your overall research aim into a research question. Finally, convert your individual objectives into sub-questions. For example, the sample objectives in Appendix E are:

> Specifically, within the context of higher education, the objectives of this research are to:
>
> 1 *Identify* the forces driving e-Learning and the barriers to the successful delivery of e-Learning programmes.
> 2 *Evaluate critically* models and frameworks relevant to supporting academic staff in coping with e-Learning.
> 3 *Explore* staff stakeholder views and practices related to e-Learning preparation, including drivers and barriers to e-Learning.
> 4 *Formulate* recommendations on staff preparation issues.

These objectives, converted into questions, now become:

> Specifically, within the context of higher education, the objectives of this research are to answer the following questions:
>
> 1 What are the forces driving e-Learning and the barriers to the successful delivery of e-Learning programmes?
> 2 What models and frameworks are available to support academic staff in coping with e-Learning and how helpful are they?
> 3 What are staff stakeholder views and practices related to e-Learning preparation, including drivers and barriers to e-Learning?
> 4 As a result of these research questions, recommendations on staff preparation issues will be formulated.

Notice that objective 4 was not rewritten as a question, but simply added as an output. Also, you can mix and match how you wish to write your overall research aim and corresponding research objectives. For example, you can state your overall research aim, not as a question, but as a simple research task ('The purpose of this research is to investigate . . .') and then shape your individual research objectives into questions, the answers to which you reckon will cover your main research aim. Or you could do the reverse: write your overall research aim as a research question to be pursued ('The main question that this research will attempt to answer is . . .') and then list the individual research tasks you consider need to be completed in order to produce an answer to your substantive research question ('Objective 1 will identify the forces driving e-Learning and the barriers to the successful delivery of e-Learning programmes; Objective 2 will evaluate critically models and frameworks relevant to supporting academic staff in coping with e-Learning . . .', etc.). Alternatively, you can decide to dispense with the matter of research questions altogether and simply list your intended overall research aim and individual research objectives. To play safe on which approach to adopt, consult your dissertation supervisor. Different institutions, and different departments in the same institution, often prefer different practices.

You do not need to justify your overall aim again, but make an effort to restate briefly why the individual objectives are important, as shown in the sample chapter ('It would be difficult to comprehend how staff ought to meet the challenge of e-Learning without knowing the drivers behind e-Learning . . .').

## Outline research methods and timescales

You need to throw some light on how you will carry out your research, for example, through a Literature Review and, perhaps, the collection of empirical data (e.g. 'In turn, two main research vehicles will be exploited to facilitate this study: an in-depth review of relevant literature and the collection and analysis of empirical data'). There is no need at this stage to explain in detail how you will gather and analyse your empirical data: you can simply refer the reader to your later section on research methods (e.g. 'The Research Methods chapter contains the details of both the research strategy and the data collection techniques to be used to obtain empirical data'). You should, however, provide *outline information*, such as your general research strategy (e.g. case study), research participants (e.g. university staff), and data collection technique(s) (e.g. interviews), but the precise details of your research choices are left to your Research Methods chapter.

The sample Introduction starts by linking specific objectives with particular research activities:

> This research will depend on a review of pertinent literature (objectives 1 and 2) and the collection of empirical data through a case study (objective 3).

Next, examples of literature sources are identified:

> The secondary data (i.e. literature review) will largely come from journals (e.g. *International Journal of e-Learning*), conference proceedings (e.g. Online Educa), seminal books (e.g. Laurillard, 2009), and recent surveys. The following library databases will, in particular, be utilised to support this research: ERIC, British Education Index (ProQuest), and JSTOR.

Followed by outline information on how the empirical study will be implemented:

> The primary data (i.e. empirical data) will be collected through a case study . . . The case unit will consist of an academic department within . . . The means of collecting the primary data will be based on an initial questionnaire to academic staff from which a subset of the target population will be subject to a detailed follow-up interview. In addition, a number of *elite staff* – those responsible for the success of e-Learning and staff training – will be interviewed.

It will also prove helpful to your reader if you include a bar chart or a Gantt chart identifying the main research activities against expected durations. Even a basic table will suffice. The way to create your pictorial representation is to list, not the objectives, but the parts that will form the substance of your dissertation (e.g. Introduction, Literature Review, Research Methods, Discussion, Conclusion and Recommendations) and the time that you expect each activity to take, in terms of either weeks or months. It is not important that your expected timescales prove accurate, merely that you recognise the need for strategic planning, that you have an awareness of the big picture and how each of the tasks connects to complete the big picture, and that you have made a reasonable estimate on how long you expect to complete the main parts of your dissertation. In other words, you are doing what good researchers do – organising your research work.

Of course, you do not pluck your timescales out of thin air: have an intelligent guess at how long you think each task will take you, taking into account time for illness (e.g. common flu), holidays, unexpected emergencies, other work, days when you might be tired, etc. Do not expect your timescale to run like clockwork – it will not.

---

**!   A common mistake by students**

A common mistake by students is not to start their dissertation when they are supposed to, but leave it as late as possible, citing other commitments and always promising that after such-and-such a time, event, etc., they will concentrate exclusively on their dissertation. It is not uncommon for students still to be struggling with their Literature Review (and, on occasion, still rewriting their individual objectives!) when they ought to have completed their chapter on Research Methods. Too often, when students are submitting their final dissertation, they complain that they wish they had more time. If only they had listened to their supervisor's advice in the first place!

---

You could, if you find it more convenient, merge sub-sections, particularly if word-count is an issue. For example, the two sub-sections 'Research focus' and 'Overall research aim and individual research objectives' could merge into one sub-section, 'Research focus'. Or, alternatively, merge 'Overall research aim and individual research objectives' and 'Outline research methods and timescales' into one sub-section, 'Overall research aim and individual research objectives'. There is nothing wrong with that approach, but if you do that, then you need to remember to combine the main elements of each sub-section.

# Value of your research

Initially in the 'Research focus' sub-section of your Introduction, you ought to justify why you are doing your research, but it can also be a good idea to have a separate sub-section, entitled 'Value of this Research' or 'Importance of this Research' or 'Beneficiaries of this Research' or 'Research Worth' or 'Added Value', where you make it crystal clear to the reader – that is, those who will be judging the merit, or otherwise, of your efforts – how your work will add value to your field of study.

> **!** **A common mistake by students**
>
> It really is not difficult to address this concept of 'added value', but unfortu-
> nately a common mistake by students is to omit any clear reference to the
> importance of what they are doing and instead, at best, tentatively hint at the
> worth of their dissertation. **BE BOLD**. Either have a paragraph or two, or have
> a new sub-section (i.e. 'Value of this Research'), where you state, unequivo-
> cally, the worth of your work.

In what ways could your work *add value*? It could be that the area you have
picked to research is lacking in critical investigation. Or you are looking at a
subject from a different angle. Or your chosen research area is topical and
urgent (e.g. important medical issues or current computer security problems).
You need to state why you think your research is important and worth doing
(think in terms of who will benefit from your work and in what ways it will shed
light on specific research issues). State quite categorically why your research
study is important: 'This research is important for a number of reasons . . .' or
'This research adds value to current research in a variety of ways . . .'.

There are a number of ways that you can tackle the question of added
value. You could break down the importance of your research into two areas:
first, why your Literature Review is important and, second, why your empirical research is important. When explaining the importance of your Literature
Review, refer to your individual research objectives and how the Literature Review
will help meet them. But also explain the *overall* importance of your Literature
Review (perhaps it provides a coherent perspective on a subject area that has
previously received scant attention, producing a deeper intellectual understanding; or it meets an urgent need to address a topical subject, e.g. medical
research or computer security issues). Next, and still on the importance of
your Literature Review, explain the value of your specific sub-sections (e.g.
barriers to e-Learning). In other words, explain why you need to do a Literature Review, the areas that you intend reviewing, and the benefits to the
research community and others (e.g. business community) of this academic
research.

Whereas students sometimes find it difficult to justify a Literature Review
(and so tend not to), they find it is much easier to justify the worth of empirical
research. It may be that your particular empirical research activity is unique
and will provide a valuable insight into a problem area (although your research
does not need to be unique to be of value). It may be that your empirical
research will complement the work of others. Or there is a call for practical research in your area (from other researchers complaining about the paucity of research in your chosen field). You can also argue in terms of the value
of comparing and contrasting theory (i.e. your Literature Review) with practice
(i.e. your empirical work). Where possible, show evidence of support for your
empirical research.

Alternatively, *with implicit or explicit reference to your research object-ives*, you could summarise how your work will add value:

This research work will contribute to the development of the discipline of e-Learning in a number of important ways: first, by providing a critical review of issues pertinent to the implementation of e-Learning (what is driving e-Learning and what can act as a barrier); second, by critically examining existing models and frameworks to support academic staff; third, by obtaining the views of a variety of staff stakeholders on existing practices in e-Learning, a rich picture of e-Learning can emerge, allowing a meaningful comparison between theory and practice, from which an improved understanding of e-Learning issues in higher education can be derived, particularly with regard to academic staff training and support in preparing for e-Learning.

Or you could simplify things by providing a general statement highlighting a generic benefit of your research to the research community (as in the sample Introduction):

This research will benefit the academic research community by con-tributing to the field of e-Learning in the area of academic staff prepar-ation. The results of this work – secondary and primary data – can be used to enrich existing research schemas, particularly in relation to staff preparation models/frameworks and staff views, thus adding incrementally to the knowledge base of e-Learning research.

Followed by benefits to specific stakeholders (in this case managers, academic staff, and students):

Although the output from this research work cannot be generalised, none-theless the literature review findings and the empirical case study can act as a focus to inform elite staff in universities on potential staff e-Learning preparation issues, encouraging management to revisit how they prepare academic staff to engage fully with e-Learning. Other beneficiaries include: academic staff themselves, who will gain from recommendations that reflect their concerns on support issues; and, ultimately, students. If staff are better prepared to deliver e-Learning programmes, then that augurs well for the student experience.

This work will raise the profile of an area of educational delivery – e-Learning – that Vermeer (2000, p. 329) once decried had often been dependent on 'the enthusiasm of the recently converted' for its success. Technology is increasingly at the heart of university education and this research will benefit all those with an interest in ensuring that technology is exploited by fully trained academic staff.

In essence, pointing out the value or importance of your intended research will aid in explaining to the reader why you have chosen to research a particular topic.

# A further suggestion

Remember, within each chapter of your dissertation you should take every opportunity to gain marks. Another way to enhance your dissertation Introduction is by tagging on, at the end of your Introduction, an outline of each chapter in your dissertation. You can do this by typing up the headings for each chapter, and then, once the dissertation is complete, fill in basic information outlining the areas covered in each of the chapters. If the Introduction of your dissertation had as its structure the sub-sections 1.1 Background; 1.2 Research focus; 1.3 Overall research aim and individual research objectives; 1.4 Outline research methods and timescales; and 1.5 Value of this Research, then the sub-section Outline structure would be labelled 1.6 Outline structure. At this stage you can type up the headings for sub-section 1.6, which are just your chapter headings:

**1.6 Outline Structure**
Chapter 1: Introduction
Chapter 2: Literature Review
Chapter 3: Research Methods
Chapter 4: Case Study Results: Academic Staff; Elite Staff
Chapter 5: Conclusion
Chapter 6: References

As you complete each chapter, you are then in a position to write down the main areas that were covered in that chapter. Note that you are not summarising the content of each chapter in your outline structure. You are merely providing the reader with a statement of the main topics addressed:

**Chapter 1: Introduction**
This chapter provides the reader with *background* information on the impact of e-Learning on the traditional teaching and learning paradigm in the University environment, including an illustration of some drivers and barriers and the need for an understanding of how staff are being prepared to make the switch from *sage on the stage* to *guide on the side*. The *focus* of this research is discussed and justified and the *overall research aim* and *individual research objectives* are identified. *Research methods and timescales* are outlined, as is the *value of this research*.

Chapter 2: Literature Review
Chapter 3: Research Methods
Chapter 4: Case Study Results: Academic Staff; Elite Staff
Chapter 5: Conclusion
Chapter 6: References

In this example, the main things that were discussed in the sample Introduction chapter in Appendix E have been highlighted: *background* information, research *focus*, the *overall research aim and individual research objectives, outline research methods and timescales,* and *value of this research.* These were easily obtained from the sub-headings in the sample chapter. Similarly, once you have completed your Literature Review, go back to your introductory chapter – Chapter 1 Introduction – and complete the relevant part of your outline structure. Once again, do this by identifying the key topics in your Literature Review, i.e. just take the sub-headings that you created for your Literature Review chapter and lift them to form the basis of your outline structure:

Every time you finish a chapter in your dissertation, return to your introduction to complete the relevant part of your outline structure. Appendix F contains a completed example of an outline structure. Not only is an outline structure helpful to the reader, importantly it can also get you extra marks. It is not difficult to do, and is another step towards convincing your supervisor that you are a top student.

### Chapter 1: Introduction
This chapter provides the reader with *background* information on the impact of e-Learning on the traditional teaching and learning paradigm in the University environment, including an illustration of some drivers and barriers and the need for an understanding of how staff are being prepared to make the switch from *sage on the stage* to *guide on the side.* The *focus* of this research is discussed and justified and the *overall research aim* and *individual research objectives* are identified. *Research methods and timescales* are outlined, as is the *value of this research.*

### Chapter 2: Literature Review
This chapter *defines* the term e-Learning, discusses *distance learning* (a driver for e-Learning), clarifies the *drivers* for e-Learning (including major reports, strategic forces, and the benefits of e-Learning to different stakeholders), explores *barriers* to e-Learning, evaluates *guidelines and models* on e-Learning support infrastructures in relation to providing support for academic staff preparation, and *justifies the need for empirical data* on academic staff preparation issues.

Chapter 3: Research Methods
Chapter 4: Case Study Results: Academic Staff; Elite Staff
Chapter 5: Conclusion
Chapter 6: References

One last point: when you are writing your dissertation, you need to decide on the *tense* used. You can write in the past tense ('This dissertation investigated . . .') or you can write in a tense that reflects the natural course of events, like an unfolding story, depending on where you are in your dissertation. For example, when you write your Chapter 1 Introduction, you have not started your research work, so you can use a tense to reflect that fact: 'This dissertation will examine . . .'; and after you complete any empirical research you then write in an appropriate tense: 'The results of the interviews show that . . .', etc.

In other words, you can either complete your research work and then write it up in the past tense, or write it up as you go along using a tense that is appropriate to where you are in your dissertation and what you are doing, will do, or have done. However, check with your supervisor first, in case your department has a preference.

## Summary of key points

- The introductory chapter to your dissertation should present the following information: background; research focus; overall research aim and individual research objectives; outline research methods and timescales; and the value of your intended research.
- The 'Background' sub-section to your Introduction should place your research area in context, referring to relevant literature sources using a variety of direct and indirect referencing techniques.
- The 'Research focus' sub-section of your Introduction can be combined with the Background sub-section, or placed in a separate sub-section. It establishes the subject of your research.
- The 'Overall research aim and individual research objectives' sub-section of your Introduction clarifies your research focus in simple terms, where your main research aim is identified and the specific research objectives needed to complete your main aim are enumerated. Both your overall aim and your individual research objectives can be transformed into research questions.
- The 'Outline research methods and timescales' sub-section provides an overview of the research methods that you will use to do your research, including time estimates to complete your major research tasks.
- Next, a sub-section, or a paragraph or two placed in previous sub-sections, should be created, explaining the value of your research, i.e. why you think your research is worth doing (think in terms of the beneficiaries of your work).
- Finally, create an outline structure, which you complete cumulatively as your progress through your dissertation. The outline structure highlights the main sub-sections contained in each of your chapters.

# Chapter 5

# The Literature Review

- *What constitutes a good Literature Review?* • *Structuring your Literature Review* • *Description versus critical evaluation* • *Learning theory and your dissertation* • *Literature search techniques* • *University library databases* • *Contextual Review* • *Further reading* • *Summary of key points*

This chapter identifies what constitutes a good Literature Review, shows you how to structure a Literature Review, emphasises the importance of critical evaluation, demonstrates how an understanding of learning theory can enhance your Literature Review, offers guidance on how to search for literature and where to look, and introduces a variation on the traditional Literature Review called a Contextual Review.

## What constitutes a good Literature Review?

What advice can one give about writing a Literature Review? It would certainly help if you understood the point of a Literature Review. You carry out a review of literature to find out who is saying what about the things you are interested in, specifically your research objectives, and to convince your supervisor/ marker that you have read widely, and in depth, and that you have the necessary skills to both interpret and evaluate such literature, or as Haywood and Wragg (1982, p. 2) put it: a review of literature should demonstrate that 'the writer has studied existing work in the field with insight'.

A *good* Literature Review is characterised by the following features:

- It lays out what research has been done by others *relevant to your research aim/objectives* (why waste your time discussing irrelevant stuff?).

- It presents the work of others in a *clear, interesting,* and *progressive manner* (to build up a coherent/logical picture).
- It provides evidence of *in-depth critical evaluation* (i.e. to show that YOU can give an opinion and support it with argument/evidence).
- It highlights *pertinent/emerging issues* (otherwise what is the point of your Literature Review?).
- It *cites a variety of relevant sources properly* (to show that you are well read and scholarly in your approach).

Below are examiner comments complimenting aspects of various student Literature Reviews, comments that you want to see written on your marked dissertation:

- '*Highly focused* Literature Review . . .'
- 'Clear evidence of *critical evaluation* . . .'
- '*Logical* structure . . . *eliciting* main issues . . .'
- 'Well done! An excellent *in-depth* review of *relevant* literature, supported by *properly cited* sources . . .'

Conversely, a *bad* Literature Review exhibits too many of the following (bad) practices:

- Irrelevant rambling (i.e. what we call '*student drift*').
- Ideas presented in no particular order (and so difficult to follow the thread of the student's discussion).
- Too descriptive (with no/little attempt to give an opinion, much less support it with reasoned argument).
- Ends abruptly, devoid of any clarification of main findings.
- Limited sources used (mainly websites), coupled with inconsistent referencing styles.

The following are other examiner comments highlighting deficiencies in student Literature Reviews (comments you hope do not appear in your marked work!):

- 'Poor standard of referencing.'
- 'Too descriptive in nature.'
- 'No evidence of critical evaluation.'
- 'Lacks focus.'
- 'Limited use of sources.'
- 'Superficial discussions.'

Common problems that students encounter when they first start to write their Literature Review include: (1) how to structure their Literature Review chapter; (2) where to find relevant literature; (3) how to review the literature that they have found; and (4) how to reference the literature that they are reviewing. Point (4) is covered in Chapter 2, 'Referencing and Plagiarism'. Points (1) to (3) will be covered in this chapter.

Let us first of all turn to a fundamental task: how to structure your Literature Review.

## Structuring your Literature Review

There is an impulse to start searching for any literature that vaguely relates to your general research topic. This is a mistake. Refrain from this impulse because you will waste precious time wandering down literary blind alleys. Instead, you need to establish a strategy of attack that is focused and efficient. To that end, work out first of all which of your research objectives will be covered by a Literature Review, structure your Literature Review accordingly, and then – and only then – start searching for literature to address those specific research objectives. In that way, you will be targeting literature sources to meet well-defined parts of your Literature Review. In terms of structure, a good Literature Review will have a brief introduction, followed by sub-section headings that reflect specific research objectives, concluding with a summary highlighting emerging issues.

 **A common mistake by students**

A common mistake by students is to, without warning, immediately start discussing literature that they have read, leaving the reader to work out how it relates to the student's research objectives. Try and avoid such impatience: carefully spell out to the reader the topics that you intend covering. It keeps you on the right track and lets the reader know what to expect.

The introduction to your Literature Review should be succinct. Keep clear of waffle. Simply remind the reader (i.e. your supervisor/marker) of your research objectives and the areas you will cover in your Literature Review. Typically, not all of your research objectives will be covered in the Literature Review. Remember to point out the value of your review. By doing this you will have a reference point to help you achieve focus, which is so important in a Literature Review. It is not uncommon for students, halfway through their Literature Review, to forget about their stated objectives and wander into other areas that, although interesting, are largely irrelevant to their work (as well as eating into their word-count).

Appendix G contains a fitting example of an introductory section to a Literature Review. It re-lists the research objectives, indicates which objectives will be tackled within the Literature Review, and reiterates the value of the Literature Review topics, and so places the relative importance of the Literature Review within the context of the dissertation.

As mentioned, a simple but clever way to avoid the pitfall of *student drift* is to create sub-sections headings in your Literature Review chapter that reflect specific research objectives. This makes it difficult to stray from what you are supposed to be writing about.

 **A common mistake by students**

A common mistake by students is to stray from their intended research focus. Too often supervisors witness muddled dissertations that meander aimlessly and fail to keep the reader focused on the student's initial research objectives. Avoid that mistake by creating sub-section headings tailored to your research objectives.

Let us now concentrate on the detail of how to structure your dissertation by looking at an example. We shall revisit the research objectives listed in the sample Introduction in Appendix E, but this time with an eye on the Literature Review:

Specifically, within the context of higher education, the objectives of this research are to:

1 *Identify* the forces driving e-Learning and the barriers to the successful delivery of e-Learning programmes.
2 *Evaluate critically* models and frameworks relevant to supporting academic staff in coping with e-Learning.
3 *Explore* staff stakeholder views and practices related to e-Learning preparation, including drivers and barriers to e-Learning.
4 *Formulate* recommendations on staff preparation issues.

The first two objectives would be tackled in the Literature Review chapter, while objective 3 would be implemented through the collection and analysis of empirical data (e.g. case study). Research objective 1 could be tackled in two related sub-sections: e-Learning drivers could form one sub-section and e-Learning barriers another sub-section. Taking into account the brief introduction, right away you have three sub-sections to your Literature Review chapter (remember to start with an *introductory* sub-section, where you let the reader know the topics that you are going to discuss and how they relate to your research objectives – see the example in Appendix G as an illustration of good practice).

If your Literature Review chapter was numbered Chapter 2 (Chapter 1 being your dissertation Introduction), then these three sub-sections could be numbered as follows:

2.1 Introduction
2.2 The Drive for e-Learning in Higher Education
2.3 Barriers to Delivering e-Learning Programmes

It is your choice whether or not to number the subheadings. Next, look at what sub-sections could be created from your second objective (*'Evaluate critically* models and frameworks relevant to supporting academic staff in coping with e-Learning'). An appropriate sub-section appears in 2.4 below, once again lifted directly from the research objective:

2.1 Introduction
2.2 The Drive for e-Learning in Higher Education
2.3 Barriers to Delivering e-Learning Programmes
2.4 Models/Frameworks to Support Academic Staff

By explicitly linking your sub-section headings to your research objectives, you ensure that your work will be very focused, thereby reducing the opportunity for waffle and student drift (= good marks).

Finally, you need to conclude your Literature Review by highlighting emerging issues, so make your final sub-section heading about emerging issues (or key issues or pertinent issues, etc.):

2.1 Introduction
2.2 The Drive for e-Learning in Higher Education
2.3 Barriers to Delivering e-Learning Programmes
2.4 Models/Frameworks to Support Academic Staff
2.5 Summary and Emerging Issues

Figure 5.1 illustrates this linkage between the specific research objectives in the example and the corresponding structure of the Literature Review, thus minimising the danger of sleepwalking into wasteful and unrelated discussion.

You can include other sub-sections as you see fit. One such sub-section commonly seen in student dissertations, which avoids ambiguity on terms used, is a sub-section on definitions. For instance, the example above is about e-Learning, so an early sub-section entitled 'Defining e-Learning' could be inserted after the Introduction:

2.1 Introduction
2.2 Defining e-Learning
2.3 The Drive for e-Learning in Higher Education
2.4 Barriers to Delivering e-Learning programmes
2.5 Models/Frameworks to Support Academic Staff
2.6 Summary and Emerging Issues

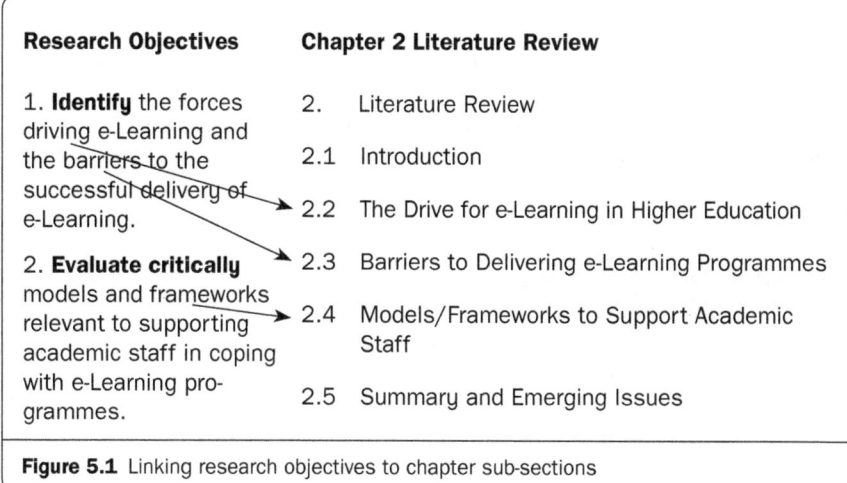

**Figure 5.1** Linking research objectives to chapter sub-sections

If your topic was, say, 'accessibility and website design', then you may wish to have a sub-section on what you mean by 'accessibility'. Similarly, if your research is focused on 'modernism and its impact on contemporary art', then a good starting point could be a sub-section on defining what you mean by 'modernism' (and/or 'contemporary art').

Now you have a very structured, focused, and logical approach to your Literature Review (= good marks), one that ought to prevent Literature Review 'drift'. Of course, as you complete your individual sub-sections, it is likely that you will also create sub-sections within sub-sections. For instance, in sub-section 2.3 above – The Drive for e-Learning in Higher Education – an appropriate collection of lower-level headings could be:

2.3 The Drive for e-Learning in Higher Education
    2.3.1 An Early Impetus: The Dearing Report
    2.3.2 Strategic Forces Driving e-Learning
    2.3.3 Benefits of e-Learning

One thing to bear in mind when you create further divisions: if you are not writing very much within each sub-section, then your Literature Review will appear superficial and thus lacking depth. One student (who rarely turned up for pre-arranged meetings) had about twenty sub-section headings in a draft Literature Review submission, with each of the twenty sub-sections containing only two or three sentences. Try and avoid writing a sub-section that contains only one or two sentences:

**2.2 Research Aim**
The aim of this research is to investigate current approaches to the development of business information systems (IS) within the public sector in terms of their cost-effectiveness.

In such a scenario, you need to remove a number of your sub-headings and merge others. Remember, in your Literature Review you are trying to convince your supervisor that you are well read and that you can critically review the work of others, which you can only achieve if you engage in meaningful discussion under each sub-section. Of course, deficient structuring and superficial comment are not confined to the Literature Review. Here is the type of structure and content that students can unwittingly replicate in the chapter on research methods:

**3.2 Research Philosophy**
    3.2.1   Phenomenology
          [Two sentences on phenomenology]
    3.2.2   Positivism
          [One sentence on positivism]
    3.2.3   Research Philosophy
          [Two sentences on research philosophy]. Etc.

At the end of your Literature Review, you want to be in a position where you have:

1 Summarised your Literature Review findings (bullet points are acceptable at this stage);
2 Highlighted emerging themes/issues; and
3 Justified the need for your empirical study (if you intend doing one).

Appendix H contains a sample conclusion for a Literature Review, based on the e-Learning example used throughout this book. Your conclusion to your Literature Review may be shorter, or longer, depending on the number of words that you have at your disposal. What is good about this sample conclusion that you might wish to replicate when concluding your own Literature Review?

First, it summarises the findings from the Literature Review ('The study of relevant e-Learning literature . . .'). Your Literature Review might be quite large and complex, so by providing a précis, you will help the reader to understand your work. A summary is also a useful *aide-mémoire* in that it ought to help you to stay focused and so avoid the potential for 'drift'.

Second, when you summarise your Literature Review findings, make sure that you emphasise what you consider to be the salient points ('The review of literature stressed the need . . .'). You do not need to go over the arguments again because that takes up valuable words: just point out what you found out in the literature *vis-à-vis* your research objectives, which, in turn, ought to be reflected in the sub-section headings. You are, in effect, summarising the content that appears under each core sub-section heading, in this case the drivers for e-Learning, barriers, and support for academic staff.

Third, if your research involves the collection and analysis of empirical data, then you ought to explain, in your Literature Review conclusion, the necessity for such empirical research. For example, perhaps the literature that you looked at expressed concern about the lack of empirical research in your field of study or perhaps current studies are incomplete in some way ('A crucial issue for the development of e-Learning . . .').

Finally, make some sort of reference to your next chapter – Research Methods – so as to provide a link for the reader ('The next stage of this research will detail the research methods to be used . . .').

By providing a summary, highlighting main points, the need for empirical research (if you are implementing empirical research), and a link to the next chapter, the conclusion to your Literature Review ought to add to the quality of your dissertation. Depending on the word-length of your dissertation, your summary may be shorter, or longer, than the sample summary given in Appendix H. If word-count is an issue, feel free to conclude with a bullet-point summary. Here is a bullet-point version of the narrative summary in Appendix H. The bullet-point summary has a word-count of 269 words, as opposed to the 423 words in the narrative version in Appendix H, a saving of 154 words without loss of meaning:

'The study of e-Learning literature revealed that:

- There was no agreed definition of e-Learning. One was produced in this dissertation, highlighting connectivity, support infrastructures, and flexibility of access and delivery.
- Strategic drivers included perceived reduced costs, access to global markets, and increased student numbers.
- Benefits to staff and students included flexibility of delivery and access, independent learning, and job opportunities.
- Barriers to e-Learning included staff resistance, student drop-out rates, student inability to cope with independent learning, opposition to globalisation, access to support facilities, inadequate student support infrastructures and, crucially, lack of staff preparation to cope with e-Learning.
- Meaningful guidelines and models were identified as a necessary prerequisite to preparing academic staff for e-Learning environments.
- Guidelines and models, however, were mainly skeletal and general in nature with relatively little advice based on evidence-based research.
- There is a continuing need for empirical data on how academic staff are preparing for e-Learning, and the aforementioned review of literature supports this claim.

To arrive at a deeper understanding of how universities are meeting the challenge of e-Learning, empirical research will be implemented. Specifically, such research will attempt to find out how academic staff are preparing for e-Learning, what motivates them to do so, and, from a wider perspective, the drivers and barriers acting on the university environment in relation to developing e-Learning programmes. The next stage of this research will detail the Research Methods to be used to capture the empirical data, including details on the research strategy to be adopted, data collection techniques, sample selection, and management of the researcher's role.'

A good Literature Review requires depth as well as structure. Now that you know how to avoid drifting from your research objectives by clearly mapping research objectives onto sub-section headings, and know how to introduce and conclude your Literature Review, let's look at how to write the actual review. To fulfil the concept of a 'review', you will need to advance beyond mere *description* of what you have read and show evidence of *critical evaluation*, otherwise your Literature Review would be more appropriately headed Literature Report or Literature Summary, and not Literature Review.

## Description versus critical evaluation

In-text referencing requires that you learn how to cite sources (see Chapter 2, 'Referencing and Plagiarism'), how to use quotations properly, and to know the difference between *describing* the work of others and *critically evaluating* their efforts.

---

**!   A common mistake by students**

A common mistake by students is to quote a source out of the blue, without any warning. A typical example of this is:

*'Software Piracy can be defined as the unauthorised copying, reproduction, use, manufacture or distribution of software products' (Source: Microsoft).*

What is wrong with this quotation? A number of things. In the first place, the actual referencing is poor: the Harvard style of referencing (author–date system) has not been applied properly - it should have read (Microsoft, 2004) instead of (Source: Microsoft). In fact, if you are quoting a literary source, you ought to give the page reference as well, for example (Microsoft, 2004, p. 12). However, the main problem with the quotation is that it forms a sentence on its own, with nothing before the quotation to prepare the reader and no comment on the quotation itself. In other words, the quotation appears out of the blue with no warning beforehand and no explanation afterwards.

---

It is important that you let the reader know when you are about to quote someone. If you are embedding a quotation in your sentence, then you can do so like this:

Thomson (2005, p. 345) has a cynical view of e-Learning: 'it is a big con'.

If the quotation is long (three or more lines), then introduce the quotation to the reader as shown in the following example:

> The Dearing Report (1997, p. 202) foresaw benefits of using ICT in higher education:
>
> > '... we believe that the innovative application of ... C&IT holds out much promise for improving the quality, flexibility and effectiveness of higher education. The potential benefits will extend to, and affect the practice of, learning and teaching and research.'

Alternatively, you can place the citation at the end of the quotation:

> An influential report foresaw the benefits of using ICT in higher education:
>
> > '... we believe that the innovative application of ... C&IT holds out much promise for improving the quality, flexibility and effectiveness of higher education. The potential benefits will extend to, and affect the practice of, learning and teaching and research' (Dearing, 1997, p. 202).

Too often students use quotations without any warning or explanation, which they then compound with poor referencing. You will have succeeded only in showing your supervisor that you can neither reference nor make appropriate use of quotations. By all means quote sources but do so in a helpful manner applying proper citation conventions.

Just as bad is the overuse of quotations. If the Literature Review part of your dissertation is full of other people's words, then you are leaving little or no room for your own voice to come through. Supervisors want to know, *inter alia*, what YOU think about the literature you are reading, so use quotations sparingly and as supporting material for *your* discussion. It is YOUR dissertation, so let YOUR voice come through.

What separates a good student from an average/poor student in the Literature Review is that the former will provide evidence of *critical evaluation* in their work, while the latter concentrates on *describing* what they have read. Here are examples of typical (negative) comments from supervisors, related to the Literature Review:

- 'Too descriptive!'
- 'Completely devoid of critical thinking.'
- 'Superficial discussion with little in the way of critical thought.'
- 'Interesting thesis let down by uncritical acceptance of relevant literature.'
- 'Referencing is shoddy and further complicated by thin assessment of important issues.'
- 'Student concentrates on describing issues to the detriment of reasoned argument.'

What is the difference between *critical evaluation* and *description*? Imagine that you have started your Literature Review, its focus is on e-Learning, and that you have decided that one of the first things that you will do is to define e-Learning. You write the following piece of text:

> Charles Clarke, the Education Secretary, in a foreword to a consultation document on e-Learning (Department for Education and Skills, 2003a, p. 1), defined e-Learning in the following simplistic terms: 'If someone is learning in a way that uses information and communication technologies, they are using e-Learning.' According to this definition, using the Internet as a vehicle for learning would qualify as e-Learning.

The aforementioned piece of text has some admirable qualities, namely: it is clear, the referencing has been applied properly, and the quotation has been successfully embedded in the body of the text. Also, the student has provided a basic description, through an example, of what he believes to be Charles Clarke's view of what counts as e-Learning. This piece of text would achieve pass marks.

However, it is better to go beyond mere description. To achieve decent marks you have to show that you can offer critical evaluation – what Haywood and Wragg (1982) call 'insight' – of other people's views. That does not mean to say that you review the work of others from a negative perspective, though on occasion that may be appropriate, but rather that you can offer your own point of view and support it with reasoned argument. For example, if the student had written the following additional piece of text (in bold for illustrative purposes), then, because of evidence of critical thinking, more marks would have been gained:

> Charles Clarke, the Education Secretary, in a foreword to a consultation document on e-Learning (Department for Education and Skills, 2003a, p. 1), defined e-Learning in the following simplistic terms: 'If someone is learning in a way that uses information and communication technologies, they are using e-Learning.' According to this definition, using the Internet as a vehicle for learning would qualify as e-Learning. **Unfortunately, the definition, although having the benefit of brevity, suffers from a lack of clarity. For example, it is difficult to think of an example of technology-enabled learning that would be excluded from this definition, i.e. it is all-inclusive and therefore unhelpful in understanding what counts as e-Learning (and what does not).**

The first two sentences are the same as the previous text. The added text (from 'Unfortunately, the definition . . .' onwards) shows that the student knows how to review the work of others in a critical way. It is irrelevant whether or not your supervisor agrees with your opinion: what your supervisor wants to see from you is that you have an opinion on the literature that you are reading and that you can support your opinion. To move towards achieving top marks for your Literature Review, adopt the following technique:

(a) Describe what you are reading (to show that you can interpret what others write).
(b) Offer your views on what you have read.
(c) Support your views (i.e. demonstrate *critical evaluation*).

Here is another example that ticks all three boxes above. The use of square brackets indicates where points (a), (b), and (c) occur (**[a]**, **[b]**, and **[c]** would obviously not appear in the original text):

There are a number of definitions that equate e-Learning with Internet-based learning. For example, Thomas (2001, p. 2) **[a]** associates e-Learning with Internet-based learning:

> *'Today's learning communities gather in the virtual space provided by the Internet – communicating at the speed of thought, on a global scale. E-Learning is the most effective, efficient means ever invented for people to get the knowledge they need, at the time when they need it most, wherever they happen to be.'*

However, **[b]** to restrict e-Learning to Internet-based learning could lead to anomalies in deciding what is accepted as e-Learning. For example, **[c]** if a university has two groups of students studying a module, with one set learning at home through the Internet, and the other set of students learning on-campus, with both sets of students using identical 'e-Learning' software, then it would be inconsistent to classify one type of learning as e-Learning, and the other not, just because it is not Internet-based. To underline this point, WebCT's course authoring software is used over the Internet and on campus, with 80% of its software used on campus (Bates, 2001), indicating that e-Learning can appear in pure e-Learning environments and also be part of a traditional teaching and learning setting.

Do not overdo the critical evaluation. You are not required to evaluate critically every piece of literature that you read, or interpret and assess the worth of every quotation that you use. To do so would create unnecessary work for yourself, significantly hinder progress in your dissertation, and make for turgid reading. There are times when you describe things and there are other times when you decide to go further and delve critically into perceived wisdom. That judgement is for you to make, but essentially you display critical evaluation when you are involved in tackling issues central to your dissertation.

A word of caution about how you use words when referring to the work of other researchers. If you write, 'Gillingham (2006) *discovered* that . . .', you are accepting his position. Alternatively, if you were to write 'Gillingham (2006) *alleges* that . . .', you are viewing his work in a suspicious light, casting doubt on his opinion. On the other hand, if you write 'Gillingham (2006) *concludes* that . . .', you are adopting a neutral stance. The verbs you use – *discovered*, *alleges*, *concludes*, etc. – can reveal to the reader what you really think about the literature that you are reading, so use them carefully. There is nothing wrong, *per se*, in using positive verbs to show that you are supportive of someone else's ideas, if that is the perception that you want to convey to your reader; similarly, there is nothing wrong in using negative verbs, such as *claims*, *distorts*, *confuses*, etc., if that is your intention. More often than not, though, when students describe the sources that they have read, they tend to re-use the same two or three verbs, again and again, such as the neutral 'Thomson (2004) *states* that . . .' or the telepathic 'Thomson (2004) *thinks* that . . .' or, worse, the lazy 'Thomson (2004) *says* that . . .'. Table 5.1 gives a snapshot of the wide variety of verbs available for your use.

**Table 5.1**  Snapshot of useful verbs

| | | | | |
|---|---|---|---|---|
| Accepts | Asserts | Compares | Convinces | Determines |
| Acknowledges | Assumes | Compiles | Cultivates | Develops |
| Acquiesces | Attempts | Complains | Dabbles | Digresses |
| Adduces | Bombasts | Concludes | Debates | Dilutes |
| Admits | Bores | Concocts | Debunks | Disagrees |
| Adopts | Builds | Concurs | Declares | Discloses |
| Advances | Cajoles | Confirms | Deduces | Discovers |
| Advises | Calculates | Confuses | Defends | Discusses |
| Advocates | Captures | Considers | Delves | Dismisses |
| Agrees | Cautions | Conspires | Demonstrates | Dispels |
| Alludes | Challenges | Constructs | Denies | Dispenses |
| Appears | Clarifies | Contemplates | Denounces | Displays |
| Argues | Clings | Contends | Derides | Disputes |
| Arrives | Clutches | Contrives | Derives | Dissents |
| Articulates | Comments | Conveys | Desists | |

Appendix I contains a comprehensive list of verbs from which you can select those that reflect what you want to write, which in turn ought to go some way to stopping you from repeating the same tired old verbs *ad nauseam*.

The appropriate use of verbs will also help towards achieving a readable, coherent, and persuasive Literature Review. In terms of critical evaluation, you want to see written on your marked dissertation the following sorts of effusive comments:

- 'Excellent. Student not only describes pertinent issues but also engages the reader with reasoned argument. Well done!'
- 'An impressive Literature Review. Relevant sources used + clear evidence of critical evaluation. Keep up the good work!'

- 'Student knows how to interpret the work of others and offer her own opinion, supported by clear and logical argument. Highly commendable.'
- 'At last your own voice is shining through! And what a voice! Enjoyed reading this work. Focused, thoughtful, and worthy of publication. Superb stuff.'

If you follow the advice given, you should be well placed to achieve such fulsome praise!

In a final attempt to get across to you the importance of critical evaluation, let us explore Benjamin Bloom's theory of learning, a theory that was developed in the middle of the last century (1956) but which still has credibility today. You will soon see that the elements in his learning theory are used by your supervisors – if not consciously, then subconsciously – when they come to judge the worth of your submitted work. Understand this theory, and how it relates to your dissertation, and you will put yourself in an excellent position to exploit its elements to the benefit of your dissertation.

## Learning theory and your dissertation

There is more than one way to learn how to do things. Learning a martial art, for example, can be achieved by reading books, watching videos, listening to friends talk about martial arts and, of course, through actual participation. Likewise, in the world of education, there are different ways that students can learn. Bloom (1956) identified three broad ways in which students learn. These involve the use of:

1 Cognitive skills (development of mental skills to acquire knowledge)
2 Affective skills (development of feelings, emotions and attitudes)
3 Psychomotor skills (development of manual and physical skills).

Learning about a martial art, for instance, will incorporate all three types of learning: understanding the theory of martial art techniques (*cognitive* skills); developing positive attitudes towards aspects of your chosen martial art (*affective* skills); and when you practise the physical techniques 'on the mat', you progress your *psychomotor* skills.

There is a symbiotic, circular relationship between the use of these skills and their actual development: as you apply them, you develop them; and as you develop them, you are better able to apply them. For instance, if you are learning how to perform a turning kick in Tae Kwon Do, a Korean martial art, then as your instructor explains the kick to you, you will make use of your cognitive skills – mental skills – to try and understand what your instructor is saying. You can apply your new-found knowledge of the turning kick when you try to perform the technique (using psychomotor skills). And as a result of your physical attempt at executing the kick, you can reflect on your performance, relating theory to practice, which means that you develop your cognitive and psycho-motor skills each time you apply the technique and reflect on your progress.

This is called *learning*, and it is an active process. It requires your involve-ment – sitting in a lecture theatre, half asleep, is *not* learning! This theory about learning is all very well, but how does it relate to succeeding with your disser-tation? In the context of your dissertation, it is your cognitive skills that you are being marked on. You need to show your marker that you have them, and that you have them at a variety of levels. Bloom categorised the different layers of cognitive learning (as he saw them), which is referred to collectively as Bloom's taxonomy of learning and is illustrated in the learning pyramid in Figure 5.2.

Let us relate this hierarchy of learning to your dissertation. Your marker will go through your dissertation looking to find evidence of higher-level cog-nitive skills (such as *analysis*, *synthesis*, and *evaluation*). If you stick to low-level cognitive skills (such as *knowledge* and basic *comprehension*), you will get low marks. If you exhibit higher-level cognitive skills, you will secure high marks. Table 5.2 shows examples of evidence for each of these cognitive skills, ranging from 1 to 6 in increasing order of importance, in your Literature Review.

Bloom's categories of learning have been updated, with some of the ele-ments retained, others moved position or merged or apparently removed (Figure 5.3). This new version by Anderson and Krathwohl (2001) replaces the low-level cognitive skill *Knowledge* with *Remembering* (to emphasise that this skill is really about showing memory skills); *Comprehension* is replaced with

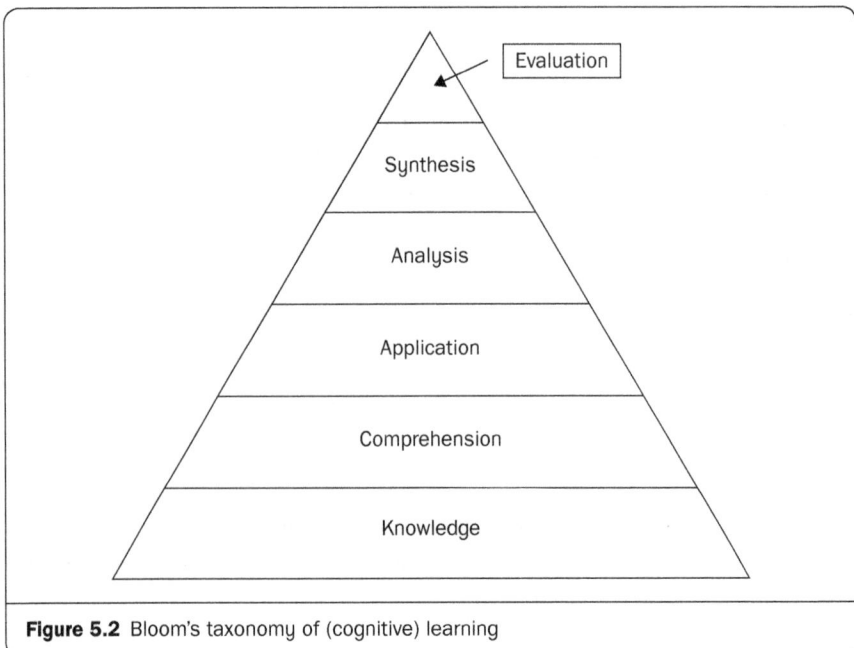

**Figure 5.2** Bloom's taxonomy of (cognitive) learning

**Table 5.2** Sample evidence of cognitive skills in your dissertation

| Cognitive skill | Evidence (in your Literature Review) |
| --- | --- |
| 1. Knowledge | Repeating what you have heard in a lecture. Writing down simple facts and figures. Quoting other authors. So, basic memory skills, but no evidence that you understand what you write about. |
| 2. Comprehension | Paraphrasing what you have heard (in a lecture) or read. Summarising material in your own words, illustrating simple comprehension skills. |
| 3. Application | Taking someone's idea or view or theory, and giving a practical example to show that you can apply this idea or view or theory. In other words, you can relate theory to the real world. |
| 4. Analysis | Breaking down arguments into constituent parts, dissecting an author's logic, identifying key issues in reports, surveys, articles, etc. |
| 5. Synthesis | Bringing together strands of your argument and discussion, voiced at different stages of your dissertation, to create a coherent message to the reader. |
| 6. Evaluation | Critically evaluating the work of other authors – combining a variety of cognitive skills above – and so presenting evidence of your ability to understand what you are reading by giving opinions and justifying them. |

*Understanding* (but basically means the same thing); *Synthesis* is removed (although it is embedded in the new top-level skill, *Create*); a new skill, *Create*, is included (although it does not necessarily mean that you create your own ideas, or theories, as such, but more commonly that you bring your thoughts together to form a coherent whole).

Do not worry about the subtle differences between the two models of learning: they both amount to roughly the same thing, even if the labels differ here and there. The key message you need to get from these models is that sticking to low-level cognitive skills in your Literature Review will get you low marks, whereas providing clear evidence of high-level skills will get you high marks. Of course, you will need to show some memory skills (e.g. quoting the work of researchers or recalling someone's idea) but you must take the opportunity to illustrate that you have high-level cognitive skills, by applying theory (through examples), analysing what you have read, collating your thoughts (synthesis), giving your opinion and backing it up with evidence and argument; all painting a rich picture of a critical, comprehensive, and coherent review of literature relevant to your research objectives. The cognitive skills that you display in your review of literature should also be replicated throughout the other major

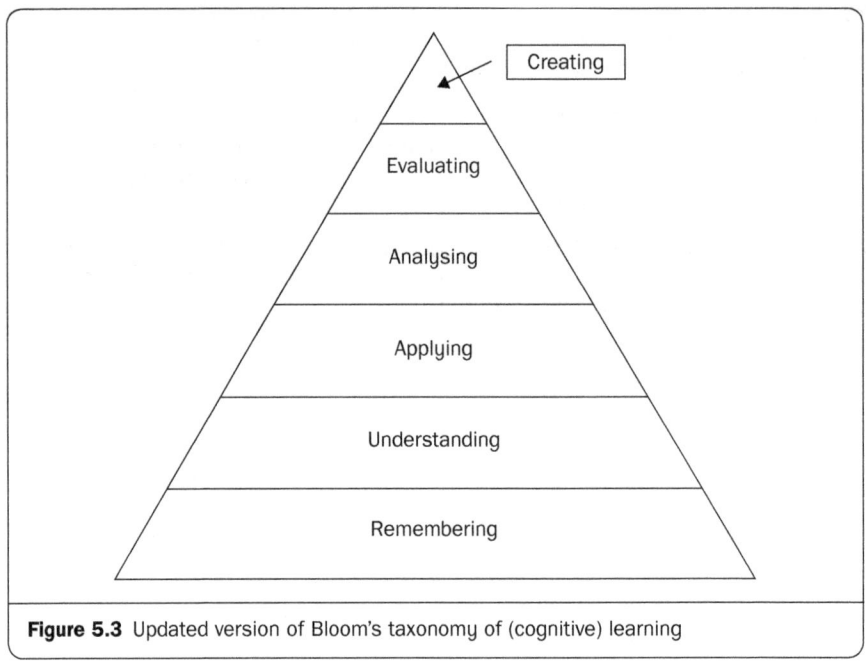

**Figure 5.3** Updated version of Bloom's taxonomy of (cognitive) learning

stages of the dissertation life cycle, *viz.*: your Research Methods, Findings, and Conclusion and Recommendations.

In summary, *describing* literature, although a necessary activity, is, in the first instance, evidence of the basic cognitive skill *Remembering* in model 2 above (called *Knowledge* in the first model); at most it is an example of *Understanding* in model 2 (called *Comprehension* in model 1). When you go further and engage in *Applying, Analysing,* and *Evaluating* literature (called *Application, Analysis, Synthesis, Evaluation* in model 1), leading to a coherent 'creation', then you have entered the realm of *critical evaluation* (= high marks). Hence the value of understanding Bloom's learning theory and the role critical evaluation plays in your Literature Review.

## Literature search techniques

To complete a Literature Review, you need to know how to search for literature. The word *literature* stems from the Latin *litteratus* = letter. In days gone by, a *literate* person was a 'man of letters', i.e. someone – usually a man, given the restricted educational opportunities open to women in the past – well versed in scholarly books, though nowadays it also has a more basic definition, meaning someone who can read and write (illiterate = someone who cannot read or write). Belonging to the *literati* (plural of *litteratus*) meant being part of a highly educated group. Taking something *literally* means interpreting something *by the letter*, i.e. straight from the source without exaggeration or embellishment.

Literature is normally equated with written published material. D.H. Lawrence's classic book *Sons and Lovers* is an example of literature. In fact, it is an example of *high literature*, a book appreciated for its artistry and originality of style (in France this literature would be called an example of *belles lettres* = fine letters, i.e. beautiful writing). Literature, however, comes in all shapes and sizes, and is not confined to 'beautiful writing'. Books, articles, reports, official publications, conference papers, theses, newspapers, encyclopaedias, all fall within the common definition of literature: they are all written, published sources.

The emergence of the Internet has also loosened the definition of literature. Digital versions of printed books now appear on the Internet (as e-books), as so do many scholarly articles, company reports, and government documents. Unfortunately, there are also literary sources of dubious quality (blogs, e-encyclopaedias, commercial sites, e-newspaper articles, etc.). If you concentrate on the latter grouping in your literature review, your work may be perceived as lacking academic credibility.

A literature search is 'a systematic and thorough search of all types of published literature in order to identify as many items as possible that are relevant to a particular topic' (Gash, 2000, p. 1). *Systematic* is a keyword in the aforementioned quotation. Attempting a literature search with only a rough idea of what you are looking for will yield only rough results. You need to be focused and use your time wisely. An effective search of literature in whatever form – books, journal articles, reports, official publications, conference papers, theses, etc. – requires a structured approach. Figure 5.4 sets out an orderly, methodical plan for achieving an effective and efficient literature search.

### Select topic

Ask yourself, what is it that you want to know? Jot down your answer in the form 'I want to know . . .'. Avoid unhelpful broad queries, such as '*I want to*

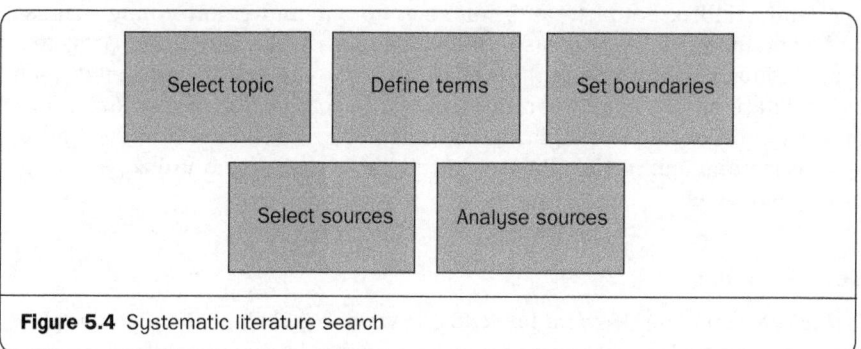

**Figure 5.4** Systematic literature search

*know* about e-Learning'. Break down what you want to know into manageable chunks and do a literature search for the different chunks. Think in terms of *subject* and *topic*, where the subject is your general area of study (e.g. e-Learning) and the topic is something that you want to know about that subject (e.g. barriers to e-Learning), yielding the query '*I want to know* about the barriers to e-Learning'. You might want to know about other things related to your research subject (e.g. benefits of e-Learning, costs of e-Learning, etc.) but when doing a literature search stick to one topic at a time. Table 5.3 gives some further examples.

**Table 5.3**  Topic selection

| Subject | Topic | What you want to know |
|---------|-------|----------------------|
| Equality legislation | Impact on employees | '*I want to know* about the impact of equality legislation on employees' |
| Pensioners | Winter Heating Allowance | '*I want to know* what percentage of pensioners applied for the Winter Heating Allowance' |
| Redundancy policies | Employer practices | '*I want to know* about employer redundancy policies' |
| University students | Plagiarism | '*I want to know* about the extent of plagiarism in universities' |

### Define terms

Think of the words that you are using: *employees, pensioners, policies, plagiarism.* Are there any other similar/alternative words that could help in your search for literature? You can use a dictionary or thesaurus to help you. For example, *plagiarism = cheat, steal, copy.* The alternative terms need not be an exact match. Also consider different spellings, particularly between British English and American English, such as analyse and analyze, behaviour and behavior, catalogue and catalog, centre and center, civilise and civilize, colonise and colonize, colour and color, commercialise and commercialize, emphasise and emphasize, fibre and fiber, grey and gray, labour and labor, maximise and maximize, metre and meter, nationalise and nationalize, neighbour and neighbor, organisation and organization, organise and organize, plagiarise and plagiarize, recognise and recognize, synthesise and synthesize, theatre and theater, utilise and utilize, visualise and visualize, etc.

### Set boundaries

Is timescale an issue? How far back do you want to go? What about geography? Do you need to confine your search to a particular country? For instance, you may be interested in employer redundancy practices in the USA over the past ten years.

## Select sources

It makes sense to select your sources only after you have: (1) identified your topic; (2) defined your terms; and (3) set your boundaries. If you know exactly what you are looking for, then that will assist you in selecting appropriate sources. For example, the query '*I want to know* about the impact of equality legislation, over the past five years, on UK employees who are from an ethnic background' might lead you to a search for government publications, such as reports, as well as legal documents and journal articles referring to case studies.

## Analyse sources

The information you get from your source ought to be *good* information, as opposed to *bad* information. Good information has the following characteristics: it is relevant, reliable, and recent. Bad information is information that is irrelevant, unreliable or dated. When assessing the value of the information derived from a literature source (e.g. from an article), it is useful to measure the information against the *3 Rs* in Figure 5.5.

*Relevant* information is information that is related to your research objectives. By this stage you ought to have created headings in your Literature Review that reflect specific research objectives. If you have a heading 'The Scottish Parliament's Strategy for Tackling Poverty in Scotland', then you only include sources in that sub-section that reflect that heading.

*Reliable* information is information obtained from credible sources. That is, sources that carry authoritative weight, examples of which include academic books, peer-reviewed articles, and government publications, much of which can be accessed through university library systems (more on this later). That does not mean to say that you have to agree with everything a source is telling you: indeed, you may wish to challenge underlying assumptions or projected implications.

The last criterion *Recent* is flexible. If you are researching activities in the distant past (e.g. First World War poetry), then obviously much of your information may not be recent. That is not to say, however, that you do not include

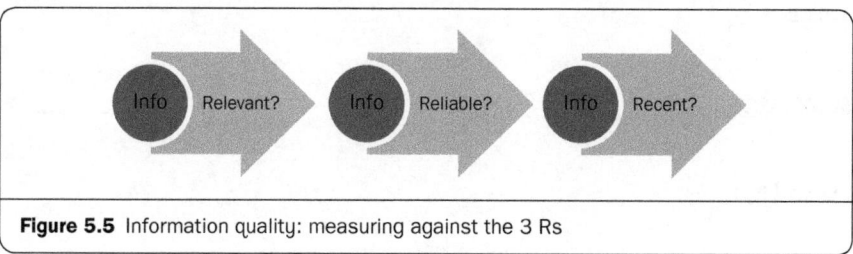

**Figure 5.5** Information quality: measuring against the 3 Rs

current interpretations of poetry in the First World War. Even if your research topic is about the here-and-now (e.g. Poverty in Modern Scotland), sometimes it can impress your supervisor to include a very old source among your current sources, either to show that the point you are making has been held for a long time and/or that you have a sound grasp of the historical development of your subject area. For example, one student, while commenting on current views on the role of the teacher, slipped in the following quotation: 'The greatest service the teacher can render the student is to increase his freedom.' The source of this quotation? Mary Parker Follett, in a speech that she made to students and staff at the University of Boston in 1922, but which was not published until 1970 (Follett, 1970, p. 137). So perhaps we should amend the 3 Rs to read: Relevant, Reliable, and Recent (or really old!).

At this point, it makes sense to keep a record of your selected source documents: where you got them, what they contain and any comment, yours or theirs, you want to highlight. You can do this on a blank piece of paper and attach it to your source documents. The comments that you might wish to raise are ones that illustrate evidence of critical thought on your part. Crystallising your thoughts in writing will help you to understand what you are reading, with the added benefit that you will have a focused summary to act as an *aide-mémoire* for later use in your Literature Review. Table 5.4 provides a template that you can recreate using the technology of your choice (or pen and paper if you prefer). Remember to write out the full reference for your source document: this will make the task of putting together your final reference list so much easier. Table 5.5 is an example of a completed *aide-mémoire* to record, summarise, and comment on your sources.

### Google it!

Or Safari it or Yahoo it – irrespective of the particular search engine you use, the Internet is a favourite resource for many students, so you may as well know how to use it to your advantage. The following *Helpful Hints* show you how to use the Internet to home in on *relevant, reliable,* and *recent* sources.

*Helpful Hint 1.* Government websites are useful resources for getting hold of statistical data, annual reports, and policy documents. To access a particular

**Table 5.4**   Source document *aide-mémoire*

REFERENCE:

SUMMARY:

COMMENT:

**Table 5.5**  Example completed source document *aide-memoire*

**REFERENCE:**

Bothwell, E. (2017) 'Pen and paper beats computers for retaining knowledge', *Times Higher Education Magazine,* 13 February. Available at: https://www. timeshighereducation.com/news/pen-and-paper-beats-computers-retaining-knowledge (Accessed: 15 February 2017).

**SUMMARY:**

Article about a recent survey report of 650 students from 10 countries by Jane Vincent, visiting fellow of LSE, entitled *Students' use of paper and pen versus digital media in university environments for writing and reading.* Author concludes that 'handwritten notes lead to greater retention of data than if it is typed'.

**COMMENT:**

Unclear how central thesis – pen and paper is better for retaining knowledge than use of technology – has been tested. No details in article of testing mechanism. Need to access full report! Question: does the report test how well students have retained knowledge with/without paper/technology? What were the testing criteria? Over what timescale? Same students? How was 'knowledge' defined?

Furthermore, report appears to be more nuanced than article heading suggests. For instance, students from different countries had conflicting views (e.g. Russian students favoured technology over paper while Chinese students preferred writing by hand). Even where students from different countries had same preferences, the reasons sometimes differed (e.g. Chinese students felt that they had more freedom to express themselves when writing by hand whereas Italian students liked the feel and smell of paper).

---

government's website, you simply enter the government's name, adding the term 'government website'. Examples: Australian government website, Indian government website, Canadian government website, etc.

*Helpful Hint 2.* To access a particular country's actual web space, irrespective of what you want to search for in that country, enter 'Google *country name*' in your browser. Table 5.6 gives some examples.

*Helpful Hint 3.* Using AND, OR and the minus sign (–).

- **AND operator.** If you type *'War' AND 'Poetry'* in your browser, you will get a list of entries reflecting war poetry. For an exact match, you should enclose what you are after within quotation marks, separated by AND. For example, if you are seeking literature on computer viruses, type *'Computer' AND 'Viruses'*.
- **OR operator.** *'War' OR 'Poetry'* will give you a listing of anything that is about war and, in addition, anything on the subject of poetry (any poetry). Using OR widens your search. It is particularly useful when you want to search for a topic that might appear under different spellings or headings:

**Table 5.6** Web links by country

| Country | Entry in browser | Web address |
| --- | --- | --- |
| India | Google India | http://www.google.co.in/ |
| Mexico | Google Mexico | http://www.google.com.mx/ |
| Australia | Google Australia | http://www.google.com.au/ |
| Japan | Google Japan | http://www.google.co.jp/ |
| France | Google France | http://www.google.fr/ |
| Canada | Google Canada | http://www.google.ca/ |

*'E-Commerce' OR 'ecommerce'; 'e-Business' OR 'ebusiness'; 'Computer virus' OR 'Computer worm'; 'Research objectives' OR 'Research aims'; 'Scientific experiments' OR 'Scientific trials' OR 'Scientific tests'.* And you can combine AND and OR operators: for example, *'ACAS Policy' AND ('Redundancy' OR 'Dismissal')* will result in any ACAS policies on redundancy as well as any ACAS policies on dismissal. Note the use of parentheses ( ) to help clarify the conditions that you want met.

- **The minus sign (–).** If you want to exclude an item, use the '–' sign immediately before the word that you want to exclude from your search, e.g. *'War poetry'* – *'Owen'* will yield war poetry excluding anything written by Owen. Similarly, *'Sport'* – *'football'* will list anything in sport except football (not always successful!).

*Helpful Hint 4.* Use Google Advanced Search. Type *Google Advanced Search* into your browser. Up pops an advanced search form. The form is a way of using AND, OR, and the minus sign (–) but getting Google to do the hard work for you.

*Helpful Hint 5.* Use Google Books. If you want to find out what books are in your subject area, then enter the Google Books website. At your browser window (Google, Firefox, Yahoo, etc.) type *Google Books*, then click on the Google Books link (or type in your country's related web address, e.g. http://books.google.co.uk, to go to Google Books directly).

*Helpful Hint 6.* Use Google Scholar. If you want scholarly material, use Google Scholar. At your browser type *Google Scholar*. Google Scholar is different from Google Books in that the former gives you access to scholarly books, journal articles, conference proceedings, pdf documents, etc., while the latter focuses on books. You can start immediately searching for a document you want to find, or for more control you can access the Advanced Search option. The option will be there somewhere on the screen. For example, on an iPad it can be found under the heading 'More'. When the Advanced Search form appears on the screen, you will notice that there is an option that allows you to restrict your search period to a particular timeframe ('Return articles dated between'). This is an excellent way to obtain up-to-date sources.

*Helpful Hint 7.* Searching within a specific website. *'Divorce' site:nytimes.com* will bring up divorce articles in the *New York Times* newspaper and *'Iraq' site:abc.net.au* will call up articles on Iraq in the Australian Broadcasting Service (ABC). Similarly, *'Henri' AND 'Matisse' site:heraldscotland.com* will give a listing of articles in *The Herald* newspaper that refer to Henri Matisse.

## University library databases

Google Scholar *et al.* are powerful free search tools not to be dismissed lightly but every university has its own collection of library databases available for student use. A university will have books, journals, conference proceedings, and magazines that have been ordered by academic departments to meet their students' needs. The library therefore should be your first port of call in any search for literature. If you have not already attended a library induction course – the most useful course you will ever attend – then librarians, helpful to a fault, will carefully explain how to find what you are looking for in the library. Unfortunately, there will be a limited number of printed books, etc. – and they are not always there when you need them most. Even when you do manage to get hold of what you are after, you normally only have a short loan period. Be aware also that some of the material on the shelves may be out of date because university departments, and libraries, have limited budgets.

On a university's home page there will be an option to link to the university's online library portal. Each university will have a name for their digital library system. The University of Toronto in Canada, for example, has a very simple name for its online library system: University of Toronto Libraries (UTL). The University of Toronto has more than one online library, hence 'Libraries'. The University of Aberdeen's online library system is shortened to LSC&M, which stands for Library, Special Collections, and Museums.

Once you have accessed the university library system, you will be presented with an array of options, including general library-related matters (library staff, services on offer, opening hours, helpful guides), the main library catalogue, and subject-specific material.

The main catalogue will show both print and electronic resources held by the library. A one-stop-search facility is the norm for finding out what material a library has in stock and how to locate it. You can also reserve items online or, if it is an eBook or eJournal or specific eArticle, you should be able to access them immediately.

Most universities have an obvious menu option from which to access material specific to your subject. Usually, the research subjects are listed alphabetically, for example from Accountancy to Women's Studies. Clicking on one subject will open a list of databases from which you can browse at your leisure. Some universities prefer, in the first instance, to allocate more generic labels to subject-specific material, such as Humanities & Social Science, Science & Engineering, Medicine & Veterinary Medicine, etc.

Your university may be so large that the online library system is partitioned into different libraries to reflect the different campuses. There may also be an agreement between your university and neighbouring universities – or even those further afield – to share library databases.

Irrespective of the physical layout of your university's library, it will contain a number of in-house database collections – online and physical – as well as a point of access to external databases for which the university will pay an annual fee. It is up to the university, based on budgetary factors and advice from subject departments, which databases they rent for student (and staff) use. The country in which the university resides may also impact on the choice of databases, for example, in the field of Law. In general, there will be a degree of commonality from university to university where the subject disciplines overlap.

For example, the University of Chicago library points students whose specialist field is Education to four external databases: ERIC (the largest education database in the world), Articles Plus (articles, books, reviews), Education Abstracts (index of periodicals, books), and Education Index Retrospective (historical periodicals). The University of Edinburgh library directs their Education students to the Australian Education Index, the British Education Index, the Education Image Gallery, the Education Source, and ERIC.

As well as the availability of subject-specific external databases, universities are increasingly making use of external multi-disciplinary databases. JSTOR (http://www.jstor.org), which is short for Journal STORage, is a US-based multi-disciplinary database of scholarly articles and primary sources used by many universities across the globe. Digital books have now been added to JSTOR's inventory. Although JSTOR leans heavily in the direction of the Humanities and Social Sciences, there is a wealth of material to be found on other discipline areas (see Table 5.7).

Web of Knowledge is another multi-disciplinary database that casts its subject-net wide: Arts and Humanities, Social Sciences, and Sciences, including Medicine. In effect, universities can choose from a wide selection of external databases, some of which are shown in Table 5.8, p. 130.

In summary, using a well-known search engine such as Google has two attractive advantages: it is free and easy to use. There is the additional advantage that up-to-date case studies can be readily accessed on the Internet. Disadvantages include the currency of the information that appears on your screen (i.e. is it relevant, reliable, and recent?). Databases recommended by your university library, on the other hand, have not been made available by accident: they have been chosen carefully to meet the needs of subject departments. As such, the currency of what is on offer is normally guaranteed. Use both the Internet and the university library but lean more heavily towards the latter.

There is no royal road to learning, and the material will not just appear in front of you as if by magic: you have to go and look for it. By all means type

**Table 5.7** JSTOR subject categories

| | |
|---|---|
| **Area Studies** | African American Studies, African Studies, American Indian Studies, American Studies, Asian Studies, British Studies, Irish Studies, Jewish Studies, Latin American Studies, Middle East Studies, Slavic Studies |
| **Arts** | Architecture & Architectural History, Art & Art History, Music, Performing Arts |
| **Business and Economics** | Business, Development Studies, Economics, Finance, Labor & Employment Relations, Management & Organizational Behavior |
| **History** | History, History of Science & Technology |
| **Humanities** | Bibliography, Classical Studies, Film, Folklore |
| **Law** | Criminology & Criminal Justice, Law |
| **Medicine and Allied Health** | Health Policy, Health Sciences, Public Health |
| **Science and Mathematics** | Aquatic Sciences, Astronomy, Biological Sciences, Botany & Plant Sciences, Chemistry, Developmental & Cell Biology, Ecology & Evolutionary Biology, Engineering |
| **Social Sciences** | Anthropology, Archaeology, Communications Studies, Education, Feminist & Women's Studies, Geography, International Relations |

keywords into your Internet browser (use Google Scholar) but also visit the university library, look at past dissertations, read relevant journals, get hold of recently published conference proceedings related to your topic, and follow up the references supplied in your lecture and seminar hand-outs. The material you need will not appear all at once, rather you will discover that one source will lead to another, one author directing you to another author, one article referring to another article, and so on. Collecting literature sources is an cumulative process that requires patience and perseverance in equal measure.

# Contextual Review

If, for the most part, you are referencing 'things' – such as software programs, sculptures, and performance pieces (plays, music, light shows, stage settings, etc.) – rather than traditional literature sources (books, articles, etc.), then you may prefer to call your Literature Review a *Contextual Review*. A Contextual Review is a variation of a Literature Review.

So what is the difference between a Contextual Review and a Literature Review? Both may make use of traditional academic sources such as scholarly

**Table 5.8** External digital databases

| Subject | External database(s) |
|---------|---------------------|
| **Arts & Humanities** | Art & Architecture Complete (EBSCO), ARTbibliograpies Modern (ProQuest), Arts & Humanities Citation Index, British Humanities Index (ProQuest), Humanities Abstracts (EBSCO), MLA International Bibliography, Social Services Abstracts, SocINDEX, ASSIA |
| **Business & Economics** | Business Source Complete (EBSCO), Emerald, FAME, Economist Historical Archive, KeyNote, Materials Business File, Mintel Reports, Osiris |
| **Education** | ERIC, Australian Education Index (ProQuest), British Education Index (ProQuest), Teacher Reference Centre (EBSCO) |
| **Environment** | Environment Abstracts (ProQuest), Environment Engineering Abstracts, Environment Impact Statements, Pollution Abstracts |
| **Human Resources** | Croner-i Human Resources |
| **Law** | CANS Advice Notes, Lawtel, LexisLibrary, HeinOnline, HUDOC, Max Planck Encyclopedia of Public International Law, Oxford Scholarship Online (Law) |
| **Medicine & Health Care** | Cochrane Library, MEDLINE, PubMed, EMBASE: Excerpta Medica, Scopus, CINAHL, PsycINFO, Web of Knowledge, Amadeo, Clinical Trials (US National Institute of Health), NICE, ScienceDirect, Social Care Online |
| **Multi-disciplinary** | JSTOR, JISC, ZETOC, Web of Knowledge |
| **Science & Engineering** | BioMed Central, Chemical Database Service, Science Direct, Science Citation Index, SciFinder, Scitation, Scopus, MathSciNet, Web of Science, ACM Digital Library, Cern Document Server, Inspec, SPIRES-HEP, ACM Digital Library, Computer and Information Systems Abstracts (ProQuest), IEEE Electronic Library, Compendex, Engineering Research Database, Engineered Materials Abstracts, Environment Engineering Abstracts |

books and journal articles. Both may well discuss *things* such as photographs or buildings or artefacts or music or plays or computer software. However, the difference is in the weighting: if the focus of the theoretical part of your dissertation concentrates predominately on using traditional sources of academic information (books, articles, etc.), then you are better served with a Literature Review; if, on the other hand, your main focus is on discussing 'things' in themselves, such as software code or art pieces or acting or musical scores (as perhaps a precursor to creating your own 'thing'), even though you may also access some traditional literature, then you may find that a Contextual Review better describes that task. If in doubt, check with your supervisor. The overall structure of your dissertation will remain the same, with the difference that where you had a Literature Review, you will now have a Contextual Review (Figure 5.6):

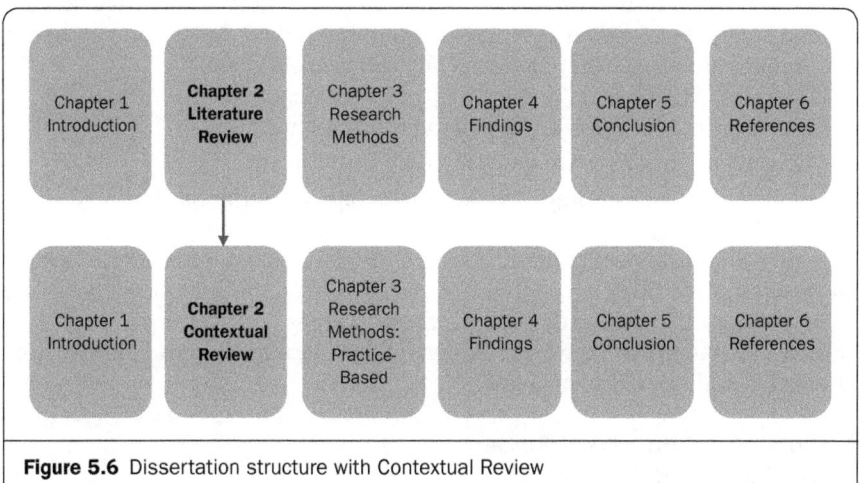

**Figure 5.6** Dissertation structure with Contextual Review

Contextual Reviews are really intended for students involved in practical subjects where they are expected to create something – software, art, theatre work, etc. – and prior to doing their own thing they might feel more at home placing their intended work in the context of other works through the vehicle of a Contextual Review rather than a Literature Review. Students engaged in such practice-based research will also require a different type of Research Methods chapter to accommodate their studies. Hence the renaming of the traditional research methods chapter from 'Chapter 3 Research Methods' to 'Chapter 3 Research Methods: Practice-based Research' (see Chapter 8, 'Research Methods 2: Artist as researcher').

The chapter headings in Figure 5.6 are not carved in stone – you can embellish them to fit in with your research topic. For example, the rather bland title 'Chapter 4 Findings' might be called 'Chapter 4 Analysis of New Musical Piece in A Streetcar Named Desire', if that is the thing that you eventually created and wanted to analyse. Similarly, you might decide upon a more descriptive title for your 'Chapter 3 Contextual Review', such as 'Chapter 3 Contextual Review: The Use of Music in Plays'. Also remember that an abstract (summary) of your dissertation will precede 'Chapter 1 Introduction'.

### Example 1: Computer Science – Software Development

Let's assume that you are a computer science student specialising in software development. For your dissertation you decide to improve upon a piece of freeware – publicly available software – designed to enhance Twitter access and usage. Before creating and testing your own contribution, you opt to place your proposed work in context via the mechanism of a Contextual Review rather than the more traditional Literature Review (reasoning that most of the literature you will review will be of the non-traditional type, e.g. software code).

As with a Literature Review, you will structure your Contextual Review around research objectives pertinent to your theoretical discussion. For example, suppose you have three research objectives as follows:

1 Clarify the role of freeware in software development
2 Critically assess freeware designed for Twitter usage
3 Develop and test prototype freeware to enhance Twitter usage.

Objective 3 above is a practical activity and would follow after your research methods chapter. Objectives 1 and 2 above are intellectual activities based on a study of software code and other literature sources, such as reports and articles, and so would form the main content of a Contextual Review, the structure of which could be as shown below:

**Chapter 2: Contextual Review**
2.1  Introduction
2.2  Role of Freeware in Software Development
2.3  Assessment of Twitter Freeware
2.4  Need for Enhanced Twitter Freeware to Improve Usage
2.5  Summary and Emerging Issues

It is good practice to bookend your main discussion with a brief introduction explaining the purpose of your Contextual Review and identifying which research objectives will be addressed (sub-section 2.1), ending with a summary of key points/issues (sub-section 2.5). Objectives 1 and 2 are specifically tackled in sub-sections 2.2 and 2.3 using headings that clearly reflect the stated research objectives. This will help prevent *student drift*. Another sub-section is included (2.4) because you ought to clarify intended software improvements to remedy identified deficiencies and so justify your intended practical work.

Within your Contextual Review you will still need to replicate the good practice exhibited in a traditional Literature Review. That is, you are still expected to show evidence of higher-level cognitive skills. Yes, place your chosen software code/program in the context of other software developments and describe what each software does, but also take the opportunity to go beyond mere description: critically evaluate that software, i.e. give your views on it, where it is deficient and how it could be improved. In other words, describe, quote, comment, and justify your comments.

Referencing will form the backbone of your review – it is, after all, a Master's dissertation. For in-text referencing, you adopt the same approach as you would if completing a Literature Review. When referencing 'things' in your

Contextual Review rather than traditional literature, you name the thing, its creator and, where known, year of creation. Here are some in-text referencing examples to highlight these points using Harvard:

> AVG anti-virus software (AVG Technologies, 2017) claims to provide fully loaded protection.

> Civilisation VI (Firaxis, 2016) is the latest version of a game that has maintained a loyal following since its inception in 1999.

> Newton is an android app by Cloudburst (2016) that allows users to access all their email addresses through one point of contact.

Here is the Harvard format, with an example, for creating a software-related entry in your References list at the end of your dissertation:

> Author (year of release) *Title* (Version) [Format, e.g. Computer program, Mobile app, Video game, Xbox 360]. Distributor: place of distribution.

If e-software:

> Author/publisher (year of release) *Title* (Version) [Format e.g. Computer program, Mobile app, Video game, Xbox 360]. Available at: URL (Downloaded: date).

> AGT Technologies (2017) *AVG anti-virus* (free) [Mobile app]. Available at: http://www.avg.com/gb-en/antivirus-for-android (Downloaded: 14 March 2017).

## Example 2: Art

In this example, let's assume that you are a sculpture student at an Art School. You want to research the role of public sculpture in fostering Romantic nationalism. You decide that your dissertation will contain a theoretical element (a review of sculpture and its use in Romantic nationalism) and a practical element (the creation of a sculptural piece to reflect Romantic Scottish nationalism). Instead of a traditional Literature Review you resolve to write a Contextual Review, reasoning that you will be primarily discussing things, in this case sculptures, rather than focusing on traditional literature sources, although it is likely that you will also be referring to traditional literature sources in the form of art books and articles. You might have four research objectives:

1  Define the term 'Romantic nationalism'
2  Review the historical role of sculpture in Romantic nationalism
3  Create a piece of sculpture to reflect Romantic nationalism in Scotland
4  Assess audience reaction to sculpture piece in terms of Romantic nationalist feelings.

The structure of your Contextual Review might appear as follows, covering objectives 1 and 2 above:

**Chapter 2: Contextual Review**
2.1   Introduction
2.2   Definition of Romantic Nationalism
2.3   Historical Role of Sculpture in Romantic Nationalism
2.4   Summary and Emerging Issues

Here are some examples of how to reference art work in your Contextual Review (or Literature Review if you so choose). Once again, you just need to remember to name the thing (in this case, an art work), its creator and, where known, year of creation.

Michelangelo's *David*, created between 1501 and 1504, is an excellent example of classical renaissance sculpture.

Rottenberg's video and sculptural piece 'NoNoseKnows' (2015) focuses on the process of transformation.

The strange thing about Van Gogh's *Café Terrace at Night*, painted in 1888, is the absence of black in a night scene.

Here is a format, with an example, for creating a reference entry for an art work in a gallery. Other formats are included in Appendix A to cover other scenarios (e.g. public art, exhibition catalogue, etc.).

Artwork in gallery:

Artist (year) *Title* [Medium] Gallery name, City.

Rembrandt, van R. (1642) *Night watch* [Oil on canvas]. Rijkmuseum, Amsterdam.

If viewed online:

Artist (year) *Title* [Medium] Available at: URL (Accessed: date).

Rembrandt, van R. (1642) *Night watch* [Oil on canvas]. Available at: https://www.rijksmuseum.nl/en/search/objects?q=Rembrandt+&p=1&ps=12&st=-OBJECTS&ii=2#/SK-C-5,2 (Accessed: 10 April 2007).

*Note*: if the exact date a work was created is not known, use n.d. ('no date') for year, or, if approximation given by source, then use c. ('circa') with approximated year, as shown in the following examples:

Botticelli, A. (n.d.) *The Birth of Venus* [Tempera on canvas]. Uffizi Gallery, Florence.

Rembrandt, van R. (c. 1628) *Self-portrait* [Oil on panel]. Rijkmuseum, Amsterdam.

## Example 3: Theatre Studies

In this example, let's assume that you are a student of theatre and that your topic of study is the use of music in plays. You decide that central to your dissertation will be (a) an academic review of the use of music in plays and (b) an empirical element wherein you intend to create an alternative piece of music for an established scene in a well-known play with a view to changing audience expectations and experience.

Once again you could, without any detriment to your dissertation, write a Literature Review to cover part (a) above. You choose instead to write a Contextual Review, reasoning that for the most part you will be reviewing musical scores, although you will also be referring to plays as well articles and books about music in plays.

The structure of your Contextual Review will closely follow your research objectives. Let's suppose further that you have four research objectives:

1  Explain the impact of music on mood and atmosphere
2  Critically explore the use of music in plays
3  Create a musical piece for a seminal scene in a famous play to alter audience expectations and experience
4  Assess audience responses to the scene in 3.

Objectives 1 and 2 will be addressed in the Contextual Review, the structure of which could be as follows:

### Chapter 2: Contextual Review
2.1  Introduction
2.2  The Impact of Music on Mood and Atmosphere
2.3  The Use of Music in Plays
2.4  Summary and Emerging Issues

Examples of in-text referencing in your Contextual Review:

Music is the unseen actor in a play (Biggam, 2017).

The background music in *Death of a Salesman* perfectly captures Willy Loman's psychological state of mind (Beckford dir. 2017).

Tennessee Williams was very specific about the use of music in his plays, as evidenced in *A Streetcar Named Desire* (1947).

Here are formats for creating some theatre-related entries in your References list.

Play (book format):

> Playwright's surname, initials (year) *Title of play*. Editor. Place of publication: Publisher.

> Beckett, S. (2006) *Waiting for Godot*. Edited by Knowlson, J. London: Faber and Faber.

When referencing a particular line or scene in a play (book format), it is simpler to cite the specific location in-text as you would a book, e.g.:

> Beckett (2006, p. 1) immediately sets the enigmatic and philosophical tone for the whole play with Estragon declaring 'Nothing to be done'.

Alternatively, you can identify the location of the play in terms of act, scene, and line number when you create your entry for your reference list; but if you are discussing several scenes in your play, then that becomes problematic as a reference entry. Hence the simpler idea to cite the specifics as an in-text reference while keeping the reference entry in your reference list as simple as possible as per the general play format given above.

Play performed live:

> *Title of play* by playwright (Year performed) Directed by director name [Place performed. Date seen].

> *The Steamie* by Tony Roper (2013) Directed by Tony Roper [Eastwood Park Theatre, Scotland. 23 October 2013].

Musical score:

> Composer (Year) *Title*. Additional information. Place of publication: publisher.

> Chopin, F. (2009) *Mazarkus*. Edited by Carl Mikuli. New York: Dover Publications.

Live (classical) performance:

> Composer (Year performed) *Title*. Performed by orchestra name conducted by conductor name [Place performed. Date seen].

> Korngold, E. W. (2017) Performed by the Scottish Symphony Orchestra conducted by John Wilson [City Halls, Glasgow. 16 March 2017].

There is no compulsion to adopt a Contextual Review rather than a traditional Literature Review. Computer science students, as well as art students and students engaged in aspects of theatre studies, could, without any detriment to their dissertation, stick to writing a Literature Review. Although some of their sources will appear in traditional academic format (i.e. books and articles), much of their writing will be about things that they can see or feel or hear (e.g. software programs, art works, performance pieces). Hence the preference to place these things within the confines of a Contextual Review rather than a Literature Review.

That is not to say that the previous advice given in this chapter on how to write a Literature Review needs to be jettisoned. On the contrary, the same advice holds. You will still need to structure your Contextual Review around your research objectives; you will still need to understand the difference between description and critical evaluation, with emphasis placed on producing evidence of the latter; you will still need to know how to reference, even though you will mainly reference objects such as computer programs or scenes from films or art works or plays or musical scores, etc.; you will still need to appreciate that an understanding of Bloom's taxonomy of learning can help you target specific cognitive skills – knowledge, comprehension, application, analysis, synthesis, evaluation – to enhance your review; and you will still need to highlight a rationale for your own empirical creation.

# Further reading

Cottrell, S. (2011) *Critical thinking skills: developing effective analysis and argument.* 2nd edn. Basingstoke: Palgrave Macmillan.

Machi, L. A. (2016) *The literature review: six steps to success.* Thousand Oaks, CA: Corwin Press.

Markey, K. (2015) *Online searching: a guide to finding quality information efficiently and effectively.* London: Rowman & Littlefield.

Oliver, P. (2012) *Succeeding with your literature review.* Maidenhead: Open University Press.

Ridley, D. (2012) *The literature review: a step-by-step guide for students.* 2nd edn. London: Sage.

## Summary of key points

- In a Literature Review, you should demonstrate that you have 'studied existing work in the field with insight'.
- A good Literature Review should be focused on your research objectives, display spread and depth to your reading, and show evidence of *critical evaluation.*
- To avoid drifting away from your research focus, create sub-headings in your Literature Review that link explicitly to your research objectives.
- Write a brief introduction to your Literature Review reminding the reader of your research objectives, the topics that you will cover, and how they relate to your research objectives.
- Describing the work of others is a basic undergraduate skill. Master's students are expected to go beyond mere description and engage in critical evaluation. Critical evaluation = description (of something) + your views (on that 'something') + reasons for holding your views.
- Use quotations to support your writing and not as a substitute for your own words. Remember to introduce quotations properly and, when you consider it appropriate, offer comment on them.
- Appendix I contains a rich variety of verbs ('accepts', 'captures', 'expresses', 'speculates', etc.) to help you to describe the work of other authors.
- Learning involves the development of cognitive skills (mental skills), affective skills (feelings, emotions), and psychomotor skills (physical skills).
- To achieve good marks, you need to exhibit the following higher-level cognitive skills in your writing: *analysis*, *synthesis*, and *evaluation* (in Bloom's taxonomy of learning) or *analysing*, *evaluating*, and *creating* (in Anderson and Krathwohl's updated model).
- Conclude your Literature Review with a summary of your main findings (relating them to your research objectives) and have a link to your Research Methods chapter.
- *Literature search skills.* Select your topic; define your terms, set boundaries, select appropriate sources; and analyse your sources. Your selected literature should be *relevant*, *reliable*, and *recent*. University library databases therefore ought to be your first port of call.
- A Contextual Review is an alternative to a Literature Review, intended for those students writing *mainly* about 'things', such as software or art works or theatre studies, rather than traditional literature sources (books, articles, etc.).
- The academic skills and knowledge required to complete a Contextual Review are the same as those required to complete a Literature Review.

# Chapter 6

# Systematic Reviews

- • *What is a Systematic Review?* • *The stages of a Systematic Review*
- • *AMSTAR: a checklist for Systematic Reviews* • *Further reading*
- • *Summary of key points*

This chapter is intended for those who have been asked to write a *Systematic Review* instead of a *Literature Review*. The stages of a Systematic Review are discussed in detail including the use of helpful protocols, such as PICO and AMSTAR.

## What is a Systematic Review?

In the context of post-graduate dissertations, it is common for students in Health-related faculties to be asked to complete a *Systematic Review* instead of a *Literature Review*. Given that the choice of literature to include in the latter can be a personal one, Literature Reviews – sometimes referred to as *Narrative Reviews* within the healthcare profession – are vulnerable to criticism: the literature chosen can be arbitrary, biased, out-of-date, limited in scope, lacking in credibility, and unrepresentative. A key criticism of Literature Reviews is that it can be difficult to replicate the findings. For example, two researchers may do a Literature Review on the same topic but it is statistically unlikely that they will choose the same literature sources, in the same order, giving the same weight to each source, with the same interpretations, resulting in the same findings. Ultimately, it is the lack of a peer-reviewed protocol that brings the trustworthiness of a Literature Review into question. In the healthcare professions, it would be unwise to make decisions that could impact on someone's health based on an uninhibited personal selection of published sources. Where lives, not to mention a substantial financial investment, are at stake, a more rigorous and reliable approach is required.

In the world of medicine, nursing, etc., there is an abundance of articles on empirical research studies written every year, which means that it is not easy to keep up-to-date with current research (Hemingway and Brereton, 2009). Hence the need for a way to review primary research findings on a specific topic that can be trusted by policy-makers, professionals in the field, and the general public. When policy-makers, such as the Secretary of State for Health in the UK or the Minister for Health and Ageing in the Australian Government, wish to make decisions on what drugs, for example, will best reduce high blood pressure, it is to their research advisers they will look to for answers. They in turn will: (a) implement a primary research project to determine the case for or against the use of certain treatments; (b) initiate a Systematic Review of existing research literature in the area in question; or (c) determine if a Systematic Review of literature has already been carried out, in which case they reflect on the review's findings.

So, what is a Systematic Review? Egger *et al.* (2001, p. 4) define Systematic Reviews as 'explicitly formulated, reproducible, and up-to-date summaries of the effects of healthcare interventions'. In addition to reviewing primary research findings on the effectiveness of a particular drug/treatment, Systematic Reviews are also being used to look at the feasibility of an intervention/ activity, as well as the appropriateness of doing so (medical intervention may be inappropriate where the patient holds certain religious beliefs, for example). A Systematic Review attempts to pool results from a number of studies, allowing the reviewer, and interested readers, to see the bigger picture: if the studies on cot deaths, for instance, had been pooled from different countries, then the dangerous practice of placing babies on their front would have ended much earlier than it did. An outline of the stages of a Systematic Review is shown in Figure 6.1.

An excellent resource on Systematic Reviews is the UK-based not-for-profit organisation The Cochrane Collaboration (http://www.cochrane.org/), which also publishes the Cochrane Library. The library contains a comprehensive database of completed Systematic Reviews on healthcare and health policy. By looking at a few of these Systematic Reviews you should get a good idea of what a review looks like and how to write one.

Although Systematic Reviews are normally associated with healthcare research, they are now being used in other disciplines such as criminology, education, and social studies. These are areas where it is too important to leave policy decisions to a traditional Literature Review. Systematic Reviews are also appearing in unexpected research areas. For instance, Sauve *et al.* (2007) published a Systematic Review on the difference between games and simulations.

The literature that is included in a Systematic Review is subject to a rigorous selection procedure and research studies that do not meet the selection criteria are automatically rejected, regardless of their providence. In this way, Systematic Reviews achieve credibility in the eyes of the research community and policy decision-makers.

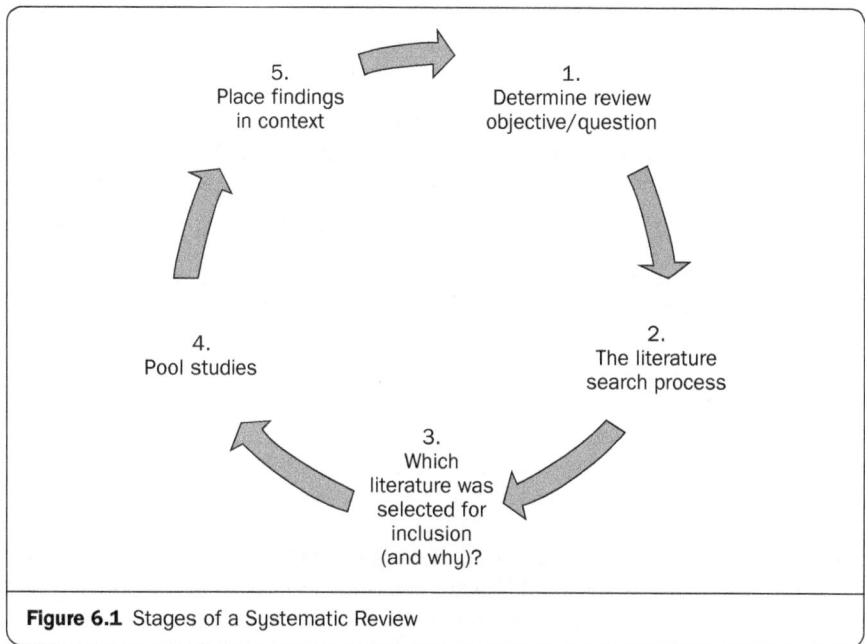

**Figure 6.1** Stages of a Systematic Review

# The stages of a Systematic Review

To achieve credibility and trustworthiness, a Systematic Review must go through a formal process that includes: (a) the establishment of the review objective/question; (b) how to find literature to enable the research question to be answered; (c) decisions on the literature to be included in the study; (d) the pooling together of results from the various studies in an effort to answer the initial research question; and (e) finally placing the results in context (e.g. in terms of their heterogeneity, quality, likely bias, etc.). The stages of a Systematic Review are now discussed in detail.

### Stage 1: Determine review objective/question

A Systematic Review needs to be transparent and well documented. The first opportunity to show such openness and attention to detail occurs when defining *the purpose of the Systematic Review*, i.e. the review objective. This can appear in the form of a *statement* or as a *question*, even though the purpose of the Systematic Review tends to occur more often in the former format rather than the latter. Examples of review objectives:

To assess the clinical effectiveness of treatments for childhood retinoblastoma (McDaid *et al.*, 2005).

To assess the effectiveness and safety of bisphosphonates in increasing bone mineral density (BMD), reducing fractures and improving clinical function in people with OI (Phillipi *et al.*, 2008).

To determine clinical effects and safety of active compression–decompression cardiopulmonary resuscitation compared with standard manual cardiopulmonary resuscitation (Lafuente-Lafuente and Melero-Bascones, 2004).

A review may have more than one objective. The following is an example from Poustie and Wildgoose (2010):

1 To assess the effects of a low-phenylalanine diet commenced early in life for people with phenylketonuria; and
2 To assess the possible effects of relaxation or termination of the diet on intelligence, neuropsychological outcomes and mortality, growth, nutritional status, eating behaviour and quality of life.

A review may have one broad aim and quite a number of sub-objectives. For instance, a broad objective could be 'to assess the evidence on the positive and negative effects of population-wide drinking water fluoridation strategies to prevent caries' (McDonagh *et al.*, 2000). This, in turn, could be refined into more manageable and achievable individual objectives (*ibid.*):

Objective 1:  What are the effects of fluoridation of drinking water supplies on the incidences of caries?

Objective 2:  If water fluoridation is shown to have beneficial effects, what is the effect over and above that offered by the use of alternative interventions and strategies?

Objective 3:  Does water fluoridation result in reduction of caries across social groups and between geographical locations, bringing equity?

Question 4:  Does water fluoridation have negative effects?

Question 5:  Are there differences in the effects of natural and artificial water fluoridation?

If you are having difficulty in framing your research question (or statement), you could try applying *PICO*, a protocol developed specifically to aid healthcare researchers in framing their research question. PICO was developed by the Centre for Clinical Effectiveness (CCE) at Monash Institute and stands for the *Patient group*, the *Intervention*, the *Comparison (or Control) intervention*, and the *Outcome*. If you can capture these elements in your question/statement, you will have made a good, solid start to your Systematic Review. Using PICO takes practice but it is worth the effort. The main benefit of applying PICO is that it forces you to concentrate on the components you consider central to your research, making life so much easier when it comes to locating the studies to be included in your review. A structured approach to applying PICO is to ask yourself the questions posed in Table 6.1.

The PICO-generated example in Table 6.1 yields the following review question (International Development Research Centre, 2010, p. 5):

> *Among the children under the age of five living in rural settings (Patient group), does the use of insecticide-treated bed nets (Intervention) lead to lower malaria prevalence rates (Outcome) as compared to when non-treated nets are used (Comparison intervention)?*

**Table 6.1**  Applying PICO

| Question | Example |
| --- | --- |
| What is your **P**atient group/setting? | *Children under the age of five living in a rural setting* |
| What is the **I**ntervention under question? | *Use of insecticide-treated bed nets* |
| **C**ompared to what? | *Bed nets that have not been treated* |
| What **O**utcome is being tested? | *Lower malaria prevalence rates* |

## Stage 2: The literature search process

After settling on your research objective, you now need to reflect on where to look for studies that meet your review question. Try to keep an open mind and avoid just sticking to pet journals, well-known researchers or Western-based publications. If you tread the usual publication paths, then from the outset you may very well fall into the trap of introducing different types of bias to your Systematic Review (Hemmingway and Brereton, 2009), such as *language bias* (favouring, for example, English publications), *publication bias* (favouring particular publications), and *selection bias* (favouring particular researchers). Where can you look for studies to be included in your review? A popular database is PubMed (https://www.ncbi.nlm.nih.gov/pubmed), a US-based site that facilitates access to the MEDLINE database of citations, abstracts, and full articles on biomedical studies. Table 6.2 gives a list of some useful databases and resources.

If your Systematic Review is not on healthcare interventions but on one of education, crime and justice, or social welfare, then The Campbell Collaboration will prove a first-rate resource well worth accessing (https://www.campbellcollaboration.org).

Do not concentrate exclusively on *published* sources. You should try and seek out *grey literature*, e.g. studies that have not been formally published in peer-reviewed forums. Grey literature covers working papers, government reports, institutional documents, market surveys, conference proceedings, technical papers, and works-in-progress (e.g. PhD studies). There is even a website on how to exploit grey literature: GreyNet International (http://www.greynet.org).

**Table 6.2** Useful resources on healthcare studies

| Resource | Website |
| --- | --- |
| PubMed | http://www.ncbi.nlm.nih.gov/pubmed/ |
| The Cochrane Library | http://www.cochranelibrary.com |
| Centre for Evidence-Based Medicine | http://www.cebm.net/ |
| Centre for Reviews and Dissemination | http://www.york.ac.uk/inst/crd/ |
| JBI Library of Systematic Reviews and Implementation Reports | http://journals.lww.com/jbisrir/pages/default.aspx |
| Clinical Trials Registry – India | http://ctri.nic.in/Clinicaltrials/login.php |

In this stage of your Systematic Review, you need to state where you sought studies to review. The following example is taken from Morrison and Agnew (2009, p. 1):

> We searched the Cochrane Cystic Fibrosis and Genetic Disorders Group Trials Register comprising references identified from comprehensive electronic database searches, hand searches of relevant journals and abstract books of conference proceedings. We searched PubMed and major conference proceedings. Most recent search of the Cystic Fibrosis Trials Register: Nov. 2008.

### Stage 3: Which literature was selected (and why)?

As you search online databases and flick through hard copies of journals, you need to make a decision on which studies to include in your Systematic Review. This ought to be an objective selection process and not one based on personal or political bias. Here is a methodical approach to assist you in deciding which studies to include and which to exclude:

1 Does the study meet each of the elements in your review question/objective? If not, reject it outright. It does not matter how eminent the authors of the study are or how brilliant the work is: if it does not contribute to answering your review question, then it has no part to play in your review. Keep a note of the studies that you reject and the reasons for your decision (this helps you to counteract claims of bias for excluding certain literature).

2 Is the study methodologically sound? If it is not, then do not include the study in your review. A study is methodologically suspect if the methodology used is not clearly stated in the literature, from the initial research question (including component parts) to the data collection and analysis techniques. One way to determine if this is the case is to ask the question: 'Is the study repeatable?' If the answer is no, then this would suggest that the authors have not clearly identified how they carried out their study. Also, in terms of

the hierarchy of preferred evidence, was the study based on a randomised control trial (RCT)? The results of an RCT are more reliable than, say, a case study. Evans (2003) produced a neat summary of the hierarchy of preferred evidence, dealing with healthcare interventions in terms not only of the effectiveness of a treatment but also its appropriateness and feasibility. RCTs appear in the top bracket of preferred evidence for systematic reviews (see Table 6.3). Automatically reject any studies that fall into Evans' 'Poor' category. However, you might not exclude a study because it is in the 'Fair' category – for example, non-randomised controlled trials – but you would need to recognise its limitations and take care when using the results of such a study. Notice that Systematic Reviews are at the very top of Evans' hierarchy of evidence. That is for a very good reason – Systematic Reviews are superior to individual studies because they are made up of a collection of the best studies available and because the Systematic Review process itself is, or ought to be, scientifically rigorous.

3   Are you looking for studies based on quantitative or qualitative data? Try and avoid mixing and matching (e.g. qualitative case studies with RCT experimental studies) because it is extraordinarily difficult to pool the results of studies that deal with different data types.

4   Who paid for the study? This may seem an irrelevant question, particularly if the study meets your PICO-derived objective and is methodologically rigorous. However, the study may be biased, although not necessarily so, if it was financed by a third party with a vested interest – commercial, personal or political – in the results.

In your dissertation make a clear statement of your selection criteria (e.g. 'Selection criteria: randomised control trials of oscillating devices compared with any other form of physiotherapy in people with cystic fibrosis'), together with the actual literature that met the selection criteria, as well as examples of literature that was not included (and reasons why not).

## Stage 4: Pool studies

Once you have reduced the number of studies to those that meet your selection criteria and are methodologically adequate, then you can attempt to pool the results of the independent but interrelated studies together to form a position on either the effectiveness of a particular intervention or the feasibility of such an intervention or even the appropriateness of such an intervention. This is referred to as synthesising your evidence, or the *evidence-synthesis* stage.

Pooling the results from different studies is easier said than done. In the first place, if the results of one study were based on quantitative RCT data and another study was derived through qualitative observational studies, then it would be inappropriate and potentially misleading to combine the results to form an aggregate 'score'. This means that the first decision you have to make before you pool the data from the various studies is in relation to the type of

**Table 6.3** Evans' hierarchy of preferred evidence

| | Effectiveness | Appropriateness | Feasibility |
|---|---|---|---|
| *Excellent* | • Systematic Reviews<br>• Multi-centre studies | • Systematic Reviews<br>• Multi-centre studies | • Systematic Reviews<br>• Multi-centre studies |
| *Good* | • RCTs<br>• Observational studies | • RCTs<br>• Observational studies<br>• Interpretive studies | • RCTs<br>• Observational studies<br>• Interpretive studies |
| *Fair* | • Uncontrolled trials with dramatic results<br>• Before and after studies<br>• Non-randomised controlled trials | • Descriptive studies<br>• Focus groups | • Descriptive studies<br>• Action research<br>• Before and after studies<br>• Focus groups |
| *Poor* | • Descriptive studies<br>• Case studies<br>• Expert opinion<br>• Studies of poor methodological quality | • Expert opinion<br>• Case studies<br>• Studies of poor methodological quality | • Expert opinion<br>• Case studies<br>• Studies of poor methodological quality |

data: is it qualitative or quantitative? The type of data that you are dealing with determines how you will collate the data from the different studies. If the data from each of the studies is qualitative, then you will engage in *meta-synthesis*. However, if it is quantitative data in each study, then you will use either *meta-analysis* or *narrative summaries*: the former if the data are homogeneous (i.e. from the same population, applying the same inclusion criteria, and using the same methodological design); the latter if the data are non-homogeneous (i.e. different population group and/or inclusion criteria and/or different methodology).

Meta-synthesis, which is applied to qualitative data, is much like critical evaluation in a Literature Review but with the added bonus that the studies that you are reviewing have been meticulously selected to meet a peer-reviewed protocol. Meta-analysis, which is applied to quantitative data, involves the use of traditional statistical techniques to arrive at an aggregate score. If the data from different quantitative-based studies are non-homogeneous, then it is a delicate and difficult task to pool the data together to produce a single statistical score that can be relied upon. In such a situation, a narrative summary is normally employed: this is a discussion about the strength of evidence on the topic under discussion with respect to intervention, feasibility or appropriateness. So, meta-synthesis is similar to a narrative summary, but the former relates to qualitative studies and the latter to non-homogeneous quantitative studies. Figure 6.2 summarises the evidence-synthesis process.

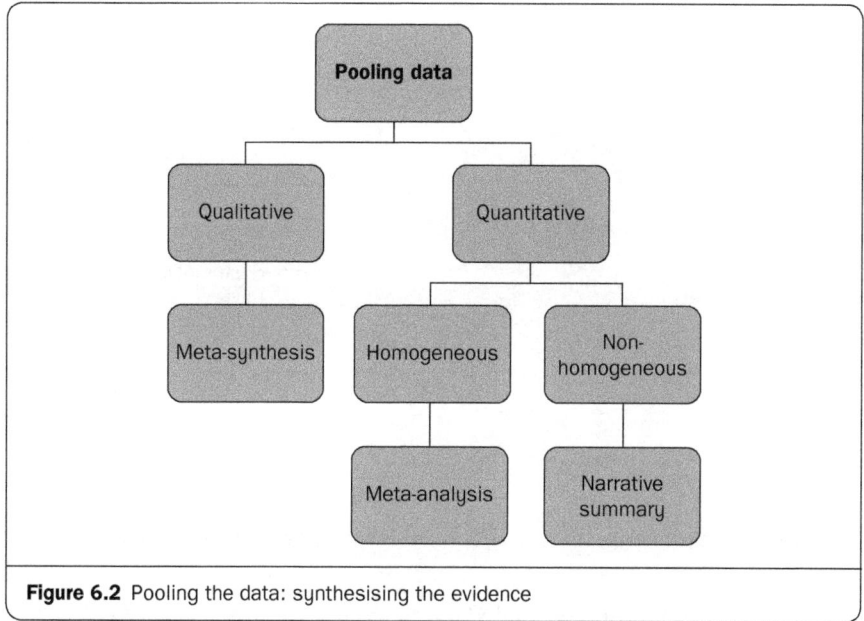

**Figure 6.2** Pooling the data: synthesising the evidence

## Stage 5: Place findings in context

It is in this final stage of the Systematic Review where you:

1 Interpret your synthesised results in the context of the initial review question.
2 Identify any limitations of your review.
3 Point out the practical implications of your findings.

If you are confident that you have a clear answer, one way or the other, to your initial review question, then say so (either a treatment works or it does not, or an intervention is appropriate or it is inappropriate, etc.). On the other hand, if the evidence from your pooled studies is inconclusive, then you must also say so. Importantly, you should place your work in the context of other studies in the same area (Figure 6.3), comparing your findings against the individual empirical work that you looked at and against other Systematic Reviews.

All studies have deficiencies, whether it is an individual study or a Systematic Review of a collection of studies. No research work is perfect and to pretend otherwise is to invite criticism. An inflated ego is not the preserve of celebrities: researchers can sometimes let the thought of fame and fortune cloud their intellectual judgement. Be upfront about any biases or shortcomings in your work and recognise and resist the dangers of exaggerating the strength and impact of your findings. For example, perhaps the data used are

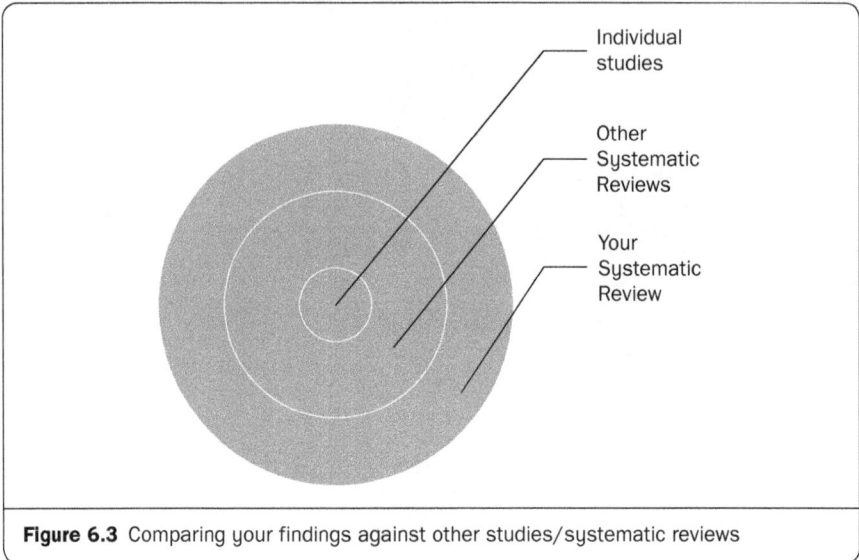

**Figure 6.3** Comparing your findings against other studies/systematic reviews

non-homogeneous or you depended too much on observational studies or you ignored grey literature or focused on studies published from one source. Identifying any defects in your study will help the reader make a more informed view on the value of your work.

Lastly, what are the practical implications of your work? Will it impact on patient care? Will it have an impact on healthcare policy and practice? Does it point to a new focus of research? Identify the practical implications, if any, of your work.

## AMSTAR: a checklist for Systematic Reviews

How can you tell if your Systematic Review is academically thorough? One way is to compare it against a reputable checklist for Systematic Reviews. There are many around but one gaining in popularity is that developed by Shea *et al.* (2007): A MeaSurement Tool to Assess Reviews (AMSTAR). This tool is based on eleven questions (Table 6.4), each of which is designed to assess cumulatively the methodological quality of a systematic review.

Shea *et al.* (*ibid.*) provide more information to help you answer each of the questions in their checklist:

**Q1. *Was an 'a priori' design provided?*** The research question and inclusion criteria should be established before the conduct of the review.

**Q2. *Was there duplicate study selection and data extraction?*** There should be at least two independent data extractors and a consensus procedure for disagreements should be in place.

**Table 6.4**  AMSTAR Checklist

| **AMSTAR Checklist** |
| --- |
| Q1 | Was an 'a priori' design provided? |
| Q2 | Was there duplicate study selection and data extraction? |
| Q3 | Was a comprehensive literature search performed? |
| Q4 | Was the status of publication (e.g. grey literature) used as an inclusion criterion? |
| Q5 | Was a list of studies (included and excluded) provided? |
| Q6 | Were the characteristics of the included studies provided? |
| Q7 | Was the scientific quality of the included studies assessed and documented? |
| Q8 | Was the scientific quality of the included studies used appropriately in formulating conclusions? |
| Q9 | Were the methods used to combine the findings of studies appropriate? |
| Q10 | Was the likelihood of publication bias assessed? |
| Q11 | Was the conflict of interest stated? |
| | ANSWERS for each of the above: Yes, No, Can't answer, Not applicable. |

**Q3. *Was a comprehensive literature search performed?*** At least two electronic sources should be searched. The report must include years and databases used (e.g. Central, EMBASE, and MEDLINE). Key words must be stated and where feasible the search strategy should be provided. All searches should be supplemented by consulting current contents, reviews, textbooks, specialised registers, or experts in the particular field of study, and by reviewing the references in the studies found.

**Q4. *Was the status of publication used as an inclusion criterion?*** The authors should state that they searched for reports regardless of their publication type. The authors should state whether or not they excluded any reports (from the Systematic Review) based on their publication status, language, etc.

**Q5. *Was a list of studies (included and excluded) provided?*** A list of included and excluded studies should be provided.

**Q6. *Were the characteristics of the included studies provided?*** In an aggregated form such as a table, data from the original studies should be provided on the participants, interventions, and outcomes. The ranges of characteristics in all the studies analysed (e.g. age, race, sex, relevant socioeconomic data, disease status, duration, severity, or other diseases) should be reported.

**Q7. *Was the scientific quality of the included studies assessed and documented?*** '*A priori*' methods of assessment should be provided (e.g. for effectiveness studies if the author(s) chose to include only randomised, double-blind, placebo-controlled studies, or allocation concealment as inclusion criteria); for other types of studies, alternative items will be relevant.

**Q8. *Was the scientific quality of the included studies used appropriately in formulating conclusions?*** The results of the methodological rigour and scientific quality should be considered in the analysis and the conclusions of the review, and explicitly stated in formulating recommendations.

**Q9. *Were the methods used to combine the findings of studies appropriate?*** For the pooled results, a test should be done to ensure the studies were combinable, to assess their homogeneity (i.e. Chi squared test for homogeneity, $X^2$). If heterogeneity exists, a random effects model should be used and/or the clinical appropriateness of combining should be taken into consideration (i.e. is it sensible to combine?).

**Q10. *Was the likelihood of publication bias assessed?*** An assessment of publication bias should include a combination of graphical aids (e.g. funnel plot, other available tests) and/or statistical tests (e.g. Egger regression test).

**Q11. *Was any conflict of interest stated?*** Potential sources of support should be clearly acknowledged in both the Systematic Review and the included studies.

The questions in Table 6.4 are there to ensure that your own Systematic Review is of a high standard. Use it in your dissertation to show your supervisor and your marker – they may well be one and same person – that you understand what makes a good Systematic Review and that, within your word-count and time limitations, you have done your best to follow professional protocols.

# Further reading

Bettany-Saltikov, J. and McSherry, R. (2016) *How to do a systematic literature review in nursing: a step-by-step guide*. 2nd edn. Maidenhead: Open University Press.

Boland, A., Cherry, M. G. and Dickson, R. (2013) *Doing a systematic review: a student's guide*. London: Sage.

Gough, D., Oliver, S. and Thomas, J. (2017) *An introduction to systematic reviews*. 2nd edn. London: Sage.

Higgins, J. and Green, S. (2008) *Systematic reviews of interventions*. Chichester: Wiley.

Jesson, J. K., Matheson, L. and Lacey, F. M. (2011) *Doing your literature review: traditional and systematic techniques*. London: Sage.

# Summary of key points

- A Systematic Review is a focused study of primary research from a number of studies to assess the effectiveness, appropriateness or feasibility of an intervention, normally, but not exclusively, in the field of healthcare. Systematic Reviews must meet peer-reviewed protocols.
- The main stages of a Systematic Review are: (1) determine the review question or objective; (2) work out the literature search process; (3) justify why literature was included/excluded; (4) pool data from each study to give, where applicable, an aggregate score or a summative view; and (5) place findings in context.
- PICO is a protocol to help you develop your review question/statement. PICO stands for: **P**atient group/setting, **I**ntervention, **C**omparison, **O**utcome.
- Avoid the different types of bias in your literature search: language bias, publication bias, and selection bias.
- How you *pool* the data together – referred to as *evidence-synthesis* – depends on the type of data to be pooled: if the data are qualitative, then the analysis technique to be used is *meta-synthesis*; if the data are quantitative and homogeneous, then use *meta-analysis*; if the data are quantitative and non-homogeneous, then the analysis technique involves a *narrative summary*.
- *Placing your findings* in context means that: (a) you interpret your results with reference to your review question and other studies; (b) you identify limitations in your work; and (c) you highlight the implications of your findings.
- AMSTAR is a professionally developed protocol based on a checklist of eleven questions that is used to assess the methodological quality of a systematic review. AMSTAR is short for: **A M**ea**S**urement **T**ool to **A**ssess **R**eviews.

# Chapter **7**

# Research methods 1: traditional approaches

> • *What's it all about?* • *Research strategy* • *Data collection* • *Frame-work for data analysis* • *Limitations and potential problems* • *Further reading* • *Summary of key points*

This chapter covers traditional research methods. If you are collecting your own data, then you will need to explain your methods. Most Master's students will adopt traditional research methods in their dissertation, both in terms of research strategy (case studies, surveys, etc.) and data collection techniques (questionnaires, interviews, etc.). If, however, you are creating something with your own hands, such as a play or a sculpture or a piece of music, or even a computer program, then Chapter 8, 'Research Methods 2: Artist as researcher' is for you. Nevertheless, if you are engaged in practice-based research, you will still benefit from reading this chapter, as it addresses research data collection techniques that you may also use, as well as offering generic advice on writing a chapter on research methods.

## What's it all about?

What is the point of a chapter on research methods? If you intend collecting your own data – that is, implementing your own empirical research – then you need to tell the reader how you propose to go about this process. Your results will not be trusted if you fail to inform the reader how you did your research. Tales abound of students who fail because they neither provide information on their research subjects – *who, when, where, why* – nor include, for example, their questionnaires, leaving their supervisor to guess the questions allegedly asked and to work out why the questions were being asked. Research studies that lack crucial information on the research methods used, and why the research was implemented, are worse than useless and cannot be trusted. The trick, therefore, is to give the reader clear and unambiguous information on these issues, so much so that, if the reader wishes, he or she could replicate your studies. Consequently, the information that you will give to the reader (your supervisor/marker) about your research methods will be highly structured and detailed, reflecting the meticulous nature of credible research work (Gill and Johnson, 1997).

You will still need a chapter, or at the very least a significant sub-section, on research methods even if you have no plans to gather your own raw data but depend purely on secondary data (e.g. a Literature Review) for your findings. In which case, you will clarify where you will get your literature (books, journal articles, government reports, the Internet), emphasising literature that will be of particular relevance to your research objectives and taking care to justify your choice of secondary sources. However, the typical scenario in a Master's dissertation is for students to complete a Literature Review (or its equivalent, e.g. Contextual Review or Systematic Review) *and* to collect and analyse their own data. This chapter will focus on the latter scenario, where you are expected, in addition to producing a Literature Review, to collect and analyse your own empirical data. Accordingly, the research methods chapter that you write relates to how you will collect and analyse your empirical data. (Note: to save rewriting 'Literature Review or Contextual Review or Systematic Review', reference will be made only to 'Literature Review' with the understanding that the same advice also applies to a Contextual Review and a Systematic Review.)

Too many students seem to be struck by *vagueitis* – a reluctance to reveal what they are doing in their own research – with the result that their chapter on research methods is often the worse aspect of their research project. In fact, it is the research methods chapter, more than any other chapter, that differentiates the top student from the average/poor student: the top student is knowledgeable and not afraid to provide crystal-clear information on the research to be undertaken, including the rationale for their chosen approach(es); the average/poor student, on the other hand, makes it only too obvious that there is a lack of understanding about what this chapter is all about and merely peppers their efforts with unexplained terminology and confusing, and often contradictory, statements.

There are a number of strands to a research methods chapter in a student's dissertation, typically including the following sub-sections:

- Introduction
- Research strategy
- Data collection
- Framework for data analysis
- Limitations and potential problems.

Table 7.1 highlights the sort of questions that a dissertation marker will be thinking about when reading your research methods chapter.

**Table 7.1** Marker's view of your chapter on research methods

| Research methods | Questions to be addressed |
|---|---|
| Introduction | *What* specific *research objective* does your empirical research relate to? *Why* are you collecting your own data? Is there any indication of how you are going to *structure* your chapter? |
| Research strategy | *What* is your overall research strategy? (Case study, survey, experimental, historical, action research, grounded theory, ethnographic research, or what?) *Why* have you chosen that research strategy? *How* do you intend sampling your target population? *Why* have you chosen that approach? |
| Data collection | *How* do you propose to collect your data? (Questionnaires, interviews, observation, organisational reports, etc.?) *Why* have you chosen to collect your data that way? |
| Framework for data analysis | Once you have collected your data, what are you going to do with it? In other words, *how* are you going to analyse your findings? |
| Limitations and potential problems | Do you see any *limitations or problems* with your empirical research? (For example, limitations in your chosen strategy or problems getting access to your research subjects?) Have you faced the twin issues of *validity* and *reliability*? (That is, are the research choices you made *appropriate* and can your work be *trusted*?) |

As you can see, there are a lot of *what* questions and *why* questions: and that is the key to completing a strong research methods chapter. State with absolute clarity the approaches you are adopting – your overall research strategy, specific data collection techniques, and means of analysing your data – and *why* you are doing things that way. It is the combination of *what* answers and *why* answers that will gain you good marks.

Hopefully by now you have the hang of writing an Introduction to a chapter, so introducing your research methods chapter should be quite straightforward:

- First of all, remind your supervisor of your specific research objectives. (This also has the effect of reminding you to keep on track!)
- Next, refer to the research objective(s) that relate to your research methods chapter: 'A valuable aspect of this research relates to Objective 3: the opportunity to study e-Learning strategy and implementation in practice . . .'
- Then, remind the reader of the need for your own research work, with reference back to your Literature Review: 'Objectives 1 and 2 were initially

addressed in the Literature Review.' Include the potential benefits of your intended research: 'Objective 3 takes this research one step further . . . By comparing theory with practice, the research will gain a fuller . . .'

- Finally, outline the topics that you will cover in your research methods chapter: 'This chapter will provide the details of the research strategy adopted to address the research issues identified above, together with the means of collecting data for analysis, including . . .'

Appendix J – 'Sample research methods chapter' – begins with a sample introduction to a research methods chapter, but your chapter may be shorter, or even longer, depending on how many words you have to play with and what you want to say.

Let us now look at the other parts that usually go to make up the research methods chapter: *Research Strategy, Data Collection, Framework for Data Analysis, Limitations and Potential Problems* – starting with your research strategy.

## Research strategy

Many students score less than average marks for this section in their chapter on research methods, principally because they do not understand what is meant by a research strategy or they fail to explain why they are using a particular research strategy, or because they select a strategy that is inappropriate for their research.

 **A common mistake by students**

A common mistake by students is to spend the bulk of their time discussing research strategies in general, with scant attention given to the one that they have chosen and, crucially, why.

In the first instance, you must identify in detail *how* you intend implementing your own research study, i.e. the strategy that you intend adopting to complete your empirical study. For instance, suppose that you were alarmed at the number of MSc. students who gained poor marks for their dissertation submissions and you wanted to find out why this was so. To begin with, you could carry out a Literature Review to find out what other researchers had to say about the subject. Suppose further that the findings from your Literature Review revealed that there was a need for empirical data, rather than anecdotal evidence; or that there were a number of empirical studies but that they concentrated on staff views rather than the views of students, and it is the latter group that you want to question. You decide to do your own practical research work to help address this deficiency. To do this, however, you need to work out your overall approach to implementing your research, i.e. your research strategy.

Rather than invent your own research strategy, there are numerous ones from which you can choose, including case studies, surveys, ethnography, and action research, to name but a few. It makes sense to use a tried-and-tested research strategy because it ought to have academic credibility (although that does not stop academics themselves arguing the merits of one approach over another!). What you have to do is to select the approach that best suits *your* research. Related to the student dissertation example above, you could select one MSc. programme in one university – that is, implement a case study – and interview a sample of students who had failed their dissertation to ascertain their views on why they think they failed.

For the moment, it is time to digress and outline some of the research strategies that are available to professional researchers, and to you, when carrying out empirical research.

## Case study

A *case study* is a study of one example of a particular type of something, e.g. Oxford University is an example of a particular type of university, ancient universities; similarly, Ryanair is an example of a particular type of airline, a budget airline. Cohen and Manion (1995, p. 106) describe a case study thus:

> *The case study researcher typically observes the characteristics of an individual unit – a child, a class, a school or a community. The purpose of such observation is to probe deeply and to analyse intensely the multifarious phenomena that constitute the life cycle of the unit.*

Case studies are very popular with students, probably because they find it easier to focus their research on one organisation or part of an organisation. When applying a case study approach, students incline towards using interviews as their main, or sole, means of data collection, although more enterprising students use a mixture of data collection techniques, such as questionnaires, individual interviews, and group interviews, aiming not only for a rich output, but higher marks.

Case study research can be based on a single case study or multiple case studies (i.e. more than one case). If you decide to do more than one case study, remember to apply the same research approach to each of your cases, otherwise it will be difficult to compare and contrast your case studies against each other. For example, suppose that you want to understand how universities in the same town view incidences of plagiarism. Let us pick the city of Glasgow in Scotland as an example, where three universities exist: the University of Glasgow, the University of Strathclyde, and Glasgow Caledonian University (incidentally, the case studies do not need to be in the same geographical vicinity). These three universities form your multiple case study research. You decide to collect the following data from each of the institutions for the last three years: (a) the number of students formally accused of plagiarism; (b) the number of students found guilty; and (c) the punishments meted out to students. However, the primary justification for a case study is to explore some contemporary issue *in depth* – in this example, plagiarism – which is normally translated as engaging in meaningful interaction with the case study units. So you need to collect the data in a way that allows for detailed responses. You could choose to interview two groups within each of the universities, students and academic staff, and design structured interviews to collect their views on their university's approach to plagiarism. Whether to do one case study or to base your research on multiple case studies is a matter for you (after, of course, taking advice from your supervisor).

Once you have made the choice whether to undertake one case study or to execute multiple case studies, you then need to reflect upon the *type* of case study research that best meets the purpose of your research, and there are three types (Figure 7.1): *explanatory, descriptive,* and *exploratory.*

*Explanatory* case studies focus on trying to find out – *explain* – why something happens. Here is an example of an explanatory case study: interviewing and observing a sample of Twitter users in an attempt to explain the attraction of social media. The phenomenon to be researched would be social media and Twitter would form the case study. If you introduced other cases of social media – YouTube, Facebook, etc. – then you would be implementing multiple case study research.

*Descriptive* case studies zoom in on producing a full description of a phenomenon, such as an organisation or an event, within its context (Yin, 2003). Descriptive case studies are not seeking to answer cause-and-effect questions.

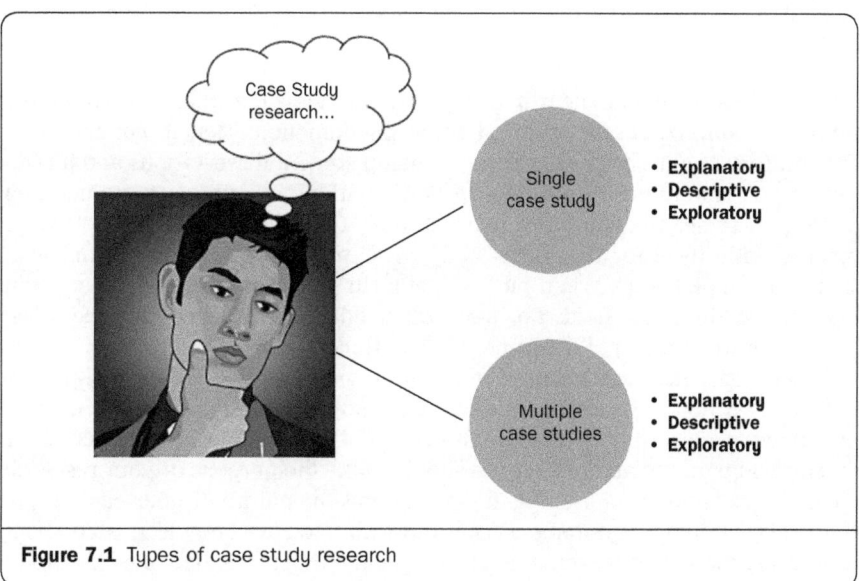

**Figure 7.1** Types of case study research

Their primary function is to gain a deeper understanding of some phenomenon. For example, suppose that you want to study trade unions and, in particular, capture a comprehensive knowledge of the work of trade union representatives. You select one particular type of trade union, in this case the University and College Union (UCU), and describe the day-to-day activities of a number of their representatives in one university: the training they receive, the meetings they attend, the casework they get involved in, their views of management, etc. The key to descriptive studies is identifying from the outset the boundaries of your research, where your description starts and where it ends. As with any research strategy, you should explain the *why* and *what*: why you are using a descriptive case study and what it is you will be describing.

*Exploratory* case studies are less common in student dissertations and are closely associated with pilot studies. Exploratory case studies are usually a precursor to a later, large-scale investigation. Their objective is mainly to determine hypotheses or research questions for a future study. Even though exploratory case studies, by their very nature, tend to be incomplete studies, they can be informative, signposting future research issues. Examples of published exploratory case studies are:

Scharzbaum, J. A., George, S. L., Pratt, C. B. and Davis, B. (1991) 'An exploratory study of environmental factors potentially related to childhood cancer', *Medical & Pediatric Oncology*, 19(2), pp. 115–21.

Azouzi, R., Beauregard, R. and D'Amours, S. (2009) 'Exploratory case studies on manufacturing agility in the furniture industry', *Management Research News*, 32(5), pp. 424–39.

Palmer, R. and Wilson, H. (2009) 'An exploratory case study analysis of contemporary marketing practices', *Journal of Strategic Marketing*, 17(2), pp. 169–87.

Dissertation students nearly always take the view that their research must involve a *comprehensive* study of some phenomenon. That is *not* the case. Exploratory studies are tailor-made for many student dissertations and it is an option you should not dismiss out of hand. Within your time constraints they allow you to set realistic objectives, study a topic in reasonable depth, and emerge with ideas for future research. An exploratory study does not mean that you can pick a generic topic (budget airlines, for example) and just study anything within that field: no, you still need to be focused (for example, 'An Exploratory Study of Customer Care in Budget Airlines').

When you write your chapter on research methods, it is not normally compulsory that you explain the type of case study research you will be using – explanatory, descriptive or exploratory – for the simple reason that your research aim and related objectives should make the purpose of your research clear. There is no harm, though, in spelling out the nature of your case study: it would certainly let your supervisor know that you are knowledgeable about case study theory. However, if you are implementing more than one case study (i.e. multiple case studies), then you need to include this information.

## Survey

A *survey* is a representative selection from the population of a particular type, for instance, a survey of 30 universities from the population of universities in the UK or a survey of 200 retail companies in Europe. There are a number of ways that you can carry out a survey: personal interviews, telephone interviews, postal questionnaires (or hand-delivered), email questionnaires (i.e. sending out a questionnaire as an email attachment), online questionnaires using online survey software such as SurveyMonkey (https://www.surveymonkey.co.uk), or group questionnaires (where you get a target population together to complete your questionnaire, e.g. a group of class mates – convenient, saves time, and ensures a high return rate).

*Personal interviews* are resource-intensive, for interviewer and interviewee, but the advantage is that responses to questions are usually more expansive than those obtained through other means. Surveys can be time-consuming, thus rather than interviewing the sampled population, students often favour questionnaires. The main questions you need to consider when designing your survey are:

- Which group of people do I wish to survey? Your target population should be an easy one to determine (business leaders, iPad users, students in debt, computer hackers, and so on).
- How many people do I need to survey? This depends on a number of variables, including the size of the main population from which your survey population is derived, the geographical considerations, the type of survey you want to use, ease of access to your target population, and expected return rate. If in doubt, seek your supervisor's counsel and have a look at past dissertations where students made use of surveys.
- Are the intended recipients easy to access? What you need to remember is that you have a dissertation to complete and by the time that you start your empirical research, your submission date will be drawing ever closer, so be realistic when making decisions about your target group.
- What should I ask them? Your questions should link directly to your research objectives. In other words, pose questions that help to answer your research objectives/questions. Make life easy for your research subjects by grouping your questions into themes, themes that reflect your research objectives. Let them know what these themes are by either telling them during your personal interview or by providing appropriate headings in your questionnaire.
- How should I ask them? There are two strands to this question: which techniques should I use (personal interview, email questionnaire, etc.) and how should I construct my questions? If you can obtain personal interviews and you have the time, then by all means do so. Or, if an email to your research subjects is easier to do, without compromising the quality of your work, then send out a questionnaire as an email attachment (or link to an online survey). If geographical location is an issue but you still want to do a personal interview, then you can carry out a telephone interview or, even better, use Skype

(http://www.skype.com), combining voice with video. The format of your questions will depend on the kind of research you are doing: is it chiefly qualitative or quantitative in nature? Qualitative research dictates an emphasis on open questions whereas quantitative research leans more towards closed questions. So the type of questions that you ask – open or closed – depends on whether or not you want qualitative or quantitative data, or both. In any event, try and avoid getting carried away with the number of questions you want to ask. It is not always the case of the more the merrier – too many questions might deter people from completing your questionnaire!

## Ethnography

Ethnography has its roots in anthropology, the study of people in their natural environment; in effect, the study of *cultures*. For example, the study of Amazon tribes would qualify as ethnographic research. Ethnographic researchers patiently record what they observe and then attempt to interpret that data. Theirs is a difficult job, not just in terms of the patience that is required, but also with respect to the difficult conditions under which they work. The traditional ethnographic researcher has to be admired. These days, however, ethnography has taken a wider meaning, referring to the study of any culture, old or modern. A modern example of ethnography would be the study of gang culture.

Field notes – a record of your daily observations – are at the heart of ethnographic research. Every time that you go out to meet/observe/interact with your research subjects, you should have already decided on how you will record the day's events. Do not rely on memory. You need to create notes about what you are witnessing. These notes will form the basis of your evidence and analysis. What sort of information should you record? Date, time, and place are essential. It is also helpful to note the purpose of a particular field trip (e.g. Purpose: to observe a day in the life of Tom, a beggar). You need to describe events and jot down initial thoughts/views/feelings that spring to mind. A standard layout that you can use is shown in Figure 7.2.

These days it is much easier to record information. You can use a mobile phone, a camcorder or a camera to capture audio and video evidence, including your own running commentary. Or you can borrow or purchase a small digital voice recorder. The advantage of a digital voice recorder is that your research subjects are more likely to view that as less intrusive than someone taking pictures or video evidence. An innovative approach would be to utilise the portability and versatility of an iPad: use an iPad app to store your written observations/comments; use another app to capture voice commentary; access the Internet for any information you might need to look up; connect to email to contact a colleague/supervisor for advice; and even store your thesis on the iPad word processor and directly update it while taking a coffee break! There are also specialised ethnographic software tools for storing and analysing qualitative data, such as E6 (http://www.qualisresearch.com).

Ethnographic research is not something that the novice student ought to attempt without clear guidance from an experienced supervisor.

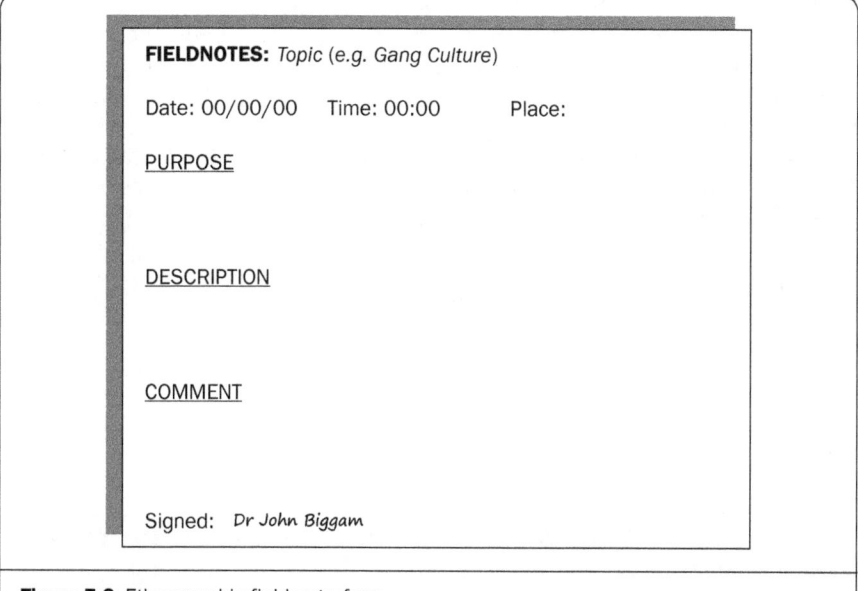

**FIELDNOTES:** *Topic (e.g. Gang Culture)*

Date: 00/00/00    Time: 00:00         Place:

PURPOSE

DESCRIPTION

COMMENT

Signed:  Dr John Biggam

**Figure 7.2** Ethnographic field note form

## Experimental research

*Experimental research* tends to be the domain of the scientist, where he or she attempts to test an hypothesis (i.e. a theory) through some type of experiment. The scientist will first try to define the problem; then formulate an hypothesis; and, finally, implement an experiment to test whether or not the hypothesis was correct. The experimental researcher is normally well versed in using statistical tools and techniques.

An hypothesis is a theory proposed by a researcher. It may be a theory that the researcher has come up with or it may be someone else's theory. An hypothesis has to be explicitly and unambiguously stated, such as:

*Hypothesis: It rains more in England than in Scotland.*

This is called the prevailing theory. Scientists love abbreviated labels and refer to a theory put forward by a researcher as $H_0$, also called the null hypothesis.

*$H_0$: It rains more in England than in Scotland.*

The alternative theory is labelled $H_1$. Why is it called the *alternative* hypothesis? This is because the suggested theory is alternative to the opposite theory, which prevails until there is evidence refuting it:

*$H_1$: It does not rain more in England than in Scotland.*

The two theories, or hypotheses, are competing against each other and after the researcher carries out an experiment, only one theory will survive. However, it is *always* the null hypothesis, $H_0$, that is tested. That is the theory that has priority and until evidence is produced to nullify or reject it, then it remains the prevailing theory.

Here are two more examples of alternative $(H_1)$ and null $(H_0)$ hypotheses. The null hypothesis, H0, is the one that the researcher is interested in refuting, to be replaced by a new theory, the alternative theory, $H_1$:

Example 1
$H_1$: There is no difference in taste between Coke and Diet Coke.
$H_0$: There is a difference in taste between Coke and Diet Coke.

Example 2
$H_1$: There is a difference in levels of intelligence between children raised in working-class environments and those raised in middle-class environments.

$H_0$: There is no difference in levels of intelligence between children raised in working-class environments and those raised in middle-class environments.

The scientific protocol used to conduct experimental research can be more formally expressed by the seven-stage process shown in Table 7.2.

1 In the first stage you write down your alternative theory, $H_1$, and the theory you are testing, $H_0$.
2 The second stage is where you identify your sample population. The size of your sample population should be large enough to allow you to make statistically significant generalisations. Be careful how you choose your sample population: if you are interested in those who vote and you select just students for your experiments, then, at the most, you will only be able to generalise about students who vote, not all voters. Also, experiments are more reliable where the research subjects are selected at random (minimises bias).
3 In the third stage you create control and test groups. Once again, these should be selected at random and, where possible, performed 'blind' or 'double-blind'. The test is blind when the participants are unaware of which group they are in; the test is double-blind when neither the participants nor the researcher are aware of which group has received the causal agent. Both the control and test groups are identical with the exception that the variable considered by the researcher to make a difference – *the causal agent* – is introduced into the test group.
4 Next you establish how often you will sample your test subjects: every minute, every hour, every day, every month? The sample period depends on the type of experiment.
5 Now you perform your experiment, adhering to your stated procedures . . .

6  … after which you analyse your data using appropriate statistical techniques.

7  Lastly, you decide whether to accept or reject the prevailing view, the null hypothesis, $H_0$. If your results support the rejection of the null hypothesis, then your alternative theory, $H_1$, is accepted and, in turn, becomes someone else's null hypothesis. The purpose of experimental research is to continuously replace one null hypothesis – the prevailing theory – with a better one.

**Table 7.2**   Experimental research protocol

| Stage | Activity |
|-------|----------|
| 1 | State alternative hypothesis, $H_1$, and null hypothesis, $H_0$ |
| 2 | Determine sample groups |
| 3 | Specify control and test groups |
| 4 | Establish sampling procedure |
| 5 | Perform experiment |
| 6 | Analyse raw data |
| 7 | Accept or reject null hypothesis, $H_0$ |

## Historical research

*Historical research*, as the name suggests, is research that focuses primarily on events that occurred in the distant past (e.g. the conditions under which soldiers lived during the First World War), but it can also deal with events in the recent past (e.g. the growth of the Internet). Historical research is a bit like ethnographic research in the sense that the researcher requires skills in observation and interpretation, except in the case of historical research the subjects under study tend to appear in documents, videos, etc., rather than in real life. You could say that historical research is akin to a detective mystery, but where all the suspects are (normally) dead! When the historical researchers investigate events in the recent past, the issue arises of whether they are engaging in historical research or contemporary research.

The immediate difficulty encountered by those seeking to find out about the past is that the past no longer exists. All they have to go on are fragments, which they have to piece together to form a coherent narrative. Their task is therefore twofold: find the right fragments and tell a credible story. Historical researchers call such fragments 'documents', which can include a whole range of primary and secondary sources: manuscripts, books, maps, voice recordings, photographs, films, government documents, etc.

In the context of historical research, a primary source is a 'document' from the period under study; a secondary source is one that refers to the same period but created by someone else at a later date. Examples of primary sources include written statements, archive film, newspapers, and diaries. Examples of secondary sources include documentaries, research papers, books and reports. Primary and secondary sources can be found in libraries, government archives, historical associations, and on the Internet. An excellent source for information on historical research is the Institute for Historical Research (http://www. history.ac.uk), which is part of the University of London.

Good historical research requires that you should be versed in core scholarship skills such as oral history (e.g. collecting oral testimonies), i-skills (finding sources, organising documents/data, Internet skills, etc.), appraising the worth of primary and secondary sources (placing it in context and being aware of potential bias), textual analysis (e.g. competent at using NVivo to manage qualitative data), understanding historical explanatory paradigms such as Marxism and psychoanalysis, and having the ability to piece all this together to form a compelling narrative.

Notwithstanding the difficulties inherent in historical research, of all the research strategies it is the one that is actually fun to do.

## Action research

*Action research* is where the researcher starts with a particular problem that needs to be solved, or understood better, usually within the environment where the researcher is working (Cunningham, 1995). A teacher could carry out action research to improve his or her teaching. Perhaps the pupils are having difficulty understanding a particular subject. The teacher would define the problem, plan a means of solving the problem (e.g. make it more interesting, introduce topical discussions, use groupwork, etc.), implement a proposed solution, and evaluate the results. The key to understanding action research is to realise from the outset that the researcher is *involved* in the research not just as a (research) observer but as a participant, i.e. the researcher is part of their own research and their participation can influence the findings. Writing about your own participation in a research project can be problematic: there is the question of objectivity and the temptation to show yourself in a good light in your findings.

To gain credibility in the research community, action research, although problem-based, nevertheless follows accepted research procedures: elucidation of research objectives, review of relevant literature, applied research, discussion of results, conclusion. Some students attempt what they think is action research, but omit the research aspect, and are left with what is in effect a work-based project rather than a well-rounded piece of credible research.

The focus of action research is on promoting change, typically in educational and organisational settings, and central to this type of research is the idea of self-reflection or self-reflective enquiry. Most researchers do research on other people but action researchers do research on themselves. Action research is more than a process (define the problem, plan a solution, implement the proposed solution, evaluate the result), it is also a commitment to solving a problem, starkly summarised in Stringer's (1999) model of action research (Figure 7.3):

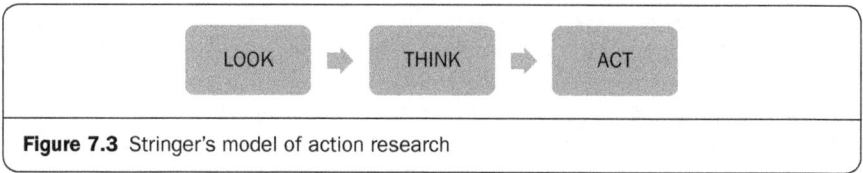

**Figure 7.3** Stringer's model of action research

LOOK:    Observe and record the context, the problem to be solved, together with participant roles and activities. For example, if you suspect that dissertation supervision in your institution could be improved, you could note the dissertation process, the types of supervision (face-to-face, email, etc.), where supervision takes place and how often, including supervision activities and obvious problems (e.g. difficulty in students contacting supervisors and receiving timely feedback).

THINK:    This is where you think about the problems in more detail and identify solutions (e.g. you might propose that the use of mobile technologies will improve dissertation supervision).

ACT:    Here you put your solution(s) into practice and evaluate the results.

Action research is an incremental activity. Very often the proposed solution is only partly effective or part of the answer, which means that action researchers require another iteration or two before they can bring their research to a satisfactory conclusion. You, as a dissertation student, do not have the luxury of repeated attempts at solving a problem. In reality, you will have one go at action research: Look once, Think once, and Act once. That in itself should not deter you from action research. You are being tested on how to complete a dissertation, not that you must solve a particular problem. As long as you go through the process and make recommendations on what still needs to be done, if that is the case, and how to do it, then you should be fine.

## Grounded theory

*Grounded theory* (Glaser and Strauss, 1967) is quite a difficult theory to apply in practice, and only a very confident student ought to attempt grounded theory. It is demanding in the sense that it does not follow the normal procedures for implementing a research project: that is, start with a clearly defined research focus, find out through a Literature Review what others have to say about your research problem, implement your own practical research, discuss the findings, come to a conclusion, etc. Instead, grounded theory is a bit higgledy-piggledy, in that you do not start with a clearly defined set of research objectives but follow where your research takes you, building up theory as you go along.

In grounded theory, you start with a rough idea of the area that you are interested in researching; next, you carry out some empirical research; then you refer to literature that you think is relevant to the work that you carried out; you then, depending on what you have read, implement further practical work; and so on, jumping back and forth between your empirical work and your review of relevant literature, until you develop a sustainable theory grounded in your practical research, but influenced by reference to appropriate literature. In other words, the relationship between the Literature Review and your practical research is not sequential but symbiotic, where one feeds off the other. It is very exploratory in nature, and so means that you need to be aware of when to call a halt to your research, otherwise it will be never-ending. It is very much like the relationship between an artist and a painting: what the artist thinks will influence what the artist paints; and what is painted will influence what the artist thinks; but at some point the artist needs to set aside the paintbrush or risk ruining a work of art.

Incidentally, some staff, and so students, refer to the aforementioned research strategies – case study, survey, etc. – as examples of a research *method* ('The research method that I will be adopting is a case study . . .'), equating a research strategy with a research method. This is fine, but it can be confusing. Your overall research strategy is only one of the *methods* that you will be using to carry out your practical research: the other methods, which you also have to discuss in your dissertation, include your *method* of data collection and also the *method* by which you expect to analyse your collected data. That is why this chapter in your dissertation is usually called the Research Methods chapter, to reflect the fact that you will be writing about a number of methods related to implementing your empirical research (research strategy, data collection techniques, framework for data analysis, etc.). Otherwise, logically, if you equate a research method only to a research strategy, and you call your chapter 'Research Methods', then all you ought to be writing about is your case study, or survey, or whatever, which is clearly wrong because you also need to discuss how you intend to collect and analyse your data. So, instead of writing 'The research *method* that will be adopted is a case study . . .', you ought to be writing either 'The research *strategy* that will be adopted is a case study . . .' or 'One research method that will be adopted, related to research strategy, is a case study . . .', but not '*The* research method that . . .'.

## Quantitative versus qualitative research

Some researchers mistakenly group research strategies under two opposing headings: quantitative and qualitative. Students often replicate this mistake. At a simple level, the former type – *quantitative* – refers to research that is concerned with quantities and measurements, such as the number of people who smoke in a given period on 5th Avenue in New York, or the success rate of dissertation students in the London School of Economics, or the proportion of a population that use a particular type of transport to get to work in Bombay. The number crunching can be more complicated than just gaining simple quantitative information. For example, it can include calculating the probability of dying before retirement for those in a given profession. Much of the scientific research that occurs, because it deals with quantifiable data, tends to be grouped under the heading quantitative research.

*Qualitative* research, on the other hand, is linked to in-depth exploratory studies (exploring, for example, *why* students pick a particular module to study), where the opportunity for 'quality' responses exists. Denzin and Lincoln (1994, p. 2) hold that qualitative research involves studying 'things in their natural settings, attempting to make sense of, or interpret, phenomena in terms of the meanings people bring to them'.

In general, quantitative research answers the *how* questions, whereas the *why* questions are left to qualitative research. Of course, the reality is that it is rare that professional researchers, and dissertation students for that matter, stick to collecting and analysing either quantitative or qualitative data. They usually mix and match (Myers, 1997). A student could be interested in quantitative issues such as how many postgraduate students picked a particular module for the taught part of their course, the number that passed that module, as well as qualitative matters such as why students selected the module in the first place and what they liked/disliked about the module. This mix of quantitative/qualitative questions is common in everyday life: someone might ask you if you attended so-and-so's party at the weekend (begging a quantitative y/n response) but also enquire what you thought of the party (encouraging a qualitative answer).

> **!  A common mistake by students**
>
> A common mistake by students is to equate *research strategies* with quantitative or qualitative research. Too many students think that it is the research strategy that determines whether their research is quantitative or qualitative in nature. For instance, it is common for students to relate surveys to quantitative research and case studies to qualitative research. Although it is generally true that a case study, for example, *suggests* a qualitative study and that a survey, for example, *suggests* a quantitative piece of research, it is not necessarily the case. It is not the research strategy – case study, survey, experimental, action research, etc. – that determines whether or not your empirical study is quantitative or qualitative in nature: that, instead, is dependent on a combination of your individual research objectives, your research strategy, and your data collection technique(s).

Suppose that you decide to do a case study of one university in Paris (e.g. the Sorbonne). A case study is normally associated with an in-depth exploratory study, so a case study of one university in Paris must be a qualitative study, yes? Well, not necessarily. If your case study was intended to determine issues surrounding pass rates, such as the number of students passing each module, the progression rates for different courses and years, including direct entrants, and that you want to collect your data through the use of closed questionnaires, then the nature of this research would be quantitative in nature because the research objectives relate mainly to *how* questions (*how* many students passed each module, etc.) and because questionnaires limit the opportunity for in-depth exploratory responses, tending to yield answers that are easily quantifiable (six people said this, four said that, etc.). On the other hand, you could implement a survey of universities in France, but instead of focusing on how many students failed modules, etc., you could focus on *why* students are failing, and collect your data through interviews. The 'why' nature of the research and the use of interviews – where the opportunity to explore matters in depth exists – provide evidence that the research would now be primarily qualitative in nature.

So do not write in your dissertation that you are doing quantitative – or qualitative – research solely because of the research strategy that you have chosen. A research strategy cannot be, in itself, qualitative or quantitative – it is the combination of your research strategy, your research objectives, and your data collection techniques that help determine the quantitative or qualitative nature of your research. When you are explaining why you have picked a quantitative (or qualitative) approach, do so by reference not only to your research strategy but also to your research objectives and your means of data collection. Do not exclude the possibility that your research is both quantitative and qualitative in nature. If so, indicate which parts are mainly quantitative and which parts relate to the qualitative aspects.

## Sampling techniques

Regardless of whether your research is quantitative or qualitative in nature, it is highly unlikely that you will be in a position to collect data from your whole target population (e.g. all customers who frequent Marks & Spencer), in which case you will need to collect data from a sample of your population (e.g. a sample of those who frequent Marks & Spencer). There are a number of sampling techniques that you can use, including: random sampling, simple random sampling, stratified sampling, cluster sampling, systematic sampling, quota sampling, and convenience sampling.

---

### Sampling techniques

- *Random sampling* is where you sample a population entirely at random. For example, if you want to know how people will vote in a local election, rather than ask everyone in that town – because it may be too costly and perhaps impossible to accomplish in a set period – you might decide to stop and ask a selection of people at random in the street. Be aware, though, that samples are often open to the accusation of bias: the street you stood in, the time of day you carried out your survey, the ▶

▶

number of people you asked, etc. Whenever politicians do not like the results of a survey, they are inclined to criticise the sampling methods employed. Nonetheless, implementing a random sample helps you to reduce bias.

- *Simple random sampling* is a variation of random sampling. In random sampling it does not need to be the case that each member of your population has the same chance of being selected (e.g. if you pick a Saturday afternoon to sample your population, then football fans, many of whom may be watching their favourite football team at the time of your sampling activity, have less of a chance of being sampled), whereas with simple random sampling every member ought to have an equal chance of being selected. If you have a large population where it is impossible to identify every member – so as to allow everyone an equal chance of being selected – then your sample may be subject to significant bias.

- *Stratified sampling* is where you break down your target population into identifiable groups (strata) and then take samples from each of these groups. For example, students attending a lecture could be classified under the strata 'male' and 'female' or 'school leaver' and 'mature entrant', and samples taken from each stratum.

- *Cluster sampling* is where you break down your target population into clusters (or groups or strata) but, unlike stratified sampling (where you immediately select samples from each of your groups), you then randomly select a sample of your clusters. From within each of your chosen clusters, you will then select random samples. It is actually quite simple to understand, as the following example shows. Suppose that you want to investigate the health of chickens in Scotland. It would be time-consuming and expensive to check on the health of every chicken, so you decide to use the different regions of Scotland as your clusters (Strathclyde, Highland, Grampian, South Lanarkshire, etc.), from which you then randomly select a subset of these regions, thus reducing the clusters that you need to target. From these clusters you randomly select the chicken plots that you will visit for inspection. You have to be careful that your clusters are of comparable size, so it may be appropriate to merge some of your clusters at the very start of your research before you randomly select the clusters that you will then explore in detail.

- *Systematic sampling* occurs when you take a sample of your target population at equal or regular intervals. For example, you select every fifth name on a list or every tenth customer record from a customer computer database.

- *Quota sampling* does not involve random sampling and is therefore vulnerable to the criticism that there is no way of telling if the results are representative of a larger population. Sampling that does not involve random sampling is sometimes referred to as non-probability sampling. In quota sampling, you decide beforehand the type and number of members (i.e. your selection quota) that you intend sampling. When you are stopped in the street and asked about your choice of breakfast cereal or how you will vote in the next election, then it is likely that you are the victim of quota sampling (you have been picked because you are one of

▶

▶ the '5 elderly males' or '10 teenage females' or '15 professionals' that
  are on their list for selection).

- *Convenience sampling* is another non-probability approach to sampling, i.e.
  it is non-random. It is implemented because, as the name suggests, it is
  convenient to the researcher. You might decide to interview fellow students for your dissertation because it is convenient for you to do so; similarly, you might interview staff in an organisation where you have worked
  and have ready access. That is not to say that your research findings will
  not prove valuable, although they must be treated with caution (if your
  sample has not been selected randomly, then it is difficult to claim that it
  is representative). Convenience sampling tends to be used as a form of
  exploratory research, giving ideas and insight that may lead to other, more
  detailed and representative research. If you are interested in exploratory
  research, and not claiming that your findings will be representative of a
  larger population, then convenience research is perfectly acceptable for a
  student dissertation.

'DEWEY DEFEATS TRUMAN' announced the *Chicago Daily Tribune* in 1948.
Quota sampling was used by Gallup to predict the outcome of the Presiden-
tial election in the 1948 US elections. Using quota sampling – which we know
is unlikely to produce results that are representative – Gallup predicted that
Truman would lose the election to Dewey. The next day the big newspapers
led with the headline story that Dewey had won the election. In fact, as
history shows, the opposite happened and it was Truman who had won the
election! Gallup quickly dropped the use of quota sampling to predict election
results and ever since that embarrassing episode Gallup has used clustered
sampling of interviews nationwide. After his victory, Truman was asked to
comment on the earlier headlines – 'DEWEY DEFEATS TRUMAN' – to which
he replied, 'This is for the books.' He was right, because it has appeared in
this book!

Another example of a disputed survey occurred when *The Herald* newspaper (2007) led with the headline 'Labour leads in new poll but 50% still to decide'.
The headline refers to the Labour Party in Scotland apparently in poll position
to win the up-and-coming elections for control of the Scottish Parliament at the
expense of the Scottish National Party (SNP). This survey contradicted all previous surveys of voter intentions, which hitherto had shown the SNP with a
sizeable lead. *The Herald* (2007, p. 2) provided details of the sampling methods
adopted:

*It surveyed a random sample of 1000 adults across Scotland by tele-
phone between March 22 and March 27. The survey was quota controlled
by geography, age, gender, and socio-economic grade, and results then
re-weighted to ensure balanced representation was obtained. The mar-
gin for error is plus or minus 3%.*

Yet the survey could be criticised on a number of fronts. First, 50 per cent of respondents identified themselves as undecided on how they would vote in the forthcoming election: that fact alone would seriously damage the credibility of the survey (or rather any claim to 'balanced representation' based on the survey). MacLeod (2007, p. 6), reporting for *The Times* newspaper, comments that 'the poll's validity was damaged by the fact that as many as 50 per cent of the respondents were "undecided" and that it was conducted by an organisation with no discernible track record on political polling'. Also, quota sampling appears to have been used to collect voter intentions (*'The Survey was quality controlled . . .'*). In quota sampling, the selection process is dependent on human judgement and so subject to bias. The attractiveness of quota sampling to organisations lies in the relatively inexpensive costs and ease of implementation, but such practical advantages may not be enough to compensate for the core methodological weakness inherent in quota sampling: lack of confidence in the results.

Sample size is an issue in quantitative research, particularly when you want to claim that your findings are representative of a larger population. Generally speaking, the larger your sample size, the more representative your results. Students who interview two people, asking each only three questions, are unlikely to convince their supervisor that the results are representative of a larger population. There are statistical software tools to help you determine your sample size with different *degrees of confidence*. The Internet site Survey System (http://www.surveysystem.com) has produced a calculator to help you determine your sample size with different *degrees of confidence*. To use the calculator, you need to understand the terms *confidence level* and *confidence interval*. To quote the site (http://www.surveysystem.com/sscalc.htm, 2017):

> The confidence interval (also called the margin of error) is the plus-or-minus figure usually reported in newspaper or television opinion poll results. For example, if you use a confidence interval of 4 and 47% of your sample picks an answer you can be 'sure' that if you had asked the question of the entire population [then] between 43% (47 – 4) and 51% (47 + 4) would have picked that answer.

> The confidence level tells you how sure you can be [about your results]. It is expressed as a percentage and represents how often the true percentage of the population who would pick an answer lies within the confidence interval. The 95% confidence level means that you can be 95% certain; the 99% confidence level means you can be 99% certain. Most researchers use the 95% confidence level.

If you are not comfortable using statistical techniques, then stick to qualitative research, where you typically use case studies, open questionnaires, and/or semi-structured interviews. You will still need to justify your sample selection, though.

## Positivism and phenomenology

Researchers can sometimes get carried away with terminology and instead of using the terms *quantitative* and *qualitative* to describe the nature of their research, they substitute the term *positivism* for quantitative research and the terms *interpretivism/phenomenology* for qualitative research. Supervisors teaching research methods to students sometimes reiterate this fusion of terminology. Unfortunately, there are occasions when students, without grasping the meaning of these new terms, mimic their supervisors with disastrous consequences. They see their supervisors using such terminology, and so they themselves feel obliged to incorporate the same terminology into their dissertations. If you do not understand what these terms mean, then why use them? You are only highlighting your ignorance, and will lose marks as a result. It is depressing for a supervisor to witness students using terms in a dissertation which they clearly do not understand, yet insist on using because they feel that is what their supervisors want to see. No! If you are not sure about research terminology, ask your supervisor. That is what supervisors get paid for – to help you. It is better to show your ignorance during the process of writing your dissertation than at the end, after you have submitted: in the former you only lose virtual marks, whereas in the latter you lose real marks.

Nevertheless, some explanation will be provided here of the terms *positivism* and *interpretivism/phenomenology,* just in case you feel the need to use them in your dissertation. A researcher with a *positivist* view of the world is someone who holds that reality is objective and independent of the observer and so can be measured and predicted (Orlikowski and Baroudi, 1991; Remenyi *et al.*, 1998). Measuring the temperature at which different types of metals melt could fall into the category of positivist research (since the melting metal is not influenced by human observation). What the positivist researcher is really saying is that their type of research – positivist research – is not influenced by the unpredictable behaviour of human beings and that, as a result, their findings are more reliable (e.g. such-and-such a metal melts at such-and-such a temperature, full stop). Positivist research is common in the world of science (mathematics, physics, chemistry, etc.) and less prevalent in the arts-based research world (e.g. sociology, history, history of art, etc.), where the latter normally involves, and is influenced by, human participation and observation. The emphasis on quantifiable data is the reason that positivist research is equated with quantitative research, but the two concepts, although similar, are not exactly the same (e.g. providing students with questionnaires to complete, with a view to obtaining quantifiable data, is an example of quantitative research, but is not an example of *positivist* research, because the questionnaire responses are dependent on human participation, and therefore human influence).

*Interpretative* researchers, on the other hand, have a very different view of the world. Interpretative researchers believe that there are many, equally valid, interpretations of reality, and that, furthermore, these interpretations are dependent on when they are made and the context in which they are made (i.e. they are *time* and *context* dependent). A student who accepts the 'ontological assumption associated with interpretative/constructivism that multiple realities exist that are time and context dependent . . . will choose to carry out [their] study using qualitative methods so that they can gain an understanding of the constructs held by people in that context' (Mertens, 1998, p. 161). If your research concentrated on, say, interviewing your fellow students on their views of dissertation supervisors, then you would be engaging in interpretative research: students would present a variety of views, some praising supervisors, others offering criticism, with a range of views expressed on why they like/dislike their supervisor. The fickleness of interpretative research is such that students who previously applauded a supervisor might change their mind if they failed their dissertation and vice versa for students who disliked their supervisor but altered their opinion after securing a high mark! One colleague carried out research where he interviewed students as they progressed from first year to third year, capturing their views on how they were coping with group-based coursework. He was adopting an interpretative philosophy to his research work in that he was interested in his students' interpretations of their groupwork experiences, which he also recognised might alter as they advanced through their studies (i.e. time and context dependent). For interpretative researchers, human participation and observation, and the context and time these occur, are fundamental to the research. The emphasis on human interpretations of events leads interpretative research to be identified, correctly, with qualitative research.

*Phenomenological* research is just a fancy word for interpretative research (i.e. the focus is on individual perceptions of events). Phenomenology has strong philosophical foundations, where the phenomenological philosopher, just like his or her later phenomenological research cousin, is interested in how the world appears to others (i.e. subjective experiences). Some researchers divide phenomenological research into two categories: phenomenological research that deals with *describing* events and phenomenological research that attempts to *explain* as well as *describe* events. Mostly it is the latter interpretation – description and explanation – that is accepted as phenomenological research: what is the value of just describing what has happened when you could go further and try and explain why something happened? Your interpretation of your qualitative data might be wrong but at least it will have value in trying to engender further debate or lead to further lines of enquiry.

One could argue that the positivist researcher's view of their research – that it is untainted by human influence and so more reliable – is erroneous and just wishful thinking. In the first place, positivist researchers are often wrong. Scientists once thought that the world was flat. That the Sun rotated around the Earth. Aeroplanes continue to crash. Missiles go astray. Economic forecasting, based on quantitative modelling, is often wrong; and so on. There is also the argument that even in the world of positivist research, human influence cannot be avoided. Once measurements have been taken, and results produced, the results themselves require human interpretation. Scientists often disagree about how to interpret the same research data (e.g. global warming), and they have been known to interpret research data that best suits their own career interests, or the interests of their political or financial masters. For instance, Dinwoodie (2007, p. 6) reports that the Director of the Information Services Division (ISD), a body that produces statistical data on health issues in Scotland, laments that:

> *The independent, neutral and honest interpretation of statistics is often lost in the middle between opposing interpretation poles ... On the one hand the media and political opposition concentrate on negative themes and interpretation. The Scottish Executive [the ruling political body] and ministers naturally press for any positives to be highlighted ... We find it difficult to steer a neutral course when publishing statistics, especially so because most of the statistical collections ... have the Executive [the ruling political body] as the main sponsor.*

That is not to say that interpretative research is any more reliable, or somehow 'better', than positivist research. Both types are useful, and have their place; and both types are fallible, because humans are fallible.

### Justifying your research strategy

After identifying the research strategy that best meets your own research objectives, you now have to do two things: first, describe that research strategy, to convince your supervisor that you understand your chosen research strategy and, second, justify why that approach best meets your research needs.

---

**!  A common mistake by students**

A common mistake by students is to select a research strategy (survey, case study, historical research, etc.) and then to try and see how it fits in with their research objectives. That is a back-to-front way of doing things. What you ought to do is to consider your main research questions/objectives and then reflect on which research strategy best meets your needs. In short, a *survey* is used when you are seeking representative views; an *experimental* strategy is required when you are interested in causal relationships; *historical* research for events that occurred in the past; a *case study* when you seek an in-depth, investigative study; and so on.

---

Of course, there are practical considerations that might influence your choice of research strategy, given the reality that students tend not to have much time in which to implement their empirical research. So, although you might decide that a survey of fifty employers, using interviews, might provide the basis for an excellent empirical study, you need to be practical: Do you have the time for such a survey (using interviews)? Will you get access to all of your research subjects? Do you have the time to analyse all the data? In brief, are you being unrealistic and over-ambitious? Practical considerations can form part of the justification for your chosen research strategy and data collection techniques.

Let us look at the e-Learning sample research objectives identified earlier in this book as an example of how to select and justify a particular research strategy:

---

1 *Identify* the forces driving e-Learning and the barriers to the successful delivery of e-Learning programmes.
2 *Evaluate critically* models and frameworks relevant to supporting academic staff in coping with e-Learning.
3 *Explore* staff stakeholder views and practices related to e-Learning preparation, including drivers and barriers to e-Learning.
4 *Formulate* recommendations on staff preparation issues.

---

Objectives 1 and 2 above could initially be covered in a Literature Review. Objective 3 ('Explore staff stakeholder views and practices . . .') is a practical objective, requiring the implementation of empirical research. Which research strategy should we adopt to meet this objective and how can we justify our selection? Central to this objective is the keyword 'explore', which implies an in-depth, exploratory study of staff stakeholder views and practices. Suppose that you have decided that a case study best allows you to implement objective 3. Within a sub-section of your research methods chapter entitled 'Research Strategy', make it clear: (a) which research strategy you have decided to adopt; (b) your understanding of what that strategy is; and (c) your justification for choosing that strategy. Saunders *et al.* (2000, p. 92) stress the importance of justifying the relevance of your chosen research strategy to your work: 'what matters is not the label that is attached to a particular strategy, but whether it is appropriate for your particular research'. Below is a sample answer tackling these very points for the above empirical research (taken from 'Appendix J: Sample research methods chapter', sub-section 'Research Strategy'). In the example below, where you see [a], [b] and [c], [a] refers to text that identifies the research strategy adopted, [b] refers to text that describes that strategy, and [c] refers to text that justifies why that strategy was chosen:

[a] The research strategy that will be used to implement the empirical research is a case study. What is a case study approach and why is it suitable for this research? [b] Cohen and Manion (1995, p.106) describe a case study thus:

> *'the case study researcher typically observes the characteristics of an individual unit – a child, a class, a school or a community. The purpose of such observation is to probe deeply and to analyse intensively the multifarious phenomena that constitute the life cycle of the unit.'*

According to this definition, a case study is therefore concerned with close observation of how a particular population group behaves in a particular context. **[c]** A case study approach facilitates this researcher's drive to probe deeply into a university's response to e-Learning, by devoting time and energy concentrating on specific aspects of e-Learning in one higher education institution. **[b]** However, there is some disagreement about what constitutes a case study. Yin (2003, p. 13), for example, defines a case study in a different way:

'*A case study is an empirical inquiry that*

- *Investigates a contemporary phenomenon within its real-life context, especially when*
- *The boundaries between phenomenon and context are not clearly evident.*'

Continuing . . .

Yin, with the above definition, is trying to distinguish a case study from other research strategies. An *experiment*, he argues, intentionally separates phenomenon from context; *historical* research, although integrating phenomenon and context, normally deals with non-contemporary events; *surveys* can investigate phenomena and context together, but lack the in-depth investigation of a case study approach. That a case study is an in-depth study of a phenomenon is not evident from Yin's definition (Cohen and Manion's definition makes the depth of study clear – *probe deeply and analyse intensely*), although his book *Case Study Research* makes it obvious that he knows that case study research is a detailed and time-consuming undertaking. **[c]** This research is concerned with an in-depth study of the phenomenon e-Learning in a contemporary context – a university environment – where the boundaries between e-Learning and a university environment are not obvious. For example, the review of literature showed clearly that there is confusion over what is meant by the term e-Learning; further, it is difficult to compartmentalise e-Learning in a teaching and learning institution; also, the boundaries, if there are any, between e-Learning and learning, a university's primary focus, whether it be through teaching or research, are not *clearly evident*.

Adding . . .

**[b]** and **[c]** Although this research meets Yin's second condition – *the boundaries between phenomenon and context are not clearly evident* – it seems likely that Yin's second condition has more to do with emphasising the interpretative/constructivist view of the world than insisting that complexity of environment is a necessary condition that needs to be satisfied to justify the use of a case study as a research strategy (in any case, the university environment is a complex environment and one that encompasses different stakeholder perspectives and interest groups). Thus, either definition of a case study, whether it be Cohen and Manion's simple, but helpful, description of a case study, or Yin's conditional definition, meets this researcher's aim of delving deeply into a contemporary phenomenon, e-Learning, within the context of a university environment.

Finishing with . . .

[c] The case study approach provides focus, emphasises depth of study, is based on the assumption that reality can only be understood through social constructions and interactions, and that the context in which the phenomena under study is situated is complex. These facets of case study strategy fit perfectly with the aim of objective 3 of this research: to implement an in-depth exploratory study of staff stakeholder views and practices related to e-Learning preparation, including drivers and barriers, focusing on a specific unit of analysis (a team of academic staff preparing for e-Learning for a particular programme), but obtaining other stakeholder views in recognition that a university is a complex environment and academic staff views need to be placed in context.

Note that the example in Appendix J also goes on to addresses perceived criticisms of the chosen research strategy: 'A case study strategy is not without its critics . . .'. It is good to face criticisms of your adopted research strategy head-on – remember, no research strategy is perfect.

Essentially, what you have to remember is that you need to **define your chosen strategy and justify why it meets your research needs**. As long as you do that, then your marker will see that you understand the strategy that you have picked and, importantly, why you have picked it (once again, it is the *what* and *why* questions that you focus on in your chapter on research methods). Try and refer to literature when laying bare your reasoning: this demonstrates that you are well read and allows you another opportunity to exhibit your skills in critical evaluation. Of course, the length of your answer will depend on the type of dissertation that you are doing and the number of words that you have to play with.

### The question of reliability (and validity)

Is your empirical research reliable? Is it valid? And what is the difference between the two? If your postgraduate dissertation is subject to a viva – an oral examination – then the question of validity and reliability is likely to be raised by your examiners. Which means that you will need to be prepared to defend against the charge that your research is invalid and unreliable. Even if you are not subject to an oral examination, your marker may expect you to address the issues of validity and reliability in your research dissertation. Play safe – include a paragraph or two on why your research is valid research and why it can be relied upon.

What counts as *valid* empirical research? Valid research is research that is acceptable to the research community. How, then, do we know what is acceptable to the research community? What is acceptable to the research community – academics and practitioners engaged in research – is research that: is based on tried and tested research strategies and data collection techniques (discussed later); uses data analysis techniques that are deemed *appropriate to your research* (discussed later); all of which are implemented properly. So, if you use a survey as your research strategy, and it is appropriate to your research (i.e. you have successfully argued the case), then you are heading towards the goal of achieving valid research. Similarly, if you collect your data using data collection techniques that are relevant to what you want to achieve (e.g. questionnaires – see Sample Questionnaire in Appendix K), then you are building up the case that your research is valid. And if you analyse the data that you have collected in a way that is relevant to your research, then you are helping to achieve research that is valid. In other words, *valid research* is all about implementing your empirical work – from selection of an overall research strategy to the collection and analysis of your data – in a way that uses research approaches and techniques suited to each of these activities.

Here are a few hypothetical examples of research that would be open to the accusation of being invalid. You seek to ascertain from the general public their views on the 2003 invasion of Iraq by Western forces, which you wish to claim are representative of the general population. You adopt a case study of those staff working in an Army Recruitment Office. This research would be invalid because the target population – Army Recruitment officers – could not be said to represent the general population; and besides, a survey would be more appropriate. You are keen to implement an in-depth discussion with old people about how they are being cared for in their old age and you decide to base your results on a survey questionnaire. This research would be invalid because a questionnaire, however detailed, would be inappropriate to your aim of achieving an 'in-depth discussion': interviews would be more appropriate, or a combination of questionnaires and interviews. *Valid* research is about the appropriateness of the choices you make in terms of your research strategy and data collection/ analysis techniques.

What counts as *reliable* empirical research? Central to reliable research is the concept of *trust*: can your results be trusted? Your work could be valid but unreliable, that is to say you could adopt a research strategy that is appropriate to your research (e.g. a case study), use data collection techniques which you consider to be relevant (e.g. interviews, sample documents), and apply a suitable means of analysing your collected data, yet your work may be untrustworthy. How could that be? If you interview your research subjects but keep no record of your interviews, then your research may be viewed as unreliable. Or if you are vague about who you interviewed and when the interviews took place, then your research may not pass the reliability test. The best way to achieve research that can be relied upon is to make available to your examiner, either in the body of your dissertation or in your Appendices, details of where you did your empirical research (i.e. research site), who you researched (i.e. sample selection information), together with evidence of what you did with the sample population (e.g. experiments, interview questions, etc.) and what you found (e.g. experiment results, transcript of interviews, etc.). Yin (2003, p. 38) states that the way to deal with reliability is to 'make as many steps as operational as possible and to conduct the research as if someone were looking over your shoulder'. That is sound advice.

The issue of bias may also impact on the reliability of your research. For instance, if you are claiming that your results are representative of a larger population but your sampling was non-random, then your results (as in the earlier 'DEWEY DEFEATS TRUMAN' example) are not reliable. Similarly, interviewing as a means of data collection is a tricky business because sometimes the respondent is trying to please the interviewer and so gives answers that will elicit approval from the interviewer (or show the respondent in a good light). Gavron (1996, p. 159) recognised the problem of eradicating bias altogether, particularly in relation to interviews: 'It is difficult to see how this [bias] can be avoided completely, but awareness of the problem plus constant self-control can help.' Even the simple act of observation is not bias-free: in trying to make sense of what we are looking at, we are influenced by our own prejudices, experiences, and personal baggage. Phillips and Pugh (2007, p. 50) agree: 'There is no such thing as unbiased observation.'

So, *valid* research relates to how you gather and analyse your empirical data – that is, the strategies and techniques that you use (e.g. surveys, interviews, etc.) – whereas *reliable* research focuses on the need for a record of evidence that you did the research (in a fair and objective way). If a supervisor, or external examiner, asks you about the validity of your research, then you need to answer in terms of the appropriateness of your research strategy, the relevance of your data collection techniques, and the (fitting) way that you analysed your data. If you are questioned on the reliability of your research, then you should answer with reference to your record of evidence (e.g. detailed information provided on your site and sample selection, sample questionnaires, interview transcripts, etc.) and the steps that you took to achieve fairness and objectivity (e.g. random selection of subjects). You can also argue that your research is reliable because you used valid strategies and techniques appropriate to your research objectives AND you have a detailed record of your research plan (e.g. people interviewed, questions asked, etc.) and its implementation (e.g. completed questionnaires, transcripts, etc.) AND you took steps to minimise bias in your work (e.g. random selection of research subjects). In other words, although valid research is not proof that your research is reliable, it can be used to strengthen the case for trusted research when combined with the other tests for reliability.

A further argument for reliability relates to the experience of the researcher. Companies that have a long record of trusted research publications, such as Ernst & Young or PricewaterhouseCoopers, have a good chance of their research output being accepted as reliable work because of their experience in the field. Similarly, many supervisors will have a record of publishing that, in turn, will add weight to the reliability of future research intentions. Although it is unlikely that you, a student, will have similar research output as your supervisor or large companies, you can argue that any classes that you attended on research methodologies, together with close supervision, will have aided you in producing research work that can be deemed reliable. If you have indeed produced a research paper that, for example, was presented at a conference, then you can certainly argue that your work, in summary form, was accepted by your peers and, hopefully, received enthusiastically!

# Data collection

### Preparation, preparation, preparation

Once the research strategy has been selected (case study, action research, etc.) and justified, you now need to identify (and justify) *where* and *how* you will collect research data using your chosen research strategy. Data collection methods include a variety of techniques: sampling (discussed earlier), secondary data (e.g. company reports), observation, interviews, and questionnaires. Researchers may use more than one technique to collect data. Using more than one technique allows you to *triangulate* results. Triangulation occurs when you use different sources of data to get a range of perspectives (particularly useful in qualitative research) and so achieve a more rounded picture, or 'thick description', of what you are looking at (Geertz, 1973). If you were to ask a fellow student about their expectations on an exam just sat, you might get the reply, 'I did fine'; but if you then decided to check the results on the examination board, you might discover that the student barely passed; and, further, if you were able to see the student's examination script and read the examiner's comments, you might get a better insight into where marks were lost and gained. Triangulation can be time-consuming but it has its rewards.

Preparation is absolutely crucial to successful data collection: making arrangements to obtain your supervisor's views on your proposed research methods; putting together, and implementing, a pilot study if you have time; negotiating access to your data subjects; development of your actual questions (interview questions, questionnaires); and giving yourself enough time to collect the empirical data and write up your results. Unfortunately, when students are asked to collect and analyse their own data, they often leave themselves little time to do justice to these tasks, and it can show in the final output: rushed, confused, superficial, and vague.

If you intend interviewing your research subjects, then plan your questions beforehand. You can impose a rigid structure to your interview by sticking strictly to your pre-arranged questions. Or you can introduce a degree of flexibility to the interview process by using a semi-structured questionnaire. That is, you can go into the interview with a limited number of pre-arranged questions but with a willingness to let the interview ebb and flow, following related leads and new issues as they arise.

Qualitative interviewing, using a semi-structured approach, makes use of *open-ended* questions to encourage meaningful responses (Patton, 1990). Open questions are so-called because the respondent is not confined to a limited number of responses. Examples of open questions are:

- What do you think of the benefits, if any, of e-Learning?
- Why did you register for this course?
- What are your views on capital punishment?
- What problems have you encountered with train travel?
- Tell me about your marriage?
- How would you define *happiness*?

The flip side of using open questions is that they can prove difficult for respondents to answer. Respondents might be tempted to give you an 'answer' that either shows themselves in a good light or which they think will please you; or they might blurt out the first thing that comes into their head! How many times have you been asked an open question and given a quick response, one that you later regret as inadequate and not reflecting what you genuinely believe or wanted to convey?

*Closed* questions are an alternative to open questions. They are used when you want a specific type of answer to a limited range of responses, such as:

---

Please indicate your sex
Male ___ Female ___

Which of the following reflects your views on capital punishment?

1  Support capital punishment ___
2  Against capital punishment ___
3  Indifferent ____

---

You can combine open and closed questions in the same interview or within the same questionnaire, or even within the same question by including the option of 'Other (please specify)' as shown below:

---

What problems have you encountered with train travel?

A. Overcrowding ___
B. Delays ___
C. Expensive ___
D. Discomfort ___
E. Other (please specify):

---

If your research is primarily quantitative in nature and you are using question-naires to collect your data, then make sure that your questions are precise and suitable for later software analysis. SPSS is a standard data analysis package that students can use to aid their quantitative research. Although SPSS stands for Statistical Package for the Social Sciences, its use is not confined to research in the social sciences. Statistical packages such as SPSS depend on you creating data sets or files, which in turn are extracted from your completed question-naires; therefore, your questionnaires need to be thought through with the data analysis process in mind.

You could work backwards and imagine the type of data file that you will be entering into your chosen statistical software package, as shown in Table 7.3 (where M = male, F = female, 0 = degree, 1 = diploma, 2 = school qualification, 3 = other). From there, you can then work out the sort of questions you need to ask to enable you to create that data file:

Please enter your age: ____
Sex: Male ____ Female ____
Qualification(s):
Degree ____
Diploma ____
School ____
Other (please specify): _____

Do not start your empirical research unprepared, hoping somehow that things will come together. Give yourself enough time to write your chapter on research methods. Seek your supervisor's advice on how you intend to collect and analyse your data (e.g. does your supervisor think that your data collec-tion techniques are appropriate?). Work out your questionnaires/interview questions in full. Ask yourself if the responses to your questions, whatever they may be, will help you meet your specific research objectives (i.e. are your

**Table 7.3**   Example of coded data file

| Age | Sex | Qualification |
|-----|-----|---------------|
| 19  | M   | 0             |
| 23  | F   | 2             |
| 30  | M   | 2             |
| 18  | M   | 3             |
| 20  | F   | 1             |
| Etc. |    |               |

questions relevant?). Plan your physical collection process (e.g. interviews with data subjects) and give yourself plenty of time to analyse your results.

## What and why?

> **!** **A common mistake by students**
>
> A common mistake committed by students when writing about the data collection techniques they intend using for their empirical research, is to be vague about what they did, and why, opting instead to concentrate their efforts on providing the reader with a dull list of data collection techniques that are available to researchers in general. This is very boring to the reader, and it is not going to get many, if any, marks.

In the Data Collection part of your chapter on research methods, you need to explain *what* you will be doing and *why*. The *what* part can often be conveniently divided into *where* and *how* questions, with justification of each as follows:

1 Identify *where* you will collect your data. For example, people coming out of a shopping centre, fans in a football stadium, employees from a number of companies, lab rats, or wherever. If sampling, then describe your approach to sampling (random, stratified, convenience, etc.), including sampling size (number of experiments/companies/people, etc.).
2 Identify *how* you will collect your data. This refers to your data collection technique(s) used to collect your data. You need to identify and describe the data collection technique(s) that you will use (interviews, observation, questionnaires, tests, etc.). You can include your sampling approach and sample size in this part of your answer rather than in part 1 above.
3 *Justify* each of 1 and 2.

As evidence of point 2 – how you will collect your data – you should place a copy of your questionnaire/interview questions (if that is how you intend to collect your data) in an appendix at the back of your dissertation.

Rather than title this sub-section Data Collection, some students prefer to divide the sub-section in two, with one part titled Data Collection: Site and Sample Selection (or another heading that best describes where you will get your data) and the other part titled Data Collection Technique(s), with each part tackling 1 and 2 respectively, with 3 addressed under each part. The 'Sample research methods chapter' in Appendix J follows this practice.

The key to your data collection sub-section, however you title it, is to provide enough detail so that the reader can, if they so choose, repeat your research. In that way, the information that you provide about your empirical work will be unambiguous and transparent, and so avoid potential examiner comments such as 'not sure how many companies this student sampled' or 'this student fails to make it clear why questionnaires have been adopted as the principal data collection technique' or 'this student has not included a copy of the questionnaire, so the actual questions asked remain a mystery!'

Let us take the e-Learning case study as an example of how to record information about your intended empirical work. In Appendix J, 'Sample research methods chapter', there are two fully worked-out sub-sections that are relevant: *Data Collection: Site and Sample Selection* and *Data Collection Techniques*. You can peruse the detail of these sub-sections at your leisure, but for now we will focus attention on specific points.

The empirical research for the e-Learning example is based on a case study of one university from which a number of staff are to be sampled to meet objective 3 of the research study ('Explore staff stakeholder views and practices related to e-Learning preparation, including drivers and barriers to e-Learning'). Hence the heading *Data Collection: Site and Sample Selection*. If your empirical work is different, then you should have a different heading. If you intend visiting a number of companies (i.e. more than one site), then change your heading accordingly, for example *Data Collection: Sites and Sample Selection*.

What forms the content of a sub-section entitled *Data Collection: Site and Sample Selection* and how do you go about recording this information? First, *you state where you are getting your data from*, i.e. what case study you have chosen and why, including *sample size* (number of research subjects) and sampling approach. If you are investigating the behaviour of crabs on a number of beaches, then say which beaches you will be using (i.e. your research sites), including how many crabs; and justify your choices (namely, why those beaches and why that number of crabs). If you intend sending out questionnaires to a number of companies about their e-security measures, then say which companies (or types of companies, if anonymity is a requirement laid down by your research subjects), the number of questionnaires, and why you have chosen those particular companies (you may have selected them at random). If you are going to interview students from a particular undergraduate programme, from a particular year-group, then state the basic details (university/course/year), the number of students, sampling technique, and why that particular site/course/year-group.

The sub-section *Data Collection: Site and Sample Selection* adopts the same *what* and *why* approach described above: the chosen case study – a university – is identified and justified; a department within the case study to be the particular focus of the study is identified and justified, including sample size; the type of sampling that will be used – in this case convenience sampling – is described and justified; other stakeholders within the case study who are part of this research are identified and their inclusion justified; and a summary chart is produced to clarify site and sample selection. All this transparency is adding to the reliability of the research study. Here's a breakdown of this detail in Appendix J:

Chosen case study:

> The case study site will be Inverclyde University (IU). This case study is not intended to be an exhaustive study of all the e-Learning initiatives operating in the university. Such a study would, in order to produce meaningful results, be enormously time-consuming and perhaps never-ending (e.g. as one moved the study from one School or Faculty to another School or Faculty, or indeed between departments, new blended e-Learning programmes may suddenly appear and others may just as quickly disappear).

Justification:

> The Commission of the European Communities (2002, p. 5) lamented that the 'most successful players [in e-Learning initiatives] to-date, however, remain the well-established and prestigious institutions'. The Literature Review supports that assertion, with many of the e-Learning initiatives coming from leading academic institutions such as Oxford, Cambridge and MIT. IU is one of the 'new' universities in the UK, known for its social inclusion policy. Researching their e-Learning strategies and implementation issues, particularly related to staff involvement and preparation, offers a chance to capture important data from a university that is neither an 'ancient' university nor a 'redbrick' university, but one that has been created in relatively recent times as a result of the removal of the binary divide in higher education.

Chosen department within case study (including sample size):

> One division within the Inverclyde Business School (IBS) will form the focus of this study. Specifically, eight academic staff involved in preparing module material for Blackboard usage on the China suite of postgraduate programmes in E-Business, Knowledge Management and Management of Information Systems. This will allow a focused, achievable approach to the study, giving academic staff the opportunity to express detailed views on e-Learning preparation.

Justification of chosen department:

> In a report entitled *The International Postgraduate: Challenges to British Higher Education*, the UK Council for Postgraduate Education (1999) raised the issue of the potential for using new technologies for teaching and learning with international postgraduate students but revealed that evidence of staff e-Learning experiences with international postgraduate students was from 'anecdotal' sources. Selecting X's postgraduate programme provides an excellent opportunity to obtain empirical data on

how X's staff prepare for e-Learning and how they prepare for the challenge of dealing with students (and staff) from a different culture.

The type of sampling to be used is identified and justified:

Convenience sampling was used to select both the university and the postgraduate programmes. It is convenient because the researcher is a student at, and works in, the university. This means that the subjects under study have not been chosen at random and that therefore there can be no claim to achieving representative views related to the broader university community. Instead, this research has as its focus the aim of achieving an in-depth and qualitative insight into e-Learning preparation issues. The review of relevant literature established that e-Learning is an area of increasing interest in the wider university community and so the results of this study will be of interest to those grappling with similar staff preparation issues. Convenience sampling is also used because of time issues and easy access to research subjects.

Other stakeholders forming part of the research are identified and justified:

In order to achieve a three-dimensional perspective of e-Learning at IU, other stakeholders need to form part of this research. To concentrate solely on staff from Division X would produce, at best, a two-dimensional perspective: experiences and views of academic staff. To gain a fuller perspective, the research needs to be widened to include staff outwith Division X. Those who have a part in training academic staff to cope with e-Learning ought to form part of the study. Similarly, *elite* staff – staff with influence,

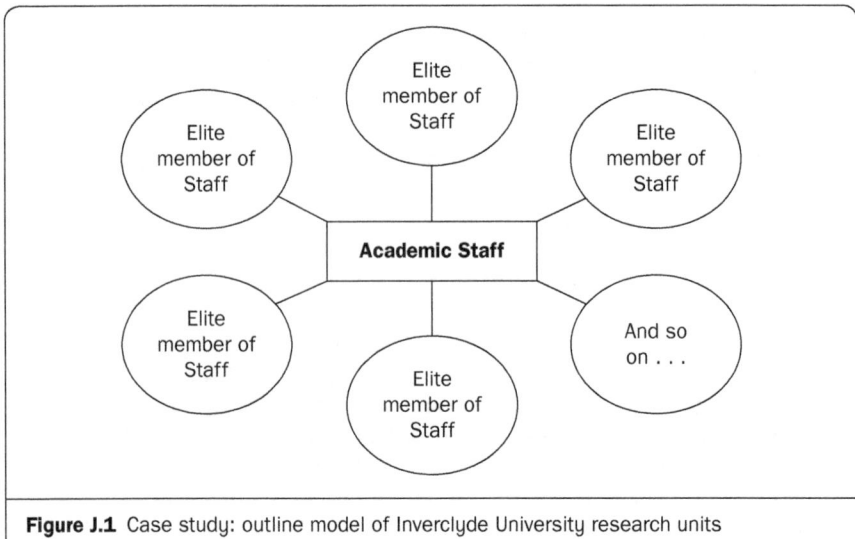

**Figure J.1** Case study: outline model of Inverclyde University research units

and who are well informed in the organisation (Marshall and Rossman, 1989) – need to be included. Figure J.1 illustrates an outline model of the research units under study, emphasising that, although the views of elite staff are important, central to this research are the views of academic staff.

To capture a School/Faculty view of e-Learning issues, the Dean of the Inverclyde Business School (IBS) will be included in the case study; similarly, the Principal and Vice-Chancellor is included to give a strategic perspective on e-Learning. The Pro Vice-Chancellor of Learning and Information Services will be part of this study, for his over-arching role in achieving strategic objectives related to the use of ICT. And because Division X is located in IBS, the C&IT Fellow located in IBS (someone with direct responsibility for encouraging and supporting e-Learning initiatives in the IBS) will also be included.

This thick view of e-Learning will be enhanced further by including members of those who have a role in best teaching practices within IU: the Head of the Academic Practice Unit (APU), and a member of the Teaching and Learning Team (LTAS). In effect, empirical data will be obtained from academic staff involved in the field of e-Learning preparation, from staff in the e-Learning Innovation Support Unit, as well as staff with a specific role in offering guidance and strategy on teaching practice; and, for a wider management perspective, data will be captured from the Head of X, the Dean of IBS and the Principal and Vice-Chancellor.

A summary chart clarifying the case study site and sampling selection is then produced:

Figure J.2 illustrates the stakeholder groups that will form the units of research for this IU Case Study on e-Learning.

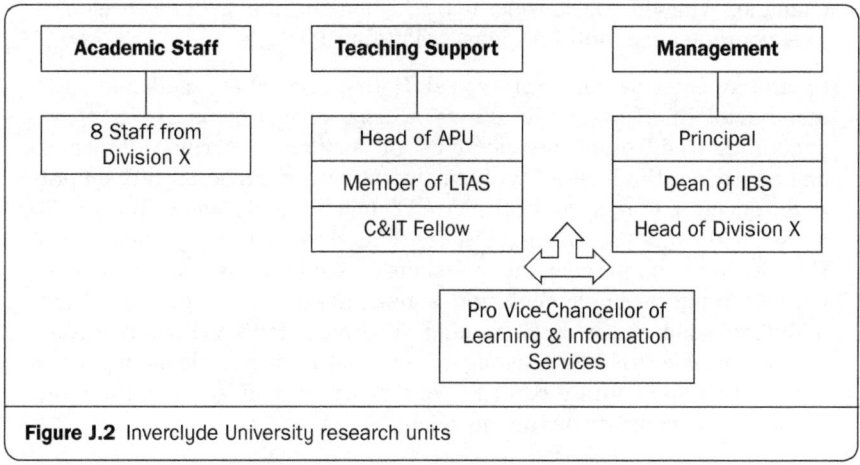

**Figure J.2** Inverclyde University research units

Now you will need to start explaining *how* you will collect data from your sources, i.e. identify and justify your data collection techniques (interviews, questionnaires, etc.). Do not get bogged down in the common mistake of just listing the general benefits of the techniques that you intend using: try and discuss the relevance/benefits of *your* chosen techniques to *your* research. In other words, articulate the type, or types, of data collection techniques that you will be adopting, indicating who will be subject to what data collection technique, and assert your rationale for using those techniques. For instance, if you want to email questionnaires to your research subjects, then state this and justify why you are using email questionnaires as opposed to, say, interviews. If you are interested in interviewing employees from a particular company, then say so, explaining how you will conduct your interviews (i.e. structured or semi-structured interviews?), who will be subject to these interviews, and how interviewing will help you collect the data that you need in order to complete your empirical research.

The following extracts from the e-Learning sample chapter on research methods in Appendix J, under the sub-section Data Collection Techniques, illustrate the previous points, *viz.*: [a] clarify your main data collection technique(s); [b] indicate who is subject to which technique and type of questions; and [c] justify your choices:

[a] Qualitative data will be obtained primarily through the vehicle of interviews. [c] This will open the opportunity to discuss, with the various stakeholders, e-Learning issues in depth. [a] However, in order to establish a framework around the interviews, and to focus on specific issues with different interviewees, the interviews will be structured with questions prepared beforehand, but the interviewer will be open to new issues and follow different, associated leads depending on the responses and willingness of the interviewee. [c] Qualitative interviewing, using structured questions, makes use of open-ended questions – such as, for example, 'What do you consider to be the benefits, if any, of e-Learning?' – to encourage meaningful responses (Patton, 1990).

[b and c] Interviewing different staff (e.g. Principal, academic staff, member of LTAS, etc.) will allow for cross-comparisons of responses, encouraging different perspectives of similar e-Learning issues to emerge (e.g. rationale for involvement, perceived barriers, staff support required, etc.). For example, the Vice-Chancellor and Dean of IBS will be questioned mainly on strategic issues related to e-Learning, whereas the Head of X, although receiving questions on strategic issues, will be questioned mainly on implementation issues linked to strategic objectives, including support for staff training. The interviews will be recorded, where possible, for two reasons: to ensure that the analysis of data is based upon an accurate record (e.g. transcript) and to allow the interviewer to concentrate on the interview.

Continuing with details of staff to be interviewed . . .

[b] The following staff will be interviewed:

1 Principal and Vice-Chancellor of Inverclyde University (IU)
2 Pro Vice-Chancellor of Learning and Information Services
3 Member of e-LISU
4 Head of Academic Practice Unit (APU)
5 The Dean of the Inverclyde Business School (IBS)
6 The Head of the Division X
7 Member of Learning and Teaching Strategy (LTAS) Team
8 C&IT Fellow
9 Academic Staff from Division X: module teaching team involved in development of teaching and learning material, using Blackboard, for the delivery of an MSc. E-Business to students in China.

Including the benefits of choosing the above stakeholders:

[c] By selecting a variety of e-Learning stakeholders, from those involved in strategic decision-making (1, 2, 4 and 5), those charged with providing training to academic staff (2 and 3), those involved in providing IT Support (2 and 5) and learning and teaching advice (3, 4, 7 and 8), and by selecting a Division that has recent experience of implementing an e-Learning strategy (6 and 9), it is expected that an enriched understanding of e-Learning will emerge, one that will better inform the e-Learning process and assist in the development of, for instance, the ingredients for improved guidance to support those faced with implementing e-Learning: academic staff.

If you are making use of secondary data (such as company records), then state explicitly what secondary data you will be using, and why:

Secondary data, in the form of university documents and academic staff teaching and learning material, will also be collected to form part of the analysis. The secondary data will come from a variety of documented sources:

• University Strategic Plan
• IBS Plan for 2002/03–2005/06
• Division X's Strategic Plan
• Learning, Teaching and Assessment Strategy (LTAS) 2000–2004
• APU E-Learning Strategy.

[c] The secondary data, coupled with the interview data, will assist in providing a rich picture of e-Learning in the university by facilitating a

comparison of the stated University/Business School/Divisional object-ives against staff perceptions, at various levels within the institution.

Finally, you should inform the reader in which appendix you will be placing your questions and raw data, for example:

Appendix A contains the collection of structured questions to be used for the academic staff; Appendix B contains the actual interview transcripts of interviews with academic staff; and Appendix C contains the questions and transcripts of interviews with elite staff.

A convenient and cost-effective way to collect qualitative data, often favoured by students, is to use *focus groups* (Marshall and Rossman, 2006). Instead of interviewing subjects on a one-to-one basis, in a formal, uninviting environment (e.g. an office), focus groups provide an opportunity to gather together a predetermined number of interview subjects, usually in a relaxed setting, to discuss their attitudes towards whatever topics you want discussed. The emphasis on capturing people's views means that focus group-based research is phenomenological in nature and linked to qualitative research. However, getting data from a focus group is not straightforward. You need to plan your discussion topics in advance, decide how to collect your data, pay attention to the flow of discussion (allowing others to contribute), recognise when to call a halt to particular discussions, as well as making every effort to minimise bias. On this last point, it is very easy to manipulate inadvertently what you want people to say by the questions that you ask and in your responses – both oral and facial – to comments given by members of the focus group. This can happen to such an extent that your input may contort what you think you are witnessing, or as Heisenberg (1958, p. 288) put it: 'What we observe is not nature itself, but nature exposed to our method of questioning.' Perhaps com-plete objectivity is a fallacy, something that can never be achieved, as posited by Zukav (1979, p. 328):

'Reality' is what we take to be true. What we take to be true is what we believe. What we believe is based upon our perceptions. What we perceive depends upon what we look for. What we look for depends upon what we think. What we think depends upon what we perceive. What we perceive determines what we believe. What we believe determines what we take to be true. What we take to be true is our reality.

Zukav's perspective on objectivity, although perhaps over-cynical, underlines the need for you not to covet deliberate bias and to make every effort to mini-mise accidental bias.

When you engage in focus groups, you are in effect participating in a form of action research. You are not a full participant because you are not answering the questions you pose. At the same time, it cannot be claimed that you are a neutral observer, because you are asking questions, directing the flow of dis-cussion, interrupting debate, inviting others to contribute, revealing unwitting approval/disapproval (a slight frown here, a quiet smile there, laughing at a joke, shaking your head at an argumentative participant, and so on). Indeed, your mere presence impacts on the group dynamics and the questions that you ask influence the nature and tone of group members' responses. It is probably more accurate to describe your role as a *participant observer*. That said, there is a dynamism to be found in focus groups that makes them suited to exploratory, in-depth qualitative studies (e.g. case studies).

Remember, you do have some flexibility on how you structure this part of your chapter on research methods. You are free to have one sub-section in your chapter to cover both your site/sample selection information and your data collection techniques (e.g. *Data Collection*) or you can subdivide this part as you see fit, i.e. there is no rule that you need to separate *where* and *how* you collect your data into different sub-sections (as done in Appendix J). As long as you give the information in a detailed and clear manner, that is what is important.

It is important to emphasise that the length of the sample in Appendix J is not indicative of how much you need to write: that all depends on the type of dissertation you are writing and the number of words at your disposal. That said, the research issues that need to be addressed and the principle of how to write your answers remain the same.

## Framework for data analysis

After you have disclosed how you propose to collect your research data, you should then go on to explain how you intend analysing what you have collected.

> **!  A common mistake by students**
>
> A common mistake by students is to collect the data with no prior plan of how to go about making sense of their raw data. The inevitable consequence is that they become quickly bogged down and confused about what to do next, and this sense of befuddlement becomes evident in their final submission.

After you get your empirical data, you need to *describe* what you have collected and then *analyse* the data (although you can describe and analyse simultaneously), producing what is called your 'empirical research findings'. Your overall research findings, in effect, are the combination of your Literature Review work and your empirical findings. Collectively, this is sometimes referred to as *synthesising* your research work, i.e. the bringing together of your main research output from your Literature Review and your empirical research. However, you first need to make clear how you will analyse your empirical data. This can be done by outlining a *framework for data analysis*.

Before you can produce such a framework, however, you need to know the difference between *data description* and *data analysis*. Suppose that you issued a questionnaire and it was completed by 100 respondents. You start to describe the results for question 1, which asked 'Do you like the [UK] Prime Minister (Y/N)?' You count how many people responded 'Y' and how many people responded 'N'. A description of what you found could be as follows: '82% of respondents stated that they do not like the Prime Minister'. (At a simpler level, describing your raw data can entail prerequisite tasks such as transcribing taped interviews or writing down notes about an organisation you recently visited.) Interpreting what this means is not so simple, and is unlikely to occur after looking at the results of just one question. Instead, analysis tends to be a cumulative process, dependent on the results from a number of question responses combined with cross-referencing of related Literature Review findings. For instance, if other parts of the same questionnaire highlighted that most people objected to the 2003 invasion of Iraq, then you might start to analyse the Prime Minister's unpopularity in terms of the war in Iraq, i.e. by combining questionnaire results you can begin to place meaningful interpretation on aspects of your collected data. Data description is a necessary step before data analysis, with the former simpler and relatively easy to do, involving a straightforward statement of what you found, while the latter takes you into the realm of interpretation, usually requiring cross-referencing of data descriptions, together with references to your Literature Review findings.

If you are attempting to analyse quantitative data, you could exploit the power of statistical data analysis software. For instance, you could use simple cross-tabulation together with elementary graphical models to convey basic statistical information (allowing you to describe your empirical data) as well as utilise more advanced features such as statistical correlation and regression, hypothesis testing, and time-series analysis (giving you evidence to support detailed analysis). Table 7.4 provides a list of some of the statistical tools and techniques that you can use. Descriptive statistics are used to help you present your quantitative data in a manageable form.

**Table 7.4** Examples of statistical techniques for quantitative research

| Descriptive statistics | Advanced statistics |
|---|---|
| **Summary statistics** (mean, median, mode, range, central tendency, standard deviation, variance) | Student's $t$-test |
| | Chi-square test |
| | Analysis of variance (ANOVA) |
| **Tabulation** (simple tabulation and cross-tabulation) | Regression analysis |
| | Correlation |
| **Graphics** (bar chart, pie chart, line chart, multi-series line chart) | Fisher's least significant difference test |
| | Time-series analysis |

In the context of a student dissertation, a framework for data analysis is usually straightforward. Once again, let us return to the e-Learning case study for illustration purposes (sub-section *Framework for Data Analysis*, in Appendix J) to see how easy it is to develop, and explain, a framework for data analysis (in this case related to qualitative research). The case study raw data come mainly from two sources: (1) interviews with academic staff who are preparing e-Learning material for a postgraduate programme, and (2) elite staff interviews, i.e. those staff who are in a position of power to influence the direction of e-Learning at Inverclyde University. How can we go about analysing these two sets of data? One way to analyse qualitative interview data is to first of all break down the interview data into easily identified *themed* subsets, and then compare and contrast staff responses to each themed group of questions. For example, if a number of questions in the interview relate to 'drivers for e-Learning', then the data for that particular theme can be described and analysed as a separate unit. Similarly, if another group of questions centre on 'barriers to e-Learning', then you can compare and contrast staff responses relative to the theme 'barriers to e-Learning', and so on. However, at some point you need to cross-reference how staff have responded to different questions in order to build up a fuller picture of what your data are telling you.

How you prepare to collect your data has an impact on how easy it will be to analyse it once collected – so, if you wish to analyse data via themes within your subject area, then incorporate these themes in your initial questionnaires/interviews, etc., using appropriate headings (e.g. Computer Security Breaches Suffered, Impact of Security Breaches, Counter-measures Adopted, Views on Government Advice, Recommendations to Other Companies, etc.). Appendix K contains a sample questionnaire that illustrates how to group your research questions into themes: there are six themes in this example and each theme is clearly headed. For instance, the first theme – e-Learning drivers – consists of questions linked to that theme:

---

### A. THEME: University Drivers for e-Learning

Question 1A
The university's Strategic Planning Document makes reference to e-Learning targets and objectives.
*Do you know what these are?*

Question 2A
The Inverclyde Business School's (IBS) plan for 2002/3 to 2005/6 also makes reference to e-Learning targets and objectives.
*Do you know what these are?*

Question 3A
*Why do you think university management wish academic staff to become involved in e-Learning?*

▶

▶ Question 4A
*What advantages do you think e-Learning will have for students?*

Question 5A
*What advantages do you think e-Learning will have for academic staff?*

The general structure of the sample questionnaire, with the themes evident from the section headings, is designed to make the task of data analysis easier:

**A. THEME: University Drivers for e-Learning**
(Questions)

**B. THEME: Barriers**
(Questions)

**C. THEME: Preparation**
(Questions)

**D. THEME: IT Infrastructure**
(Questions)

**E. THEME: Academic Staff Motivation**
(Questions)

**F. THEME: Reflections and Future Directions**
(Questions)

It makes sense when you are preparing your data collection techniques to reflect on your questionnaire/interview design in terms of the impact on your later data analysis. Grouping related questions together under an appropriate heading, as above, will make life easier for you when you eventually get around to undertaking your data analysis.

Returning to the e-Learning example, a useful start would be to explain to whoever is reading (and marking) your dissertation that the analysis of the interview data, obtained from the academic staff and the elite staff, will revolve around the idea of themes. As such, these themes have to be made apparent to the reader:

To help focus the interviews in terms of reflecting the main objectives of this research and ease the analysis of the qualitative data, the interviews will be structured according to themes. These themes reflect the overall aim and objectives in this research and also echo the main areas arising from the review of literature: *University Drivers for e-Learning, Barriers, Preparation, IT Infrastructure, Academic Staff Motivation,* and, to conclude, *Reflections and Future Directions.* It is important not to view these themes as separate topics: they are interrelated. All of the topics could have been placed under the heading 'Preparing for e-Learning'. For example, questions on academic staff motivation relate specifically to what motivates/demotivates staff to become involved in e-Learning; similarly, IT Infrastructure concerns the IT support suitable for an e-Learning environment. The themes are there to help the interviewer and interviewees focus, and as an aid to the analysis of the transcripts.

If you want, you could also indicate the spread, or type, of questions to your stakeholders:

Further, as an indication to the quest for depth as well as focus to this research, academic staff will be asked 4 questions on Drivers, 5 questions on Barriers, 2 questions on IT Infrastructure, 5 questions on Motivation, 3 questions on Reflections and Future Directions, and over 30 questions (including sub-questions) on Preparation. Table J.1 reveals the breakdown of questions (including sub-questions) under each theme, for academic staff and elite staff. An additional theme – e-Learning Strategy – is included for elite staff, to reflect their role in the strategic shaping and delivery of e-Learning.

**Table J.1**  Case study: breakdown of themes and questions=

| Theme | Academic staff questions | Elite staff questions |
| --- | --- | --- |
| X. e-Learning Strategy | — | 10 |
| A. Drivers | 5 | 4 |
| B. Barriers | 5 | 6 |
| C. Preparation | 33 | 12 |
| D. IT Infrastructure | 2 | 6 |
| E. Academic Staff Motivation | 6 | 3 |
| F. Reflections and Future Directions | 3 | 4 |

Using a diagram or table is an effective way to communicate summary information, adding a professional touch (e.g. Table J.1, from Appendix J).

Although the e-Learning example explains that interview questions will be analysed in terms of themes – drivers, barriers, etc. – there is still the big picture to consider. By that, one means your general approach to data analysis. For the e-Learning example, this involves collecting interview data, describing it (i.e. interview transcriptions, simple written statements of who said what), followed by interpretation of the descriptions (= analysis). Wolcott (1994) refers to this approach as a process of *description, analysis*, and *interpretation*, while Miles and Huberman (1984) and Creswell (1997) emphasise that such an approach is non-linear, involving repetition and reflection.

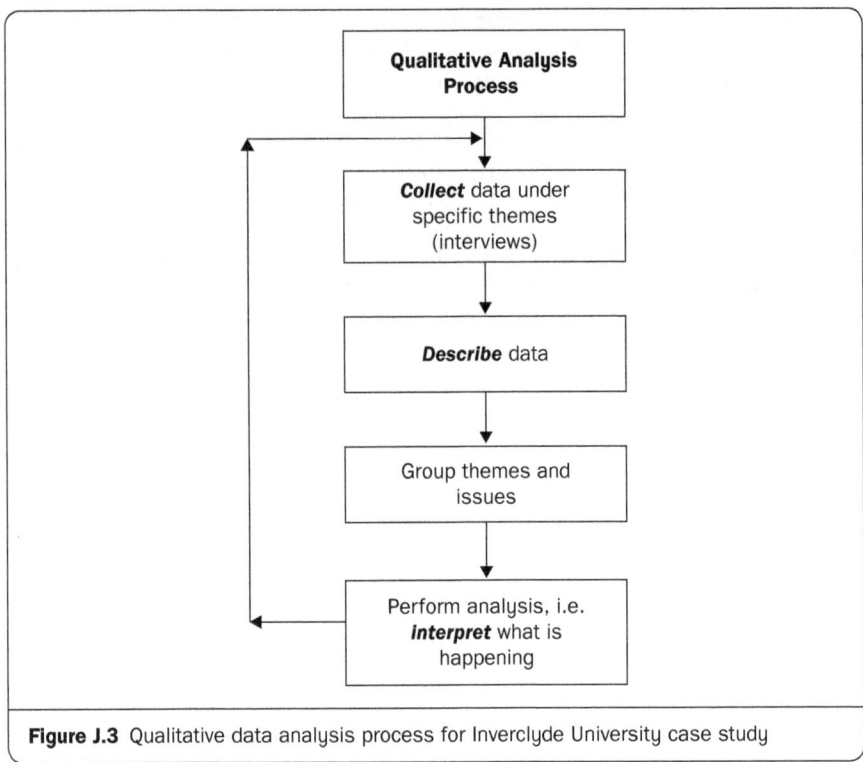

**Figure J.3** Qualitative data analysis process for Inverclyde University case study

Once again, where possible, produce a diagrammatic summary of your approach to data analysis with a little preamble to introduce it. From Appendix J:

> Figure J.3 illustrates graphically the approach that will be adopted to analyse data from the case study, based on the iterative process *of description, analysis* and *interpretation* (Wolcott, 1994) of the collected data, particularly with regard to extracting and understanding emerging themes. However, analysis of qualitative data is not a linear activity and requires an iterative approach to capturing and understanding themes and patterns (Miles and Huberman, 1984; Creswell, 1997).

You might also wish to raise any issues about how you collected your data (from transcribing, to data protection issues, use of notes, dependence on memory, etc.), as shown in the e-Learning example:

> The question of how to record the interviews is one that has been given much consideration in this case study. Taking notes as respondents talk is one simple alternative. However, the disadvantage of having to write as respondents are talking, and so failing to give respondents your full

attention and, in turn, perhaps omitting crucial comments and nuances, together with the problem of having to interpret summary comments some time after the event, in the end made this mode of recording unsuitable. Instead, all interviews will be recorded on tape and transcribed. Such an activity will prove time-consuming, but the resulting data will aid in the researcher's aim of gathering enriching, qualitative data. Overriding advantages include the freedom to concentrate on the interview process and, crucially, the capture of everything said by the respondents. As each interview will be structured under the themes mentioned earlier (Drivers, Barriers, etc.), the transcriptions for each interview will not form one mass of oral text, but rather be categorised under predetermined topics and sub-topics, in turn aiding the analysis phase. One last point on transcribing: all the interviews will be transcribed. As Strauss and Corbin (1990, p. 31) recommend: 'better more than less'. The researcher has decided to err on the side of caution and have all interviews transcribed.

Data analysis rarely consists of only description and analysis of themed groups of sub-questions in isolation (i.e. looking at Theme A, then Theme B, then Theme C, and so on). For the richer dimension it is often necessary to cross-reference respondent data, linking different sub-groups of data (or, in this case, 'themes'), adding cumulative meaning through an iterative process, and, particularly in the context of a student dissertation, comparing and contrasting your raw data description and analysis with your Literature Review findings. Therefore, if you have some raw data under a theme entitled e-Learning Barriers, then you could interpret your raw data findings not only in relation to what your respondents tell you within that specific theme, but also what they told you in other related themes that might give you a better understanding of their views, and against what the literature said about the barriers to e-Learning. In other words, you are comparing and contrasting your raw data at a number of levels. In your chapter on research methods, you can let your supervisor know how you will analyse your collected data:

An important part of this research is to analyse the case study data, comparing and contrasting different stakeholder perspectives (as above), and to reflect on the case study results with respect to the findings in the Literature Review. Figure J.3 is updated (Figure J.4) to show this overarching reflective process.

Even if you think your diagram is self-explanatory, take your reader through your diagram. This helps remove any misunderstanding and shows your supervisor that you have a clear understanding of your data analysis framework. A summary of Figure J.4 could be as follows (notice that the summary finishes with a quotation, taking the opportunity to add academic weight to your approach to data analysis):

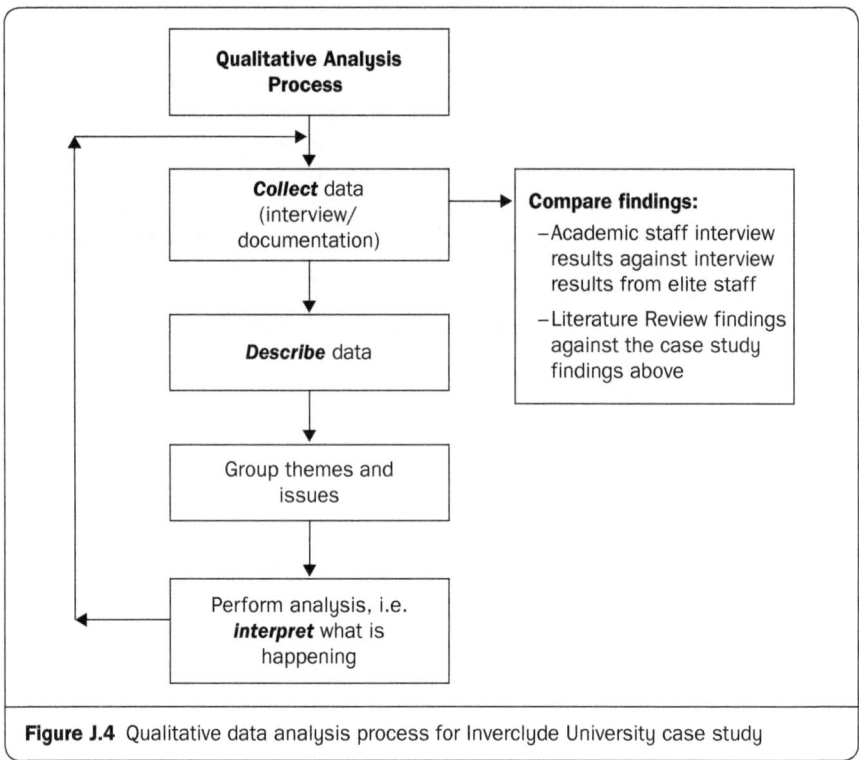

**Figure J.4** Qualitative data analysis process for Inverclyde University case study

In terms of analysis, there will be a two-pronged approach: first, the academic staff case study findings will be described and analysed; second, the elite staff case study findings will be described and analysed, not only comparing elite staff findings against each other, but also comparing elite staff findings against academic staff findings. However, it is in the second phase that, as well as comparing elite staff findings against academic staff findings, relevant Literature Review findings will also be compared and contrasted against the case study findings (this is to avoid repetition of comment with reference to the findings in the Literature Review). The essence of this qualitative analysis paradigm reflects accepted practice in dealing with qualitative data, and is perhaps more succinctly described by Bogdan and Biklen (1982, p. 145) as 'working with data, organising it, breaking it into manageable units, synthesising it, searching for patterns, discovering what is important and what is to be learned, and deciding what you will tell others'.

Too often, students populate their dissertations, from beginning to end, with unexplained diagrams. Worse, students can be seen embedding diagrams in their dissertation yet fail to refer to these diagrams in the body of their text, in which case the diagrams are not even acknowledged by the students themselves and so serve no purpose, and therefore gain no marks, and might even lose some!

There are many approaches to data analysis. This sub-section has merely described one approach, based on the concept of *themes*, using the e-Learning case study example to illustrate key points. The important factors that you should take on board are:

1  You ought to inform the reader how you intend analysing your data.
2  How you implement your data collection techniques can impact on your data analysis, so think carefully about how you design your interviews, questionnaires, experiments, etc.
3  Your data analysis framework will involve *data description* followed by *data interpretation*.
4  Cross-referencing of data results, coupled with references to related Literature Review findings, will help produce a more meaningful analysis of your empirical data.
5  Remember to illustrate your data analysis approach through the use of diagrams/figures/tables. And do not forget to explain your diagrams/figures/tables!

## Limitations and potential problems

It is unusual for researchers, at any level, not to recognise limitations in their own work. In a paper published in *Women in Management Review* by Ogden *et al.* (2006, p. 43), for example, the authors acknowledged the limitation of using a case study as their research strategy but justified it with an appeal to capturing a rich picture of individual human experiences:

> *Due to the combination of the depth and sensitivity of the research topic, a case study approach is adopted (Yin, 1994). Although the lack of probability sampling inherent in the case approach means the results cannot be generalised, the results provide a rich and detailed picture of the experiences and perceptions of individuals working within the industry. Analysis of this data provides a valuable insight into contemporary inhibitors and enablers of females' career development in financial services.*

Similarly, the student dissertation that is problem-free or not limited in some way does not exist, so do not try and fool your examiner and pretend otherwise. On the other hand, your examiner is not interested in every single problem that you have encountered while doing your dissertation, from perceived bad supervision to your initial inability to find relevant literature. If you include a section on 'Limitations and potential problems' (or whatever you want to call it) within your chapter on Research Methods, then it is limitations and problems related to your empirical research work that your examiner expects to read about, not problems in general. By facing possible criticisms of how you conducted your empirical research, you are displaying a certain level of research maturity. Of course, do not go overboard and undermine your good work!

As stated above, in such a section – *Limitations and Potential Problems* – you ought to focus on issues connected to your empirical research and not your dissertation as a whole. These issues tend to concentrate on your chosen research strategy, data collection techniques, including site and sample size and selection where appropriate, and analysis of collected data.

---

**Questions that you can reflect on:**

- What are the known criticisms of my chosen research strategy? (If you read the literature on your chosen research strategy, then you are bound to unearth criticisms – every research strategy has its critics as well as its supporters, some more vociferous than others!)
- Is my approach to collecting data limited in any way? (For example, why am I using questionnaires when interviews might give me more meaningful results? Perhaps you are unable to get access to your research subjects or they are so geographically dispersed that it is impractical to visit them.)
- Is my sample population big enough? (For example, a criticism may be that your experiment/questionnaires/interviews, etc., are limited in number, but the lack of time available to you, as a student, may form part of your justification.)
- Is my research open to the accusation that it is invalid? (That is, have I argued successfully that the way I approached my research is appropriate to achieving my research objectives/questions?)
- Am I vulnerable to the claim that my empirical work is unreliable? (That is, have I provided enough detail to show that I did the research and that my findings are trustworthy, e.g. provided site and sample selection information, questionnaire samples, made efforts to reduce bias, etc.?)
- Can I generalise as a result of my empirical work? (Does it matter if I can't?)
- What efforts have I made to ensure that my empirical research is, as far as possible, fair and free from bias? (For example, if you know the research subjects – for instance, they may be fellow students whom you wish to interview – what mechanisms have you set in place so that your views of them and, equally, their views of you, do not influence your findings?)

---

It is important to recognise potential problems and to show how you have addressed them. Avoid producing just a *list* of issues. Identify perceived limitations of your work/potential issues and *explain* what you have done to negate or minimise those risks. It is the top students who do well in this section because they are confident in putting up a stout defence of their work, even with identified shortcomings.

To help clarify the question of limitations/potential problems linked to your research methods, a defence of potential issues in the empirical sample e-Learning dissertation will now be developed. To begin with, below is recognition that a case study – the chosen research strategy for the practical research – is limited because generalisations cannot be made from case studies. However, a defence of the case study is also given, with the author appealing to *relatability* as his goal rather than *generalisability*:

> There are limitations to this research, as well as issues related to imple-menting a case study in an environment where one is both a student and employed. The results of this study cannot be generalised to the wider research community. Indeed, the results of this research cannot even be generalised to represent the university under study: although key elite staff will be interviewed, and strategic documentation will be referred to, the study of a different programme team in the institution, preparing for e-Learning, may lead to different results. The question of the validity of case study research, in the sense that generalisations cannot normally be made, has already been discussed and addressed. This researcher is using a tried and tested research strategy, appealing to the concept of *relatability* rather than *generalisability*, although it was also argued that generalisa-tion, although not immediate, can take place over a period of time – incre-mental generalisability – as more empirical research case studies are implemented. This researcher is sacrificing immediate generalisability for depth of study.

Next, the issue of the reliability of the research work is discussed:

> Nonetheless, there is also the question of the *reliability* of using such a strategy, particularly when interviews are used as the main means of data collection. In the first place, there is the matter of studying one instance of one phenomenon, the results of which are not open to imme-diate generalisation. Next, there is the question of depending on a data collection technique – interviews – that relies on personal opinion, and so is open to bias and inaccuracy. Even more problematic, how can the researcher maintain *objectivity* when he interviews colleagues in an environment wherein he works?

> In terms of the reliability of case study research, Yin (2003, p. 38) states that the way to deal with reliability in a case study is to 'make as many steps as operational as possible and to conduct the research as if some-one were looking over your shoulder'. This research work meets this test of reliability by providing details of the appropriateness of the case study strategy to this research, as well as the data collection techniques to be used, the site selected, the type of staff to be interviewed, their roles, the specific themes that will be addressed, the actual interview questions, and the method of data analysis. In addition, full transcripts are provided. Reliability is sought through a highly structured, transparent and detailed

approach to this study, using a research strategy and data collection techniques that have validity in the research community.

And then dealing with the question of bias:

> The issue of depending on interviews as the main source of data, when interviewees can exhibit bias or poor memory recall, was dealt with by ensuring that the researcher was not depending on his results from only one or two respondents, but on a number of sources. To begin with, a team of academics preparing for a new suite of programmes will be interviewed. A number of views are collected on the same issues, from staff working on the same programmes, ensuring that the researcher is not dependent on one or two respondents for key data. Second, staff from outwith this programme will be interviewed, further removing the dependence on opinion that may be factually wrong or skewed and to place academic staff views in a wider context, lessening the opportunity for bias or misinformation. Third, the interview questions are extensive and detailed, where some of the same issues are tackled in different themes (e.g. barriers to e-Learning), which presents an opportunity for staff to consider some topics in different contexts and acts as a check on the consistency of staff views. Fourth, documentation will be used as a means of understanding the university's e-Learning objectives and implementation issues, and also used to compare against interview answers. It must also be accepted that people are not robots and that to err is human, both in terms of expressing occasional bias and making honest errors of recollection; but that for the most part respondents will answer interview questions in a professional, competent manner. Nonetheless, by adopting the aforementioned procedures, it is expected that any bias or misinformation will be minimised.

If your research subjects are people known to you – work colleagues or student friends or staff you know, for example – then you need to be prepared to meet the claim that your work is vulnerable to bias. The findings from the sample e-Learning research case study are based, for the most part, on interviews of some people known to the researcher. This is openly recognised in the discussion below, but, in addition, the researcher outlines how he intends to achieve objectivity and, therefore, trust in his findings:

> Interviewing one's colleagues raises the issue of objectivity. Implementing a case study within one's place of employment has the comforting advantage of access to subjects. However, such a scenario brings with it problems that, if not managed properly, may hinder the research and endanger relationships between the researcher and the participants in the research project. There may be the concern expressed that 'how can a colleague, albeit one engaging in research, not be influenced by his prior knowledge of his fellow colleagues' views and bring such knowledge to

bear when interpreting transcripts of interviews?' To minimise such an influence, the researcher will adopt the following strategy: until he has secured all staff interviews and completed the transcripts, the researcher will refrain from attending any e-Learning seminars within Division X (to avoid directly or indirectly presenting his views of e-Learning or acquiring the views of his research subjects); after the transcription of interviews, staff names will be replaced by codes (Lecturer A, Lecturer B, Senior Member of Staff A, and so on); and a deliberate and significant time-gap created between the transcriptions and transcription analysis to further minimise the possibility of bias when interpreting staff views. Furthermore, as far as is practical, staff transcriptions will be edited to remove identifying comments. This may help allay any concerns that staff may have concerning their transcriptions, with the added benefit that they may speak more freely.

Still on the theme of reliability, the researcher now attempts to reduce fears that, while carrying out his interviews, his colleagues may have difficulty in perceiving him as a researcher rather than just a colleague:

> Another issue, connected to objectivity, is that it may prove more difficult for colleagues to view the researcher other than a colleague than it may be for the researcher to view current colleagues as research subjects. This is a danger that the researcher is aware of and will attempt to minimise by clarifying the researcher's role and by informing participants of the purpose of the research, the uses of the collected data and the manner in which participants could assist in the research. The fact that the researcher is recognised within Division X as a researcher with publications in the field may go some way to gaining the respect and trust of colleagues.

As you can see, what you have to do is confront openly any perceived limitation of your research methods (selected research strategy, site and sample selection, data collection issues, etc.) and associated problems, such as achieving objectivity in your findings. The aforementioned issues do not exhaust all the possible problems that you might encounter in your empirical work. For example, if you are new to implementing empirical research, like most students who embark on a major dissertation, then you might claim with some justification that your lack of experience in this area, and shortage of practical skills (e.g. in carrying out interviews, questionnaire design, data analysis, etc.) present a possible limitation in implementing your empirical research. If this is your first attempt at a dissertation, then it will be a learning experience, one where you will make mistakes (and hopefully learn from them). Nevertheless, you should not submit yourself as incompetent! Explain how your attendance at classes on research methods, sage advice from your supervisor, your own learned reading and, where appropriate, pilot testing have all contributed towards mitigating this apparent limitation.

Another potential barrier that might hinder the smooth implementation of your empirical work is the possibility that you may encounter difficulty in getting access to your research subjects when you want them – the answer may lie in the timing of your practical research and maintaining regular contact with those whom you want to 'research'. Too many students fail to appreciate how time flies. Naïvely, they leave their empirical research to the last minute and neglect to consider the possibility that their research subjects might be too busy to see them.

Student complaints about lack of time are quite common, particularly as submission deadlines approach, and are usually evidence of a lack of planning and foresight on the part of the student. Year after year, supervisors witness numerous dissertation students, at various levels, leaving their dissertation work to the stage where the best that the student can hope for is a basic pass. Plan your work from the start; as far as possible adhere to your anticipated milestones; do a bit of work on your dissertation every week; and keep in touch with your supervisor.

With respect to your intended empirical work, try and maintain contact with your research subjects, from the moment that they have agreed to participate in your research up until the moment you make use of them, or they might forget all about you! It is not uncommon for students to approach their supervisor with a hang-dog expression, complaining that the people who had agreed to be interviewed three months ago are no longer available or have changed their mind. Do not leave your empirical work to chance: be organised. And leave enough time to accommodate mishaps.

Lastly – this was mentioned before but it merits repeating – the tense you adopt is normally yours to decide. For example, you could write in the future tense '8 staff will be interviewed' or you could write in the past tense '8 staff were interviewed.' As always, check with your supervisor.

# Further reading

Blair, J., Czaja, R. and Blair, E. (2013) *Designing surveys: a guide to decisions and procedures*. London: Sage.

Buglear, J. (2013) *Practical statistics: a handbook for business projects*. London: Kogan Page.

Creswell, J. (2013) *Research design: qualitative, quantitative and mixed methods approaches*, 4th edn. London: Sage.

Davies, C. A. (2007) *Reflexive ethnography: a guide to researching selves and others*. 2nd edn. London: Routledge.

Denzin, N. K. and Lincoln, Y. S. (2011) *The Sage handbook of qualitative research*. 4th edn. London: Sage.

Dey, I. (1999) *Grounding grounded theory: guidelines for qualitative inquiry*. San Diego, CA: Academic Press.

Ekinci, Y. (2015) *Designing research questionnaires for business and management students*. London: Sage.

Emerson, R., Fretz, R. and Shaw, L. (2011) *Writing ethnographic fieldnotes.* 2nd edn. London: University of Chicago Press.

Gillham, B. (2008) *Developing a questionnaire.* 2nd edn. London: Continuum.

King, N. and Horrocks, C. (2010) *Interviews in qualitative research.* London: Sage.

Reason, P. and Bradbury-Huang, H. (2013) *The Sage handbook of action research: participative inquiry and practice.* London: Sage.

Saldana, J. (2015) *The coding manual for qualitative researchers.* 3rd edn. London: Sage.

Saunders, M., Lewis, P. and Thornhill, A. (2015) *Research methods for business students.* 7th edn. Harlow: Pearson Education.

Silverman, D. (2013) *Doing qualitative research: a practical handbook.* 4th edn. London: Sage.

Urquhart, C. (2012) *Grounded theory for qualitative research: a practical guide.* London: Sage.

Yin, R. K. (2014) *Case study research: design and methods.* 5th edn. London: Sage.

## Summary of key points

- Your research methods chapter is where you describe the methods that you will use to implement your research and, importantly, explain the reasons behind your choices. An appropriate structure would cover: research strategy, data collection techniques, approach to data analysis, and acknowledged limitations of your work.
- The research *strategy* refers to your over-arching approach to your empirical research, and there are a number of tried and tested strategies to choose from, examples of which include: case study, survey, ethnographic, experimental, historical, action research, and grounded theory. You must *identify* your research strategy, *describe* it, and *explain* why it is appropriate to your research.
- The question of whether your research is *quantitative* or *qualitative* in nature, or a mixture of the two, depends not on your choice of research strategy alone but on the combination of your research strategy + research objectives + data collection techniques.
- *Sampling* is the process of selecting a portion of a target population. Sampling techniques available to you include: random sampling, simple random sampling, stratified sampling, cluster sampling, systematic sampling, quota sampling, and convenience sampling.
- *Positivist research* is research that is objective and independent of the observer and which can be measured and predicted. *Interpretative/ phenomenological research*, on the other hand, accepts that there are many interpretations of phenomena and that these interpretations are time – and context – dependent.
- Your research work should be *valid* and *reliable*. Valid research is about the appropriateness of the choices you make in terms of your research strategy and data collection/analysis techniques pertaining to your research objectives. *Reliable* research refers to the trustworthiness of your research findings, which you achieve through transparency on how you implemented your research.
- In your sub-section on data collection techniques, you need to state from where you will get your data (a football stadium, employees from a number of companies, or wherever), your sample size (number of experiments/companies/people), your sampling technique (random, stratified, quota, convenience, etc.), and how you will extract your data (interviews, observation, questionnaires, tests, etc.). Justify your choices.
- A *framework for data analysis* is an outline of how you expect to analyse your collected data.
- Identify perceived limitations of your work and/or potential issues and explain what you have done to reduce those limitations and/or potential issues.

# Chapter  8

# Research methods 2: artist as researcher

> • Who is this chapter for? • Practice as research • Writing about your research methods • Further reading • Summary of key points

This chapter clarifies the intended audience, justifies the need for a bespoke research strategy, including associated data collection and analysis methods, to accommodate artists as researchers, and takes the student artist-researcher through the process of writing a chapter on research methods for their dissertation.

## Who is this chapter for?

This chapter is primarily intended for artists who need to critique something they have created and are required to write a chapter on their research methods. Dictionary.com (http://www.dictionary.com/browse/artist, 2017) defines an artist as follows:

1  A person who produces works in any of the arts that are primarily subject to aesthetic criteria.
2  A person who practices one of the **fine arts**, especially a painter or sculptor.
3  A person whose trade or profession requires a knowledge of design, drawing, painting, etc.: a commercial artist.
4  A person who works in one of the **performing arts**, as an actor, musician, or singer; a public performer; a mime artist; an artist of the dance.

It is this definition of artist that is used as a basis in this chapter, i.e. someone in the fine arts or performance arts. However, although fine arts are often associated with more obvious art forms, such as painting and sculpture, the definition is widened in this chapter to include all types of creative art forms: painting, sculpture, embroidery and weaving, video art, ceramics, poetry, music, and so on. Thus this chapter is intended for students in the **fine arts** (as widely defined above) and also those in the **performance arts** who are tasked with producing an 'artefact' (painting, sculpture, play, musical score, dance, etc.) and need to write about it within the framework of a Master's dissertation.

Although this chapter is mainly directed towards artists, students in computing departments who create computer software or computer apps or computer videos, and who are required to write about their creation, could also find a natural home here. Indeed, the traditional world of computer and technological development has crossed over so much into the world of art and drama that sometimes it can be difficult to disentangle the science from the art. The advice given in this chapter on how to write a chapter on research methods – where the thing created is central to the research output – applies equally to the dual creating/reviewing roles to be found in software development of one kind or another.

## Practice as research

For the best part of two centuries, the prevalent approach to research has been based on selecting a research strategy from a well-defined collection of research strategies (experimental, case study, survey, ethnography, etc.) and then to choose, once again from an established list, a method of data collection (tests, questionnaires, interviews, etc.) from which either quantitative or qualitative results, or a combination of the two, are produced. Other research strategies, such as grounded theory and action research, have been added to the strategy list, as have other data collection techniques, such as participant observation and specific types of reflection; but they have all been developed with the traditional academic researcher in mind.

Then along came art and drama tutors who wanted to do research. They also wanted to encourage their students to do research. And why not? They have things to say about their work, so let them say it. Unfortunately, the academic research community wasn't sure how to deal with those who create art and drama and want to write about what they have created; and art tutors and drama tutors were similarly tentative about how to do research where an object of creation (a painting, a scene from a play, a musical score, etc.) was the main research output.

At the heart of the problem is the realisation that the traditional research strategies are ill-suited to those who wish to create something and write about their creation in a critical way. For example, which traditional research strategy helps an art school student create a painting? A case study? Not really – the student may do various versions of one painting. Multiple case studies? Not really – the versions may be in different media for different purposes. A survey? A painting is not a survey. Experimental? No – although there may be experimental aspects to painting a picture, the student may be applying tried and tested art techniques that best suit his or her skills-set. Action research? Not quite – the student may not be trying to solve a problem. And so on.

The painting student would encounter the same problem when trying to select a data collection technique to facilitate critical commentary on what has been painted. A questionnaire might be useful but it is not the normal way to judge paintings. Interviews? Same issue. Textual analysis? A painting is not a piece of text. And so on.

The problem is that a painting student, at a push, *could* exploit one or two traditional research strategies, and *could* exploit one or two traditional data collection techniques too, but as a principal means of researching an art piece created by the student artist, it would be like asking a footballer to wear house slippers during a game of football – it could be done, and the footballer might even score a goal, but it would be an odd fit.

The difficulty that a painter has trying to develop and critique their work using traditional research methods would also apply to others involved in the creative arts, from sculptors to weavers. Performance artists too, such as dancers, actors, and musicians, would similarly struggle to apply research strategies and techniques to their work that are more geared towards either quantitative reductionism or textual analyses rather than performance art. Even software development students would toil to align their array of software development models and testing protocols with traditional research paradigms.

What all these students have in common is that they are creating something – a painting, a dance, a piece of music, a scene from a play, etc. – and the thing being created partly speaks for itself, i.e. it is, de facto, an integral part of the research: 'it is not an optional extra' (Haseman, 2006, p. 6). In addition, students have to write about the thing they have created in a way that satisfies academic rigour – and that comes with its own special problems. Such students need guidance but traditional research methods do not naturally meet their research needs.

Academics in the creative and performance arts recognise this problem and have made significant progress since the 1960s in producing an alternative meta research strategy to accommodate the needs of their students. To cut a long story short, it is now accepted practice for art and drama students to produce an 'artefact' as a main research output, supported by critical reflection. However – there is always a 'however' in any intellectual development – the name to give this research strategy is still debated among artists themselves. The examples below highlight the ongoing search for an appropriate nomenclature:

- Cindy (2006, p. 3) calls this meta strategy *practice-based research*, and gives a simple, easy-to-understand definition of what she means: 'if a creative artefact is the basis of the contribution to knowledge, the research is practice-based'. The term 'artefact' should be interpreted widely to refer to a physical object (e.g. a painting), a performance (e.g. a dance), a textual work (e.g. a play), sounds (e.g. a musical piece), a digital creation (e.g. a video), or software (e.g. a computer program), and so on.

- Nelson (2013, p. 9) prefers the label *Practice as Research* (PaR), and writes that PaR takes place where 'practice is a key method of inquiry and where, in respect of the arts, a practice (creative writing, dance, musical score/performance, theatre/performance, visual exhibition, film or other cultural practice) is submitted as substantial evidence of early enquiry'.
- Haseman (2006, p. 7) adopts the term *performative research*: 'This paper proposes that performative research represents a move which holds that practice is the principal research activity – rather than only the practice of performance – and sees the material outcomes of practice as all-important representations of research findings in their own right.'

All the above terms refer to the same thing: the artist as practitioner-researcher. Sometimes other terms are introduced and used instead; sometimes these other terms, confusingly, are used to mean something else! *Practice-led research* is a case in point. Here are two different definitions of practice-led research: the first one can be used interchangeably with the terms practice-based research, PaR, and performative research; the second one is very different:

**Definition 1**
Rust *et al.* (2007, p. 11): 'Research in which the professional and/or creative practices of art, design or architecture play an instrumental part in an inquiry.'

**Definition 2**
Creativity and Cognition Studios (https://www.creativityandcognition.com/research/practice-based-research/differences-between-practice-based-and-practice-led-research/, 2017): 'Although practice-based research has become widespread, it has yet to be characterised in a way that has become agreed across the various fields of research where it is in use. To complicate matters further, the terms 'practice-based' and 'practice-led' are often used interchangeably. In fact we can distinguish between different types of research that have a central practice element and that distinction is summarised here as follows: If a creative artefact is the basis of the contribution to knowledge, the research is practice-**based**. If the research leads primarily to new understandings about practice, it is practice-**led**.'

In the first example, the authors (of a Review Report) expand on their definition of practice-led research to support the view that by practice-led research they mean research where an artefact is produced and is supported by critical commentary: '. . . a design or artwork can provide new insights . . . the knowledge associated with the artefact . . .' (p. 12). In the second example, it is clear that practice-led research is viewed as something different from practice-based research. Practice-led research, in their view, is research influenced by practice but does not involve the production of an artefact. An art historian, nurse or accountant doing research about the practice of art, nursing or accountancy would fall into this category. To make matters even more confusing, those involved in health care research often refer to their research as practice-based research or evidence-based practice research!

Do not panic about the label you use for your research. This chapter is assuming that you are creating some sort of artefact and that you will be providing critical reflection on that artefact. Irrespective of the generic term that you use to describe your research strategy – practice-based research, PaR, performative research, or practice-led research – as long as you make it clear to the reader the nature of your research (artefact + commentary), then you will cover all bases.

The structure for your dissertation (the written part of your submission) is not a million miles away from a traditional university dissertation:

Chapter 1: Introduction
Chapter 2: Contextual Review (or Literature Review if that is what you did)
Chapter 3: Research Methods
Chapter 4: Findings and Discussion
Chapter 5: Conclusion

How to write an Introduction, a Literature Review, and a Contextual Review have already been covered in this book, as have traditional approaches to research. What follows is advice on how to write a chapter on research methods for those who are creating an artefact and are required to review their creation.

## Writing about your research methods

To start with, you could give your chapter on research methods one of the following titles:

'Research Methods: Practice-based Research'; or
'Research Methods: Practice as Research'; or
'Research Methods: Performative Research'; or
'Research Methods: Practice-led Research'.

The label is not important provided that it is clear what you mean by *practice-based* or *practice-led* or *practice as research* or *performative research*. Alternatively, you could go for the simple option and call your chapter 'Research Methods'. Irrespective of the chapter title you settle on, there are three main activities that need to be addressed in your chapter: your research strategy (or strategies), your data collection technique(s), and how you intend to analyse your created artefact and data about your artefact (you may have collated views from others).

Let's assume that you stick with the simple option: 'Chapter 3 Research Methods', and it is placed after 'Chapter 1 Introduction' and 'Chapter 2 Contextual Review (or Literature Review)'. You could structure such a chapter along traditional lines:

3.1   Introduction
3.2   Research Strategy
3.3   Data Collection Techniques
3.4   Framework for Analysis
3.5   Limitations and Potential Problems

Given that this type of creating/critiquing dissertation will be considerably shorter in length than traditional dissertations, you need to cut your cloth accordingly. Accordingly, you might find it more convenient to treat your chapter as a mini-essay without the need for the formal sub-headings. Nevertheless, you would still address the content expected in 3.1–3.5:

Chapter 3: Research Methods
(Write short intro . . .)
(Write about your research strategy . . .)
(Write about how you will collect data on your creation . . .)
(Write about how you will analyse that data . . .)
(Write about any limitations of your research . . .)

Your research strategy, data collection technique(s), and method(s) of data analysis are collectively known as your research methods. Let's now explore how to write the various parts that go to make up a chapter on research methods.

### Writing a brief introduction

By this stage you should already know how to write a short introduction to a chapter. In this case, remind the reader of the research objective(s) that refer to your creation and outline the topics your chapter will cover. For example:

The objectives in this research were identified as follows:

1 . . .
2 . . .
3 . . .
4 . . .

Objectives 2 and 3 refer to the creation of a piece of ceramic art and the evaluation of that piece [if that is the case]. This chapter will identify the research strategy to facilitate these objectives. Specifically, the research strategy to be adopted will be discussed and details of how the artefact will be created and reviewed will be explained, including data collection and analysis techniques. In addition, limitations of this research work will be addressed.

## Writing about your research strategy

Students tackling a traditional dissertation have a number of research strategies from which to choose: case study, experimental, historical, action research, and so on (see Chapter 7). This is both a blessing and a curse: they will never be short of research strategies from which to choose but they need to tread carefully and pick one that is a best fit for their research. You, on the other hand, have your research strategy handed to you on a plate. You research strategy is **PaR** (let's stick with that label for illustrative purposes for now but other terms can be used interchangeably). Completing this part of your chapter on research methods should be straightforward, as long as you answer the *what, why, how,* and *where* questions.

*What is your research strategy and why are you using this research strategy?* Your research strategy is PaR (or an equivalent label). However, you need to describe that strategy to show that you understand what it is. You can do so with reference to a definition of research-based research (this shows that you are well-read).

> The research strategy to be used in this research is called Practice as Research (PaR). What is PaR? So-and-so defines it as '___'. A central feature of PaR is the requirement . . .

Importantly, do not automatically exclude traditional research strategies in support of your main research strategy – PaR – just because you don't recognise them as arty. If the hat fits, wear it. For example, you might want to experiment with ceramics at different kiln temperatures. In which case you will be creating an artefact, thus identifying your main research strategy as PaR, but it will be supported by another type of research strategy: experimental research. Similarly, if you wanted to show the influence of music in a play, you could take key scenes from a famous play and introduce music to change audience perception. For example, you could have comical music playing in 'A Streetcar Named Desire' whenever Stanley and Blanche interact. You would then be exploiting two research strategies, one modern and one traditional: PaR and case study research. If you are using another research strategy in support of PaR, then you also need to explain what it is.

The *why* answer is also obvious. You are using PaR because of the nature of your research (i.e. your stated research objectives). So, justify your use of PaR with reference to your research objectives:

> The nature of this research work aligns with the definition of PaR . . . The following artefact will be created to meet Research Objective 2 . . . This

reflects the definition of PaR . . . Also, the need to review an artefact that one has created (Research Objective 3) requires data collection and analysis techniques sympathetic to the creative process . . .

If you have also included other strategies, then justify their use too (see Chapter 7 for justification of traditional research strategies).

Do not confuse PaR, practice-based research, practice-led research, performative research – whatever you want to call it – with another type of research activity: Action Research. The juxtaposition of opposites in the title (*Action* and *Research*) suggests a similarity of purpose replicated in *Practice as Research, practice*-based *research, practice*-led *research,* and *performative research*. To understand the purpose of Action Research, and hence the difference between it and PaR, etc., we can do no better than turn to an article written by Kurt Lewin, the founder of Action Research.

In 1946, Lewin wrote an article with the title 'Action research and minority problems'. He wanted to use a form of social engineering, which he called 'action research', to improve intergroup relations, particularly to the benefit of those in society who were often disadvantaged in work and/or the wider community. In his own words (1945, p. 35), his idea can 'best be characterised as research for social management or social engineering . . . a comparative research on the conditions and effects of various forms of social action and research leading to social action'. It involved holding workshops 'to face the problem squarely and really to do something about it' (p. 34) with a view to improving intergroup relations. The person leading the workshops would be knowledgeable in social management or social engineering and would participate in the resolution of issues and observe the impact of the workshop (i.e. he or she would play the role of a 'participant observer'). Every page of Lewin's article repeats the desire to repair intergroup relations:

*'help in the field of group relations'* (p. 34);

*'Social research should be one of the top priorities for the practical job of improving intergroup relations'* (p. 35);

*'to improve intergroup relations'* (p. 36);

*'fact-finding on intergroup relations'* (p. 37);

*'devoted to improving intergroup relations'* (p. 38);

*'betterment of intergroup relations'* (p. 39);

*'to lead to long-range improvements in the field of intergroup relations'* (p. 40);

*'the power of the participants to bring about the desired change'* (p. 41);

*'in the field of intergroup relations . . . building productive, hard-hitting teams with practitioners'* (p. 42);

*'close integration of action, training, and research holds tremendous possibilities for the field of intergroup relations'* (p. 43);

*'results of research on group interrelations'* (p. 44);

*'for the improvement of intergroup relations'* (p. 45);

*'A large scale effort of social research on intergroup relations . . .'* (p. 46).

Social improvement is not a pre-condition of artistic practice-based research; nor is the betterment of intergroup relations; nor the need to solve a problem; or hold a workshop. Although Action Research has loosened its parameters to include any group and not just disadvantaged minority groups, it still revolves around the notion of problem solving through some form of groupwork for the benefit of that group. Artists as researchers ought not to be constrained by these conditions. If, on the other hand, the purpose of your work is to improve the lot of a particular group (however you define that group), where you observe the impact of your creation on that group, thereby resolving a problem in whole or part, then it could be said that you are exploiting two types of research strategies: practice-based research and Action Research.

*How* will you create your piece? *Why* are you creating your piece and *where* are you creating it? The trick at this stage is to provide enough detail that someone with the same level of skills as you could have a good bash at repeating your research work (that is not to say that they will end up with the same painting, sculpture, dance, play, musical piece, video, computer game, etc.). For example:

A papier mâché sculpture of a calf humpback whale will be made and left to rot on a beach. A tape of a baby crying will be placed inside the whale. The papier mâché will be constructed as follows . . . Figure 1 illustrates the design and dimensions of the whale. The sculpture will be placed on the following beach . . . The purpose of this piece is to . . . A calf whale was chosen, rather than, for example, a horse, because it serves the artist's purpose of . . .

## Writing about your data collection techniques

To review your art work, whatever it is, you will need to collect data about that art work. Once again, it is the what- and why-type questions that are important:

*What* data collection techniques will you be using and *why* those techniques? There are a host of ways that you can collect data about your artefact. There is nothing stopping you using well-established traditional data collection techniques, such as interviews, questionnaires, and focus groups. Practitioner-based research tends to be associated with qualitative research. So rather than closed questions, the emphasis tends to be on open questions that help to answer two core questions: *what do I think about my work?* and *what do others think about my work?* You are trying to record thoughts and feelings about your work. Data about thoughts and feelings are normally captured through observation and conversation, both casual and formal. If using observation and conversation, you will need a way to record what you observe about your work and the reaction of others to your work. Options for recording observations and views include: a diary, voice recording, photographs, video, sketches, Post-It® notes, transcripts, noting facial expressions, visitor response sheets, etc. Once again, there is nothing stopping you mixing and matching traditional and less traditional data collection techniques (e.g. formal interviews and Post-It® notes). You will need to identify who will be subject to what data collection technique (include yourself). You also need to justify your choices. For example:

> Data will be collected from a number of sources using a variety of techniques. How the artist views his own work will be recorded in a diary and through the use of a recording device. This will allow for immediate personal observations to be recorded in situ. A relaxed focus group of fellow students will be used to capture views of one's peers in a non-threatening environment. The group will be asked to discuss specific issues (e.g. 'what do you think the artist was trying to achieve?'). The specific themes for the focus group are attached in Appendix . . . An anonymised transcript of the focus group meeting is in Appendix . . .

> Two formal semi-structured interviews will also take place between the artist and an environmentalist: before the creation of the work and after its creation. An environmentalist was chosen because the work is a comment on the environment. Interviewing before and after helps capture the expectations of the environmentalist before the art work was created and her views after its creation. Semi-structured interviews give focus to the interview and, at the same time, allow the respondent the opportunity to 'open up'. The questions to be asked, including transcripts of the interviews, are included in Appendix . . .

If you are creating a software app, computer program, video game, etc., then more traditional data collection techniques are likely to appear in your analysis alongside self-reflective techniques used in practice-based research. Your main concern will be that the app, program, video, etc. does what it is supposed to do and so you will get much of your data from testing your creation at different levels and at different stages. Software developers have well-established testing protocols and institutions normally make these available to students for use.

### Writing about how you will analyse your artefact

Here you outline your general approach to analysing your empirical work. For traditional dissertations, the generic approach is to **describe** the collected data, **interpret** what it is telling you, then compare and contrast the findings with the results of the Literature Review. This last stage is called **synthesis**. That accumulative process of **description–interpretation–synthesis**, leading to a rounded evaluation, is no different for practice-based research with the caveat that you are not only analysing data, you are also analysing data about something you created. That means there is the artefact and views about the artefact from you and, perhaps, others that require critical discussion. To accommodate this duality, practice-based researchers often make use of a two-fold reflection process:

1 Reflection-in-action; and
2 Reflection-on-action.

*Reflection-in-action*, in the context of practical art work, occurs when you have cause to reflect during the creation of the artefact, usually when key decisions have to be made. You might be reflecting on different design ideas or having to change course as a result of a resource issue, in which case you can take the opportunity to record your choices and decisions, including rationale. You can make use of a variety of tools to record your thought processes, examples of which include: a diary, a voice recorder, sketches, photographs, etc. Figure 8.1 is an example of reflection-in-action, where a postgraduate art student reflects on ideas for a sleeping bag she wants to weave.

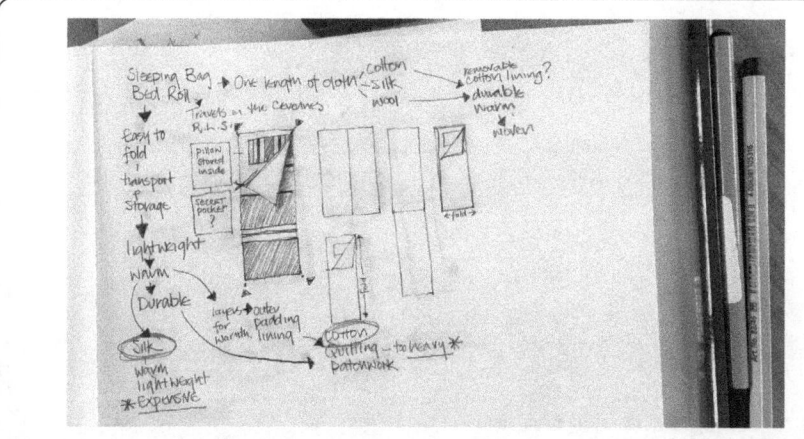

**Figure 8.1** Example of reflection-in-action

Reflection-**on**-action occurs when you reflect on your work after the creation of your artefact. Figure 8.2 (p. 218) shows the finished artefact from Figure 8.1. Reflecting on the completed artefact can involve personal observation from the artist as well as the artist reflecting on the views of others.

You begin to achieve synthesis when you compare and contrast your empirical findings with what you found out in your Literature Review or Contextual Review. Figure 8.3 (p. 218) summarises a generic framework for practice-based research. There are other, equally valid, frameworks.

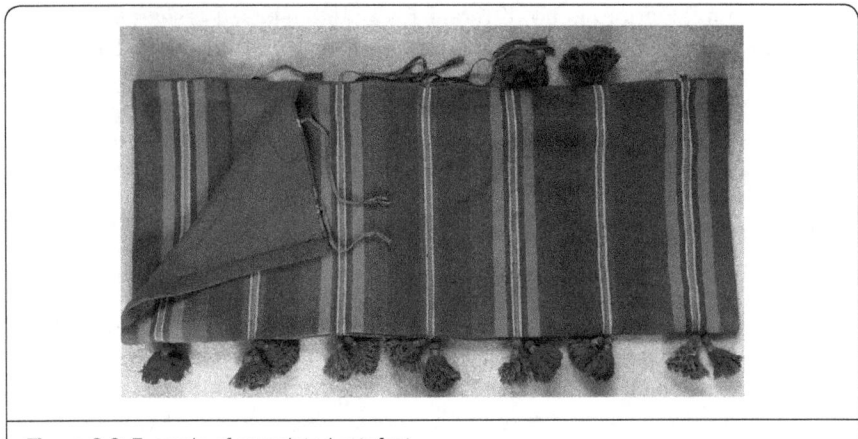

**Figure 8.2** Example of completed artefact

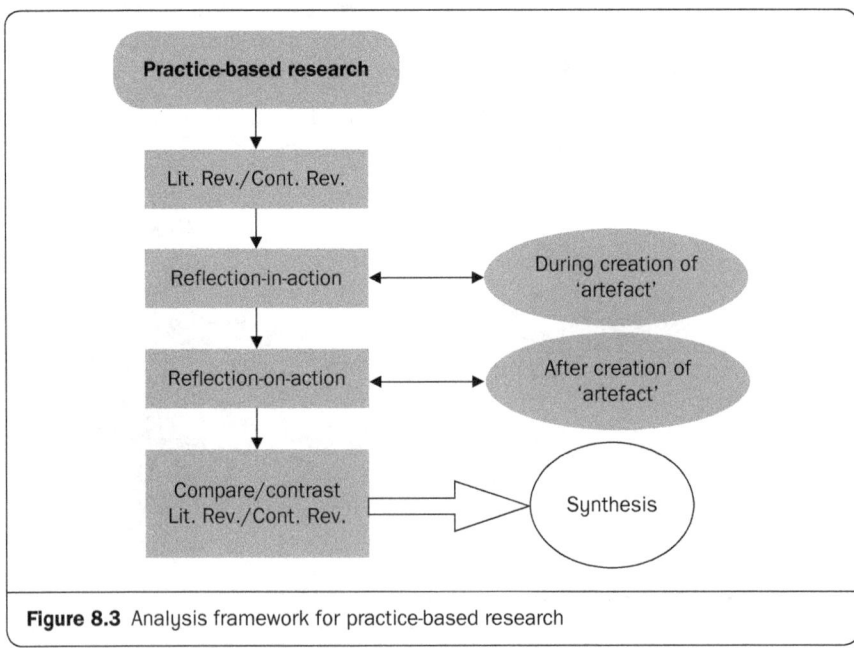

**Figure 8.3** Analysis framework for practice-based research

The first stage – the implementation of a Literature Review or Contextual Review – will normally have been completed before you start your empirical work. Although the second stage, reflection-in-action, will take place during the creation process, the results of that activity will appear in the Findings chapter, as will the third stage of the model (reflection-on-action) and stage 4 (comparison/contrast with the results of stage 1 (Literature Review or Contextual Review)); all of which will allow the reader to get a complete picture of practice-based research from development to creation.

Another model for your practice-based research might be to drop the idea of recording reflection-in-action altogether, i.e. create the artefact and then reflect on your creation (Figure 8.4). This is perfectly acceptable. Depending on what you are creating, the pressure of time constraints might push you in that direction anyway. Nonetheless, the opportunity to reveal your thought processes through reflection-in-action adds a certain richness and insight that are normally welcomed in the creative arts, where the creation process itself is often viewed as just as important as the finished product. Furthermore, although recording reflection-in-action might appear time-consuming, it will in fact make the job of completing your final write-up so much easier: your past thoughts will have been accurately recorded *in situ* and available to hand. In any event, you would still be expected to compare/contrast your practical findings against your Literature Review/Contextual Review findings.

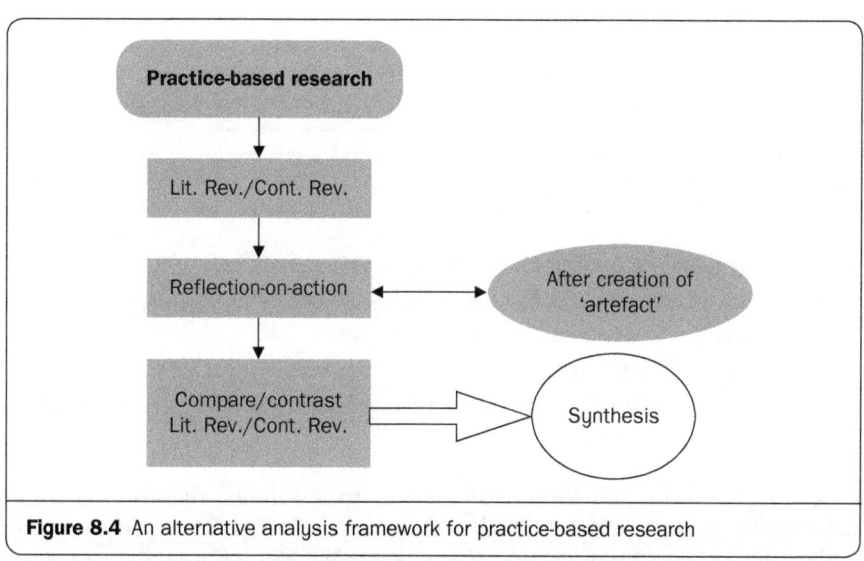

**Figure 8.4** An alternative analysis framework for practice-based research

Before giving advice on completing the last part of your mini-essay – writing about the limitations of your research and potential problems – it is necessary to digress and provide a deeper understanding of what is meant by *reflective practice* so that you can apply it in your research from an informed position.

'Reflecting' is not a new concept. Dewey (1933) believed that there was thinking and there was thinking well, and that the latter could only be achieved through reflection, which he defined as an 'active, persistent, and careful consideration of any belief or supposed form of knowledge in light of the grounds that support it and the further conclusions to which it tends' (p. 9). For Dewey, learning was achieved if you faced problems by challenging existing beliefs; and you did this by reflecting on personal experience and, based on lessons learned, planned accordingly for the next experience (*ibid.*, p. 100): 'The function of reflective thought is, therefore, to transform a situation in which there is experienced obscurity, doubt, conflict, disturbance of some sort into a situation that is clear, coherent, settled, harmonious.' His ideas were developed specifically to encourage teachers to reflect on their classroom experiences and, through reflection, make themselves better teachers.

Kolb (1984, p. 38) held similar views to Dewey about learning from experience: 'Learning is the process whereby knowledge is created through the transformation of experience.' He went further, though, and developed a four-phase model which he called the *experiential learning cycle* (Figure 8.5). Learning takes place after the completion of all four phases of the learning cycle.

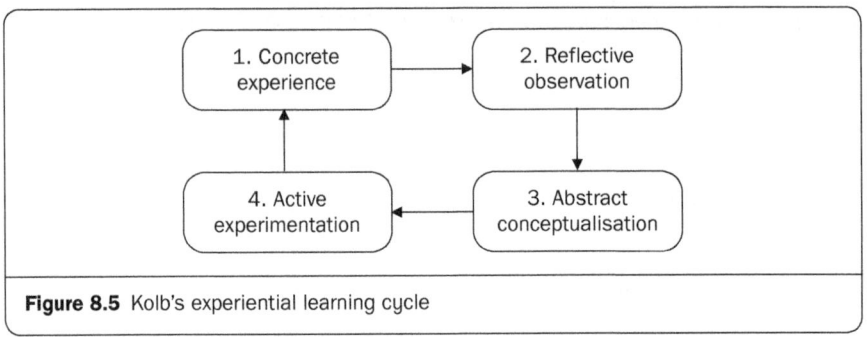

**Figure 8.5** Kolb's experiential learning cycle

1 *Concrete experience*: individual has an experience.
2 *Reflective observation*: individual reflects on that experience, particularly with reference to expectations and anomalies.
3 *Abstract conceptualisation*: new idea to improve experience crystallises.
4 *Active experimentation*: new idea planned for next concrete experience, and so on.

Although Dewey and Kolb gave impetus to the notion of *thinking about thinking* to improve practice, their theories viewed reflection as an incremental learning process taking place after an experience or before the next experience. It was Schön (1983) who came up with the concept of reflecting during practice to accompany reflection after practice, naming them reflection-in-action and reflection-on-action respectively. Here is Schön's take on reflection-in-action (p. 50):

> *'There is a puzzling, or troubling, or interesting phenomenon with which the individual is trying to deal. As he tries to make sense of it, he also reflects on the understandings which have been implicit in his actions, understandings which he surfaces, criticizes, restructures, and embodies in further action.'*

While Dewey and Kolb's advice on reflecting between experiences find a natural home in scientific research – experience a problem, reflect on what went wrong, make adjustments, have another go, etc. – it is clear that Schön's reflection-in-action to complement reflection-on-action is particularly suited to those involved in the creative arts, where reflection is a fluid, intuitive activity to cope with uncertain, ongoing situations. Schön's two modes of reflection can be differentiated as shown in Table 8.1:

**Table 8.1** Schön's models of reflection

| Reflection-in-action | Reflection-on-action |
|---|---|
| Thinking about something 'in the moment' | Thinking about something after the event |
| Thinking about what to do | Thinking about what to do next time |
| Making a decision there and then | Making a decision next time |

You don't need to reflect on everything when implementing reflection-in-action. It is much more sensible to reflect on key events involving the creation of your artefact. Figure 8.6 is a simple two-stage protocol that you can adopt to record your thoughts.

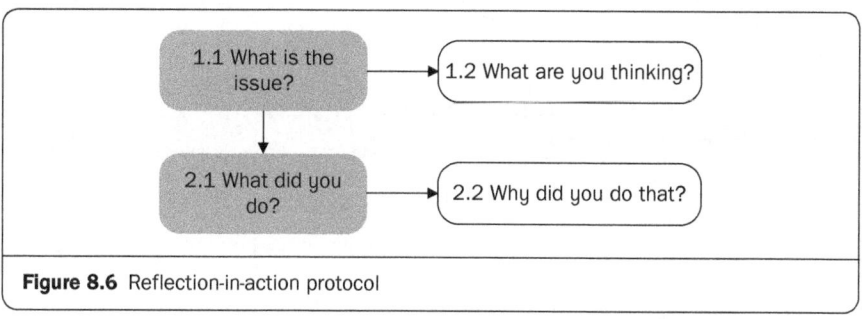

**Figure 8.6** Reflection-in-action protocol

How you record the data in reflection-in-action is up to you. You can use a diary, Post-It® notes, annotated sketches (see, for example, Figure 8.1), a word-processed document, a journal, a blog, photographs, videos, voice recordings, or whatever you find convenient. Table 8.2 gives an example of a tabular template mirroring the reflection-in-action protocol in Figure 8.6. An additional question is included to try and capture your feelings at the time. The factors that could influence your decisions could be advice from your supervisor, comments from peers, something you saw or read, or from your own reasoning, or practical matters such as time constraints or access to resources.

If you record your reflection-*in*-action using Table 8.2, page 222 or similar, then the data in that table will act as a data collection technique to be used when you apply reflection-*on*-action in your write-up. In other words, reflection-in-action now serves a double purpose: initially, it is used as a quick analysis tool to help you think 'in the moment' in order to progress the creation of your artefact; but the data that you record while engaging in reflection-in-action can then feed into your reflection-on-action activity when you look back over your work.

**Table 8.2** Reflection-in-action log

| Date | Reflection-in-action |
|---|---|
| What is the issue?<br>What are you thinking?<br>What are you feeling?<br>What did you do?<br>Why did you do that? | |

If you are developing a piece of software, then it is likely that your reflection-in-action would also involve applying a standard software testing protocol every so often and making decisions based on the results.

Remember, unlike reflection-*in*-action, reflection-*on*-action takes place after you have created your artefact. In the context of a dissertation, your reflection-on-action is principally about reflecting on your created artefact. Table 8.3 provides a template for reflecting on your created artefact. You can include other questions as you see fit, but Table 8.3 presents a good starting point.

**Table 8.3** Reflection-on-action protocol

| Artefact: < Title of artefact > | Reflection-on-action |
|---|---|
| What were you trying to achieve?<br>Did you achieve that?<br>What are your views on what you achieved?<br>What do others think about your artefact?<br>Where is there a similarity/difference of opinion?<br>What are your feelings?<br>What key factors influenced the final product?<br>On hindsight, what lessons have you learned? What was good? Bad? Is there anything you would do differently? | |

It may be the case that you are not seeking views from others about your artefact, i.e. you create it and then you reflect on what you have created. This is an unlikely scenario but it is a possibility. Even if you do not have a formal focus group or issue questionnaires, etc., your supervisor will have an input about your work and there may be unsolicited views that crop up during informal discussions with fellow students or members of the public.

To achieve synthesis – that is, an all round in-depth evaluation of your work – you need to compare and contrast the findings about your created artefact against what you wrote in your Literature Review or Contextual Review.

## Writing about limitations and potential problems

You need to face these issues head-on. Practice-based research projects, in the context of artist as researcher, are open to the charge that they are highly subjective because a creative art form is produced and reviewed by the person who created it. The results of the research are therefore vulnerable to personal bias. All true, none of which reduce the standing of practice-based research. The artist as researcher can rightly appeal to the twin foundations upon which all credible research is built – *validity* and *reliability* – and to the 'no difference' defence, where all research strategies, data collection techniques, and methods of analysis are subject to one criticism or another and practice-based research is no different:

- A valid research strategy, irrespective of any inherent limitations, is one that is the best fit for a particular type of research. Practice-based research, where an artefact is created by the artist and reviewed by the artist, is a valid research strategy for artists because it is the only research strategy that is designed to meet the needs of the artist as a researcher.
- All research strategies have inherent limitations. The results of a case study cannot be generalised, historical research cannot wholly reconstruct the past, experimental research answers 'what-if' questions, not 'why' questions, and so on. Limitations do not disqualify research strategies: lack of validity and reliability does. The perfect all-purpose research strategy has not yet been invented.
- The inherent limitation of practice-based research is that, although the research can answer what, why, and how questions, it can only do so in relation to one artefact by one artist (or group of artists if groupwork is performed). In terms of validity, the fact that the artist and the reviewer are one and the same person is neither here nor there. Researchers in traditional research strategies regularly review their own research work without outcry. For example, action researchers will posit a solution to a problem, try it out with a group of people, then review the results; a scientist will create an experiment, test it, and review that experiment; and so on. If independence were a crucial criterion to validate a research strategy, then all research would have someone thinking up the research approach, someone else implementing it, and someone else reviewing it. That does not happen. Independent reviewers do exist after the event and their expert opinions are welcome. The world of art and performance-based research, though in its infancy relative to other research paradigms, is also not short of other equally independent and expert voices.
- All data collection techniques have their limitations. Questionnaires lack the in-depth responses found in qualitative interviews; interviews are time-consuming and dependent on the responsiveness of the interviewee; observation is subjective and time- and place-dependent; data from tests are only as good as the tests; and so on. Practice-based research is dependent on: (a) the artefact itself (painting, dance, musical piece, etc.); (b) data about

the artefact (from the artist and other voices); and (c) reflection about the object and data about the object (reflection-in-action and reflection-on-action). Products are standard outputs in other research (e.g. missiles, new drugs, new models, etc.); data about these objects, from researchers and others, are regularly accepted as valid forms of input; and reflection is a tool that has been used by traditional researchers for centuries. Reflection-in-action and reflection-on-action are appropriate data collection and analysis techniques because that is how artists develop their work.

- Reflection-in-action and reflection-on-action can reduce to a tick-box exercise, where pre-determined questions are summarily completed in a mechanical fashion (Boud and Walker, 1998). It is not the pre-determined nature of the questions that is the problem – in fact, that is good planning – it is the answers, or lack of, that can cause concern. Unthinking reductionism can be avoided by adopting an honest and open approach to recording thoughts and feelings and by engaging in *critical* reflection.

- The analysis strategy of achieving synthesis by comparing and contrasting empirical results against stated research objectives/questions and the results of a Literature Review or Contextual Review is standard practice in the world of research.

- All research, not just practice-based research for art and drama, is vulnerable to personal bias. To think otherwise is to assign an unfailing model of human perfection to researchers that does not exist in the rest of society. Examples of bad science, based on bias, abound on the Internet. Research bias can also occur as a result of incompetence rather than personal prejudice. Incompetence is a human fault. It is not an element of any research method.

- Reliable research is research that can be trusted. To win trust, every key step of the research process is made transparent as proof that the research was indeed carried out and to allow others the opportunity to repeat the research if they so wish. All research projects ought to meet the test of reliability and practice-based research is no different: research activities should be recorded and described in detail.

In addition to convincing the reader that your research is valid and reliable (that is, you have an *appropriate* research strategy and you will be *transparent* about your research work), you ought to highlight limitations and potential problem areas specific to your research project – and, importantly, how you will tackle these issues. That is what good researchers do. For example, is time an issue? What you want to do and what you have time to do can be two very different matters. Is access to resources an issue? Do people you know form part of your research (e.g. fellow students commenting on your work)? If so, how will you get them to view you as a researcher and not as a friend whom they wish to please?

This last point above leads to a bigger danger: drowning in an egotistical quagmire of Me, Me, Me. This strikes at the heart of conventional criticisms of practice-based research: the personal nature of it and getting around the difficulty of criticising your own work. The answer lies in viewing yourself not as an artist but as an artist-researcher. You recognise the duality of that role and you act accordingly. You are a *participant-observer* in every sense of the term and intend living up to that label: the artist part of you is *participating* in developing an artefact and the artist part of you is *observing* the results; similarly, the researcher part of you is *participating* in designing the research methods (choosing the research strategy, or strategies, choosing the data collection techniques, and choosing how to analyse the artefact and data about the artefact) and *observing* the results. Also, to maintain a balanced equilibrium between the professional and the personal, appeal to the concepts of validity and reliability (see above).

You can also argue that even in the minutiae of recording reflection-in-action and reflection-on-action you phrase questions in such a way as to encourage the artist to see him or herself as a participant-observer. For example, the reflection-in-action questions are not directed to the artist personally – they are directed to the researcher in the artist: 'What is *the* issue?', not 'What is *my* issue?'; 'What are *you* thinking?', not 'What was *I* thinking?', etc. This arm's-length approach is replicated in the reflection-on-action questions in Table 8.3: 'What were *you* trying to achieve?', not 'What was *I* trying to achieve?'; 'Did *you* achieve that?', not 'Did *I* achieve that?', etc.

In short, address limitations and potential problems of your work, including ones of a general nature and ones specific to your research project. Make sure that you write how you will deal with them. It may be that you take the practical path trodden by all researchers at one time or another – that research design and implementation are all about trade-offs. Accepting some limitations and some problems is the price you pay for creating what you want to create in the timescale that you have, using the resources that you have access to.

# Further reading

Dewey, J. (1933) *How we think: a restatement of reflective thinking to the educative process.* Boston, MA: D. C. Heath.

Gherardi, S. (2013) *How to conduct a practice-based study: problems and methods.* Cheltenham: Edward Elgar Publishing.

Kershaw, B. and Nicholson, H. (2010) *Research methods in theatre and performance.* Edinburgh: Edinburgh University Press.

Kolb, D. A. (1984) *Experiential learning: experience as a source of learning and development.* Englewood Cliffs, NJ: Prentice-Hall.

Leavy, P. (2015) *Method meets art: arts-based research practice.* London: Guilford Press.

Nelson, R. (2013) *Practice as research in the arts: principles, protocols, pedagogies, resistances.* Basingstoke: Palgrave Macmillan.

Schön, D. A. (1983) *The reflective practitioner: how professionals think in action.* New York: Basic Books.

Smith, H. and Dean, R. T. (2009) *Practice-led research, research-led practice in the creative arts.* Edinburgh: Edinburgh University Press.

Vaughan, L. (2017) *Practice based design research.* London: Bloomsbury Academic.

## Summary of key points

- There are valid and reliable research methods available to artists intent on creating and critiquing an artefact. 'Artist' is interpreted loosely to include anyone involved in creating artefacts. 'Artefact' is also interpreted loosely to include any art form, examples of which include paintings, a dance, a piece of music, a scene from a play, a video, and a computer app.
- The *research strategy* for artists is known under different names – Practice as Research (PaR), practice-based research, practice-led research, and performative research – but the terms can be used interchangeably provided two criteria are met: (1) an art form is created by the artist and (2) it is critiqued by the artist.
- The principal *data collection and analysis technique* favoured by artists is based on critical thought called *reflection*. There are two types of reflection: *reflection-in-action* and *reflection-on-action*. Reflection-in-action occurs during the creation of the artefact and is a means of collecting data about a current issue and doing something about it there and then (i.e. thinking on one's feet); reflection-on-action takes place after the creation of the artefact and is a means of making sense of the finished work with an eye on lessons learned.
- A *reflection-in-action log* is a useful tool to record key thoughts and feelings during the creation process. A *reflection-on-action protocol* consisting of summative questions is a useful tool to aid reflection after the creation of an artefact.
- A generic model for practice-based research includes: (1) the implementation of a Literature Review or Contextual Review to place the proposed artefact in context; (2) reflection-in-action during the creation of the artefact; (3) reflection-on-action after completion of the artefact; (4) a comparison of what was done and how it is viewed (by the artist and perhaps others) against the Literature Review or Contextual Review findings. This last stage is done to achieve *synthesis*.
- All research strategies, data collection techniques, and analysis techniques have inherent limitations. Practice-based research is no different.
- Traditional research methods should be exploited where they add value.
- *Valid research* is research that is appropriate for a particular type of research project. *Reliable* research is research that can be trusted. Reliability is achieved through transparency about the research process.
- A chapter on research methods for practice-based researchers ought to identify and justify the chosen research strategy, data collection techniques, and method of analysis. In addition, any limitations and potential problems should be identified and addressed. In defence, while all research strategies, data collection techniques, and methods of analysis have limitations, and practice-based research is no different, it is to the concepts of validity and reliability that the student appeals in support of their chosen research methods.

# Chapter

# Writing up your findings

- Writing up the findings: traditional dissertations • Writing up the findings: art and performance-based dissertations • Further reading
- Summary of key points

This chapter is in two parts. The first part – *Writing up the findings: traditional dissertations* – is intended for those students completing a traditional dissertation, i.e. one where traditional research methods have been used (case study, survey, experimental research, questionnaires, interviews, etc.); the second part – *Writing up the findings: art and performance-based dissertations* – is intended for artists involved in practice-based research, i.e. where an art form has been created (painting, sculpture, dance, music piece, etc.) and is to be reviewed by the artist.

## Writing up the findings: traditional dissertations

The conventional approach to completing a dissertation typically involves an extensive Literature Review followed by the implementation of empirical research using well-established research methods. A case study supported by interviews using structured questionnaires is an example of this type of research. The task of writing up your results is a necessary and, for the most part, mechanical process. If you have worked out a way to analyse your results beforehand, then your job will be made that much easier. By this point you should have completed the first three stages of your dissertation, including your empirical research, and are now in the position to write up your empirical findings:

**Chapter 1: Introduction**
**Chapter 2: Literature Review**

**Chapter 3: Research Methods**
Chapter 4: Findings
Chapter 5: Conclusions and Recommendations

 **A common mistake by students**

A common mistake by students is to write their chapter on research methods devoid of any reference to data analysis, with the result that when they eventually have the data in front of them, they are not sure what to do with it!

Create a simple structure for your *findings* chapter. Have an uncomplicated title, such as 'Findings: Case Study Results', if you carried out a case study, or 'Findings: Survey Results', if you implemented a survey. Better still, you could call your chapter 'Survey Findings: Description, Analysis and Synthesis', thus identifying the type of empirical research that you did – in the latter case, a survey – as well as informing the reader that you will partake in three main types of intellectual activity:

1  A simple description of your results;
2  Discussion about what you found; and, finally,
3  An integrative analysis of your empirical data against your Literature Review findings (i.e. the synthesis bit).

If you give your write-up chapter the minimalist title, as one student did and others still do, 'Chapter 4: Findings' – assuming it is the fourth chapter, after Introduction, Literature Review (or Contextual Review), and Research Methods – then you will be missing an easy opportunity to signpost your work. Much better is the student who used her title to remind the reader of her main research strategy (a case study) and of the academic activities the reader would encounter in her write-up:

**Chapter 4 Case Study Findings: Description, Analysis and Synthesis**

Although your chapter title may give the impression that the content is purely about your empirical findings, this is not the case – yes, you are expected to report on the data that you have collected but you are also expected to compare and contrast your empirical findings against what you discovered in your Literature Review (or its equivalent), otherwise what was the point of initiating a review of literature?

Give a brief introduction to your chapter. By now you should be well versed in writing an introduction to each of your chapters. Start by [a] reminding the reader of what you *set out to do*, followed by [b] a brief description of how *you intend approaching* the write-up of your empirical results. You should also [c] place your empirical research *in context*. For example, if your data were derived from a case study of an organisation, then give some background information about that organisation, as in the sample e-Learning case study:

> **[a] This chapter reveals** the results of the case study described in Chapter 3 Research Methods . . . The research concentrates on two groups of stakeholders: academic staff within Division X, located in the Inverclyde Business School (IBS) at Inverclyde University (IU) and recently involved in preparing teaching and learning material on an e-Learning environment, and senior staff in Division X, IBS and ICU who have an influence on the implementation of e-Learning in the university, i.e. *elite* staff . . . **[b] The case study is approached in a highly structured way**. First, a description is provided of academic staff results, theme by theme . . . The gathering of empirical data for this research is based on a case study, to allow an analysis of real problems in a set context. Prior to a description and analysis of the case study results, a profile of related aspects of ICU will now be made **to set the study in context [c]** . . . It is in the context of these developments, self-perceptions, and aspirations in which the context of this study is implemented. It should be appreciated that universities are complex organisations and that the above is not an attempt to *explain* ICU or describe fully its operation or culture, but merely to place the study in context . . .

Also, let the reader know [d] *in which appendix* they will find evidence of your interviews, experiments, questionnaire responses, as in the example above: 'The transcripts of the interviews for academic staff can be found in Appendix B; the transcripts from the senior staff interviews are in Appendix C.' The following is an example of a bad effort at writing the introduction to the findings:

### 4.1 Chapter Introduction
This chapter will discuss the findings of this research. These findings will include views of managers and others in the field as well those affected by the policy decisions.

There are a number of deficiencies in this Introduction that you need to avoid. It is *too* brief, lacking in any meaningful information. There is no mention of the research strategy or the data collection techniques (a full description is not required – just a sentence or two to remind the reader of how the research was carried out). There is no indication of how the student will approach the write-up. 'These findings will include the views of managers . . .' – which managers? Views related to what issues? Who are the 'others' and in which 'field'? What policy decisions? Also, there is no need for the word 'Chapter' to be included in the sub-section heading – '4.1 Introduction' will suffice.

The heart of the chapter on your empirical findings will revolve around the tasks of *description* (of your empirical data), *discussion/analysis* (of what you have described), and *synthesis* (of your discussed empirical results against your literature findings). It is worth repeating Bogdan and Biklen's description of this process: 'working with data, organising it, breaking it into manageable units, synthesising it, searching for patterns, discovering what is important and what is to be learned, and deciding what you will tell others' (1982, p. 145). You cannot evaluate the worth of your research findings unless you have made an attempt at going through the intellectual exercise of description → analysis → synthesis.

If you recall Bloom's (1956) taxonomy of learning, you are being tested that you have the cognitive skills illustrated in his learning triangle (basic knowledge → comprehension → application → analysis → synthesis → evaluation); and the higher up his learning triangle you go, the more marks you get! Your ultimate goal is to show that you can *evaluate* what you are looking at with reference to your Literature Review + Empirical Findings. You need to describe your empirical data before you can discuss/analyse it; and you need to have discussed/analysed your descriptions before you can synthesise your empirical results with your Literature Review findings. Only then can you evaluate the worth of your findings and decide if you have met your specific research objectives and, in turn, your overall research aim. The actual evaluation of your overall research work should appear in your Conclusion chapter, not this one. Figure 9.1 captures the cyclical nature of writing up your empirical findings, culminating at some stage (usually in your concluding chapter) in a self-evaluation of your overall findings.

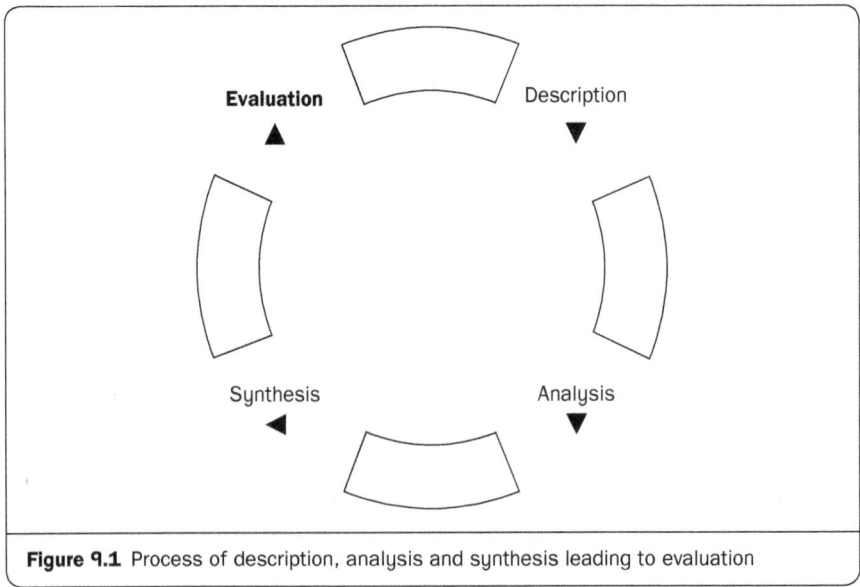

**Figure 9.1** Process of description, analysis and synthesis leading to evaluation

Once you have carried out your description, analysis, and synthesis (and leaving the overall evaluation to your final chapter, the Conclusion), it is good practice to provide a summary of your findings. Even here, if you are running short of words, you can make the alternative decision to summarise your findings in your Conclusion chapter. This makes sense because if you summarise your findings in this chapter, you will also find yourself having to repeat this summary, in whatever form, when you discuss your conclusions and recommendations in your final chapter. If you have plenty of words to spare, then there is no harm in doing both; if you are running close to your word-count, then think strategically and put the summary of your findings in your Conclusion.

A meaningful structure for your 'Chapter 4 Findings' (assuming you did a case study) that reminds you of the tasks to be completed could be:

Chapter 4 Findings: Case Study Results
4.1  Introduction
4.2  Findings: Description and Analysis of Results
4.3  Synthesis of Findings with Literature Review
4.4  Summary

There are alternative structures that are dependent on how many things your are writing about. For example, if you implemented interviews with some staff and gave others a questionnaire to complete, then you need to alter your structure accordingly to make that clear:

Chapter 4 Findings: Case Study Results
4.1  Introduction
4.2  Findings: Interviews
4.3  Findings: Questionnaire
4.4  Synthesis of Findings with Literature Review
4.5  Summary

Alternatively, you could decide that it is more convenient to synthesise your results as you go along, rather than wait until stage 4.4 above. This would mean that in 4.2 above you would describe and analyse the results of the interviews and then compare the results against the Literature Review findings. Then in 4.3 above you would describe and analyse the results of the questionnaire *and* compare those results against the interview results *and* compare them against the Literature Review findings. In other words, there would be no need for a separate synthesis sub-section. Whether or not to synthesise your results as you go along or to leave that activity to a separate sub-section is your choice.

To demonstrate data *description, analysis,* and *synthesis* in practice, we will revisit the e-Learning case study, where two sets of university staff – academic staff and senior staff – were interviewed on aspects of e-Learning. The early stages of reporting on responses to questionnaires or interviews tend to yield basic information, with little to get your teeth into, as illustrated in the following example interview question and answer:

**Question 1A**
*The University's Strategic Planning Document makes reference to e-Learning targets and objectives. Do you know what these are?*

### Response

Seven of the eight members of the programme team replied 'No' and one member of staff answered 'Eh, to be honest with you, I don't. I know that there is some vague push for e-Learning but I'm not clear on the specifics.' Thus, no members of staff knew what the university's strategic objectives and associated targets were in relation to e-Learning.

It is only when you get deeper into your reporting that you can then begin to show cognitive skills beyond mere description. Suppose both sets of staff were asked the question: 'What, in your view, is the rationale behind the university's drive for e-Learning environments?' The early part of your empirical findings chapter will necessarily involve much basic description of your results, which you build up with cross-referencing to empirical data, as shown in the following example.

### Question 3A

*What, in your view, is the rationale behind the university's drive for e-Learning?*

### Response

Three members of staff viewed it as a cost-saving exercise. Two members of staff believed the university's interest in e-Learning was driven by their competitors and perhaps cosmetic. Two members of staff gave the combined reasons of efficient use of resources coupled with university image. One member of staff held a positive view, believing that the university management did not intend that e-Learning be seen as 'a replacement for traditional modes of delivery, but to complement traditional modes of delivery' and that there existed the potential for professional development initiatives for those 'who can't attend traditional face-to-face modes'.

Summarising academic staff views as follows:

Of the eight respondents, only one viewed management intentions in a wholly positive light, with the majority suspicious that management were introducing e-Learning to make cost-savings or to 'look good' or a combination of both. Only one member of staff made any explicit reference to university management intentions as an attempt to 'enhance the student experience as well'.

Next, we could describe the responses from the senior staff to the same question. At this stage, we might still only be engaged in simple description – the analysis and synthesis will come later. Note that the question number – labelled Question 3A for academic staff but Question 2X for senior staff – might be different because the number of questions, and type, might differ from one group to another. So, starting with:

### Question 2X

*What, in your view, is the rationale behind the university's drive for e-Learning environments?*

**Response**
One respondent responded curtly: 'I don't know. But I know what the Business School's is.' Another did not answer the question directly other than to say that the university has 'a good rationale in terms of its vision for the future of where the university is to go and how e-Learning can support that', but added that 'what it hasn't considered is how it will embed e-Learning in the systems throughout the university'. One member of staff thought that 'there wasn't a big overall university picture' and that there were many perspectives on the subject. Emphasising that he was presenting his own personal perspective, he conjectured that the rationale behind the university's drive for e-Learning was linked to student freedom of choice in terms of 'how, when, where, what to learn', in effect, issues related to flexibility of access and delivery.

Continuing with basic reporting, peppered with supporting quotes. . .

The above four senior staff then went on to suggest a university rationale for e-Learning. One member conjectured that he would like to think that it had reasons to do with 'effectiveness of learning', but suspected that the rationale was more to do with efficiency, specifically releasing staff from teaching duties to pursue research income and consultancy activities. A second member agreed that the rationale might be linked to efficiency – 'I can give you a rationale' – in making the university more cost-effective by enhancing quality and reducing costs at the same time. However, he made it clear that he did not agree with this rationale and that, contrary to this rationale, the quality–cost trade-off remains the same: 'I think all the evidence so far is that the quality–cost trade-off stays the same, em, in other words if you use e-Learning, if you invest in e-Learning you push quality up but you also push costs up . . . I don't believe it actually.'

The two other staff members cited the same two reasons behind the university's push for e-Learning: to compete with other universities engaging in e-Learning ('that competitive element, a need to go for a wider global market'; 'maintaining some degree of presence relative to other universities') and to implement the university's objective of wider access ('wider access in terms of outreach to more remote communities'; 'widen our inclusiveness and accessibility').

Building up your descriptions and cross-referencing of the data . . .

One member of staff explained the IBS's e-Learning strategy:
'. . . we want to roll out Blackboard in a sequential way, year on year, eh, as the delivery mechanism, em, that we are now up to level 3 modules . . . So, level 3 modules will be rolled out next year . . . So that's part 1 of the strategy, to roll out with the, em, the framework. And secondly to broaden*

*that, em, across all modules through a period of time. And thirdly, our strategy is to deepen our engagement with the VLE and with, with web-based learning, em, through, em, eh, further staff developments . . .'*

In essence, the IBS plan is in the first instance, to convert year 1 under-graduate modules onto the VLE software platform Blackboard; do the same with year 2 modules of the School framework, then years 3 (along with Master's programme modules) and 4. Currently, modules in years 1 and 2 of the undergraduate framework have been placed on Blackboard and year 3 and Master's (at the time of interview) were planned for Semester A of the academic year 2003–2004.

Another member of staff explained that Division X had no e-Learning strategy as such, but that the Division was implementing the university's Learning and Teaching Assessment Strategy (LTAS), 'and the LTAS plan has very clearly this kind of dimension of e-Learning within it, and that's quite implicit as well, you know, this kind of moving responsibility to the student for learning etc.' He did add that although there was not an e-Learning strategy in Division X, the Divisional Plan had 'a number of objectives which relate specifically to e-Learning' and that he was in the process of creating an e-Learning Task Force. As well as the aforemen-tioned activities, Division X was implementing the IBS's e-Learning strategy.

Although the descriptions above are quite prosaic, with no analysis, quotations have been included to colour and support the descriptive process. When you are describing raw data, particularly people's views on a topic, then it is also worthwhile to put together a summary of what you have described, particu-larly if there are salient points that you wish to highlight:

No member of staff stated that they knew the rationale behind the uni-versity's drive for e-Learning. One respondent said categorically that he did not know, another respondent offered a view on the rationale with-out saying what she thought it was, and five others made it clear that they had a personal view on what it might be. Two staff suggested that the rationale may be about efficient use of resources (with one member suspecting this to be the unstated university rationale, and the other disagreeing with the logic of that rationale); two staff thought that it might concern the twin elements of competitiveness and student access; with one member of staff suggesting that the rationale was connected to student freedom of choice. Even where the staff offered a suggested rationale, their suggestions were varied.

Various tools and techniques exist that you can use to describe and analyse your empirical findings, ranging from simple descriptive graphs, such as bar charts and tables, to more complicated statistical analysis. It all depends on the type of data that you have and what you want to do with that data. If your research is essentially qualitative in nature, then using themes (as in the case study example) coupled with basic descriptive tools will suffice; if your research is mainly quantitative in nature, then you will exploit quantitative instruments for measurement and analysis.

Once you have assembled a certain level of description, you can then enrich your work by offering intelligent comment (i.e. analysis). You can now take the opportunity to show off your analytical skills by expressing an opinion on the views given by both sets of staff. In this case, the analysis occurs through the vehicle of cross-referencing, which, for the purpose of highlighting, appears in **bold:**

> Academic staff were asked a similar question. Three academic staff members believed it to be a cost-saving exercise; two that the drive for e-Learning was driven by their competitors (and perhaps cosmetic); two that it was linked to efficient use of resources and university image; and one that it was to enhance the student learning experience. **The replies from the elite staff and the academic staff suggest that neither the senior staff nor the teaching staff had a consistent idea among their own group of the university's rationale for e-Learning. However, some staff produced suggestions that coincided in two similar groupings (competitiveness, cost-cutting/efficiency); but elite staff members also introduced the idea of accessibility (not mentioned by academic staff) and academic staff offered a less charitable gloss on the university's reasons for advancing e-Learning. Also of interest is that whereas five of the eight academic staff viewed cost-cutting/efficiency as a reason for the university wishing to engage e-Learning, only two elite staff believed the rationale was linked to cost-cutting/efficiency.**

In effect, when you are *analysing* your empirical data, you are offering comment that you support with reference to your described data. Finally, findings from the Literature Review on the forces driving e-Learning can then be recalled with a view to synthesising theory with practice, adding another layer of understanding and depth:

> The Literature Review highlighted a number of forces driving e-Learning, with the main drivers reflecting a desire to improve *quality, flexibility* and *effectiveness* of educational delivery (with the latter referring to value for money), all within the context of the Government's target of achieving substantial increases in the student population (Dearing, 1997; Jung, 2000; Farrell, 2001; Epic, 2002; Department of Education and Skills, 2003). Only one member of staff interviewed (an academic) referred to enhanced quality as a driver, with the other staff, elite and academic, highlighting either flexibility of delivery (e.g. on and off campus) or cost-cutting/efficient use of resources as primary motivators for Inverclyde University adopting e-Learning.

The primary focus for introducing new technologies in an educational environment ought to be to enhance the student learning experience, i.e. improve the quality of educational delivery. Indeed, SHEFC (2003) warn against introducing e-Learning as a way to cut costs, reflecting that it can cost six times as much to develop an e-Learning programme than a traditional programme. Similarly, a report for the CIPD (Sloman and Rolph, 2003) echoed SHEFC's views by stating that if institutions believe that e-learning will automatically save them costs, then they will be disappointed.

It is interesting to note that in the interviews above, it was mainly the academic staff that saw the rationale behind e-Learning as a cost-cutting/efficiency exercise, not the elite staff. Perhaps this reflects the earlier point raised in the Literature Review that an e-Learning strategy is important, not only to convey an institution's direction in e-Learning, but also to explain the rationale behind its usage, and so remove potential misconceptions.

A student, who was carrying out research on the elderly and their views on social media (Facebook, Twitter, etc.), epitomised how to develop the findings chapter, progressively addressing the need to describe, analyse, and synthesise. The chapter on her findings had a very simple structure:

Chapter 4 Case Study Findings: Description, Analysis and Synthesis
4.1   Introduction
4.2   Findings
    4.2.1   Focus Group 1
    4.2.2   Focus Group 2
    4.2.3   Focus Group 3
4.3   Summary of Findings

The introduction to her findings recalled her research strategy and data collection techniques: a case study of three focus groups of elderly citizens living in a community centre. The reason for the study – to ascertain their views/uses of social media – was repeated for the benefit of the reader. She also provided some background information on the community centre. There was a sub-section for each focus group: Focus Group 1, Focus Group 2, and Focus Group 3. Within each of these sub-sections there was a further sub-division, reflecting the student's specific research objectives:

Theme 1   (Research Objective 1): clarification of the terms 'elderly' and 'social media').
Theme 2   (Research Objective 2): elderly use/views of social media.
Theme 3   (Research Objective 3): barriers to use of social media.

The mini-write-up of the Focus Group 1 results was, as expected, mainly descriptive with some attempt at basic analysis. When the student wrote about her Focus Group 2 results, she once again began by describing the focus group discussions against each of her research themes. However, she was now in a position, because she could compare her results against those of Focus Group 1, to offer a more meaningful analysis. When she got to Focus Group 3, she described her results and then compared and contrasted her findings against those from Focus Group 1 and Focus Group 2. By the time the student completed the mini write-up of the Focus Group 3 sub-section, she had quite comprehensively and cumulatively described and analysed her case study findings. She then addressed the matter of synthesising her empirical findings against her Literature Review findings, once again relative to her research themes/objectives. She also included a final sub-section in her write-up chapter in which she bullet-pointed her main findings. The type of academic activity that took place in this example is shown in Table 9.1.

**Table 9.1** Academic activity in student's write-up

| Section 4.2 Findings | Activity | Cumulative activity |
|---|---|---|
| 4.2.1 Focus Group 1 | Reporting of Group 1 results | → description |
| 4.2.2 Focus Group 2 | Reporting of Group 2 results | → description |
| | + | |
| | Comparison with Group 1 results | = analysis |
| 4.2.3 Focus Group 3 | Reporting of Group 3 results | → description |
| | + | |
| | Comparison with Groups 1 and 2 | = analysis |
| | + | |
| | Comparison with Literature Review | = synthesis |

The student could have taken a slightly different approach to writing up her results: she could have inserted a separate section for the comparison/contrast of her collective focus group results with her Literature Review (highlighted in bold for emphasis):

Chapter 4 Case Study Findings: Description, Analysis and Synthesis
4.1  Introduction
4.2  Findings
    4.2.1  Focus Group 1
    4.2.2  Focus Group 2
    4.2.3  Focus Group 3
**4.3  Synthesis of Findings with Literature Review**
4.4  Summary of Findings

Alternatively, she could have made the comparison with her Literature Review findings as she encountered the results from each focus group (Table 9.2).

**Table 9.2** Alternative approach to write-up

| Section 4.2 Findings | Main academic activity | Cumulative activity |
| --- | --- | --- |
| 4.2.1 Focus Group 1 | Reporting of Group 1 results | = description + analysis |
| | Comparison with Literature Review | = synthesis |
| 4.2.2 Focus Group 2 | Reporting of Group 2 results | = description + analysis |
| | Comparison with Group 1 results | = analysis |
| | Comparison with Literature Review | = synthesis |
| 4.2.3 Focus Group 3 | Reporting of Group 3 results | = description + analysis |
| | Comparison with Groups 1 and 2 | = analysis |
| | Comparison with Literature Review | = synthesis |

When to compare your empirical results with your Literature Review findings is a matter of personal choice.

As you can see, at each stage of description/analysis/synthesis, you are building up a thick account of your results. It is a tedious process but one that is necessary if you want to do justice to your research.

You can summarise your findings in a paragraph or two or provide a bullet-point list of key points. There is a technique to writing a summary, irrespective of the format you choose:

- Introduce your summary in one sentence (use the word 'summary' to make it clear that you are providing one). Example: 'In summary, the main points from this empirical work are as follows.'
- For each sub-section in your Findings, capture the main points in one or two sentences. However, if the main sub-sections are substantive, as in the e-Learning example, then introduce other summative sentences as you see fit. In the e-Learning example, there are five sub-sections in the Findings chapter: 4.1 Introduction, 4.2 Findings: Interviews, 4.3 Findings: Questionnaire, 4.4 Synthesis of Findings with Literature Review, and 4.5 Summary. You can ignore 4.1 Introduction and 4.5 Summary, giving three core sub-sections that need summarising: results from the interviews, results from the questionnaire, and comparison of both results against the Literature Review Findings.
- Conclude, in one sentence, with a final point. This is optional, particularly if your summary is in bullet-point format.

Alternatively, you can choose to leave your summary to your concluding chapter when you summarise all your work, mixing mini-summaries of your Literature Review and empirical work with concluding points for each research objective, as shown in the next chapter: Chapter 10, 'Concluding your dissertation'.

# Writing up the findings: art and performance-based dissertations

There is much in common between the write-up of the findings in a traditional dissertation and the write-up of the findings in an art or performance-based dissertation. You will still need a title, an introduction, something you will be writing about (in your case, something you have created), and a summary (though that can appear in your concluding chapter instead); and all with a keen eye on *describing* your results, *analysing* them for the reader (i.e. giving your view of the results), and achieving all-round *synthesis* by comparing and contrasting your empirical work with the results of your Contextual Review (or Literature Review). Let's assume that you completed a Contextual Review rather than a Literature Review, though it makes no difference in terms of the technique of writing up your findings. By this stage, you ought to have completed the first three stages of your dissertation and had a good bash at creating whatever it is you said you would create:

**Chapter 1: Introduction**
**Chapter 2: Contextual Review**
**Chapter 3: Research Methods**
Chapter 4: Findings
Chapter 5: Conclusions and Recommendations

A generic structure for your *findings* chapter, assuming it is Chapter 4, could be along the following lines:

Chapter 4 Findings
4.1   Introduction
4.2   Findings: Description and Analysis of Results
4.3   Synthesis of Findings with Contextual Review
4.4   Summary [Optional. Can be placed in Conclusion instead]

Let's assume further that the artefact you created was a woven sleeping bag (the one in Chapter 8) and that your findings will consist of two perspectives: your views on what you created and opinions expressed by others (irrespective of how they expressed them). We can now add more meaningful detail to your heading and sub-headings:

Chapter 4 Findings: Woven Sleeping Bag
4.1   Introduction
4.2   Critical reflection on woven sleeping bag: the artist's perspective
4.3   Critical reflection on woven sleeping bag: how others see it
4.4   Synthesis of Findings with Contextual Review
4.5   Summary [Optional. Can be placed in Conclusion instead]

Alternatively, you could omit sub-section 4.4 and instead reflect on your Contextual Review as you complete 4.2 and 4.3:

> Chapter 4 Findings: Woven Sleeping Bag
> 4.1   Introduction
> 4.2   Critical reflection on woven sleeping bag: the artist's perspective
> 4.3   Critical reflection on woven sleeping bag: how others see it
> 4.4   Summary [Optional. Can be placed in Conclusion instead]

Remember, there were two main tools (described in Chapter 8) to help you reflect: a *reflection-**in**-action* log used to record your thoughts and feelings at important moments during the actual creation process, and a *reflection-**on**-action* protocol (essentially a list of directed questions) to help you reflect on what you finally produced.

Let's now go through each of the stages for 'Chapter 4 Findings: Woven Sleeping Bag' and discuss the content to give you an idea of what you should be doing. You can remove the need for a formal structure, with numbered sub-headings, if you prefer, but you still need to cover the content.

**4.1 Introduction.** The Introduction to your *findings* chapter is straightforward. Keep it simple. Let the reader know what they can expect in this chapter and take the opportunity to remind the reader how you will go about describing, analysing, and synthesising your work, including views expressed by others about your work. Include any contextual information that you feel would better prepare the reader to understand this chapter. Here is an example Introduction:

> This chapter presents the findings of this practice-based research dissertation: reflections on the creation of a woven sleeping bag by the artist. This is in accordance with research objective 3 of this dissertation: 'To evaluate the created artefact stated in research objective 2 through the vehicle of critical reflection.'
>
> There will be a three-stage approach to this reflection. First of all, the artist will critically reflect on her created work of art; then views expressed by others will be presented and discussed; lastly, the views of the artist and others will be discussed in relation to the Contextual Review.
>
> The reflection-on-action protocol outlined in the Research Methods will be used in stages 1 and 2 above. A record of key events was kept during the creation process using the reflection-in-action log presented in the Research Methods chapter. A record of the logs is located in Appendix . . . The data from these logs will be used to aid reflection-on-action. A notebook of sketches made during the creation process (Appendix . . .), including photographs (Appendix . . .), will also be used to support reflection-on-action.
>
> Other opinions on the artefact were obtained via a focus group. The themes discussed are listed in Appendix . . .

**4.2 Critical reflection on woven sleeping bag: the artist's perspective**. If you are using the reflection-on-action protocol discussed in Chapter 8, 'Research Methods 2: Artist as researcher' (Table 8.3, reproduced below for your convenience) to direct your critical reflection, then answer each of the questions in turn, providing in-depth commentary. The questions that you ought to be addressing in this part of your findings are *italicised* for emphasis.

**Table 8.3**   Reflection-on-action protocol

| Artefact: < Title of artefact > | Reflection-on-action |
|---|---|
| *What were you trying to achieve?* | |
| *Did you achieve that?* | |
| *What are your views on what you achieved?* | |
| What do others think about your artefact? | |
| Where is there a similarity/difference of opinion? | |
| *What are your feelings?* | |
| *What key factors influenced the final product?* | |
| *On hindsight, what lessons have you learned? What was good? Bad? Is there anything you would do differently?* | |

If you completed reflection-in-action logs during the creation of your artefact to reflect on your actions, then you can also use the data from those logs as a record of your thoughts and feelings at the time. This data could be used to help answer some of the questions asked in the reflection-on-action protocol in Table 8.3. The reflection-in-action log is reproduced below for your convenience (Table 8.2). You can also refer to sketches and photographs of your work in your discussion.

**Table 8.2**   Reflection-in-action log

| Date | Reflection-in-action |
|---|---|
| What is the issue? | |
| What are you thinking? | |
| What are you feeling? | |
| What did you do? | |
| Why did you do that? | |

**Apply the process of *description-analysis***. First, describe the artefact and your views on it at a basic level, making use of reflection-in-action logs and/or photographs/sketches/notes, etc. where appropriate. Next, offer critical commentary on those descriptions. In other words, start with basic 'what' questions and add depth by providing 'why' answers: *What did I set out to do? Why did I want to do that? What did I eventually create? How did I create it? Why did I do it that way? Did I achieve what I set out to do? Why do I think that? Did my views change over time? Why?* And so on. It is the explanations that differentiate *critical* reflection from mundane recall. You can see that the list of questions in the reflection-on-action protocol is a starting point to critical reflection. Once you get in the groove, you will find yourself adding/changing the questions to fit your particular scenario. Build up another 'thick account' using the same process of *description-analysis* when you come to review how others see your work.

**4.3 Critical reflection on woven sleeping bag: how others see it.** Remind the reader how you captured the views of others. If you are using the action-on-reflection protocol (Table 8.3) as a vehicle for reflection, then it is the following two questions from that protocol that you need to answer:

- What do others think about your artefact?
- Where is there a similarity/difference of opinion?

Provide explanations and contextual information as you see fit. If the opinions expressed by others occurred during the creation of your artefact, then how did you respond to them? Did they have any influence on what you produced? You can also discuss the question *'What are you feeling?'* in relation to the views expressed by others.

Make sure that you still **apply the process of** description-analysis. Start with basic descriptive questions and then analyse the answers. *What do others think about your artefact? Do they offer an explanation of their thinking? What do you think about these views/explanations? Why do you think that? Where is there a difference of opinion about their views and yours? Why do you think that is?* And so on.

It is in the next sub-section where you can complete the tripartite cycle of *description-analysis-synthesis* when you compare/contrast all the views/ explanations with reference to your earlier Contextual Review.

**4.4 Synthesis of Findings with Contextual Review.** At this point, you reflect on your views on what you created and the views of others (if there are others) in relation to your Contextual Review. Two sets of questions you need to consider:

1 What are the *similarities* between what your Contextual Review was telling you, what you produced, your views on what you produced, and the views of others on what you produced?

2 What are the *differences* between what your Contextual Review was telling you, what you produced, your views on what you produced, and the views of others on what you produced?

There might be practical questions you want to consider. For example, perhaps the Contextual Review assumed the creation of your type of 'artefact' using professional resources supported by a team of seasoned experts, but that your design decisions had to be altered to fit time and resource constraints.

**Important reminder:** instead of leaving the synthesis to the last, as evidenced in this sub-section, you could refer to your Contextual Review when you describe and discuss your views and then when you describe and discuss how others see your work. As an artist, you may find that embedded approach more natural.

**4.5 Summary.** Here is an example summary for the woven sleeping bag example. Note that one sentence is used to introduce the summary ('In summary, the salient points from the findings of this practice-based research work – to replicate traditional Bedouin weaving in a modern setting – are as follows.'), and each core sub-section in the Findings chapter is summarised in turn. In the woven sleeping bag example, there were five sub-sections in the Findings chapter: 4.1 Introduction, 4.2 Critical reflection on woven sleeping bag: the artist's perspective, 4.3 Critical reflection on woven sleeping bag: how others see it, 4.4 Synthesis of Findings with Contextual Review, and 4.5 Summary. However, you can exclude 4.1 Introduction and 4.5 Summary, which leaves summative commentary required for three sub-sections: the artist's views on the completed woven sleeping bag, how others see it (in this case a focus group), and comparison of both sets of views against the Contextual Review.

In summary, the salient points from the findings of this practice-based research work – to replicate traditional Bedouin weaving in a modern setting – are as follows. The woven sleeping bag was successful on two levels: as a practical utility and as a work of art. The material and skills used remained true, although a tapestry loom was used instead of a traditional Bedouin ground loom, resulting in a travelling utility item that, with its strong horizontals and earthy red colours and traditional tassels, held aesthetic appeal. However, practical considerations, particularly time and weight constraints, forced changes to design. For example, the level of ornamentation had to be stripped back to exclude shells and coins. The focus group concentrated on design rather than function, praising the artistic skills used and the aesthetic results. Only once the nature of Bedouin weaving was explained did they begin to see the artefact as both an art piece and a utility item. As a result, the artist will ensure that a brief commentary on the practical purpose of Bedouin weaving will be displayed alongside the woven sleeping bag.

Alternatively, you can leave the summary to your concluding chapter where you have to tie everything together.

Everything you do in your dissertation leads to your concluding chapter – Conclusions and Recommendations – wherein you collate your work, underline your main conclusions and, based on these, make pertinent recommendations.

This means that your concluding chapter is a crucial one because it is where you capture the essence of your research output, achieving what supervisors call 'cyclical closure'. So do not dismiss your final chapter lightly: it is an integral part of your dissertation.

# Further reading

Barrett, E. and Bolt, B. (2010) *Practice as research: approaches to creative arts enquiry.* London: Routledge.

Flick, U. (2014) *An introduction to qualitative research.* 5th edn. London: Sage.

Gibbs, G. (2008) *Analysing qualitative data.* London: Sage.

Guest, G., MacQueen, K. M. and Namey, E. E. (2012) *Applied thematic analysis.* London: Sage.

Harding, J. (2013) *Qualitative data analysis from start to finish.* London: Sage.

Kershaw, B. and Nicholson, H. (2010) *Research methods in theatre and performance.* Edinburgh: Edinburgh University Press.

Macleod, K. and Holdridge, L. (2009) *Thinking through art: reflections on art as research.* London: Routledge.

Miles, M. B., Huberman, A. M. and Saldana, J. M. (2013) *Qualitative data analysis: a methods sourcebook.* 3rd edn. London: Sage.

Pallant, J. (2016) *SPSS survival manual: a step by step guide to data analysis using IBM SPSS.* 6th edn. Maidenhead: Open University Press.

Rapley, T. (2008) *Doing conversation, discourse and document analysis.* London: Sage.

Sapsford, R. and Judd, V. (2006) *Data collection and analysis.* 2nd edn. London: Sage.

Silverman, D. (2015) *Interpreting qualitative data.* 5th edn. London: Sage.

Smith, H. and Dean, R. T. (2009) *Practice-led research, research-led practice in the creative arts.* Edinburgh: Edinburgh University Press.

## Summary of key points

- Create an appropriate chapter heading identifying the nature of your research: 'Case Study Findings: Description, Analysis and Synthesis' or 'Survey Findings: Description, Analysis and Synthesis' or 'Findings: Woven Sleeping Bag' or 'Findings: Musical Score', etc.
- Write a brief introduction. Identify the content of your chapter and describe how you will analyse your findings. Include useful information to place your findings in context.
- If engaged in writing a traditional dissertation: present your empirical data in an incremental way, using the process of *description-analysis-synthesis*, to achieve a rich picture.
- *Description* is a simple process, entailing the basic reporting and chronicling of empirical results (who said what, etc.).
- *Analysis* is intelligent interpretation of the aforementioned descriptions.
- *Synthesis* occurs when you compare and contrast your empirical findings against your Literature Review findings, or their equivalent (e.g. Contextual Review).
- If engaged in writing a practice-based dissertation where an art form of some kind is created: give your views on your 'artefact', reflect on how others see it (if there are others), and place both perspectives in relation to your Contextual Review (or Literature Review), making use of a reflection-on-action protocol and reflection-in-action logs as appropriate. The process of building up a rich picture of your findings through *description-analysis-synthesis* still applies.
- A summary of your findings requires summative commentary on each core sub-section, either in the form of a single paragraph or a bullet-point list.

# Chapter **10**

# Concluding your dissertation

> • *What's in a Conclusion?* • *Research objectives: summary of findings and conclusions* • *Recommendations* • *Contribution to knowledge* • *Self-reflection* • *Summary of key points*

This chapter demonstrates, through example, the art of achieving *cyclical closure* in your dissertation.

## What's in a Conclusion?

*Cyclical closure* is where you metaphorically wrap up your work in a nice big bow. There is a technique to achieving cyclical closure, which this chapter will now take you through.

By this stage, you are probably mentally exhausted and sick of the sight of your dissertation. Besides, you may have exams to concentrate on or holidays to arrange or employment opportunities to explore. Reject the temptation, however appealing, to scribble down a quick ending to allow you to submit your work and finally see the back of it. It is at this stage when you need to make a final push and finish with a flourish. If your concluding chapter is epitomised by unstructured and ill-disciplined rambling, then you will leave your dissertation marker with the clear impression that you lacked the necessary skills to compose an acceptable Conclusion and/or you lost interest in your own work. A Conclusion is the final big piece of the dissertation jigsaw and your supervisor/marker is expecting it to contain certain things.

So, what is in a Conclusion? Quite a lot, actually! Here is what is expected, as a minimum, in your Conclusion:

- Research Objectives: Summary of Findings and Conclusions;
- Recommendations.

If you omit either of these elements, you are missing out on potential marks. If, in the Conclusion, a student has not summarised the work or arrived at an informed conclusion or outlined a way forward, then substantial marks will be lost. So include these things and avoid throwing away marks. Doing so shows discipline and a structured mind, i.e. a research-based approach to rounding off your dissertation.

One other point: for most postgraduate dissertations, you are not expected to contribute *new knowledge*, so you can normally omit this requirement. The exception is the PhD. For PhD students (a route you may wish to take after your Master's), an acceptable structure for a Conclusion could be:

- Research Objectives: Summary of Findings and Conclusions;
- Recommendations;
- Contribution to knowledge.

Additionally, regardless of the type and level of dissertation, inserting a sub-section on self-reflection adds a little something different to a dissertation. As with most chapters in your dissertation, you should also begin with a short introduction. A solid structure for a dissertation might look like this:

Introduction
Research Objectives: Summary of Findings and Conclusions
Recommendations
[Contribution to knowledge – optional]
Self-reflection

Although the sub-section in square brackets – *Contribution to knowledge* – is directed at those students studying for a PhD, it may be that, even as a Master's student, you have indeed produced new knowledge, in which case by all means include a sub-section on 'Contribution to knowledge', but be warned, this is a rare event for non-PhD student work.

If you did not cover the limitations of your work in your Research Methods chapter, then you can include it here, giving you a comprehensive concluding chapter (see Figure 10.1), resulting in:

Introduction
Research Objectives: Summary of Findings and Conclusions
Recommendations
[Contribution to knowledge – optional]
Limitations
Self-reflection

Alternatively, you can embed limitations in either sub-section 'Research Objectives: Summary of Findings and Conclusions' or sub-section 'Recommendations'. It is also acceptable to combine some of the above sub-sections

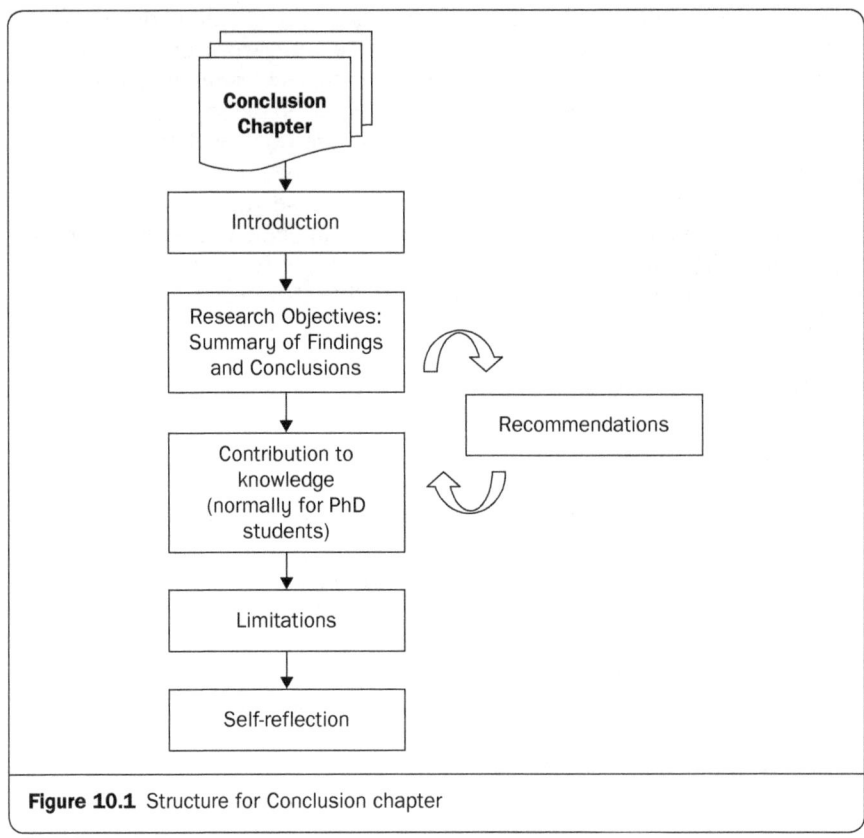

**Figure 10.1** Structure for Conclusion chapter

(e.g. 'Findings and Conclusions/Recommendations', 'Contribution to Knowledge and Self-Reflection'), particularly if you are running close to your dissertation word limit. Very often it is just a matter of personal choice. Advice is now offered on how to write up each of these sub-sections. The sub-section 'Limitations' was covered in the Research Methods chapter, so will not be covered here in any great depth.

## Research objectives: summary of findings and conclusions

Prior to summarising your findings, it is good practice to present a brief introduction at the start of your Conclusion, before your first sub-section 'Research Objectives: Summary of Findings and Conclusions', reminding the reader of your initial research objectives, and setting out what you intend to cover in your Conclusion chapter. Keep things simple, using matter-of-fact language. To begin with, remind the reader of your overall research aim, together with the individual objectives that you set out to meet in order to achieve your overall research aim: 'The overall aim of this research was to advance an understanding of . . . The specific research objectives were . . .'. Then list your objectives. For example:

---

The overall aim of this research was to advance an understanding of e-Learning in the university environment, particularly in relation to academic staff preparation issues. The specific research objectives were, within the context of higher education, to:

1 *Identify* the forces driving e-Learning and the barriers to the successful delivery of e-Learning programmes.
2 *Evaluate critically* models and frameworks relevant to supporting academic staff in coping with e-Learning.
3 Explore staff stakeholder views and practices related to e-Learning preparation, including drivers and barriers to e-Learning.
4 *Formulate* recommendations on staff preparation issues.

---

Next, state the sub-sections that your Conclusion will cover. You are not expected to *discuss* the actual content of these sub-sections at this stage. Just let the reader know what they are, for example:

> This concluding chapter will revisit the research objectives above, summarise the findings of this research work, and offer specific conclusions in relation to each stated research objective. Recommendations for future research will be outlined. Importantly, the contribution of this research to the development of e-Learning will be clarified. Additionally, a section reflecting on the research process that has been undertaken is included. By adopting this rounded approach the researcher aims to achieve cyclical closure.

The sub-section 'Research Objectives: Summary of Findings and Conclusions' is a simple matter. All that is required is that you answer two straightforward questions:

1 As a result of your Literature/Contextual Review (or equivalent) *and* empirical research (if you did both), what did you find out in relation to your individual research objectives?
2 What conclusions have you come to?

You do not need to go through all the swirling and interlinking analysis that you went through in the Literature/Contextual Review and write-up of your data collection. No, at this stage of your dissertation you can put aside your debating skills. Information rather than persuasion is the goal of your concluding chapter: you are *informing* – rather than *persuading* – the reader about your summary findings, your conclusions, your research limitations, and your recommendations.

In the sub-section 'Research Objectives: Summary of Findings and Conclusions', you are, in effect, writing a summary of the work you carried out to fulfil each of your research objectives; and at the end of each of these summaries you are coming to some sort of conclusion about your work. Think of 'conclusions' as key points you wish to make about the findings **for each of your research objectives**. So, when you write about what you found out for your first research objective, you then make a *key point* that you think captures what your findings are telling you in relation to that research objective. You then approach your other research objectives in the same way: summarise your findings for each objective, ending each time with a key point. Your structure for the sub-section 'Research Objectives: Summary of Findings and Conclusions' could take the following shape ('→ Summary of Findings' and '→ Conclusion' are not sub-headings, they are merely indicating the content under the headings '**Research Objective 1**', etc.):

**Research Objective 1**
→ Summary of Findings
→ Conclusion

**Research Objective 2**
→ Summary of Findings
→ Conclusion

**Research Objective 3**
→ Summary of Findings
→ Conclusion
Etc.

For example, if you were the researcher involved in the e-Learning example, did you 'identify the forces driving e-Learning and barriers to the successful delivery of e-Learning programmes' (objective 1) and, if so, what did you find out from your Literature Review and your empirical work? What 'models and framework relevant to supporting academic staff in coping with e-Learning' (objective 2) did you examine and what were your findings? Similarly, what were the 'staff stakeholder views and practices related to e-Learning' (objective 3)? If you have a research objective that is phrased in terms of making recommendations as a result of your work, as in objective 4 of the e-Learning example ('formulate recommendations on staff preparation issues'), then this objective would be addressed when you get to the Recommendations sub-section within your Conclusion chapter.

As described above, a convenient way to tackle your summary is to create separate headings in your 'Research Objectives: Summary of Findings and Conclusions' chapter that cover each of your individual research objectives, and under each heading summarise what you found out related to that research objective, ending with a relevant conclusion. Such a structure, related to the e-Learning example, might look like this:

5   CONCLUSION
(brief intro)

   5.1   Research Objectives: Summary of Findings and Conclusions

      5.1.1   Research Objective 1: e-Learning Drivers and Barriers
              → Summary
              → Conclusion

      5.1.2   Research Objective 2: Models and Frameworks
              → Summary
              → Conclusion

      5.1.3   Research Objective 3: Staff Stakeholder Views and Practices
              → Summary
              → Conclusion

Fleshing out research objective 1 above, to illustrate the structure in practice:

### 5.1.1 Research Objective 1: e-Learning Drivers and Barriers

The literature identified the main reasons why universities have become involved in e-Learning:

* external pressures from government to accommodate greater student numbers;
* wider access;
* flexible delivery;
* competition;
* access to global markets;
* prudent use of resources;
* assumed inherent benefits to staff and students (enhancing the educational environment).

Yet, the empirical study showed that, in practice, the picture was not so clear-cut. Those in charge of shaping e-Learning in an institution (elite staff) may not have a firm collective view of why they are introducing e-Learning, other than to be viewed as 'modern' by potential students and be different from their competitors; and that academic staff may hold an erroneous view of why their institution is pushing e-Learning (as a cost-cutting exercise, a view the elite staff were at pains to dismiss). Such misunderstandings may be complicated further by imperatives to integrate e-Learning into teaching environments without the rationale being discussed with, or explained to, academic staff, as in this case study.

Continuing with . . .

> In the case study, the elite staff held that the main benefit of e-Learning to academic staff was the opportunity for them to become reflective practitioners, whereas academic staff either did not see any benefits for them or were concerned or cautious. Both sets of staff identified similar benefits of e-Learning to students (flexible access), but academic staff were not convinced that these benefits would materialise. In terms of drivers for, and benefits of, e-Learning, it is clear that a major discrepancy can occur between theory and practice, and between different stakeholders, with elite stakeholders having a positive view of the impact of e-Learning, and those who have to implement e-Learning, academic staff, having a cynical view of elite stakeholder intentions.

Concluding with:

> **[Conclusion 1]**
> **A lack of communication is at the heart of much of the confused picture for the reason behind why an institution wishes to integrate e-Learning into their environment and the perceived benefits to the different stakeholders.**

Followed by your findings on the barriers to e-Learning . . .

> The Literature Review highlighted many barriers that can impede e-Learning initiatives, including fear of high costly failure, inadequate IT infrastructure, opposition to distance learning through globalisation, job insecurity, intellectual property rights, and perceived poor progression rates, but the main barrier identified in the literature was a lack of pedagogical training for academic staff.

> In the case study, the main barriers hindering academic staff becoming involved in e-Learning were inadequate training on e-learning *and* lack of time. Although the academic staff under study contributed to a blended e-Learning environment, staff knowledge and expertise depended on e-nthusiasts, rather than a coherent training programme. Other discouraging factors included: the compulsory manner in which e-Learning was implemented, suspicion over management intentions, and lack of confidence in IT support. However, a crucial factor in preventing staff enthusiasm for, and involvement in, e-learning was the expectation that staff would engage in e-learning initiatives in parallel with mainstream duties – teaching, marking, supervision, research, attending committees, etc. – without a reduction in their workload.

Concluding with:

> **[Conclusion 2]**
> **The two main barriers hindering academic staff in meaningful and voluntary involvement in e-Learning programmes are a lack of**

**pedagogical training on e-Learning and a lack of time to learn
about e-Learning (and prepare associated teaching material).**

You then repeat the above process for each of your research objectives: summarise your Literature Review findings and your empirical research, ending, in
each case, with a conclusion (or conclusions, as in the above example). You
can, if you wish, provide an additional (overarching) summary statement, a
final paragraph in your sub-section 'Research Findings: Summary of Findings
and Conclusions' that looks at your work in the round. Or you may introduce an
unexpected conclusion, something that you did not set out to study but which
became apparent through your research:

> There is one other, unexpected, conclusion that this research work has
> uncovered, and that is that **although there is no agreed definition of
> e-Learning among e-Learning gurus, nonetheless the absence of
> one at a local, institutional level is a hindrance to meaningful
> discussion of e-Learning itself.** The Literature Review showed that
> e-Learning definitions varied widely, that there was no consistent defin-
> ition and that some prominent figures in e-Learning concluded that any
> attempt to provide an absolute definition was an impossible task ('herd-
> ing cats', 'comparing apples to oranges', etc.). This may be true but during
> the case study staff were repeatedly peppering their responses with
> phrases such as 'well, depends on what you mean by e-Learning'. This
> suggests that a lack of a definition of e-Learning may present an initial
> barrier to progressing discussions about e-Learning, and that definitions
> are not abstract, academic activities unrelated to practical concerns. It
> may not be important as to the actual definition of e-Learning that an
> institution decides upon, but that one is required is evidenced from above.

Or you may take the occasion to remind the reader that your research, although
solid, has some limitations and that your work has to be placed in this context:

> The conclusions have to be viewed in terms of a caveat. The conclusions
> are based on an extensive review of related literature and a case study,
> which means that the conclusions are linked to these two sources only.
> One is not generalising that what was concluded in this research automat-
> ically applies to all other institutions in higher education. Instead, this
> research is appealing to the concept of *relatability*: that what was
> researched in this study will be of interest to other researchers and insti-
> tutions interested in e-Learning and that it will add, incrementally, to the
> patchwork of research in e-Learning.

Ending with . . .

> Another limitation is that student perspectives on e-Learning have not
> been explored. Such empirical data would have added further richness to
> the study, but this would have compromised the focus of the research and

perhaps made the burden of work unmanageable (the decision to include so many elite staff, although of enormous benefit to the study, did dramatically increase the workload).

# Recommendations

Normally your supervisor will want to know what recommendations you are making as a result of your research work. It would be very odd indeed if you finished your dissertation and you offered the reader no advice on what you think should happen next, so much so that you might be in danger of losing marks. Having said that, some institutions do not require their dissertation students to make recommendations in relation to their research findings, so check with your institution's regulations and your supervisor on whether or not you are required to do so.

---

**!** **A common mistake by students**

A common mistake by students is to hide their recommendations by embedding them in a sentence or two within an obscure paragraph. If the marker has to look hard to find them, then you are at risk of, once again, losing marks. Either have a full sub-section in your Conclusion headed 'Recommendations' or group together an obvious collection of paragraphs dealing with the implications of your completed research. Remember, though, if one of your research objectives referred explicitly to making recommendations, as in objective 4 of the e-Learning example case study ('Formulate recommendations on staff preparation issues'), then it is best that you devote a properly headed sub-section to your recommendations.

---

There are two types of recommendations that you can make: (1) recommendations specific to the evidence presented in your study, and (2) suggestions for future research. If your dissertation was on how governments make the decision to go to war with other countries and that your work concluded – based on a case study of the UK and the 2003 invasion of Iraq – that there was scant regard both to democratic process and the need for concrete evidence of the case for war, then you might recommend that, in the future, procedures are in place to ensure Parliament has a crucial role to play before war is declared and that part of that process necessarily involves the independent collection and analysis of any data related to such a decision. In terms of future research, you might propose that other researchers examine why some countries, under the same pressures, decide not to go to war.

One way to deal with your recommendations is to link them to your previous conclusions (which in turn were linked to each of your specific research objectives). For example, if one wished to make recommendations based on the e-Learning case study, then one would look to see what conclusions were made for each of the research objectives, and then write recommendations specific to those individual research objective conclusions. If you adopt this approach, make sure that you remind the reader what your conclusions were so that they do not have to keep flipping back over your dissertation to find them. Looking at the conclusion for objective 1 of the e-Learning example case study, related recommendations could develop as follows:

> Conclusion 1 stated that **a lack of communication is at the heart of much of the confused picture for the reason behind why an institution wishes to integrate e-Learning into their environment and the perceived benefits to the different stakeholders.** From Conclusion 1, the first recommendation to be made is that elite staff should be aware of why they are introducing e-Learning, the external factors influencing their university's decision to engage in e-Learning, the benefits to staff and students, and, importantly, the need to ensure that the e-Learning strategy is clear, justified (in terms of rationale), and communicated to those charged with integrating e-Learning into the teaching and learning environment, i.e. academic staff.

Also, try to explain the benefits of your recommendation(s). Don't just present the reader with an unexplained recommendation (or list), unless you feel that what you are recommending is blatantly obvious and requires no explanation. Explaining the above recommendation:

> This recommendation would have a number of benefits. First, elite staff themselves would understand collectively why e-Learning is important to the university and what the benefits are to the institution as a whole, as well as to staff and students, and so they would be in a much better position to win staff 'buy-in'. Communicating the rationale – whatever it turns out to be – to academic staff would remove any misunderstandings of university intentions and may help avoid cynical guesswork. Further, a university's e-Learning strategy should be clearly headed and be easy to find (whether it be on a website, or contained in university strategic planning documents) and not buried under obscure objectives such as, for example, 'Campus Development'. In effect, e-Learning strategy, rationale, and benefits should be visible and communicated to management and teaching staff.

You are entitled to group recommendations together, as follows:

> From conclusion 2, it is recommended that to encourage staff to become involved in e-Learning, a 'reward' in the form of time to prepare for e-Learning, both in terms of studying e-Learning and preparing e-Learning material, is made available. And, importantly, from Conclusions 2 and 3 – related to shortfalls in pedagogical training – it is recommended that

academic staff receive meaningful pedagogical training, in a structured way, that is aimed specifically at preparing academic staff for integrating e-Learning into their teaching, covering the following topics: benefits of e-Learning, practical advice on the changing role of staff and students, including supporting infrastructures and guidance on what works and what does not.

Where possible, try and show your recommendations diagrammatically. And do not neglect to explain your diagram (a common failing by students). For example:

The recommendations are represented in diagrammatic form in Figure 10.2. This diagram conveys the essence of the conclusions and recommendations, underlining that each of the recommendations interconnect to provide a sensible framework which universities can adopt to prepare their academic staff for e-Learning. First, a university should develop its e-Learning strategy. This strategy should be readily accessible to staff, supported by a local definition of the term e-Learning, details of the approach to be adopted (e.g. voluntary, blended, etc.), including a rationale of why the university wishes to become involved in e-Learning. Next, this strategy should be communicated to all elite staff with a part to play in shaping the direction of e-Learning. Then, the strategy should be communicated to academic staff. Following that, academic staff should receive training on e-Learning. This research showed that two types of training were necessary to prepare academic staff for e-Learning: technical training (to cope with the software platform to be used, as well as to cover necessary computer skills), and training on e-Learning pedagogy. There was a great deal of evidence to show that technical training predominated and that pedagogical training to help staff prepare for e-Learning was largely omitted. Staff should also be given time to engage in e-Learning activities.

The above recommendations are examples of the first type of recommendation, ones that originate from your specific research findings. Remember that you can also make more general recommendations, based on possible avenues for future research. To help you handle this type of recommendation, ask yourself the question: 'If I had to recommend to someone else – another student – who was interested in picking up where I left off, how would I advise that student on how to progress my work?' You are really asking yourself to reflect on the second type of recommendation: recommendation(s) for future research. You do not need to go into convoluted detail for this type of recommendation, just a sentence or two might suffice (e.g. 'Although thorough research has been conducted for this dissertation, there are other related areas of study that could aid our understanding of cybercrime [if that was your dissertation area]. For example, further research could focus on areas that were touched on only briefly in this dissertation, such as legislative or technological developments in the context of cybercrime . . .').

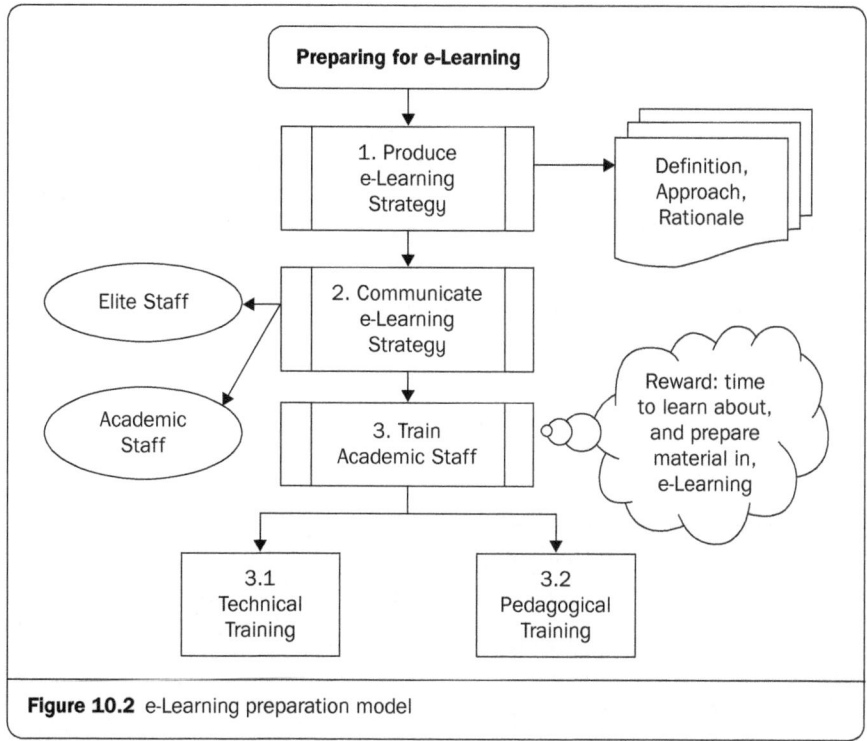

**Figure 10.2** e-Learning preparation model

Finally, you might want to offer advice on how to implement your specific recommendations (a common issue at a viva):

Another recommendation concerns the implementation of the proposed e-Learning preparation model. The culture of an organisation can impact on staff development and on how a model can be received. For example, this study illustrated that some teaching staff were resistant to change, others were amenable, whereas others, still, were cynical but interested in e-Learning. Similarly, senior staff exhibited different types of traits towards staff development: for example, some held the view that it was part of the tutor's job to engage in e-Learning and that a tutor should not be rewarded for doing so, while others believed that staff should be rewarded. These traits, or *leanings*, were reflected throughout a number of themes, from views on e-Learning strategy, to the benefits of e-Learning, through to motivational issues, perhaps demonstrating different cultural stances by the various stakeholders. To offer an improved chance of the model being adopted successfully, it would be fruitful to revisit the university under study and, applying a framework of organisational behaviour, try and determine the detail of the various cultures in operation at Inverclyde University. A formal understanding of the culture (or cultures) of an institution through the deliberate mapping of cultural traits against a credible behavioural framework would allow the proposed model to be implemented in a way that was appropriate to different cultures within a university.

To reflect the importance of making recommendations in a Master's dissertation, students often call their final chapter 'Conclusions and Recommendations', rather than simply 'Conclusions'. Regardless of the title of your concluding chapter, central to a praiseworthy sub-section on recommendations are a number of elements, *viz.*:

- Base your recommendations on your research conclusions.
- Explain your recommendations.
- Present them diagrammatically, where convenient.
- Offer advice on how to implement your recommendations.

Figure 10.3 may help you to remember these salient points.

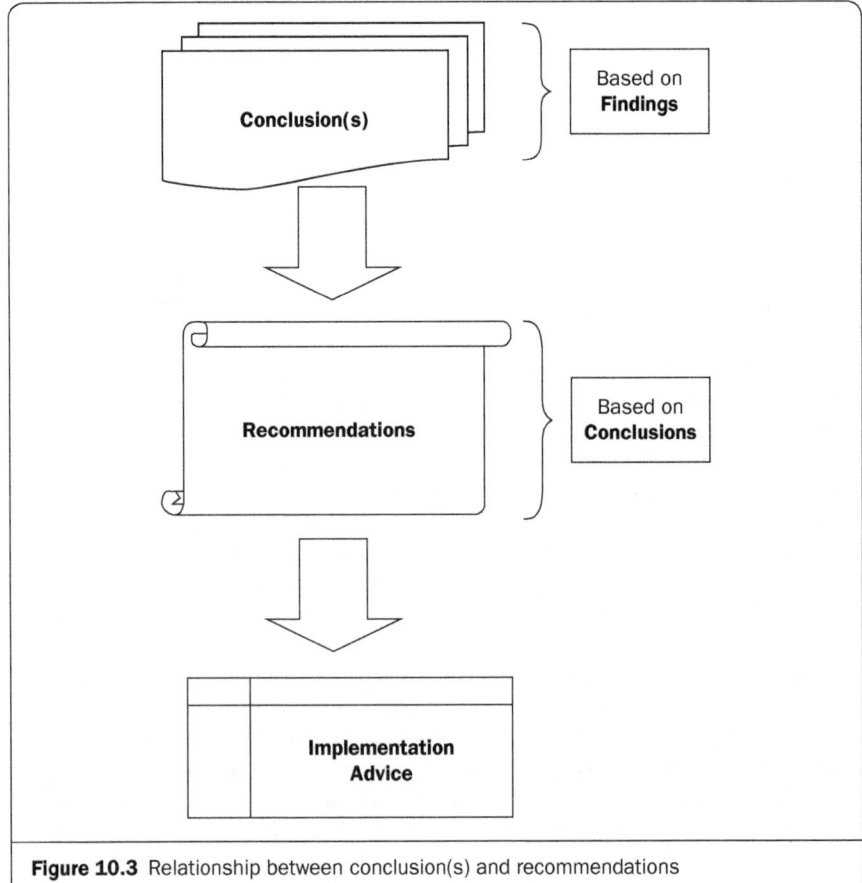

**Figure 10.3** Relationship between conclusion(s) and recommendations

**A common mistake by students**

A common mistake by students is to produce recommendations 'out of the blue', i.e. recommendations that have no or little obvious link to the research conclusions. If you follow the aforementioned advice, you should avoid that mistake.

# Contribution to knowledge

It is unusual for MSc./M.Litt./MPhil. postgraduate students to be challenged on how their work has *contributed to new knowledge*. Usually such a requirement is reserved for a special type of postgraduate dissertation: the PhD. If you are studying for a PhD, then you will need to confront the question of how your research has enhanced existing knowledge. If you are studying for a Master's but wish to progress your work to PhD level, or if you believe that your Master's work is exceptional, then you should understand how to answer the question: 'So, what's different about your work?' One way to tackle this question is to have a sub-section in the concluding chapter devoted to how your work has contributed to the field of x, y or z. 'Contribution to knowledge' is as good a title as any but how do you deal with this issue?

Let us look at what a 'contribution to knowledge' means. Implicit is the idea that you are required to make an *original* contribution to knowledge, that there is something unique about aspects of your work, either what you studied, or how you researched something, or the specific problems that you addressed, or the angle from which you approached a subject area, or the light that you have shed on a rarely researched subject, and so on. Doing the same research, in the same way, and coming to the same conclusions as others are unlikely to be viewed as making a (original) contribution to knowledge.

However, it is almost impossible to produce *completely* unique research. In some way, however distant, original work owes much to what has gone before. Even Albert Einstein's work on relativity was built on the shoulders of giants. Do not panic that you might be expected to invent a new branch of physics or emerge with the meaning of life. Here lies the clue to managing your approach to writing about your contribution to knowledge: articulate how your research compares and contrasts with research done by others in your field, eliciting what is *different* about your work.

Be bold. Do not try and avoid the issue of your contribution. Be confident. Meet the matter head on: 'How has this research work contributed to knowledge? In terms of . . .'. There are two areas where you can look for an original contribution to knowledge: in your Literature/Contextual Review and in your empirical research. For example, if in your Literature/Contextual Review you explored a facet of an important subject area that had hitherto been neglected or treated superficially, or erroneously, and your detailed study of secondary sources revealed new insights, then you can claim to have made an original contribution to knowledge. In which case, say so:

> The review of literature made it clear that e-Learning usage is fragmentary in the world of education and that there is an acute lack of in-depth research of e-Learning practices. This study has redressed that anomaly in a number of valuable ways. Firstly, the review of literature provides a critical investigation of e-Learning theory pertinent to institutions, dovetailing into a critique of guidelines and frameworks as they relate to preparing academic staff for e-Learning. Knowledge derived from this review of literature can educate and further inform debate on the drivers and barriers to becoming involved in e-Learning (too often, literature uncritically lists drivers and barriers, failing to give a more rounded, research-based picture). Secondly, . . .

Your main contribution to knowledge, however, probably lies in your empirical work. It is less common, although not unheard of, for the Literature/Contextual Review to be the principal source of an original contribution. If your experiment/survey/case study/action research/etc., is unique, then you could be making an original contribution to knowledge. Even if you do the same type of study as someone else, you still might be making an original contribution to knowledge. For example, suppose that a previous researcher implemented a survey looking at student debt. Suppose further, that the study was done in the USA. You use the same, or very similar, survey questions, but your target population is UK students. Your work compares and contrasts the two sets of results, producing new knowledge. At a simple level, even if you think up, for example, a case study from scratch, designing your own questions and selecting a specific target population, then it is statistically unlikely that someone else has carried out the *exact* same study as you. So, if your empirical work is unique, then say why that is the case, as in the following example:

> The empirical research work is unique: no other researcher has carried out a study of such depth within Inverclyde University, interviewing elite staff on strategic e-Learning issues and academic staff on e-Learning preparation, including issues surrounding drivers and barriers to e-Learning. The lack of empirical data to support research theory was recognised as a particular failing in much of the current e-Learning literature. In that respect, this research offers an insight into the views of two important university stakeholder groups on e-Learning that other institutions can relate to and learn from, allowing practice to be fed back into theory. The richness of material provided is, without doubt, fascinating. The themes addressed, in terms of their collectivity, are unique in one case study in e-Learning: e-Learning strategy, drivers, barriers, preparation, IT infrastructure, academic staff motivation, and future directions. The findings help in understanding issues related to these themes, and provide other researchers with a unique spotlight on two different types of stakeholders within an institution.

One other source of evidence to support your 'contribution to knowledge', other than your Literature/Contextual Review and your actual practical work, can be found in your recommendations. It is likely that your recommendations contain proposals that are different in some respects from what has been produced before. If, for example, you have developed some sort of model or paradigm, which you believe, if implemented, can resolve a problem that you identified earlier, then your model/paradigm itself becomes part of your original contribution to knowledge. Imagine that in the e-Learning case study example, two models were produced in the Recommendations sub-section: a Pedagogical Training Framework (on training content) as well as an e-Learning Preparation Model (outlining strategy). These models could be argued as making an important contribution to knowledge:

> The specific e-Learning models produced at the end of this research – the *e-Learning Preparation Model* and the *Pedagogical Training Framework* – encapsulate what needs to be done to encourage academic staff to engage meaningfully with e-Learning initiatives, ranging from the need to develop an e-Learning strategy that is clear, defines e-Learning, and justifies the rationale for introducing e-Learning and the approach adopted, to the communication of this strategy to elite staff and academic staff, and the crucial importance of pedagogical training on specific areas. In effect, a collective framework has been created that is specifically devoted to e-Learning preparation and based on in-depth research. This has been a highly successful piece of research with many points of learning for both theory into practice and practice into theory, resulting in a significant contribution to knowledge.

An obvious way to show your contribution to knowledge is to identify what other researchers have done and how your work builds on theirs; but importantly in what respects your work differs:

> How has this research made a contribution to knowledge? To date, the work produced by other researchers has concentrated on ... This research, on the other hand, differs in the following respects ... The importance of this work, compared to what has been produced hitherto, lies in ...

It would also be worthwhile, prior to your viva (if you are subject to one), to attend a conference – or if you cannot afford that, then try and get hold of the conference proceedings – and obtain up-to-date evidence that continues to offer support on the need for your research. For example:

> At the recent Ed-Media 2004 Conference (attended by this researcher), Zellweger (2004, p. 161) complained that anecdotal advice can be found on how to use e-Learning in universities but that 'so far there is a lack of systematized scientific knowledge'. The lack of methodical research into

e-Learning in Higher Education continues to this day to be an area of concern, but this research study, by adopting a highly disciplined and structured research-based approach to acquiring knowledge on e-Learning, has made an important and unique contribution, as discussed above, to an understanding of e-Learning in Higher Education. As more researchers adopt a research-based approach to e-Learning, then less will we hear the sentiments expressed by concerned researchers such as Zellweger.

Finally, if you have published aspects of your research in journals or conference proceedings, then that in itself can support the claim that you are making a contribution to knowledge:

> Furthermore, research publications produced as a result of this research have contributed to the field of e-Learning in that the opportunity to publish and discuss e-Learning issues with one's peers has not only engendered fruitful debate but also allowed other researchers to have access to research deemed by conference committees as making a contribution to the e-Learning academic community. These publications are listed below . . .

As you can see, the question of how to cope with writing about your contribution to knowledge is not as problematic as it first appears. Basically, look to see what aspects of your Literature/Contextual Review are unique, or different, from what others have done; look at how your empirical work contributes to knowledge; and look to your recommendations in terms of making a contribution. In short, look at what other research has been done in your field and how your contribution differs, and if you have publications to boast of, then your work has already achieved academic recognition!

# Self-reflection

*Self-reflection* is a form of *reflection-on-action* (see Chapter 8). Reflection-on-action is about your views on something specific you did but it can also take on board views expressed by others. With self-reflection, the focus is on you, and not just in respect of something you created or developed: it encompasses a reflection, in this context, on the dissertation journey.

How do you reflect upon an activity that has become an integral part of your life? Throughout the life-cycle of your dissertation, from submitting your proposal to writing your concluding chapter, a wide range of conflicting emotions have been experienced: the excitement of starting a large research project; angst at trying to get a handle on your subject area; delight at reading the work of other, more experienced, researchers; confusion over the plethora of material; frustration at following blind leads; satisfaction in structuring one's own thoughts and arguments; the pain of having to remove work that is, on hindsight, not relevant; and relief in completing the concluding chapter. Panic, pride, tedium, exhilaration . . . there are many words that could be used in equal measure to convey the feelings that you will have experienced in undertaking your dissertation. Of more practical benefit may be the need to reflect on lessons learned.

Placing a sub-section in your concluding chapter entitled 'Self-Reflection' lets the examiner see that although you did the dissertation because it was an academic requirement, it was also a learning process for you. If you are running close to your word-limit, and the sub-section on self-reflection is not compulsory, then you can be clever and include it as an appendix (anything in an appendix is not normally included in the word-count). Make sure that you let the reader know where to find your self-reflection (e.g. 'Appendix H Self-Reflection contains a personal narrative on the dissertation journey, including lessons learned').

Try and recall how you overcame difficulties at the various stages of your project. If you have kept a diary, then that will make this sub-section easier to complete. When you are mulling back over the stages of your dissertation, you could focus on two questions: 'What advice would you give to other students?' and 'If you had to do it again, what would you do differently, if anything?'

Be honest (but fair to yourself and others), or there is no point in the exercise. For instance, if your work started badly then say so, explaining why:

> This research work started badly. The (first) research topic was e-Learning and Knowledge Management, with a vague idea of some sort of connection between the two, and an ill-defined view that managing knowledge in e-Learning was problematic. A full chapter was then written, comparing how Knowledge Management researchers define knowledge against how philosophers down the ages (such as Descartes and Locke) defined knowledge. However, the overall area of study lacked adequate focus and was approached with little enthusiasm. As a result, this work was abandoned and a new research topic started from scratch.

And do not forget to offer advice to future students:

> The first piece of advice would be to select a topic that genuinely interests you. This researcher's academic interests have deep roots in education and e-Learning is an area that will have a huge impact on teaching. Bringing together an interest in teaching with research on e-Learning was an exciting prospect. Accordingly, the research focus was changed to accommodate a genuine interest in teaching, rather than what seemed clever and innovative.

The above scenario highlights a common student scenario: an initial failure to find a research topic. Another big problem area for students tends to be the chapter on research methods. For many students, it is such a difficult part of the dissertation to comprehend yet it is so pivotal to their empirical work.

Sometimes the problem lies in the concepts used in the teaching of research methods, where terms such as 'phenomenology', 'positivism', 'ontological', etc., are so abstract that they can confuse students; or perhaps there is a problem deciding whether or not the approach you are taking to collect and analyse your data is indeed the right one for your research, as discussed below:

> The Research Methods chapter was, initially, unbalanced in that it was biased towards providing details on how the research would be implemented with little attempt at justifying the choices made. There needs to be a balance, but in the initial Research Methods chapter this was missing. Sometimes the researcher can be too close to their work and so fail to notice obvious deficiencies. Listen to your supervisor. A trick suggested, which worked, was to have a few days break, return to the work, but select a page at random and try to determine how one could justify what was written, and work backwards to see if indeed that is how you approached the discussion related to the selected text. Not all the research work relates to justification of arguments, but nevertheless such an exercise does prove interesting, if only to improve the flow of what is written.

It is good to warn students that research is not a smooth, seamless activity, that things can and do go wrong:

> The case study required careful planning, not only in working out the thematic structure of the interviews (based on issues from the Literature Review) and the questions to ask within those themes, but also in terms of how to analyse the data. Despite such planning, one has to be prepared for hiccups. For example, during the transcription process it was discovered that part of a respondent's replies to a number of interview questions were missing from the tapes! During the interview, the tape had stopped and this had gone unnoticed. One has to admit the mistake and simply re-do that part of the interview.

Similarly, a dissertation does not always follow an uninterrupted linear path, where the Introduction is completed to order, followed by the Literature/ Contextual Review, then the Research Methods, etc. The reality is that the stages of the dissertation tend to be undertaken in an iterative fashion, even within the one sub-section, as detailed in the following narrative:

> When writing about barriers to e-Learning, one would discover an interesting article that was relevant to the section on e-Learning definitions, and so serious consideration would be given to revisiting that earlier section, even if the research work was at an advanced stage or one had believed that an earlier section was complete. This was time-consuming, and in some cases led to much re-thinking, but it was beneficial and gave a freshness to the work, making it as up-to-date as possible.

You can also remind the reader of the limitations, as you see it, of your work. However, you do not need to concentrate all the time on the problems you encountered, or perceived limitations of your work. You can also let others know what worked well:

> The analytical structure that was decided beforehand – deal with academic staff first, compare their answers against each other, deal with elite staff next, compare their answers against each other, then compare elite responses against academic staff responses, then compare and contrast both sets against the findings from the review of literature – forced the researcher to concentrate on processes rather than people, which helped to minimise potential bias when it came to interviewing people whom the interviewer knew.

One piece of useful advice is this: do not undersell your research findings. Too often, students are reluctant to boast about their work and it is common for supervisors to read concluding chapters that are reticent in expressing what has been achieved. The results are understated, offering tentative concluding remarks. Students, even though they produce good work, are still disinclined to express their contribution in positive terms. Sometimes they think it is ridiculous, or embarrassing, or even ill-mannered, to praise oneself, and so they underplay their achievements. You are not expected to engage in an unseemly paroxysm of self-eulogy, but you can, and ought to, assert and defend your good work with confidence.

Research is a discipline, but one that should be done with genuine conviction in an area that is of interest to you. Writing a dissertation is a demanding intellectual odyssey, but it should also be an enjoyable experience. If there is one concluding piece of advice that one can give to those contemplating a similar research journey, it is that there is no royal road to research. It takes hard work, and a disciplined mind, but the finished product is something to reflect on with pride. Or, in the words of Nick, a rebellious character in Shakespeare's *King Henry VI*, Part 2 (Proudfoot *et al.*, 2001, p. 520), who, when defending his craft, quotes with pride a common saying: 'Labour in thy vocation.' George, his rebellious comrade, echoes that sentiment when he responds: 'Thou has hit it; for there's no better sign of a brave mind than a hard hand.'

## Summary of key points

- A comprehensive concluding chapter could comprise the following sub-sections: Introduction; Research Objectives: Summary of Findings and Conclusions; Recommendations; Contribution to Knowledge (normally only expected of PhD students); Limitations; and Self-reflection.
- In the *Introduction*, refresh the reader's memory about your research objectives and give a quick run-down on the content of your concluding chapter.
- In the *Research Objectives: Summary of Findings and Conclusions*, answer the following questions: 'As a result of your Literature/Contextual Review and empirical research (if you did both), what did you find out in relation to your individual research objectives?' and 'What conclusions have you come to?' That is, for each research objective, inform the reader of your summary findings and offer a view on what your research is telling you.
- Your conclusions are derived from your research findings and your recommendations are based on your conclusions. In your *Recommendations*, you deal with two types of recommendations: recommendations linked to your conclusions and suggestions for future research. Explain your recommendations and, if you find it convenient, summarise them in the shape of a diagram. Finally, offer advice on how to implement your recommendations.
- Normally it is not a requirement that Master's students make a contribution to knowledge. However, if it is, then insert a sub-section in your concluding chapter entitled *Contribution to Knowledge* and consider your contribution in two ways: as a result of your Literature/Contextual Review findings and as a result of your empirical work. Emphasise your contribution by comparing and contrasting your work/findings against the work of other researchers.
- In the *Limitations*, qualify your research work with reference to perceived limitations, e.g. inability to generalise your findings (if that is the case), lack of time to do more (in-depth) research, restrictions on access to research subjects. It is not absolutely necessary to create a Limitations sub-section, as long as you refer to the limitations of your work somewhere in the Conclusion. You can, cleverly, turn some of the limitations of your research into recommendations ('This research revealed valuable insights into staff views of e-Learning. It is recommended, for a wider perspective, that students also be interviewed . . .').
- In the *Self-reflection*, reflect on two questions: 'What advice would you give to other students?' and 'If you had to do it again, what would you do differently, if anything?'

# Chapter

# Writing the abstract

- *What is an abstract?* • *How to write an abstract* • *Abstract template*
- *Summary of key points*

This chapter teaches you how to write an abstract. The elements that an abstract ought to contain are highlighted through examples of good and bad practice.

## What is an abstract?

Postgraduate students are normally required to include an *abstract* in their dissertation. An abstract is essentially a *synopsis* of your work. If an abstract is mandatory, it may not necessarily be assessed formally. This section will assume that you need to write an abstract for your dissertation and that it is assessable, but find out from your university's regulations whether one is needed and the weighting, if any, of marks accorded to the abstract.

An abstract is the first piece of work that readers encounter in your dissertation. It is a summary of your work and normally appears after your Title Page and Acknowledgements. It should capture the essence of your research in a lucid and succinct way. Some institutions differentiate between a *descriptive* abstract and an *informative* abstract: the former concentrates on the structure of the dissertation and not its content (and so is of limited value), whereas the latter provides a condensed summary of the actual work carried out by the researcher. It is the informative abstract that is the norm in postgraduate dissertations and, consequently, the one covered in this chapter.

Unfortunately, students often treat the (informative) abstract as an afterthought. Ignorance of what an abstract is, and how to write one, further undermines students' attempts to put together a competent abstract. Yet it is so easy to score marks in this area, despite the claim by Saunders *et al.* (2000, p. 418) that 'writing a good abstract is difficult'.

Like everything else in your dissertation, there is a technique to writing an abstract. A good abstract will normally contain the following four elements:

1  A statement of the problem/issue that you are investigating, including an indication of the need for your research.
2  Your research methods.
3  Your results/findings.
4  Your main conclusion(s) and recommendation(s).

Importantly, try and keep your abstract to one paragraph and to one page. Some institutions will also require your abstract to be *italicised*. Each of the above aspects that collectively form an abstract will now be discussed in detail. You should take into account the preferences of your examining institution as well as the preferences of your supervisor, who may well be marking your dissertation.

# How to write an abstract

If your abstract is to be assessed formally, it might only be worth about 10 marks at most, but it is very easy to obtain a high score, though it is also just as easy to lose silly marks. Students who gain few marks for their abstract do so because they have no idea what an abstract is or how to write one. You can learn by examining the following example abstracts against the criteria set down below of what an abstract ought to contain:

1  A statement of the problem/issue that you are investigating, including an indication of the need for your research.
2  Your research methods.
3  Your results/findings.
4  Your main conclusion(s) and recommendation(s).

### Example 1 (an abstract on cybercrime)

**Abstract**
The purpose of this dissertation is to explore the adverse effect of Internet crime on the modern business community. *Cybercrime* is a recent computer security issue that has evolved quickly without adequate opportunity for the issues surrounding it to become widely acknowledged and subsequently acted upon. Although there has been an abundance of tools to try and protect organisations from cyber breaches, existing research shows that e-security breaches are commonplace. Furthermore,

cyber-related legislation has been slow to keep pace with computer security breaches, even to the extent of creating additional barriers for those attempting to combat crime.

Out of 10, this abstract would get a mark of 1 or 2, for a number of reasons:

- The abstract identifies the research area only in vague terms: something to do with 'cybercrime'. There is no indication of *what* area in cybercrime the dissertation tackles, although it does suggest the motivation behind the study: the continued proliferation of cyber attacks on organisations. So, in terms of the first task that a student ought to do in an abstract – identify the research area and motivation behind the research – this abstract has failed to be specific about the research area.
- Worse, easy marks have been thrown away by failing to address the other aspects that ought to be covered in a good abstract: the research approach (e.g. research strategy and data collection techniques), the findings, and conclusions and recommendations.
- In effect, the abstract is quite empty and devoid of meaningful information.

An improved abstract is as follows (for the purpose of emphasis, the key abstract elements are in **bold**, and in square brackets – they would not appear so in the finished version):

**Abstract**

**[Motivation]** *Cybercrime – crime on the Internet – is of growing concern in the business community. Despite UK Government initiatives (such as BS7799) and growing sales in software solutions (e.g. anti-virus software), cyber attacks are on the increase.* **[Research Focus]** *This dissertation focuses on ways to assess the effectiveness of current preventative measures to cybercrime and to understand why organisations continue to be vulnerable to cybercrime.* **[Research Methods]** *This dissertation met these twin research aims through an extensive study of relevant literature and the implementation of practical research. The latter was carried out through a Case Study with Company XXX using semi-structured interviews with key I.T. security personnel.* **[Findings]** *This research produced a number of key findings: recent surveys confirm a significant increase in the incidences of cybercrime and their impact on the business community but also the types of cybercrime (viruses, hacking, spam, identity theft, fraud, privacy issues, web vandalism, etc.); organisations lacked the security expertise to deal with cybercrime and so depended too much on readily available technical ways to combat cybercrime; organisations were not aware of Government recommendations on how to address internet-based security issues; and Governments and law enforcement agencies tended to localise cybercrime, allocating scant resources to a global solution.* **[Conclusions]** *The main conclusions drawn from this research were* *that current approaches to fighting cybercrime are deficient because they fail to embrace an holistic approach, instead opting for a narrow local software-based focus, and that a lack of communication between major stakeholders at local, national and international level has hindered security development.* **[Recommendation]** *This research argues for a multi-pronged model to reduce incidences of cybercrime. One that takes into account Risk-Assessment models, local management of company policies, implementation issues (including proper resourcing and review policies), the need for global support infrastructures, and a means of fostering communication networks.*

Notice that each of the features expected of a good abstract – research focus, motivation behind the research, research methods, findings, and conclusions/recommendations – are to be found in the rewritten version. Note also that you can start with the motivation before identifying your specific research focus.

 **A common mistake by students**

A common mistake by students is to think up their abstract from scratch, without taking into account what they have written in their completed dissertation. This is harebrained, because you can get the information about your research work – motivation, research focus, research methods, findings, and conclusions/recommendations – by referring to the relevant chapters in your dissertation and summarising the appropriate segments, then sticking them in your abstract. For instance, when summarising your *research focus* for the abstract, go to your dissertation Introduction, locate your specific research objectives, summarise them into one or two sentences, and insert this summary into your abstract. Do the same for the other parts that go to make up your abstract. Students often lose stupid marks in their abstract by either ignoring what they have written in their dissertation or, worse, contradicting their own work!

## Example 2 (an abstract on software piracy)

**Abstract**
The aim of this project is to examine the impact of software piracy facing the modern business. With the Internet becoming an ever-present phenomenon, in homes and the business community, the problem of software piracy – in all its various guises – appears inexorable. As a result, many organisations continue to toil in the on-going battle to prevent this phenomenon escalating. The question has to be posed: is software piracy a problem that is solvable or do organisations have to concede that it is here to stay? This project tackles these difficult

questions. However, it is possible to deal with piracy in a strategic and cost-effective way.

Once again, as in Example 1, this is a poor abstract, deserving of only 2 or 3 marks out of a possible 10. Why?

- To begin with, although the research area is made clear ('The aim of this project . . .') and suggests the importance of the work ('With the Internet becoming an ever-present phenomenon . . .'), the abstract fails to identify the research methods.
- It is also unclear if the sentence beginning 'As a result . . .' is personal opinion or based on the research findings.
- Similarly, is the last sentence ('However, it is possible . . .') a conclusion based on the research or is it a personal comment plucked out of thin air?
- And what is specifically recommended as a result of this research? This vagueness has cost marks.

What follows is an improved version, incorporating the main abstract elements (research focus, motivation behind the research, how the research was implemented, findings, and conclusion/way forward):

**Abstract**

**[Research Focus]** *The aim of this dissertation is to investigate the extent and nature of software piracy, concentrating on three types of software piracy facing organisations today: applications software piracy, music piracy and movie piracy.* **[Motivation]** *The use of modern technology, in particular the Internet, to facilitate new avenues for software piracy makes the need for this research timely.* **[Research Methods]** *This research project was based on a Literature Review and questionnaires sent to one organisation in Scotland.* **[Findings]** *The findings underline that there is an increase in software piracy and that different types of piracy have different markets (e.g. applications software piracy directed at the business community whereas music piracy is aimed at the young) and, correspondingly, different, although overlapping, solutions.* **[Conclusion]** *The main conclusion to be drawn from this work is that software piracy is both a criminal problem and a cultural issue,* **[Recommendation]** *at the heart of which lies a solution based on ethical awareness training.*

*Keywords:* *software piracy, music piracy, movie piracy, ethics, training.*

Notice that the abstract includes a line for 'keywords'. This is good practice: it quickly helps the reader to get a handle on what your research is about and adds a professional touch that ought to meet with approval from your supervisor. Try to use no more than five keywords or key terms, otherwise it just becomes confusing for the reader.

### Example 3 (an abstract on plagiarism)

What follows is an example of a very good abstract (on Plagiarism), even though the 'motivation' part drags on somewhat:

**Abstract**

**[Motivation]** *In this digital age where plagiarism is a growing phenomenon in universities, it is imperative that senior management and academic staff understand collectively how to deal with the problem. The term plagiarism itself is often vague, leading to misunderstandings about what is acceptable and unacceptable practice. Similarly, at the chalk-face level, tutors may lack the skills necessary to detect plagiarism. At a wider, institutional level, procedures may lack coherence and consistency, leading to potential claims by students of unfair treatment.* **[Research Focus]** *This dissertation develops a workable definition of plagiarism, explores how students plagiarise, offers guidance on how to detect plagiarism, and presents a formal model on how to deal with cases of suspected plagiarism.* **[Research Methods]** *The research methods consisted of a wide review of relevant literature on plagiarism, coupled with the collection and analysis of empirical data. The latter is based on a survey of staff from 10 universities in the UK, using structured questionnaires via SurveyMonkey.* **[Findings/Conclusions]** *The findings from this research show that the term 'plagiarism' is often misunderstood; that the Internet is a core vehicle for plagiarism; and that central to combating plagiarism is the need for a coherent, consistent university-wide approach.* **[Recommendations]** *This dissertation recommends such an approach, one based on a Staff Awareness and Training module.*

***Keywords:*** *plagiarism, e-plagiarism, cheating, plagiarism software, essay banks.*

What is good about this abstract? It contains all the ingredients of a complete abstract:

- It provides a statement of the 'problem/issue' – in this case, plagiarism – including 'an indication of the need for' the research (growing problem, lack of staff understanding on how to deal with it).
- It identifies the chosen research methods (Literature Review + survey of staff from 10 universities).
- It outlines the findings (confusion over the term plagiarism, use of the Internet to facilitate plagiarism, etc.).
- It points to a way forward (adoption of a Staff Awareness and Training module).
- Finally, keywords are included to add a nice, professional touch.

Note that you can merge your findings and conclusions together if you find it convenient to do so, as in the above example.

**Example 4 (an abstract on practice-based research: embroidery and weaving)**

What follows is an excellent abstract on practice-based research where an artist creates an artefact, in this case, a woven sleeping bag. Once again, the text in bold is for your convenience and does not appear in the final abstract.

**Abstract**

**[Motivation]** *The artist was influenced by the (dying) tradition of Bedouin weaving, particularly the use of colour, strong horizontals in pattern, and decorative tassels and braids in the production of common-place objects of use, such as tents, rugs, and storage bags. The intention was to replicate this utility-based art form in a modern setting.* **[Research Focus]** *The work focused on producing a modern sleeping bag in the Bedouin style that could be used in practice and viewed as a work of art in its own right.* **[Research Methods]** *A Contextual Review was implemented to place the proposed artefact in the context of literature in Bedouin weaving and related objects of interest found in art galleries and camping shops. A practice-based strategy was then adopted as it best fits with the artist's aim of creating an art work and reviewing it. Data about the art work was based on personal observation, reflection-in-action logs, and a focus group made up of the artist's peers. A reflection-on-action protocol was used as a basis for critical reflection. Critical reflection was achieved through the technique of description-analysis-synthesis in order to gain an incremental 'thick account'.* **[Findings/Conclusions]** *The main findings show that art as utility and utility as art can be successfully integrated; and ancient technique can be replicated to an extent, increasing awareness and skills; but that each of these facets, when combined, multiply in proportion to the different, but inter-related, tasks to be overcome.* **[Recommendations]** *The principal lesson learned from this work is that an artist needs to balance design sensibilities and intentions with immediate reality, taking into consideration crucial time and resource constraints.*

*Keywords: Bedouin weaving, sleeping bag, artist as researcher, critical reflection.*

This is an excellent abstract because it covers all bases – motivation, research focus, research methods, findings/conclusion, recommendations – in one concise, clear, consistent, and fluid paragraph. Notice that the recommendation is more about a lesson learned, implying a generic recommendation to other artists: 'Bear in mind time and resource constraints!' This is perfectly acceptable, particularly in practice-based research where an art work, in whatever form, has been created and reviewed by the artist.

The next section provides an *abstract template* to help you write an abstract.

# Abstract template

As an *aide-mémoire*, an *abstract template* has been created which highlights the main elements that you ought to include in your own abstract (i.e. research problem, need for your research, how you did your research, your findings, and your recommendation(s)). You can refer to this template when you are doing your own abstract. In that way, you should avoid missing out key abstract elements and so, in turn, create a favourable impression with your dissertation supervisor/marker.

> **Abstract**
> The focus of this research *is in the area of*... Such a study is important in order to... The research approach adopted *in this dissertation includes*... The findings from this research *provide evidence that*... The main conclusions drawn *from this study are*... This dissertation recommends that...
>
> **Keywords:** *a, b, c, d, e.*

For tidiness, try and keep your abstract to one paragraph and no more than one page (a third of an A4 page normally suffices). Your institution's dissertation guidelines might even indicate the maximum number of words for your abstract. If your abstract starts to stretch over several paragraphs, there is the real danger that you are drawn into writing a disjointed, incoherent mini-essay, rather than concentrating on what you are supposed to be doing: writing an abstract. Keeping your abstract to one paragraph, as indicated in the abstract template, should assist you in the task of producing a tidy, coherent, and focused abstract.

If you find the business of writing an abstract initially difficult, then you are not alone: even academics can sometimes struggle with writing an abstract. It is commonplace for academics to submit their research, in the form of a research paper, to up-and-coming conferences, with the aim of disseminating their recent research work to the wider research community. As part of their paper submission, they must include an abstract, summarising their work. However, for their paper to get accepted, it is first judged by 'reviewers', fellow academics trusted by the conference committee to review submitted papers. One of the criteria that conference paper submissions are judged on is the quality of the abstract. When reviewers come to rate the full paper, they also tend to mark the quality of the abstract as well. On occasion, paper submissions are returned with comments such as 'abstract is lacking in detail' or 'no indication of type of study employed' or 'abstract requires to elucidate main findings'. Paper reviewers apply the above abstract template, if not consciously, then intuitively, when judging the quality of an abstract. For example, here is one such abstract (with the subject topic altered to avoid identification) that was reviewed, together with the reviewer's comments:

> **Abstract**
> This paper will delineate the efforts that have been done in applying technology as a scalable, adaptable, harmonised resource among

geographically distributed employers, employees and customers, in the context of the business community. By implementing this technology in the world of commerce, using web service and agent technology, we are able to reuse functionalities in a flexible and high performance manner. This way, many service and content providers can contribute in developing a very large-scale integrated technology-based business community, giving rise to more acceptable, and accepted, computer systems.

***Keywords:*** Grid, Resource Sharing, Technology, Web service, Agent.

**Reviewer's Comments** (related to abstract): The abstract is too short (approx. 80 words). Need to state *methodological approach* adopted and clarify your *findings* (see conference website for guidance on writing an abstract).

As you can see, writing an abstract can be problematic, even for academics. When you write your dissertation abstract, make sure that your abstract can answer the following questions:

- Have I identified the focus of my research?
- Have I indicated my motivation/rationale behind this study?
- Have I stated how I did my research?
- Have I summarised my findings/results?
- Are my main conclusions and recommendations included?

If you follow the abstract template – that is, you have addressed the above questions – then you should have an abstract that avoids the common pitfalls and is a credit to your dissertation.

## Summary of key points

- An informative abstract, sometimes referred to as a *synopsis*, is a summary of your work.
- In the abstract you should: identify the focus of your research; point out the rationale for your research; reveal your research methods; state your main findings/conclusions; and, where applicable, specify your way forward/recommendations.
- Write your abstract in a single *italicised* paragraph.
- At the end of the abstract, in a separate line, include up to five keywords that you feel best capture the nature of your dissertation.
- To help you write an abstract, use the following abstract template as an *aide-mémoire*:

**Abstract**

**The focus of this research** *is in the area of* . . . **Such a study is important in order to** . . . **The research approach adopted** *in this dissertation includes* . . . **The findings from this research** *provide evidence that* . . . The main conclusions drawn *from this study are* . . . **This dissertation recommends that** . . .

*Keywords: a, b, c, d, e.*

# Chapter **12**

# Finally: viva, dissertation marking scheme, and summary of good/bad practice

> • *Preparing for a viva* • *The dissertation marking scheme* • *Dissertation writing: summary of good practice to adopt and bad practice to avoid*

This final chapter offers advice on coping with a viva and understanding marking schemes. Summary notes on good dissertation practice to adopt and bad dissertation practice to avoid, from writing an abstract to concluding a dissertation, are presented as an *aide-mémoire*.

## Preparing for a viva

If you are lucky, once you write and hand in your dissertation to be marked, your part in the dissertation process will be over. On the other hand, some institutions also submit their students to an oral examination, i.e. a *viva*. A common mistake by students is not to prepare properly. In fact, many students often seem taken aback when asked even the most simple of questions, such as 'Tell me, Linda, why did you pick this topic?' or 'Joseph, in one sentence – what is your research about?' This sub-section will guide you on how to prepare yourself for a viva.

A *viva* is an oral examination. Students have many a sleepless night worrying about their viva. There are things that you can do to improve your performance and increase the chances of a successful viva:

- Long before your viva, summarise your work into manageable chunks. Take each of your dissertation chapters – from your Introduction right through to your Conclusion – and summarise them in a bullet-point list, using one A4 sheet of paper for each chapter. This will make it easier for you to revise. An alternative, or additional, approach to summarising your dissertation is to do so using mind-maps, delving into as much detail as you wish (see Chapter 1, 'Introduction' under sub-section 'Developing your i-skills', part 6: 'Communication skills').

- Write down who you think are the main players in your research area, identifying in what respect they are important (make use of one or two particularly memorable quotations). You will look incompetent if you are unable to talk about authors whom you have cited in your dissertation as key players. One postgraduate student, who referred frequently to a book by one particular author, was asked at an oral examination to name the colour of the book cover!

- Anticipate questions and prepare your answers. Do not panic, because most of the questions will be straightforward. The examiners are not your enemy – they are genuinely interested in what you have to say. It is generally not difficult to anticipate the type of questions you will be asked, although there will always be one or two from 'left field'. The questions tend to follow the structure of your dissertation, so take a blank sheet of paper for each chapter of your dissertation and reflect on questions that could be asked. Examples of typical questions that crop up again and again are:

  - In one sentence, what is your work about?
  - What led you to do this research?
  - Why is this work worth reading?
  - Can you explain your research objectives to us?
  - You say so-and-so has such-and-such a view. Are you sure about that?
  - Who would you say are the main players in your field?
  - I don't agree with your interpretation of so-and-so's model . . .
  - Your references are pretty old. Why haven't you used more up-to-date sources?
  - Are you really saying that your approach to empirical research is the only way to do research? No other way counts?
  - Explain your procedure for ensuring that your survey was random.
  - You cannot claim that your case study is representative, can you?
  - Why should we rely on your research?
  - You know the people you interviewed, so surely your work is biased?
  - You created the art work. Surely your views on what you did are therefore open to the accusation of bias?
  - Can you explain to us how you analysed your empirical data?
  - Do you think you achieved your research objectives?
  - I'm not sure that your conclusions follow from your empirical work . . .
  - What would you say are the practical implications of your research?
  - Can you elaborate on your recommendations, particularly on how you see them being implemented?

- What's good about your work?
- If you had to do this research work again, what would you do differently?
- Why do you think this work deserves a pass?
- So, what would you say is your contribution to knowledge?
- Why should we award you an MSc./MPhil. etc.?

- When an examiner is asking a question, do not interrupt. Politely and patiently wait for the question to be concluded. In fact, as the question is being formed, write it down. That gives you time to think about what you are being asked and shows the examiners that you are treating their questions seriously. Take your time answering a question. Once you have written down the question, take a long, deep breath before beginning your answer. In a viva, patience is a virtue. Interrupting examiners and rushing answers will do you no favours.

- If there is a question that you do not understand, then say so. Ask your examiner to rephrase any question, or to elaborate, where you are unsure of the question's meaning. It takes confidence to do this, but do not ask an examiner to re-phrase every question! If there is a question that you find difficult to answer, then graciously admit 'That's a good question!' Your comment will ease the tension, and if you are lucky, the examiner might offer you some clues as to how to answer it!

- On the other hand, if there is a question that you are unable to answer or you are in a situation where you are having difficulty persuading the examiner on some moot point, then accept a difference of opinion – even defeat if the issue in question is not central to your work – and move on. If you believe the examiner to be right, then you can say so but think carefully before you concede. You are there to defend your work, and examiners are testing that you can do that. So, defend, defend, defend! If you concede points too readily, you may be vulnerable to the accusation that although your work was well written and persuasive, your oral defence of your work was feeble. Concede where you genuinely agree with the examiner. Put up a robust defence of your work, but if things are getting hostile, and you do not want to give in, then agree to disagree.

- The examiners will have read your work in detail before the viva. They will have recorded their initial impressions, including whether or not your work is deserving of a pass (you do not see these comments). They will also have written down specific points to examine you on. As you enter the room, your examiners may already have considered your work worthy of a pass, which means that it is yours to lose! It is much worse to be in the position where your written work is initially assessed as a fail, or borderline fail: this is very difficult, though not impossible, to turn around to a pass in your viva.

- The examiners' questions might not always follow a linear path, i.e. starting with questions on the Introduction, then the Literature Review/Contextual Review, followed by Research Methods, and so on. If they have specific issues they want to explore, then it is to these issues they will direct their questions, probably in order of importance. For instance, if they decided among themselves beforehand that they had problems understanding aspects of your concluding chapter, then that is where the first set of questions are likely to be directed. So be prepared for different 'angles of attack'.

- Find out who your examiners will be. If they are external examiners, look them up on the Internet to see what their research interests are, and get hold of their recent publications. That way you will get an idea of their views about your research area (they are your examiners because they have expertise in your field of research). For example, if your research is in e-Learning and you have argued in your dissertation that there are many barriers to e-Learning but one of your examiners, in a recent publication, takes a different stance, then you will at least be forewarned and better able to prepare a response to a possible difference of opinion.

- Remember, the examiners are not your enemy – nor you theirs. They want you to pass, and will be the first to congratulate you, but only if your work is of an acceptable standard. They are asking you probing questions, not because they do not rate your work, but because it is their job as guardians of academic standards to be convinced that: (a) it is your work; (b) you can defend your work; and (c) you are a competent researcher when judged against university and national standards.

A *mock viva* is worth considering (Hartley and Fox, 2004). This is where your supervisor and/or another academic attempt to replicate a 'real' viva by inviting you to defend your work, usually two or three weeks before your formal viva. It is normally up to you, the student, to request a mock viva. It is a worthwhile exercise – the atmosphere is non-threatening and the questions and debates that take place can throw up issues you had not previously considered. For example, at one mock viva a student had been queried on her research strategy, that she had not fully justified the case for focus groups. She had no time to amend her dissertation prior to her formal viva. At her viva, the same issue was raised, i.e. the absence of a detailed explanation for using focus groups in her empirical research. However, having been forewarned at her mock viva, she was prepared for this line of attack. Her response was immediate, authoritative, informative, and comprehensive, gaining the approval of her examiners. That is the advantage of a mock viva.

A viva can be a nerve-wracking experience, but, believe it or not, it can also be an enjoyable one. If you are well prepared beforehand, then – nerves notwithstanding – you ought to be looking forward to the experience so that you can show the examiners the fruits of your labour, something that you should take pride in and be prepared to defend. Figure 12.1 identifies the preparation that you ought to do before your viva, together with a sensible approach to adopt during the viva. In short, know your own work (through your summaries); anticipate questions related to each stage of your dissertation; develop answers to these questions; request a mock viva; and at the actual viva write down questions and take your time answering them (think

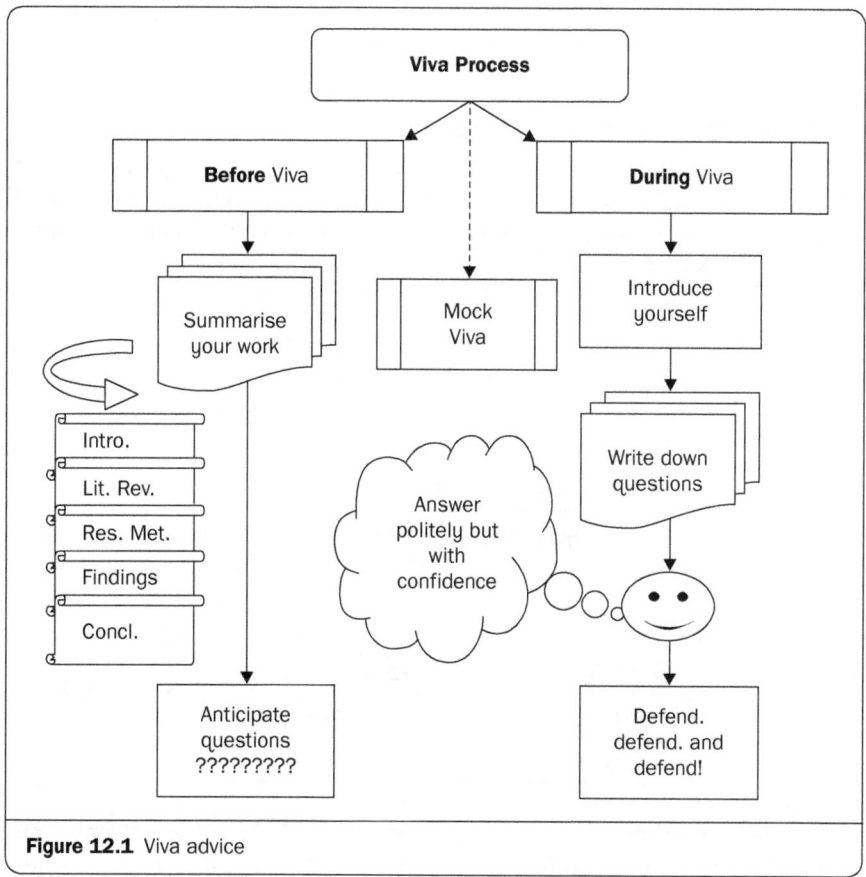

**Figure 12.1** Viva advice

about what you are being asked). Finally, defend what you wrote in your dissertation, and be polite!

# The dissertation marking scheme

When an examiner starts to mark your written work, it is normally with reference to a 'marking scheme'. Marking schemes are used for a number of reasons. First, the alternative is to depend on the examiner arriving at a pass mark (e.g. '85%') based on personal taste; or worse, failing a student, but on what basis? Second, a marking scheme introduces guidelines that all staff can use and against which student dissertations can be judged, ensuring consistency of approach and fairness to students. Third, marking schemes allow institutions to keep a record of student work, including assessment rationale, so that external auditors can see that the assessment and work are of an appropriate standard befitting a university. Finally, marking schemes are there to assist *you*, the student, in understanding how your work will be assessed.

> ! **A common mistake by students**
>
> A common mistake by students is to develop their dissertation without refer-ence to the marking scheme. This is stupid. You are being tested that your dissertation meets pre-determined criteria, so why ignore the stated criteria or pay it lip service?

What does a marking scheme look like? Marking schemes normally equate a particular range of marks with expected standards of achievement. In its sim-plest form, a marking scheme equates a marking range against the various types of pass or fail (Table 12.1).

**Table 12.1**  Generic marking scheme

| Mark range (%) | Result |
| --- | --- |
| 70+ | Distinction |
| 60–69 | Very good pass |
| 50–59 | Pass |
| 40–49 | Bare pass |
| 0–39 | Fail |

There are variations of the marking model in Table 12.1. For example, the School of Engineering and Informatics at the University of Sussex (http://www.sussex.ac.uk/ei/internal/forstudents/informatics/masters/dissertations/marking-criteriamsceasy, 2017) views a mark in the range 60–69 as 'a good pass' rather than 'a very good pass' and a mark in the 30–49 range as a fail (Table 12.2).

**Table 12.2**  Generic marking scheme: University of Sussex

| Mark range (%) | Result |
| --- | --- |
| 70+ | Excellent |
| 60–69 | Good |
| 55–59 | Satisfactory |
| 50–54 | Borderline |
| 30–49 | Fail |

Similarly, other institutions might have different marking schemes. Often, the 70+ mark is split into two types of distinction and a mark in the region 60–69 is classified as a Merit (Table 12.3).

**Table 12.3**  Generic marking scheme: distinction sub-divided

| Mark range (%) | Result |
| --- | --- |
| 80+ | Outstanding Distinction |
| 70–79 | Distinction |
| 60–69 | Merit |
| 50–59 | Pass |
| 40–49 | Bare pass |
| 0–39 | Fail |

One university's 'Outstanding Distinction' is another university's 'Brilliant Distinction', and yet another's 'Exceptional Distinction'. Similarly, one institution's 'Bare Pass' is another's 'Condonable Pass' and yet another's 'Borderline Pass'. Regardless of the different ranges and classifications, universities will often provide the detail of what they mean by 'distinction', 'pass', and so on. In effect, they are stipulating the criteria that you need to meet in order to obtain a mark in a particular range. The criteria for the higher marks (70+) are generally peppered with synonyms like 'authoritative', 'excellent quality', 'independent critical thought', 'excellent comprehension and analysis', and 'coherent and compelling'. Work that is 'outstanding in every respect' and 'publishable' is easily in the 90+ range. The criteria for the different types of passes should be available in your dissertation handbook and your university department's website. There is no reason for the different passing (and failing) criteria to be a government secret.

As well as *marking schemes*, there are *marking sheets*. When supervisors get down to marking your submitted dissertation, they normally have to complete a marking sheet. The marking sheet will have more granularity than is in the marking scheme. For example, the sample marking sheet in Appendix L allocates maximum marks achievable for each major part of a traditional dissertation, with the total adding up to 100: Aim and Objectives (10 marks), Literature Review (15), Research Methods (15), Findings and Discussion (20), Conclusion(s) and Recommendations (15), Referencing (5), Abstract (10), Structure and Quality of Written English (10).

Another institution may adopt a different marking sheet, one that allows markers to mark elements of the dissertation out of 100 but weight the different parts according to their perceived importance (for an example, see Table 12.4, p. 284).

Thus, each of the elements would be marked out of 100, then multiplied by their respective weighting to arrive at a final mark for that element. So, in this scenario, if a student scored 70% for Research Methods and Research Methods had a weighting of 0.2 (i.e. Research Methods were deemed to be worth 20% of the dissertation mark), then the final mark for that element would be $70 \times 0.2 = 14$, and so on. Table 12.5 shows a completed example of the weighted marking sheet given in Table 12.4.

**Table 12.4** Weighted marking sheet

| Aspect | Mark (%) | Weight | Weighted Mark |
|---|---|---|---|
| Abstract, Introduction | _____ | 0.1 | _____ |
| Literature Review | _____ | 0.2 | _____ |
| Research Methods | _____ | 0.2 | _____ |
| Findings/Discussion | _____ | 0.3 | _____ |
| Conclusion | _____. | 0.1 | _____ |
| Referencing, presentation | _____ | 0.1 | _____ |
| | | **TOTAL (out of 100)** | _____ |

**Table 12.5** Completed weighted marking sheet

| Aspect | Mark (%) | Weight | Weighted Mark |
|---|---|---|---|
| Abstract, Introduction | 66 | 0.1 | 66 × 0.1 = 6.6 |
| Literature Review | 60 | 0.2 | 60 × 0.2 = 12 |
| Research Methods | 70 | 0.2 | 70 × 0.2 = 14 |
| Findings/Discussion | 76 | 0.3 | 76 × 0.3 = 22.8 |
| Conclusion | 76 | 0.1 | 76 × 0.1 = 7.6 |
| Referencing, presentation | 68 | 0.1 | 68 × 0.1 = 6.8 |
| | | TOTAL (out of 100) | 69.8 = 70 |

The University of Manchester School of Computer Science operates a similar model, with weightings flexible and depending on specific MSc requirements.

Dissertation marking sheets come in all shapes and sizes, but they have certain elements in common, regardless of how they are constructed. They will have a place for the student's name to be entered (usually at the top of the page), the specific areas that the student dissertation is to be marked on (together with the maximum marks achievable for each area), a space for the actual marks to be entered, including the total mark achieved, and a section for the examiner's comments.

Let us look closely at the completed marking sheet in Appendix M, which is reproduced here in a smaller version (Figure 12.2). Notice that there are two different marks: a total mark of 85% (bottom right-hand of marking sheet) as well as an 'AGREED MARK' of 87% (near the top right-hand corner of the marking sheet). Why is this? This is because it is unlikely that your dissertation will be marked by a single member of staff. To ensure consistency of marking, it is normal practice for two members of staff to mark the same dissertation, as a

| **STUDENT NAME:** | Pat Houston | | |
|---|---|---|---|
| 1st Marker: | Dr John Biggam | | |
| 2st Marker: | Dr Alan Hogarth | | AGREED MARK: **87%** |

| **Aspect** | **Possible Mark** | **Actual Mark** |
|---|---|---|
| 1. Aim and Objectives | 10 | 10 |
| 2. Literature Review | 15 | 11 |
| 3. Research Methods | 15 | 12 |
| 4. Findings and Discussion | 20 | 17 |
| 5. Conclusion(s) and Recommendations | 15 | 12 |
| 6. Referencing | 5 | 5 |
| 7. Abstract | 10 | 10 |
| 8. Structure and Quality of Written English | 10 | 8 |
| | 100 TOTAL: | **85%** |

**Figure 12.2** Sample completed marking sheet

means of providing checks and balances. The different marks for Pat Houston's dissertation occur as a result of one member of staff (Dr John Biggam) giving a mark of 85% while another member of staff (in this case Dr Alan Hogarth) arrives at a different mark. The fact that the student's mark has been increased from 85% to 87% suggests that the mark given by Dr Alan Hogarth was higher than Dr John Biggam's mark, although not significantly so, and that they have come to an agreement on what mark to award the student. If markers cannot work out their differences, a third marker may be called in to adjudicate or an external examiner may be asked to offer a view.

Irrespective of the marking scheme used by your institution, when you submit your final dissertation you ought to ask yourself what mark you would give your own dissertation. When you are reviewing your work, either individual sections or the final submission, it is a worthwhile exercise to consider what mark *you* believe your work merits, using either the straightforward quantitative approach ('I think this is worth a 65') or using a qualitative model ('This is *good* so I reckon I deserve between 50 and 59') or the more generic marking scheme ('This is in the band 60–69 because throughout my dissertation it meets the criteria in that band'). In that way, you will begin to think like a marker, checking your efforts against the set criteria. You can even have some fun by getting your friends to 'mark' yours, while you reciprocate for them, each giving the other a completed marking sheet, including comments.

Getting good marks is not rocket science. It requires hard work and an understanding of what is expected of you. There are easy marks to pick up for your *abstract, referencing,* and *aims and objectives.* If you have grasped how to write an abstract, follow a style of referencing, and know how to clarify your overall aim and related objectives, then you really ought to be securing top marks in each of these tasks, as did Pat Houston in the sample marking sheet. Students who lose marks for each of the aforementioned areas do so because they do not know what they are doing and are reduced to guessing about how to complete each of the tasks.

For the *Literature Review* (or *Contextual Review*), you are essentially getting your marks for the breadth and depth of literature studied, relevant to your overall aim and research objectives, in a way that is not merely descriptive, but exhibits critical evaluation of pertinent literature. For the *Research Methods*, you gain marks for explaining and justifying your design decisions, that they are appropriate for your study. Marks for the *Findings* and *Discussion* concentrate on your ability to analyse the results of your empirical research in relation to your Literature Review (or Contextual Review) and your declared research objectives. Your *Conclusion* needs to provide cyclical closure, i.e. that you summarise your results, provide final comments, make recommendations, and review your own work (either from a critical perspective or lessons learned, or both).

When you start your dissertation, get a copy of the marking scheme that will be used by your supervisor, as well as any accompanying explanatory notes. Make sure that you understand it and use it as a checklist to ensure that, as you develop your dissertation, you are ticking all the right boxes ('Have I justified the need for my research?', 'Are my research objectives clear and achievable?', 'Is my review of literature extensive, showing critical evaluation?', and so on). When you attend meetings with your supervisor, ask your supervisor the same questions ('Are you convinced that I have justified the need for my research?', 'In your view, are my research objectives clear and achievable?', and so on). Prior to submitting your completed dissertation, go over the marking scheme again to check that you have made no damaging omissions (a colleague recalls one student failing to notice that he had absent-mindedly forgot to include his list of references!).

One last point on dissertation marking schemes: if there is no marking scheme, or set of marking guidelines, then you can legitimately ask your institution how they – markers – arrive at a mark for your work and, at the same time, ensure consistency of approach. They may be leaving themselves open to the claim that their approach to dissertation marking is overly subjective and thus inherently unfair.

## Dissertation writing: summary of good practice to adopt and bad practice to avoid

Forewarned is forearmed. This book has taken you through the things that you need to do to complete a dissertation. In doing so, it has also highlighted the common mistakes that supervisors observe their dissertation students making, again and again, year in year out. As a memory aid, this information is summarised for easy reference in two tables:

- Table 12.6 Dissertation writing – summary of *good* practice to adopt
- Table 12.7 Dissertation writing – summary of *bad* practice to avoid

Tables 12.6 and 12.7 concentrate, respectively, on the good and bad things that occur in the typical phases that go to make up the written dissertation (Research Proposal, Abstract, Introduction, Literature Review/Contextual Review, Research Methods, Findings and Discussion, and Conclusion). In addition, these tables make reference to the viva and dissertation marking scheme.

There are other matters that you need to consider when completing your dissertation, from picking a topic that is of genuine interest to you, to creating a dissertation template at the start (to give you an idea of what lies ahead), to making the most of meetings with your supervisor, to keeping an eye on your word-count. Above all, doing a dissertation ought to be an enjoyable experience, an opportunity to show what you can do, but it requires serious effort on your part. It is an intellectual journey that demands your active participation: passengers rarely pass. Being forewarned about the common pitfalls to avoid, together with the skills required to get through the dissertation process, will allow you to start your dissertation odyssey with confidence.

**Table 12.6**  Dissertation writing – summary of *good* practice to adopt

| Phase | Summary of good practice to adopt |
| --- | --- |
| Dissertation Proposal | – Provide background information on research topic<br>– Justify the need for your study<br>– Identify overall research aim and specific research objectives<br>– Outline your research methods<br>– Estimate duration of dissertation phases<br>– Complete a Research Ethics Approval Form or NHS equivalent<br>– Adhere to the core ethical principles of *transparency, confidentiality, voluntary* participation, *no harm* to your participants (or you), and *impartiality* |
| Abstract | – Write it last!<br>– Identify the problem/issue that you investigated<br>– Outline how you did your research (i.e. your research methods)<br>– State your main findings/conclusion(s)<br>– Indicate your recommendations<br>– Include keywords<br>– Keep to one paragraph (it is not an essay!)<br>– Apply the abstract template! |

(continued)

**Table 12.6** (Continued)

| Phase | Summary of good practice to adopt |
| --- | --- |
| Introduction | – Provide a clear structure (similar to research proposal):<br><br>→ Background information<br>→ Research focus<br>→ Overall aim and research objectives<br>→ Outline research methods and timescales<br>→ Value of your research<br>→ Outline structure of dissertation<br><br>– Show initiative (in sourcing information)<br>– Produce clear, achievable research objectives<br>– Emphasise the value of/need for your research |
| Literature Review/ Contextual Review | – Remind the reader of your research objectives<br>– Let the reader know about the topics you intend covering<br>– Develop meaningful discussions, providing evidence of critical evaluation (offer views, support views)<br>– Use wide variety of sources (websites, journals, books, reports, etc.)<br>– Reference sources properly<br>– Avoid dissertation *drift* – keep focused on your research objectives<br>– Summarise main findings and highlight emerging issues<br>– Provide link (and justification) for empirical research |
| Systematic Reviews | – Frame your research question using PICO<br>– Find literature to meet your research question, adhering to Evans's hierarchy of preferred evidence<br>– Exploit online resources (e.g. MEDLINE)<br>– Justify exclusion of literature<br>– Pool data<br>– Place findings in context<br>– Use AMSTAR checklist |
| Research Methods: Traditional Methods | – Identify and describe your research strategy (case study, survey, grounded theory, experimental research, etc.)<br>– Justify why your chosen research strategy meets your research needs<br>– Identify, describe, and justify your data collection techniques (interviews, questionnaires, documents, observation, types of experiments, etc.)<br>– Explain where you will get your data, and state your sample size<br>– Summarise the above, using diagrams where possible<br>– Explain how you will analyse your collected data (framework for data analysis)<br>– Outline limitations/potential problems (but explain why your work is valid and reliable) |

**Table 12.6** (Continued)

| Phase | Summary of good practice to adopt |
|---|---|
| Research Methods: Practice-based Research | – As above with traditional methods but with a focus on practice-based research as the research strategy (also known as Practice as Research (PaR), practice-led research, and performative research) and associated data collection and analysis techniques (e.g. reflection-in-action logs and reflection-on-action protocol). |
| Findings and Discussion | – Keep it simple: describe the data, analyse it, compare/contrast with Literature Review/Contextual Review findings<br>– Stick to your framework for analysis (if you have one!)<br>– Keep focused on relevant research objective(s), thus avoiding *drift*<br>– Summarise main empirical findings<br>– Place evidence of (non-confidential) empirical research in appendices (questionnaires, interview transcripts/notes, experiment results, etc.) |
| Conclusion | – Remind reader of your initial research objectives<br>– Summarise Literature Review/Contextual Review and Empirical Research findings (related to research objectives)<br>– Elicit main conclusions from your findings<br>– Offer recommendations (specific to your research objectives), including ideas about implementation<br>– Include self-reflection (limitations of study, lessons learnt, advice to others) |
| The viva | – Prior to your viva, summarise, for revision purposes, your dissertation chapters<br>– Anticipate questions (and prepare answers):<br>  → on preliminary issues (e.g. research focus, need for your research, etc.)<br>  → aspects of your Literature Review/Contextual Review (scope, depth, focus, range of sources, relevance, your interpretation of what other people are saying, etc.)<br>  → your research methods and data collection techniques (relevant, justified, clearly explained?)<br>  → how you analysed your empirical work<br>  → your conclusions (justified?) and associated recommendations<br>– Have a mock viva<br>– Write examiner questions down<br>– Take your time answering questions<br>– Defend your work! |

(continued)

**Table 12.6** (Continued)

| Phase | Summary of good practice to adopt |
|-------|-----------------------------------|
| The marking scheme | – Get hold of how your dissertation will be marked<br>– Use it as a checklist as you do the work (are your research objectives clear?, do you show evidence of critical evaluation? Etc.)<br>– Pick up easy marks (for abstract, dissertation structure, referencing, research objectives)<br>– Make sure that you know what you are getting the big marks for in your dissertation<br>– Before submission, have a go at marking it yourself! |

**Table 12.7**  Dissertation writing – summary of *bad* practice to avoid

| Phase | Summary of bad practice to avoid |
|-------|----------------------------------|
| Dissertation Proposal | – Lack of subject focus<br>– Vague research objectives – over-ambitious<br>– Unrealistic timescales<br>– Not justifying need for research<br>– Failing to complete a Research Ethics Approval Form<br>– Ignoring the core ethical principles of *transparency*, *confidentiality*, *voluntary* participation, *no harm* to your participants (or you), and *impartiality* |
| Abstract | – Write it without having a clue what you are supposed to be doing!<br>– Engage in mini Literature Review/Contextual Review (not the place for that)<br>– Fail to provide basic information about your work<br>– Write an essay (it is an *abstract*, not an essay) |
| Introduction | – Paying scant attention to background reading<br>– Too dependent on supervisor for research ideas<br>– Devoting too much attention to background reading!<br>– Lack of continuity between sub-sections<br>– Unconvincing rationale (or no rationale!) on the value of the work |
| Literature Review/ Contextual Review | – Ill-structured<br>– Superficial, skeletal sub-sections (lists, simple descriptions, lack of discussion)<br>– Concentrating almost exclusively on web sources<br>– Not offering, or justifying, your own views (i.e. devoid of critical evaluation)<br>– Lack of development of ideas<br>– Inconsistent referencing styles |

**Table 12.7** (Continued)

| Phase | Summary of bad practice to avoid |
|---|---|
| | – Plagiarising work<br>– No sense of direction<br>– No obvious relevance to research objectives<br>– No evidence of need for empirical research<br>– Ends abruptly with no obvious link to next section (Research Methods) |
| Systematic Reviews | – Vague research question<br>– Unmethodical literature search process<br>– Publication bias<br>– Focusing at the lower end of Evans's hierarchy of preferred evidence (uncontrolled trials, expert opinion, etc.)<br>– Inappropriate pooling of data<br>– Failing to place results in context |
| Research Methods: Traditional Methods | – Spending the bulk of your time describing a whole realm of research strategies (case studies, ethnography, experimental research, surveys, etc.)<br>– Not justifying your chosen research strategy<br>– Misunderstanding the nature of qualitative/quantitative research<br>– Introducing unexplained philosophical terms!<br>– Producing a long descriptive monologue on the different ways that data can be collected (questionnaires, interviews, etc.)<br>– Lack of detail on how and where *you* will collect data or what *you* intend doing with the data once you get it<br>– Pretending that there are no limitations to be addressed or potential problems to be minimised in relation to your research methods and particular project. |
| Research Methods: Practice-based Research | – Waffling about matters that are unrelated to your research methods<br>– Not explaining the nature of your research strategy in terms of what it is, why you are using it, what you intend creating, how you will create it, and why you are creating it<br>– Lack of detail on how and where *you* will collect data or what *you* intend doing with the data once you get it<br>– Pretending that there are no limitations to be addressed or potential problems to be minimised in relation to your research methods and particular project. |
| Findings and Discussion | – Having an unstructured, confusing approach to analysing your collected data or using inappropriate analysis techniques, or using appropriate techniques incorrectly!<br>– Coming to conclusions without any evidence of meaningful discussion<br>– Not relating your findings/discussion to your research objectives/Literature Review/Contextual Review |

(continued)

**Table 12.7** (Continued)

| Phase | Summary of bad practice to avoid |
|---|---|
| Conclusion | – Not revising your research objectives to check on whether or not you have achieved them (as a result of your Literature Review/ Contextual Review and empirical research)<br>– Not linking your conclusions, if you have any, to your Literature Review/Contextual Review or empirical research findings<br>– Not summarising your work<br>– Offering no recommendations on the way forward<br>– Treating your Conclusion as if it were another Literature Review!<br>– Ending abruptly! |
| The viva | – Not anticipating obvious questions<br>– Rushing your answers<br>– Arguing with the examiners (there is a difference between having a professional disagreement and rudeness)<br>– Giving monosyllabic answers<br>– Not referring to your dissertation when answering questions (you are being tested on the work that you have submitted, so it is to your work that you refer when giving answers) |
| The marking scheme | – Ignoring the things that you are getting marked on |

# Appendix A: Harvard referencing formats (with examples)

The following reference templates are based on the style of Harvard referencing advocated by Pears and Shields (2016) in their popular book *Cite Them Right*.

## Art work

*Artwork in gallery*

Artist (year) *Title* [Medium]. Gallery name, City.

Rembrandt, van R. (1642) *Night watch* [Oil on canvas]. Rijkmuseum, Amsterdam.

If viewed online:

Artist (year) *Title* [Medium] Available at: URL (Accessed: date).

Rembrandt, van R. (1642) *Night watch* [Oil on canvas]. Available at: https://www.rijksmuseum.nl/en/search/objects?q=Rembrandt+&p=1&ps=12&st=OBJECTS&ii=2#/SK-C-5,2 (Accessed: 10 April 2007).

*Temporary exhibition*

*Title of exhibition* (year) [Exhibition]. Place exhibited. Date(s) of exhibition.

*NoNoseKnows* (2015) [Exhibition]. Glasgow International 2016, Tramway Gallery. 8–25 April 2016.

If viewed online:

*Title of exhibition* (year) [Exhibition]. Available at: URL (Accessed: date).

*A world view: John Latham* (2017) [Exhibition]. Available at: http://www.serpentinegalleries.org/exhibitions-events/world-view-john-latham (Accessed 19 March 2017).

*Artwork in public space*

Artist (year) *Title* [Medium]. Location, City.

Niki de Saint Phalle (1996) *Tympanum* [Mirror mosaic]. Glasgow Gallery of Modern Art, Scotland.

### Exhibition catalogue

Author (year) *Title of exhibition*. Place of exhibition, date(s) of exhibition [Exhibition catalogue].

Humphrey, P. (2012) *The Essence of Beauty: 500 years of Italian Art*. Exhibition held Kelvingrove Art Gallery and Museum, Glasgow, 6 April–12 August 2012 [Exhibition catalogue].

### Article found on the internet

Author's surname, initials (year) 'Title of article'. Available at: URL (Accessed: date).

Haseman, B. (2006) 'A manifesto for performative research'. Available at: http://eprints.qut.edu.au/3999/1/3999_1.pdf (Accessed: 12 January 2017).

### Book

Author's surname, initials (year) *Title of book*. Edition if not first. Place of publication: Publisher.

Neville, C. (2016) *The complete guide to referencing and avoiding plagiarism*. 3rd edn. London: Open University Press.

### Chapter in a book

Author's surname, initials (year) 'Title of article', in Editor name(s) (eds) *Title of book*. Place of publication: Publisher, page(s).

Elsky, M. (1982) 'Words, things, and names: Jonson's poetry and philosophical grammar', in Summers, C. J. and Pebworth, T. L. (eds) *Classic and cavalier: essays on Jonson and the sons of Ben*. Pittsburgh, PA: University of Pittsburgh Press, pp. 31–44.

### E-book

Author's surname, initials (year) *Title of book*. Edition, if not first. Available at: URL (Downloaded: date).

Taylor, M. and Mayled, J. (2009) *OCR Philosophy of Religion*. Available at: https://www.amazon.co.uk/OCR-Philosophy-Religion-AS-A2/dp/0415468248 (Downloaded: 18 March 2017).

## Cinema film

*Title of film* (Year) Directed by director name [Film]. Place of distribution: distributor.

*King: Skull Island* (2017) Directed by Jordan Vogt-Roberts [Film]. California: Warner Bros.

## Classical music

*Musical score*

Composer (Year) *Title*. Additional information. Place of publication: publisher.

Chopin, F. (2009) *Mazarkus*. Edited by Carl Mikuli. New York: Dover Publications.

If viewed online:

Composer (Year) *Title*. Additional information. Available at: URL (Accessed: date).

Kratz, T. (2016). Joy. For piano. Available at: https://www.kratz/joy (Accessed: 14 May 2017).

*Live performance*

Composer (Year performed) *Title*. Performed by orchestra name conducted by conductor name [Place performed. Date seen].

Korngold, E. W. (2017) Performed by the Scottish Symphony Orchestra conducted by John Wilson [City Halls, Glasgow. 16 March 2017].

## Company report

Author or Company Name (Year) *Title*. Place of publication: publisher.

Tesco (2016) *Strategic report*. London: Addison Group.

If viewed online:

Author/Company (Year) *Title*. Available at: URL (Accessed: date).

Tesco (2016) *Strategic report*. Available at: https://www.tescoplc.com/media/264194/annual-report-2016.pdf (Accessed: 10 October 2017).

## Conference paper

Author's surname, initials (year) 'Title of paper', *Title of conference*, location, dates of conference. Place of publication: publisher, page(s).

Bloom, J. (2017) 'Picasso turns blue', *Straight from the artist's mouth*, Art Institute, Falkirk, 2–3 March 2015. London: Artbooks, pp. 36–40.

If viewed online:

Author's surname, initials (year) 'Title of paper', *Title of conference, location, dates of conference, page(s) if available*. Available at: URL (Accessed: date).

Conole, G., Oliver, M., Isroff, K. and Ravenscroft, A. (2004) 'Addressing methodological issues in e-learning research', *Proceedings of the Networked Learning Conference*, Lancaster University, UK, 5–7 April. Available at: www.sef.ac.uk/nlc/Proceedings/Symposa4.htm (Accessed: 2 October 2004).

Or (using *et al.*):

Conole, G. *et al.* (2004) 'Addressing methodological issues in e-learning research', *Proceedings of the Networked Learning Conference*, Lancaster University, UK, 5–7 April. Available at: www.sef.ac.uk/nlc/Proceedings/Symposa4.htm (Accessed: 2 October 2004).

### Government publication

Author's surname, initials (year) *Title of publication*, Place of publication: Publisher.

Goulding, A. and Cavanagh, B. (2013) *Charges reported under the Offensive Behaviour at Football and Threatening Communications (Scotland) Act in 2012–2013*, Edinburgh: Scottish Government Social Research.

If viewed online:

Author's surname, initials (year) *Title of publication*, Place of publication: Publisher. Available at: URL (Accessed: date).

Sosenko, F., Livingstone, N. and Fitzpatrick, S. (2013) *Overview of food aid provision in Scotland*, Edinburgh: Scottish Government Social Research. Available at: http://www.gov.scot/Resource/0044/00440458.pdf (Accessed: 23 July 2016).

If author unknown but government department known:

Department name (year) *Title of publication*, Place of publication: Publisher.

Justice Analytical Services (2013) *An examination of the evidence of sectarianism in Scotland*, Edinburgh: Scottish Government Social Research.

If viewed online:

> Department name (year) *Title of publication*, Place of publication: Publisher. Available at: URL (Accessed: date).

> Animal Health and Welfare Division (2013) *Promoting responsible dog ownership in Scotland: microchipping and other measures*, Edinburgh: APS Group Scotland. Available at: http://www.gov.scot/Resource/ 0044/00441549.pdf (Accessed: 14 March 2014).

### Journal paper

> Author's surname, initials (year) 'Title of article', *Name of Journal*, volume number (issue number), page(s).

> Burns, E. (1994) 'Information assets, technology and organisation', *Management Science*, 40(12), pp. 645–662.

If viewed online:

> Author's surname, initials (year) 'Title of article', *Name of Journal*, volume number (issue number), page(s) if available. Available at: URL (Accessed: date).

> Gwatipeda, J. and Barbier, E. B. (2013) 'Environmental regulation of a global pollution externality in a bilateral trade environment: the case of global warming, China and the US', *Economics*, 2013 (60), pp. 1–43. Available at: http://www.economics-ejournal.org/economics/discussionpapers/ 2013-60 (Accessed: 18 August 2014).

### Module material

> Tutor name (Year) 'Title'. *Module number: module title*. Available at: URL (Accessed: date).

> Roe, K. (2017) 'Notes'. P101: Poetry. Available at: https://www.clyde.ac.uk/ notes (Accessed: 3 May 2017).

### Newspaper article

> Author's surname, initials (year) 'Title of article', *Name of Newspaper*, day and month of publication, page(s).

> Riddell, P. and Webster, P. (2006) 'Support for Labour at lowest level since 1992', *The Times*, 9 May, p. 2.

Where the author is not known, then use the name of the newspaper instead:

> *Name of newspaper* (year) 'Title of article', day and month of publication, page(s).

*The Indian Agra News* (2007) 'Carbon footprints and economic globalisation', 18 April, p. 4.

If viewed online:

Author's surname, initials (year) 'Title of article', *Name of Newspaper*, day and month of publication. Available at: URL (Accessed: date).

McArdle, H. (2013) 'Officials say new Forth bridge on schedule', *The Herald*, 30 December. Available at: http://www.heraldscotland.com/news/13138238. Officials_say_new_Forth_bridge_on_schedule/ (Accessed: 30 December 2013).

Where the author is not known, then use the name of the newspaper instead:

*Name of newspaper* (year) 'Title of article', day and month of publication. Available at: URL (Accessed: date).

*The Herald* (2013) 'Officials say new Forth bridge on schedule', 30 December. Available at: http://www.heraldscotland.com/news/13138238.Officials_say_ new_Forth_bridge_on_schedule/ (Accessed: 30 December 2013).

## Photograph

Photographer (Year) *Title* [Photograph]. Place of publication: publisher.

Eisenstaedt, A. (1945) *The Kiss* [Photograph]. New York City: Life.

If viewed online:

Photographer (Year) *Title* [Photograph]. Available at: URL (Accessed: date).

Eisenstaedt, A. (1945) *The Kiss* [Photograph]. Available at: http://100photos. time.com/photos/kiss-v-j-day-times-square-alfred-eisenstaedt (Accessed: 27 May 2017).

## Play

### Book format

Playwright's surname, initials (year) *Title of play*. Editor. Place of publication: Publisher.

Beckett, S. (2006) *Waiting for Godot*. Edited by Knowlson, J. London: Faber and Faber.

### Live performance

*Title of play* by playwright (Year performed) Directed by director name [Place performed. Date seen].

*The Steamie* by Tony Roper (2013) Directed by Tony Roper [Eastwood Park Theatre, Scotland. 23 October 2013].

## Radio

*Title of radio programme* (Year) Station, date.

*Bob Harris Sunday* (2017) BBC Radio 2, 19 March 2017.

## Social media

### Blog

Author (Year site posted) 'Title of article', *Title of site*, date posted. Available at: URL (Accessed: date).

Snowdon, K. (2012) 'Rescuing lions – an exclusive interview with Captured in Africa', *Kate on conservation*, 28 April 2016. Available at: https://kateconservation.wordpress.com/2016/04/28/rescuing-lions-an-exclusive-interview-with-captured-in-africa/ (Accessed: 27 April 2017).

### Facebook

*Title* (Year page posted) [Facebook] date posted. Available at: URL (Accessed: date).

*University of Liverpool* (2017) [Facebook] 20 March. Available at: https://www.facebook.com/UniversityofLiverpool/ (Accessed: 22 March 2017).

### Twitter

Author (Year of tweet) [Twitter] date posted. Available at: URL (Accessed: date).

Obama, B. (2017) [Twitter] 8 March. Available at: https://mobile.twitter.com/BarackObama?ref_src=twsrc%5Egoogle%7Ctwcamp%5Eserp%7Ctwgr%5Eauthor (Accessed: 22 March 2017).

### YouTube

Name of poster (Year video posted) *Title of video*. Available at: URL (Accessed: date).

Newspoliticsinfo (2015) *Martin Luther King's last speech 'I've been to the mountain top'*. Available at: https://m.youtube.com/watch?v=Oehry1JC9Rk (Accessed: 14 January 2016).

## Software (Computer program, mobile app, video game, etc.)

Author (year of release) *Title* (Version) [Format, e.g. Computer program, mobile app, video game, Xbox 360]. Distributor: place of distribution.

Arkane Studios (2017) *Prey* [PS4]. Bethesda Softworks: Rockville, Maryland.

If e-software:

Author/publisher (year of release) *Title* (Version) [Format, e.g. Computer program, Mobile app, Video game, Xbox 360]. Available at: URL (Downloaded: date).

AGT Technologies (2017) *AVG anti-virus* (free) [Mobile app]. Available at: http://www.avg.com/gb-en/antivirus-for-android (Downloaded: 14 March 2017).

## Television

*Title* (Year broadcast) Channel, date.

*Dr Who* (2014) BBC One, 15 April 2014.

Specific episode of a series:

'Episode title' (Year) *Series title*, Series number, episode number, Channel, date.

'The Zygon Inversion' (2015) *Dr Who*, series 9, episode 8, BBC One, 13 November 2015.

## Theses and dissertations

Author's name, initials (year) *Title of thesis/dissertation*. Level of award. Institution.

Aitken, R. (2008) *Exploring the role of laughter in the workplace*. PhD thesis. Inverclyde University.

If viewed online:

Author's name, initials (year) *Title of thesis/dissertation*. Level of award. Institution. Available at: URL (Accessed: date).
Bancroft, T.D. (2016) *Scalar short-term memory*. PhD thesis. Wilfrid Laurier University. Available at: http://scholars.wlu.ca/cgi/viewcontent.cgi?article=2927&context=etd (Accessed: 24 March 2017).

## Website

Author's name, initials (year) *Title of web page*. Available at: URL (Accessed: date).

Brender, A. (2004) *Speakers promote distance education to audiences in Asia*. Available at: www.chronicle.com (Accessed: 12 November 2015).

If no author, then use website name or organisation name.

# Appendix B: Typical dissertation proposal form

MASTER'S DISSERTATION PROPOSAL FORM        University of XXXX

Student name:

Matriculation number:

Programme:

Department:

WORKING TITLE:

Research aim/question:

Specific research objectives:

Place your research in context:

Why is your research worth doing?:

How are you going to meet your overall
research aim?

Provide a timetable of activities:

What key literature influenced your choice
of research topic?:

Are there any ethical issues to consider?
If yes, please complete Ethical Proposal Form:

▶

▶ **Please complete and submit a printed copy to
the POSTGRADUATE Admissions Office.**


**Signed and dated (student):**


**Signed and dated (supervisor, if known):**

# Appendix C: Research objective keywords

| | | | | |
|---|---|---|---|---|
| Analyse | Determine | Generate | Outline | Solve |
| Apply | Develop | Highlight | Prescribe | Sort |
| Appraise | Devise | Identify | Prioritise | Specify |
| Assess | Diagnose | Illuminate | Probe | Standardise |
| Calculate | Differentiate | Illustrate | Process | State |
| Categorise | Discern | Implement | Produce | Streamline |
| Clarify | Discover | Improve | Progress | Study |
| Classify | Distinguish | Indicate | Prove | Synthesise |
| Collate | Establish | Integrate | Quantify | Tabulate |
| Compare | Estimate | Invent | Query | Test |
| Construct | Evaluate | Investigate | Recommend | Trace |
| Contrast | Examine | Itemise | Reconstruct | Transform |
| Create | Execute | Judge | Refine | Translate |
| Critique | Expand | Justify | Reform | Underline |
| Demonstrate | Experiment | List | Reveal | Understand |
| Derive | Explain | Locate | Review | Unite |
| Describe | Explore | Measure | Scrutinise | Use |
| Design | Fix | Modify | Show | Validate |
| Detect | Formulate | Organise | Simplify | Verify |

# Appendix D: Sample dissertation proposal

---

**DISSERTATION PROPOSAL**

**UNIVERSITY OF INVERCLYDE**

**Name of student:** Joseph Bloggs

**Programme/Year:** MA Educational Studies 2014/2015

**Dissertation title:** Preparing University Academic Staff for e-Learning: A Study of Drivers, Barriers and Preparation Models/ Frameworks

---

## 1.1 Background

The traditional approach to teaching and learning in universities involves a mix of face-to-face lectures, seminars/tutorials, individual tuition/supervision and, where relevant, laboratory work – all reinforced with independent self-study. The use of Information and Communication Technology (ICT) over the last two decades has increased the means of enhancing student knowledge. This is reflected in the prevalence of PowerPoint-based lectures, digital library databases, mobile technologies (e.g. iPad/iPhone), the Internet, and managed Virtual Learning Environments (VLEs). When ICT is used to support independent study, it is generally given the term 'e-Learning'. E-Learning is now a core strategy for universities, reflected in their investments in VLEs such as WebCT, Blackboard, and Moodle (OLTF, 2011).

However, an area of consistent concern is the preparedness of academic staff to contribute meaningfully to e-Learning environments (Salmon, 2011; Thuraya *et al.*, 2014). Indeed, as early as 1997, Dearing highlighted in his report (1997, p. 36) that 'many academics have had no training and little experience in the use of communications and information technology as an educational tool'. As the technology has increased down the years, so have the voices expressing apprehension over staff training to cope with a new pedagogy that places staff from the *sage on the stage* to a *guide on the side* (Laurillard, 2009; MacKeogh and Fox, 2009; Slade and Readman, 2013). Mayes and De Freitas (2013, p. 28) recognise that 'positioning empowered individual learners at the centre of the technology-enhanced design process will clearly impact on the role of the educator' and that there is a need for universities to articulate a teaching and learning pedagogy that allows academic staff to bridge the gap between theory and practice. A critique of staff preparation models/frameworks will form the central plank of this research.

Academic staff engagement is crucial to the success of e-Learning in universities (Dyment and Downing, 2013). If academic staff do not accept the educational benefits of e-Learning, then they may be less likely to be willing participants in e-Learning initiatives, irrespective of the professional nature of staff training programmes. Schneckenberg (2009) argued that there is a need to understand the staff barriers to meaningful involvement in e-Learning, citing staff motivation as an example. Tomei (2006) highlighted the negative impact of online teaching on academic staff 'load'. As such, it makes sense as part of the study of academic staff preparedness for e-Learning, to clarify the university drivers for e-Learning (and how they are communicated to academic staff) and the main barriers to academic staff becoming involved in e-Learning.

These concerns over staff training issues necessitate an exploratory study on how academic staff are being prepared for e-Learning. Furthermore, technology is changing rapidly with students no longer solely dependent on face-to-face instruction – and so universities need to adapt to this changing educational landscape. A failure by universities to ensure that their academic staff can meet the challenges of an ever-developing digital world will impact adversely on the student learning experience and, in effect, the ability of a university to meet its core e-Learning strategy. Having an academic body well versed on e-Learning pedagogy will be to the benefit of senior management, academics, and students.

## 1.2 Research aim and research objectives

The overall aim of this research is to advance an understanding of the issues surrounding the preparation of university academic staff to support student e-Learning. Within the context of higher education, the specific objectives of this research are to:

1 *Identify* the forces driving e-Learning and the barriers to the successful delivery of e-Learning programmes.
2 *Evaluate critically* models and frameworks relevant to supporting academic staff in coping with e-Learning.
3 *Explore* staff stakeholder views and practices related to e-Learning preparation, including drivers and barriers to e-Learning.
4 *Formulate* recommendations on staff preparation issues.

## 1.3 Research methods and timescales

This research will depend on a review of pertinent literature (objectives 1 and 2) and the collection of empirical data through a case study (objective 3). The secondary data (i.e. literature review) will largely come from journals (e.g. *International Journal of e-Learning*); conference proceedings (e.g. Online

Educa); seminal books (e.g. Laurillard, 2009); and published surveys/reports (e.g. Walker *et al.*, 2012: 'Survey of technology enhanced learning for higher education in the UK'). The following library databases will, in particular, be utilised to support this research: ERIC, British Education Index (ProQuest), and JSTOR.

The primary data (i.e. empirical data) will be collected through a case study. A case study is a study of a single unit (Cohen *et al.*, 2005), allowing exploratory research in depth (Yin, 2003). The case unit will consist of an academic department within Inverclyde University. The means of collecting the primary data will be based on an initial questionnaire from which a subset of the target population will be subject to a detailed follow-up interview. In addition, a number of *elite staff* – those responsible for the success of e-Learning and staff training – will be interviewed. The combination of a literature review and empirical research will allow theory and practice to be compared, from which a rich picture of academic staff preparation should emerge.

This research does not aim to generalise the status of staff preparation in e-Learning but, instead, seeks an in-depth understanding of the elements that constitute e-Learning preparation, including drivers and barriers. Hence the use of a case study to support an extensive literature review.

Table D.1 shows the expected timescales for this dissertation proposal, from finalising initial research objectives to submission of dissertation.

**Table D.1** Breakdown of dissertation timescales

| Dissertation activity | Duration (in weeks) | Month |
| --- | --- | --- |
| Clarify Aim/Objectives | 2 | June |
| Literature Review | 4 | June–July |
| Research Methods | 2 | July |
| Data Collection | 3 | August |
| Findings | 3 | August–September |
| Conclusion | 2 | 25 September |

Full details of the research methods used for this research, including justification for the chosen methods, will appear in a chapter entitled Research Methods within the dissertation proper.

## 1.4 Beneficiaries of this research

This research will benefit the academic research community by contributing to the field of e-Learning in the area of academic staff preparation. The results of this work – secondary and primary data – can be used to enrich existing research schemas, particularly in relation to staff preparation models/frameworks and staff views, thus adding incrementally to the knowledge base of e-Learning research.

Although the output from this research work cannot be generalised, nonetheless the literature review findings and the empirical case study can act as a focus to inform elite staff in universities on potential staff e-Learning preparation issues, encouraging management to revisit how they prepare academic staff to engage fully with e-Learning. At the very least, this work will raise the profile of an area of educational delivery – e-Learning – that Vermeer (2000, p. 329) once decried had often been dependent on 'the enthusiasm of the recently converted' for its success. Technology is increasingly at the heart of university education and this research will benefit all those with an interest in ensuring that technology is exploited by fully trained academic staff: senior management, students, and academic staff.

## 1.5 Ethics

There are no ethical issues requiring approval from the University's ethical committee. Academic staff will be interviewed as part of this research but their responses will be anonymised, with no identifying data used (unless permission is explicitly given), in line with Data Protection principles.

## 1.6 References

Cohen, L., Manion, L. and Morrison, K. (2005) *Research methods in education*. 5th edn. London: Routledge.

Dearing, R. (1997) *Higher education in the learning society* (The Dearing Report). London: HMSO.

Dyment, J. and Downing, J. (2013) 'Framing teacher educator engagement in an online environment', *Australian Journal of Teacher Education*, 38(1), pp. 133–149.

Laurillard, D. (2009) 'The pedagogical challenges to collaborative technologies', *International Journal of Computer-Supported Collaborative Learning*, 4(1), pp. 5–20.

MacKeogh, K. and Fox, S. (2009) 'Strategies for embedding e-Learning in traditional universities: drivers and barriers', *Electronic Journal of e-Learning*, 7(2), pp. 147–154.

Mayes, T. and De Freitas, S. (2013) 'Technology-enhanced learning', in Beetham, H. and Sharpe, R. (eds) *Rethinking pedagogy for a digital age*. New York: Routledge, pp. 17–30.

OLTF (2011) *Collaborate to compete: seizing the opportunity of online learning for UK higher education*. London: Higher Education Funding Council for England (HEFCE).

Salmon, G. (2011) *E-moderating*. 3rd edn. New York: Routledge.

Schneckenberg, D. (2009) 'Understanding the real barriers to technology-enhanced innovation in higher education', *Education Research*, 51(4), pp. 411–424.

Slade, C. and Readman, K. (2013) 'Research and development in higher education: the place of learning and teaching', *Higher Education Research and Development Society of Australasia*, 36, pp. 404–413.

Thuraya K., Crinela P. and Abdussalam E. (2014) 'Trends and policy issues for the e-Learning implementation in Libyan universities', *International Journal of Trade, Economics and Finance*, 5(1), pp. 105–109.

Tomei, L. A. (2006) 'The impact of online teaching on faculty load: computing the ideal class size for online courses', *Journal of Technology and Teacher Education*, 14(3), pp. 531–541.

Vermeer, R. (2000) 'Review of internet based learning: an introduction and framework for higher education and business', *Computers & Education*, 35(4), pp. 327–333.

Walker, R., Voce, J. and Ahmed, J. (2012) *Survey of technology enhanced learning for higher education in the UK*. Oxford: UCISA.

Yin, R. K. (2003) *Case study research: design and methods*. 3rd edn. Thousand Oaks, CA: Sage.

**Student signature:**      Joseph Bloggs

**Date:**      15 April 2014

# Appendix E: Sample Introduction

## Chapter 1: Introduction

### 1.1 Background

The traditional approach to teaching and learning has, for millennia, rested on the central premise that for instruction to take place, the tutor and student co-exist in the same place at the same time. Aristotle's lectures, preserved in the writings of Plato, are examples of such an approach, where the student is educated on particular topics through the mechanism of illuminating conversations – *dialogues* – between tutor and student (Taylor, 1955). However, few universities have the generous resources required to support one-to-one tuition as the prevailing mode of educational delivery; rather, the common method consists of a combination of lectures, seminars/tutorials and, where appropriate, laboratory work; where each of the aforementioned ways of imparting knowledge involves face-to-face instruction and discussion.

Information and Communication Technologies (ICT) are used frequently to support the traditional teaching and learning paradigm. Academic staff use technology, for example, to prepare and deliver lectures, as well as for administrative purposes. Haywood *et al.* (2004) believe that students arrive at university with high expectations that they will have access to modern technology. Universities have also moved rapidly to acquire dedicated software platforms that allow them to offer educational programs free from the shackles of time and place (Farrell, 2001), with Moe and Blodget (2000, p. 104) emphasising that 'the next big killer application for the Internet is going to be education'.

Online learning, networked learning, distributed learning, flexible learning, avirtual learning, these are some of the terms used to describe learning that uses technology as a vehicle for educational delivery (Salmon, 1998; Britain and Liber, 1999; Jung, 2000; Collis and Moonen, 2001; Rosenberg, 2001). Another, more commonly used term is *e-Learning* (Ryan, 2001; Sloman and Rolph, 2003). Tearle *et al.* (1999, p. 14) urge universities to engage with e-Learning, particularly for distance learning, and warn that 'it is no longer possible to opt out'. As early as 1997, the Dearing Report foresaw benefits of using ICT in higher education:

> ... *we believe that the innovative application of ... C&IT holds out much promise for improving the quality, flexibility and effectiveness of higher education. The potential benefits will extend to, and affect the practice of, learning and teaching and research* (Dearing, 1997, 13.1).

It is not difficult to find examples of universities responding to the call to develop e-Learning initiatives. FutureLearn, a private company owned by the Open University, offers free high-calibre online courses. FutureLearn's partners and educational contributors are wide-ranging and include, among other prestigious institutions, Shanghai Jiao Tong University, Trinity College Dublin, the University of Auckland, the University of Glasgow, the British Council, the British Library and the British Museum. The Centre for Instructional Technologies, a unit of the Division of Instructional Innovation and Assessment at The University of Texas at Austin, has embraced enthusiastically the concept of e-Learning by creating an online 'World Lecture Hall', whereby online course materials are provided free to any interested parties, who, in turn, can also contribute new material if they wish.

Technological advances, however, increasingly present a serious and genuine challenge to the traditional teaching and learning model (Collis and Moonen, 2001; Laurillard, 2002). Tomei (2006), for example, highlights the impact of online teaching on academic staff 'load', warning that the ideal class size for online teaching ought to be twelve students. Jones *et al.* (2004) point out that e-Learning students expect staff to respond expediently to their online queries, and no later than 48 hours. Hodges (2004) argues that e-Learning tutors need to incorporate techniques to motivate students involved in subjects that are delivered through e-Learning. Increased staff workload, response times and online motivational techniques are some of the issues that academic tutors involved in e-Learning ought to be trained to cope with, particularly if they are new to making the transition from teaching and learning in the traditional environment to one where e-Learning technologies are to be used.

E-Learning environments are changing the role of the university tutor, where tutors need to learn to become guides and facilitators, rather than the main source of knowledge, as in the traditional teaching and learning environment, with Salmon (2000) underlining that such a transition requires new skills, including time management skills, the ability to monitor the student learning process, and the skill to change teaching methods to meet the needs of e-Learning students.

## 1.2 Research focus

There is some confusion about the benefits of e-Learning. Serious issues are being raised concerning possible barriers to the successful adoption of e-Learning. For example, there have been concerns over student drop-out rates (Flood, 2002), inadequate IT infrastructures to support e-Learning (Cowan, 2004), and the need to ensure that e-Learning software facilities can accommodate students with disabilities (UK eUniversities Worldwide, 2003). Massey (2002), in a European survey on quality and e-Learning, lamented that only 1 per cent of respondents – a mixture of Higher Education (HE) teachers, Further Education (FE) teachers, HE and FE managers, and private trainers – rated the quality of e-Learning courses as excellent, with 61 per cent of all respondents rating the overall quality of e-Learning negatively.

In particular, e-Learning commentators are warning that academic staff in universities need to be prepared to cope with e-Learning, to make the shift from *sage on the stage* to *guide on the side*. The Dearing Report (1997, 13.2) bluntly stated that 'the concept of the higher education experience will need to be altered radically', complaining that many academics had little experience of the use of ICT as an educational tool. Laurillard (2001) argues that e-Learning requires new skills to deal with new pedagogy. Straub (2002), the director of eLearning Solutions and chairman of the European e-Learning Industry Group, complains that 'e-learning [is not] taking off [in Europe] in our daily lives – in schools, companies and universities', concluding that key reasons for this include, *inter alia*, the lack of 'professional development of educators' and a failure to engage 'new pedagogy'.

Critical to this study is an understanding of the type of support that is required to prepare academic staff from making the change from *sage on the stage* to *guide on the side*, the type of support that is available to prepare staff for e-Learning, and what recommendations can be made to help improve existing support frameworks. Understanding how academic staff are being prepared for e-Learning, and their views on their preparation experiences, is therefore an area worthy of study and one that would contribute knowledge to the e-Learning research community. A critique of staff preparation models/frameworks, including staff views on their own experiences, will form a central plank of this research.

The importance of research in this field of e-Learning becomes even more apparent when other researchers mourn the lack of research in this area. Vermeer (2000, p. 329) complains of too little research of staff experiences in e-Learning and that much commentary is anecdotal in nature, mainly coming from 'the enthusiasm of the recently converted', while Coppola *et al.* (2001, p. 96) urge that 'there is a critical need for study of faculty experiences'; and as far afield as New Zealand there is a national priority for 'more research into the effectiveness and theoretical base of e-Learning' as a result of practitioners 'finding their progress restricted by the lack of available research into e-Learning' (Ministry of Education, 2004, p. 1).

If academic staff do not accept the educational benefits of e-Learning, then they may be less likely to be willing participants in e-Learning initiatives, irrespective of the professional nature of staff training programmes. Schneckenberg (2009) argued that there is a need to understand the staff barriers to meaningful involvement in e-Learning, citing staff motivation as an example. As such, it makes sense as part of the study of academic staff preparedness for e-Learning, to clarify the university drivers for e-Learning (and how they are communicated to academic staff) and the main barriers to academic staff becoming involved in e-Learning.

To gain a deeper understanding of these issues related to academic staff preparation, two main activities will need to be tackled: a review of relevant literature to ascertain current research findings on e-Learning preparation issues, including drivers and potential barriers; and empirical data collection on academic staff experiences of preparing for e-Learning.

### 1.3 Overall research aim and individual research objectives

The overall aim of this research is to advance an understanding of the issues surrounding the preparation of university academic staff to support student e-Learning. Within the context of higher education, the specific objectives of this research are to:

1 *Identify* the forces driving e-Learning and the barriers to the successful delivery of e-Learning programmes.
2 *Evaluate critically* models and frameworks relevant to supporting academic staff in coping with e-Learning.
3 *Explore* staff stakeholder views and practices related to e-Learning preparation, including drivers and barriers to e-Learning.
4 *Formulate* recommendations on staff preparation issues.

It would be difficult to comprehend how staff ought to meet the challenge of e-Learning without knowing the drivers behind e-Learning or the potential barriers, both strategic and personal; and given the confusion between those who predict an exponential e-Learning utopia and those who raise some concerns, it is all the more important to try and clarify e-Learning drivers and barriers (objective 1). To improve staff preparedness for e-Learning it is necessary to understand and assess existing guidelines supporting staff and student needs (objective 2). Theory is important but to gain a meaningful insight into what staff think of how they are being prepared to cope with e-Learning, it is necessary to explore their experiences and views (objective 3). The ultimate point of this dissertation is to make recommendations on the findings (objective 4).

### 1.4 Outline research methods and timescales

This research will depend on a review of pertinent literature (objectives 1 and 2) and the collection of empirical data through a case study (objective 3). The secondary data (i.e. literature review) will largely come from journals (e.g. *International Journal of e-Learning*); conference proceedings (e.g. Online Educa); seminal books (e.g. Laurillard, 2002), and recent surveys. The following library databases will, in particular, be utilised to support this research: ERIC, British Education Index (ProQuest), and JSTOR.

The primary data (i.e. empirical data) will be collected through a case study. A case study is a study of a single unit (Cohen *et al.*, 2005), allowing exploratory research in depth (Yin, 2003). The case unit will consist of an academic department within Inverclyde University. The means of collecting the primary data will be based on an initial questionnaire to academic staff from which a subset of the target population will be subject to a detailed follow-up interview. In addition, a number of *elite staff* – those responsible for the success of e-Learning and staff training – will be interviewed. The combination of a literature review and empirical research will allow theory and practice to be compared, from which a rich picture of academic staff preparation should emerge.

This research does not aim to generalise the status of staff preparation in e-Learning but, instead, seeks an in-depth understanding of the elements that constitute e-Learning preparation, including drivers and barriers. Hence the use of a case study to support an extensive literature review.

Table E.1 shows the expected timescales for this dissertation proposal, from finalising initial research objectives to submission of dissertation.

**Table E.1**   Breakdown of dissertation timescales

| Dissertation activity | Duration (in weeks) | Month |
| --- | --- | --- |
| Clarify Aim/Objectives | 2 | June |
| Literature Review | 4 | June–July |
| Research Methods | 2 | July |
| Data Collection | 3 | August |
| Findings | 3 | August–September |
| Conclusion | 2 | 25 September |

Full details of the research methods used for this research, including justification for the chosen methods, will appear in a chapter entitled Research Methods within the dissertation proper.

## 1.5 Value of this research

This research will benefit the academic research community by contributing to the field of e-Learning in the area of academic staff preparation. The results of this work – secondary and primary data – can be used to enrich existing research schemas, particularly in relation to staff preparation models/ frameworks and staff views, thus adding incrementally to the knowledge base of e-Learning research.

Although the output from this research work cannot be generalised, nonetheless the literature review findings and the empirical case study can act as a focus to inform elite staff in universities on potential staff e-Learning preparation issues, encouraging management to revisit how they prepare academic staff to engage fully with e-Learning. Other beneficiaries include: academic staff themselves, who will gain from recommendations that reflect their concerns on support issues; and, ultimately, students. If staff are better prepared to deliver e-Learning programmes, then that augurs well for the student experience.

This work will raise the profile of an area of educational delivery – e-Learning – that Vermeer (2000, p. 329) once decried had often been dependent on 'the enthusiasm of the recently converted' for its success. Technology is increasingly at the heart of university education and this research will benefit all those with an interest in ensuring that technology is exploited by fully trained academic staff.

The next chapter – Chapter 2 Literature Review – examines literature pertinent to the objectives of this research, beginning with an investigation of what is meant by the term *e-Learning*.

# Appendix F: Sample chapter outline

## Outline structure

### Chapter 1: Introduction

This chapter provides the reader with *background* information on the impact of e-Learning on the traditional teaching and learning paradigm in the University environment, including an illustration of some drivers and barriers and the need for an understanding on how staff are being prepared to make the switch from *sage on the stage* to *guide on the side*. The *focus* of this research is discussed and justified and the *overall research aim* and *individual research objectives* are identified. *Research methods and timescales* are outlined, as is the *value of this research*.

### Chapter 2: Literature review

This chapter *defines* the term e-Learning, discusses *distance learning* (a driver for e-Learning), clarifies the *drivers* for e-Learning (including major reports, strategic forces, and the benefits of e-Learning to different stakeholders), explores *barriers* to e-Learning, evaluates *guidelines and models* on e-Learning support infrastructures in relation to providing support for academic staff preparation, and *justifies the need for empirical data* on academic staff preparation issues.

### Chapter 3: Research methods

This chapter discusses and justifies the *research strategy* (a case study) and *data collection techniques* (centred on structured interviews) to be adopted in the empirical collection of data for this study. Details on the *site and sample* are provided, together with a *framework for analysis* of the qualitative data. In addition, the *limitations* of the adopted approach to this research are discussed, in terms of validity and reliability, as well as *potential problems* related to implementing a case study at Inverclyde University.

### Chapter 4: Case study results: academic staff; elite staff

This chapter reports on the findings from the case study. In the first instance, the results of the *interviews with academic staff* are discussed (under the themes: Drivers, Barriers, Preparation, IT Infrastructure, Academic Staff Motivation, and Reflections and Future Directions); next, the findings from *interviews with elite staff* – university staff with an influence on the shape and direction of e-Learning in the institution under study (mainly senior management) – are discussed. It is in the section on the elite staff findings that *analysis and synthesis take place*: the empirical findings from both stakeholder groups (academic staff and elite staff) are analysed against each other and then synthesised, once again in terms of soft comparison and contrast, against the findings from the literature review. Thus, this chapter describes, discusses, analyses, and synthesises the empirical findings and the findings from the literature review.

### Chapter 5: Conclusion

This chapter revisits the overall aim and specific objectives of this research study. The *findings are summarised* against each of the stated objectives. *Conclusions* from this research work are derived and linked to the research objectives, and based on these conclusions, *recommendations* are made. The *limitations* of this work are also highlighted. Importantly, the issue of *managing* the implementation of the recommendations is addressed. The *contribution of this research to knowledge* is also clarified. Lastly, a section on *Self-reflection* is included, providing the reader with a personal reflection on the process that has been undertaken to complete this work.

### Chapter 6: References

This chapter contains an alphabetical listing of the sources referred to in this work. The Harvard system of referencing (author–date system) is used.

# Appendix G: Sample Literature Review introduction

## Sample introduction to a Literature Review

This Literature Review will examine the main issues surrounding the drive for e-Learning environments within the university sector, impediments to the successful implementation of e-Learning, and guidelines that are available to assist academic staff in tackling identified issues. The study within this review of literature focuses on objectives 1 and 2 below (the third objective will be met through the vehicle of empirical data collection and analysis, while the final objective – objective 4 – is derived as a result of the findings from objectives 1, 2, and 3):

1 *Identify* the forces driving e-Learning and the barriers to the successful delivery of e-Learning programmes.
2 *Evaluate critically* models and frameworks relevant to supporting academic staff in coping with e-Learning.
3 *Explore* staff stakeholder views and practices related to e-Learning preparation, including drivers and barriers to e-Learning.
4 *Formulate* recommendations on staff preparation issues.

By exploring the above areas of literature, a significant contribution will be made to this research. The strategic forces pushing universities to engage in e-Learning, together with the benefits to staff and students, will be evaluated.

Similarly, barriers to e-Learning involvement in universities will be examined, such as individual and social barriers, opposition to globalisation, inadequate student infrastructures, and the need for academic staff support. Importantly, guidelines to support academic staff will be assessed in terms of their relevance to preparing academic staff for e-Learning. In effect, the value of studying the aforementioned literature areas will be to provide a meaningful discussion and analysis of e-Learning, in a structured way, to facilitate a critical understanding of academic staff preparation issues.

At the end of this major section, it is hoped that a critical understanding of key issues is exhibited, that the reader will be better informed in these areas and that there will emerge a clear focus, and justification, for empirical research in the field of e-Learning in higher education. In the first instance, a sensible starting point is to investigate what is meant by the term *e-Learning*. Additionally, the educational phenomenon referred to as *distance learning* – seen by many as an obvious use of e-Learning – will be explored to help place in context drivers and barriers to e-Learning.

# Appendix H: Sample Literature Review conclusion

## Emerging issues and need for empirical research

The study of relevant e-Learning literature revealed that e-Learning is a complex and moving landscape. To begin with, there was no agreed definition of e-Learning. One was produced, highlighting connectivity, support infrastructures, and flexibility of access and delivery.

Although there were many strategic drivers (perceived reduced costs, access to global markets, increased students, etc.) and potential educational benefits to staff and students (such as flexibility of delivery and access, independent learning, job opportunities, etc.), there were also many barriers that were identified that could impact on universities and staff contemplating involvement in e-Learning: staff resistance, concerns over student drop-out rates, student inability to cope with independent learning, opposition to globalisation, access to support facilities, inadequate student support infrastructures, and, crucially, lack of staff preparation to cope with e-Learning.

The review of literature stressed the need to have in place an infrastructure to support academic staff. There was concern that universities may not train their staff, or have available for reference guidelines on how to support their staff in the development and management of e-Learning. Guidelines and models on e-Learning support infrastructures were reviewed. Meaningful guidelines were identified as a necessary prerequisite to preparing academic staff for e-Learning environments. However, the guidelines and models, although useful in part, tended to concentrate on the needs of students or, where advice on preparing staff for e-Learning was given, were mainly skeletal and general in nature with relatively little advice based on academic staff experiences.

A crucial issue for the development of e-Learning in universities is that recommendations on future directions ought to be based on research. Unfortunately, empirical data on university approaches to staff training were shown to be few and far between. In other words, there is a continuing need for empirical data on how academic staff are preparing for e-Learning, and the aforementioned review of literature supports this claim.

To arrive at a deeper understanding of how universities are meeting the challenge of e-Learning, empirical research will be implemented. Specifically, such research will attempt to find out how academic staff are preparing for e-Learning, what motivates them to do so, and, from a wider perspective, the drivers and barriers acting on the university environment in relation to developing e-Learning programmes. The next stage of this research will detail the Research Methods to be used to capture the empirical data, including details on the research strategy to be adopted, data collection techniques, sample selection, and management of the researcher's role.

# Appendix I: Comprehensive set of useful verbs

| | | | |
|---|---|---|---|
| Accepts | Acknowledges | Acquiesces | Adduces |
| Admits | Adopts | Advances | Advises |
| Advocates | Agrees | Alludes | Appears |
| Argues | Arrives at | Articulates | Asserts |
| Assumes | Attempts | Bombasts | Bores |
| Builds | Cajoles | Calculates | Captures |
| Cautions | Challenges | Clarifies | Clings |
| Clutches | Comments | Compares | Compiles |
| Complains | Concludes | Concocts | Concurs |
| Confirms | Confuses | Considers | Conspires |
| Constructs | Contemplates | Contends | Contrives |
| Conveys | Convinces | Cultivates | Dabbles |
| Debates | Debunks | Declares | Deduces |
| Defends | Delves | Demonstrates | Denies |
| Denounces | Derides | Derives | Desists |
| Determines | Develops | Digresses | Dilutes |
| Disagrees | Discloses | Discovers | Discusses |
| Dismisses | Dispels | Dispenses | Displays |
| Disputes | Dissects | Dissents | Distils |
| Distinguishes | Distorts | Diverges | Diverts |
| Dodges | Drags | Drifts | Earns |
| Eases | Echoes | Effaces | Effects |
| Effuses | Elaborates | Elucidates | Embarks |
| Embellishes | Embraces | Emphasises | Employs |
| Enables | Enchants | Endears | Endorses |
| Engages | Engineers | Enlightens | Enthrals |
| Entices | Enunciates | Epitomises | Equates |
| Erects | Errs | Eschews | Espouses |
| Establishes | Evaluates | Evangelises | Evokes |
| Exaggerates | Excels | Exhibits | Expands |
| Explains | Explores | Expresses | Expunges |
| Extricates | Fabricates | Faces | Fails |
| Falters | Favours | Fawns | Feigns |
| Ferments | Fiddles | Fields | Finds |
| Fluctuates | Forges | Forms | Formulates |
| Fortifies | Frees | Fulfils | Fusses |

▶

▶

| | | | |
|---|---|---|---|
| Gambles | Gathers | Gauges | Generates |
| Gets | Gilds | Gives | Glides |
| Glorifies | Grafts | Grapples | Grasps |
| Grates | Grinds | Gropes | Guesses |
| Hampers | Handles | Hankers | Has |
| Hatches | Hedges | Helps | Heralds |
| Hesitates | Highlights | Hijacks | Hikes |
| Hinders | Holds | Identifies | Ignores |
| Illuminates | Illustrates | Imagines | Imbues |
| Imparts | Impedes | Impels | Impinges |
| Implants | Implicates | Implies | Implores |
| Imposes | Impregnates | Impresses | Improves |
| Impugns | Imputes | Incites | Inclines |
| Includes | Inculcates | Indicates | Induces |
| Indulges | Infers | Infests | Inflames |
| Inflates | Inflicts | Influences | Informs |
| Infringes | Inhibits | Injects | Inquires |
| Insinuates | Insists | Inspects | Inspires |
| Instigates | Instructs | Insults | Integrates |
| Intends | Interferes | Interjects | Interprets |
| Intertwines | Interweaves | Intimates | Introduces |
| Intrudes | Inundates | Invalidates | Inveighs |
| Invents | Investigates | Invigorates | Invites |
| Involves | Irritates | Iterates | Joins |
| Jostles | Jumps | Justifies | Juxtaposes |
| Knows | Kowtows | Labours | Lacerates |
| Lags | Laments | Lampoons | Lances |
| Lapses | Lauds | Launches | Lays |
| Leads | Leans | Learns | Lectures |
| Lends | Lets | Likes | Limps |
| Lingers | Links | Lists | Litters |
| Livens | Loads | Lobs | Locates |
| Loiters | Looks | Lurches | Magnifies |
| Maintains | Makes | Maligns | Maltreats |
| Manages | Manifests | Marks | Marvels |
| Massages | Masters | Mauls | Means |
| Measures | Meddles | Mediates | Mentions |
| Merges | Merits | Militates | Milks |
| Minces | Miscalculates | Misfires | Misinforms |
| Misinterprets | Misjudges | Misleads | Misrepresents |
| Misses | Mistakes | Misunderstands | Misuses |
| Mitigates | Mixes | Moans | Mocks |

▶

▶

| | | | |
|---|---|---|---|
| Models | Modifies | Modulates | Motivates |
| Moulds | Mounts | Moves | Muddles |
| Mulls | Muses | Musters | Nags |
| Names | Narrates | Needs | Negates |
| Neglects | Negotiates | Niggles | Notes |
| Notices | Nullifies | Nurtures | Obeys |
| Obfuscates | Objects | Obliges | Obliterates |
| Obscures | Observes | Obsesses | Obstructs |
| Obtains | Occupies | Offends | Offers |
| Omits | Oozes | Operates | Opposes |
| Oppresses | Opts | Ordains | Organises |
| Oscillates | Ostracises | Outlines | Outwits |
| Overawes | Overcomes | Overindulges | Overlooks |
| Overreaches | Overreacts | Overworks | Pads |
| Paints | Panders | Panics | Papers |
| Parables | Paraphrases | Participates | Peddles |
| Pens | Penetrates | Peppers | Perceives |
| Percolates | Perfects | Performs | Permeates |
| Permits | Perpetrates | Perpetuates | Perseveres |
| Persists | Personifies | Persuades | Pervades |
| Perverts | Pierces | Pilfers | Pillories |
| Pinions | Pioneers | Placates | Places |
| Plans | Plods | Plucks | Plugs |
| Plummets | Plunders | Plunges | Poaches |
| Points | Pollutes | Ponders | Pontificates |
| Populates | Portends | Portrays | Poses |
| Positions | Possess | Postures | Praises |
| Prances | Prattles | Preaches | Precedes |
| Precipitates | Predicts | Pre-empts | Prefers |
| Prejudices | Prepares | Prescribes | Presents |
| Preserves | Presses | Presumes | Pretends |
| Prevails | Prevaricates | Prevents | Probes |
| Processes | Proclaims | Procures | Prods |
| Produces | Professes | Proffers | Profiles |
| Profits | Profligates | Progresses | Proliferates |
| Promotes | Prompts | Pronounces | Propagates |
| Proposes | Propounds | Proscribes | Prostrates |
| Protests | Provides | Provokes | Publishes |
| Puffs | Pulverises | Pursues | Pushes |
| Postulates | Puts | Qualifies | Quantifies |
| Quarrels | Queries | Questions | Quibbles |
| Quotes | Radiates | Rages | Raises |

▶

▶

| | | | |
|---|---|---|---|
| Rallies | Rambles | Rants | Rates |
| Rationalises | Raves | Reaches | Reacts |
| Realises | Reasons | Reassures | Rebels |
| Rebuffs | Rebukes | Rebuts | Recants |
| Receives | Reciprocates | Recites | Reckons |
| Recognises | Recommends | Reconciles | Reconsiders |
| Reconstructs | Records | Recreates | Rectifies |
| Redeems | Redresses | Reduces | Refers |
| Reflects | Reforms | Refrains | Refuses |
| Regales | Regards | Regrets | Reinforces |
| Reiterates | Rejects | Relapses | Relates |
| Relents | Relies | Relishes | Remains |
| Remarks | Remedies | Reminds | Removes |
| Renders | Repairs | Repeats | Repels |
| Repents | Replies | Reports | Represents |
| Reprimands | Reproaches | Repudiates | Repulses |
| Requests | Requires | Rescinds | Rescues |
| Researches | Resembles | Resents | Resists |
| Resolves | Resorts | Respects | Responds |
| Restricts | Retains | Retracts | Retreats |
| Retrieves | Reveals | Reviews | Revises |
| Revokes | Resolves | Rids | Ridicules |
| Rues | Ruminates | Sabotages | Salvages |
| Samples | Sanctions | Satirises | Satisfies |
| Savages | Schemes | Scintillates | Scorns |
| Scrambles | Scrapes | Scrutinises | Searches |
| Secures | Seems | Sees | Seizes |
| Selects | Sacrifices | Sends | Senses |
| Separates | Serves | Sets | Settles |
| Shapes | Shares | Shies | Shines |
| Shirks | Shocks | Shoulders | Shows |
| Shrinks | Shrouds | Shuns | Shuts |
| Shifts | Signals | Signifies | Simplifies |
| Simulates | Sinks | Sketches | Skims |
| Skips | Skirts | Slams | Slanders |
| Slants | Slays | Slights | Slings |
| Slips | Slots | Smears | Smothers |
| Snubs | Softens | Solicits | Solidifies |
| Solves | Sorts | Sources | Sparks |
| Spearheads | Speculates | Spends | Spins |
| Spoils | Spots | Spouts | Spreads |
| Squabbles | Squanders | Squares | Stands |

▶

▶

| | | | |
|---|---|---|---|
| Starts | States | Stiffens | Stimulates |
| Stirs | Stops | Strafes | Strains |
| Strays | Strengthens | Stresses | Stretches |
| Strives | Structures | Struts | Studies |
| Stumbles | Subjects | Submits | Subscribes |
| Substantiates | Subverts | Succeeds | Succumbs |
| Suffers | Suffices | Suggests | Summarises |
| Supplants | Supplies | Supports | Supposes |
| Suppresses | Surmises | Surmounts | Surpasses |
| Surrounds | Surveys | Suspects | Sustains |
| Sways | Symbolises | Sympathises | Synthesises |
| Tabulates | Taints | Takes | Talks |
| Tarnishes | Taunts | Teases | Teeters |
| Tempers | Tempts | Tends | Terminates |
| Testifies | Tests | Thanks | Theorises |
| Thrives | Thrusts | Tirades | Toils |
| Tolerates | Touches | Traces | Tracks |
| Transcends | Transforms | Transgresses | Transmits |
| Traverses | Treats | Tricks | Tries |
| Triumphs | Trivialises | Trumpets | Trumps |
| Trifles | Tweaks | Typifies | Unburdens |
| Undercuts | Underestimates | Undergoes | Underlines |
| Undermines | Underrates | Understands | Understates |
| Undertakes | Undervalues | Unearths | Unfolds |
| Unifies | Unites | Unloads | Unlocks |
| Unravels | Untangles | Unties | Unveils |
| Unwinds | Upholds | Upsets | Urges |
| Uses | Utilises | Validates | Values |
| Vents | Ventures | Verges | Views |
| Vilifies | Vindicates | Violates | Vituperates |
| Vocalizes | Voices | Volunteers | Wades |
| Waffles | Wallows | Wanders | Wants |
| Warms | Warrants | Wastes | Wavers |
| Waxes | Weaves | Welcomes | Wheedles |
| Whines | Whittles | Wills | Winds |
| Wishes | Withdraws | Withers | Withstands |
| Witnesses | Wobbles | Wonders | Works |
| Wrenches | Wrestles | Wriggles | Wrings |
| Writes | Yanks | Yearns | Yields |
| Zaps | Zings | Zips | |

# Appendix J: Sample research methods chapter

> • Introduction • Research strategy • Data collection: site and sample selection • Data collection techniques • Framework for data analysis • Limitations and potential problems

## Research Methods

### Introduction

This research study has a number of inter-related objectives set within the context of Higher Education:

1 *Identify* the forces driving e-Learning and the barriers to the successful delivery of e-Learning programmes.
2 *Evaluate critically* models and frameworks relevant to supporting academic staff in coping with e-Learning.
3 *Explore* staff stakeholder views and practices related to e-Learning preparation, including drivers and barriers to e-Learning.
4 *Formulate* recommendations on staff preparation issues.

A valuable aspect to this research work relates to objective 3: the opportunity to study e-Learning strategy and implementation in practice in a subject that, although generating much discussion and demand, is in terms of usage and research within the wider university community, in its embryonic stages. The opportunity, therefore, to gain a variety of stakeholder views ought to contribute significantly not only to the study of e-Learning in general, but to a richer understanding of staff training issues in particular.

Objectives 1 and 2 were initially addressed in the Literature Review; objective 3 takes this research one step further through the collection and analysis of empirical data obtained from a university setting. Importantly, although a focus of the empirical work will be to gather data on academic staff training to cope with e-Learning, data will also be collected on stakeholder views on perceived drivers and barriers to e-Learning within a university setting, thus providing the opportunity to explore why a university is becoming involved in e-Learning and what a variety of university stakeholders consider to be impediments to e-Learning. By comparing theory with practice – i.e. comparing the Literature Review findings with the 'real world' – the researcher will gain a fuller understanding of the issues surrounding the implementation of e-Learning and so be better placed to contribute useful knowledge in relation to e-Learning in the university environment.

This chapter will provide the details of the research strategy adopted to address the research issues identified above, together with the means of collecting data for analysis, including site and sample selection, and the analysis approach to be adopted. In addition, the reader will be directed towards the thorny issue of potential limitations and problems with the chosen research strategy and its implementation.

## Research strategy

The research strategy that will be used to implement the empirical research is a case study. What is a case study approach and why is it suitable for this research? Cohen and Manion (1995, p. 106) describe a case study thus:

> 'the case study researcher typically observes the characteristics of an individual unit – a child, a class, a school or a community. The purpose of such observation is to probe deeply and to analyse intensively the multifarious phenomena that constitute the life cycle of the unit.'

According to this definition, a case study is therefore concerned with close observation of how a particular population group behave in a particular context. A case study approach facilitates this researcher's drive to probe deeply into a university's response to e-Learning, by devoting time and energy concentrating on specific aspects of e-Learning in one higher education institution. However, there is some disagreement about what constitutes a case study. Yin (2003, p. 13), for example, defines a case study in a different way:

> 'A case study is an empirical inquiry that
>
> • Investigates a contemporary phenomenon within its real-life context, especially when
> • The boundaries between phenomenon and context are not clearly evident.'

Yin, with the above definition, is trying to distinguish a case study from other research strategies. An *experiment*, he argues, intentionally separates phenomenon from context; *historical* research, although integrating phenomenon and context, normally deals with non-contemporary events; *surveys* can investigate phenomena and context together, but lack the in-depth investigation of a case study approach. That a case study is an in-depth study of a phenomenon is not evident from Yin's definition (Cohen and Manion's definition makes the depth of study clear – *probe deeply and analyse intensely*), although his book *Case Study Research* makes it obvious that he knows that case study research is a detailed and time-consuming undertaking.

This research is concerned with an in-depth study of the phenomenon e-Learning in a contemporary context – a university environment – where the boundaries between e-Learning and a university environment are not obvious. For example, the review of literature showed clearly that there is confusion over what is meant by the term e-Learning; further, it is difficult to compartmentalise e-Learning in a teaching and learning institution; also, the boundaries, if there are any, between e-Learning and learning, a university's primary focus, whether it be through teaching or research, are not *clearly evident*.

Although this research meets Yin's second condition – *the boundaries between phenomenon and context are not clearly evident* – it seems likely that Yin's second condition has more to do with emphasising the interpretative/ constructivist view of the world than insisting that complexity of environment is a necessary condition that needs to be satisfied to justify the use of a case study as a research strategy (in any case, the university environment is a complex environment and one that encompasses different stakeholder perspectives and interest groups). Thus, either definition of a case study, whether it be Cohen and Manion's simple, but helpful, description of a case study, or Yin's conditional definition, meets this researcher's aim of delving deeply into a contemporary phenomenon, e-Learning, within the context of a university environment.

The case study approach provides focus, emphasises depth of study, is based on the assumption that reality can only be understood through social constructions and interactions, and that the context in which the phenomena under study is situated is complex. These facets of case study strategy fit perfectly with the aim of objective 3 of this research: to implement an in-depth exploratory study of staff stakeholder views and practices related to e-Learning preparation, including drivers and barriers, focusing on a specific unit of analysis (a team of academic staff preparing for e-Learning for a particular programme), but obtaining other stakeholder views in recognition that a university is a complex environment and academic staff views need to be placed in context.

This research is also interested in comparing what was discovered in the Literature Review with the results of a case study. Saunders *et al.* (2000, p. 92) believe that a case study approach meets that objective: 'we would argue that case study [*sic*] can be a very worthwhile way of exploring existing theory and also provide a source of new hypotheses'. Although the intended output of this research is not a set of 'new hypotheses', it is nevertheless worthwhile in that existing theory (found in the Literature Review) will be compared against the behaviour of one institution and, as a result, an improved understanding – rather than 'new hypotheses' – will be developed to aid universities in their quest to address e-Learning. Specifically, the findings of the case study will be compared and contrasted with the Literature Review findings in terms of views on the drivers and barriers to e-Learning and staff preparation to deal with e-Learning.

A case study strategy is not without its critics and there are limitations in adopting this approach that require to be addressed. In the first place, the researcher is aware of the difficulty of making generalisations as a result of one case study (Adelman *et al.*, 1977; Borg, 1981), in this case selecting one university in which to study aspects of e-Learning. Bell (2005, p. 11) comments that 'critics of the case-study approach draw attention . . . that generalisation is not always possible . . .'.

The use of a case study in this research instead exploits the concept of *relatability*, where other institutions in relating to situational aspects of the case study and recognising similar issues and problems described in this research work can learn from the findings. Bassey (1981, p. 85), for example, is a strong supporter of the concept of relatability and believes that 'relatability of a case study is more important than its generalisability'.

It is not expected that the fruits of this research will be representative of all universities undertaking e-Learning. It is expected that, in the fullness of time, as more case studies are implemented by other researchers, then the contribution to the e-Learning academic community will be progressively amended and developed accordingly. This view of the contribution of case studies to the research community is one held by Nunes and McPherson (2002, p. 24) who, in their revealing case study of an MA programme in IT Management, accept that it is difficult to make generalisations from one case study – 'it is important to reflect whether theory can be generalised from a single case study' – but who also believe that such a view does not minimise their findings or their contribution to knowledge, for, as further studies are implemented, the body of knowledge in their field of interest will progressively increase and they, in turn, will have contributed. In addition, when the results of a case study are related to a large body of work such as a review of relevant literature, then the contribution to knowledge can prove meaningful and worthwhile to the wider research community.

Yin believes that the criticism against case study research on the basis of an inability to generalise is harsh. He argues that the same type of criticism can be directed towards other types of research. For example, he writes (2003, p. 10): 'However, consider for a moment that the same question [how can you generalize from a single case?] had been asked about an experiment: "How can you generalize from a single experiment?"' He concludes that generalisation is typically arrived at through repeated experiments, and that generalisations from a case study are similarly arrived at through repeated case studies. This is the intention and expectation of this researcher: that the results of this research are used to contribute incrementally to the body of knowledge in the e-Learning community and that, as other research is implemented, then so generalisations can be made in time.

Another criticism of case study research is its validity as a research approach in the research community. Conole *et al.* (2004), although recognising the need for research on e-Learning guidelines for staff, complain that research into e-Learning is often ill-defined and lacking in theoretical underpinning, lumping case study research with anecdotal activities. They favour research that yields results which allow generalisation and so, in their view, are 'more authentic'. Inherent in their interpretation of case study research, is that it lacks academic rigour and is only marginally better than anecdotal evidence. This is to mis-understand the nature of case study research and to ignore the wide uses of case study strategy in the world of, for example, education research. Yin believes that such critics confuse case study research with case study teaching. The latter is used by academics to illustrate a particular point, and though use-ful in serving a purpose in highlighting specific contextual issues to students, is not subject to the same rigour applied to the former and is open to the accusation of bias. In the end, Yin puts this misunderstanding of what case study research is down to two factors: it is not easy to understand and it is not easy to do. To understand case study research requires an attempt to appreciate the factors that constitute a case study, together with its philosophical underpinning (as discussed earlier). To do case study research, he argues, can be time-consuming, and so not an easy option for a researcher. Hoaglin *et al.* (1982, p. 134) – five statisticians – accept the benefits of a case study approach to their research, but recognise that it is not easy to understand or implement and that as a result it receives criticism that is undeserved:

> '*Most people feel that they can prepare a case study, and nearly all of us believe we can understand one. Since neither view is well founded, the case study receives a good deal of approbation it does not deserve.*'

To remove any accusation of (a) not understanding the nature of case study research and (b) sloppy or ill-defined approaches in designing and applying case study strategy for this research, this researcher has done four things. Firstly, the nature and philosophical underpinning of case study research have been discussed openly and related to the nature of this work; secondly, well-established data collection methods will be used to collect the empirical data; thirdly, a structured, disciplined, approach to data analysis will be adopted; and fourthly, precise details of data collection and data analysis techniques applied to this empirical research will be described in detail, be transparent and available for scrutiny.

## Data collection: site and sample selection

The case study site will be Inverclyde University (IU). This case study is not intended to be an exhaustive study of all the e-Learning initiatives operating in the university. Such a study would, in order to produce meaningful results, be enormously time-consuming and perhaps never-ending (e.g. as one moved the study from one School or Faculty to another School or Faculty, or indeed between departments, new blended e-Learning programmes may suddenly appear and others may just as quickly disappear).

The Commission of the European Communities (2002, p. 5) lamented that the 'most successful players [in e-Learning initiatives] to-date, however, remain the well-established and prestigious institutions'. The Literature Review supports that assertion, with many of the e-Learning initiatives coming from leading aca-demic institutions such as Oxford, Cambridge and MIT. IU is one of the 'new' universities in the UK, known for its social inclusion policy. Researching their e-Learning strategies and implementation issues, particularly related to staff involvement and preparation, offers a chance to capture important data from a university that is neither an 'ancient' university nor a 'redbrick' university, but one that has been created in relatively recent times as a result of the removal of the binary divide in higher education

One division within the Inverclyde Business School (IBS) will form the focus of this study. Specifically, eight academic staff involved in preparing module material for Blackboard usage on the China suite of postgraduate programmes in E-Business, Knowledge Management and Management of Information Systems. This will allow a focused, achievable approach to the study, giving academic staff the opportunity to express detailed views on e-Learning preparation.

In a report entitled *The International Postgraduate: Challenges to British Higher Education*, the UK Council for Postgraduate Education (1999) raised the issue of the potential for using new technologies for teaching and learning with international postgraduate students but revealed that evidence of staff e-Learning experiences with international postgraduate students was from 'anecdotal' sources. Selecting X's postgraduate programme provides an excellent opportunity to obtain empirical data on how X's staff prepare for e-Learning and how they prepare for the challenge of dealing with students (and staff) from a different culture.

Convenience sampling was used to select both the university and the postgraduate programmes. It is convenient because the researcher is a student at, and works in, the university. This means that the subjects under study have not been chosen at random and that therefore there can be no claim to achieving representative views related to the broader university community. Instead, this research has as its focus the aim of achieving an in-depth and qualitative insight into e-Learning preparation issues. The review of relevant literature established that e-Learning is an area of increasing interest in the wider university community and so the results of this study will be of interest to those grappling with similar staff preparation issues. Convenience sampling is also used because of time issues and easy access to research subjects.

In order to achieve a three-dimensional perspective of e-Learning at IU, other stakeholders need to form part of this research. To concentrate solely on staff from Division X would produce, at best, a two-dimensional perspective: experiences and views of academic staff. To gain a fuller perspective, the research needs to be widened to include staff outwith Division X. Those who have a part in training academic staff to cope with e-Learning ought to form part of the study. Similarly, *elite* staff – staff with influence, and who are well informed in the organisation (Marshall and Rossman, 1989) – need to be included. Figure J.1 illustrates an outline model of the research units under study, emphasising that, although the views of elite staff are important, central to this research are the views of academic staff.

To capture a School/Faculty view of e-Learning issues, the Dean of the Inverclyde Business School (IBS) will be included in the case study; similarly, the Principal and Vice-Chancellor is included to give a strategic perspective on

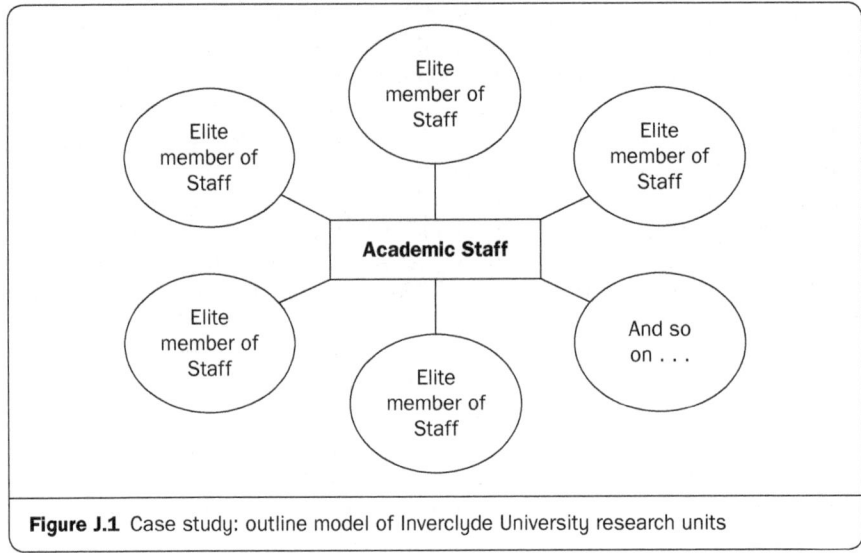

**Figure J.1** Case study: outline model of Inverclyde University research units

e-Learning. The Pro Vice-Chancellor of Learning and Information Services will be part of this study, for his over-arching role in achieving strategic objectives related to the use of ICT. And because Division X is located in IBS, the C&IT Fellow located in IBS (someone with direct responsibility for encouraging and supporting e-Learning initiatives in the IBS) will also be included.

This thick view of e-Learning will be enhanced further by including members of those who have a role in best teaching practices within IU: the Head of the Academic Practice Unit (APU), and a member of the Teaching and Learning Team (LTAS). In effect, empirical data will be obtained from academic staff involved in the field of e-Learning preparation, from staff in the e-Learning Innovation Support Unit, as well as staff with a specific role in offering guidance and strategy on teaching practice; and, for a wider management perspective, data will be captured from the Head of X, the Dean of IBS and the Principal and Vice-Chancellor. Figure J.2 illustrates the stakeholder groups that will form the units of research for this IU Case Study on e-Learning.

### Data collection techniques

Selecting the means by which to collect empirical data is just as important as choosing an appropriate research strategy. This research is interested in capturing qualitative data. As such, the use of postal or email questionnaires, although useful in gathering quantitative data, would not satisfy the researcher's desire for detailed input from staff on their experience of and views on e-Learning. That, in turn, would make it difficult for the researcher to compare and contrast his findings in any meaningful way with the findings from the literature review. Any advice or strategy on a way forward, with regard to

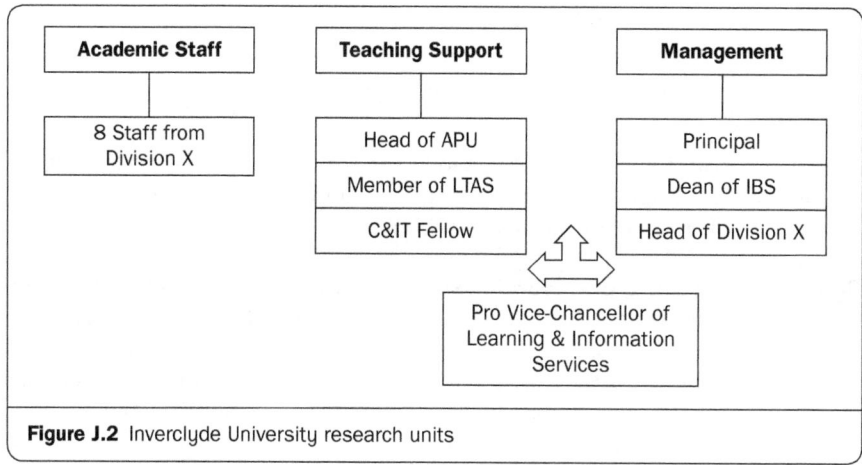

**Figure J.2** Inverclyde University research units

preparing academic staff for e-Learning, would be significantly weakened by the lack of qualitative data from a case study.

Qualitative data will be obtained primarily through the vehicle of interviews. This will open the opportunity to discuss, with the various stakeholders, e-Learning issues in depth. However, in order to establish a framework around the interviews, and to focus on specific issues with different interviewees, the interviews will be structured with questions prepared beforehand, but the interviewer will be open to new issues and follow different, associated leads depending on the responses and willingness of the interviewee. Qualitative interviewing, using structured questions, makes use of open-ended questions – such as, for example, 'What do you consider to be the benefits, if any, of e-Learning?' – to encourage meaningful responses (Patton, 1990).

Interviewing different staff (e.g. Principal, academic staff, member of LTAS, etc.) will allow for cross-comparisons of responses, encouraging different perspectives of similar e-Learning issues to emerge (e.g. rationale for involvement, perceived barriers, staff support required, etc.). For example, the Vice-Chancellor and Dean of IBS will be questioned mainly on strategic issues related to e-Learning, whereas the Head of X, although receiving questions on strategic issues, will be questioned mainly on implementation issues linked to strategic objectives, including support for staff training. The interviews will be recorded, where possible, for two reasons: to ensure that the analysis of data is based upon an accurate record (e.g. transcript) and to allow the interviewer to concentrate on the interview.

The following staff will be interviewed:

1  Principal and Vice-Chancellor of Inverclyde University (IU)
2  Pro Vice-Chancellor of Learning and Information Services
3  Member of e-LISU
4  Head of Academic Practice Unit (APU)

5  The Dean of the Inverclyde Business School (IBS)

6  The Head of Division X

7  Member of Learning and Teaching Strategy (LTAS) Team

8  C&IT Fellow

9  Academic Staff from Division X: module teaching team involved in development of teaching and learning material, using Blackboard, for the delivery of an MSc E-Business to students in China.

By selecting a variety of e-Learning stakeholders, from those involved in strategic decision-making (1, 2, 4 and 5), those charged with providing training to academic staff (2 and 3), those involved in providing IT Support (2 and 5) and learning and teaching advice (3, 4, 7 and 8), and by selecting a Division that has recent experience of implementing an e-Learning strategy (6 and 9), it is expected that an enriched understanding of e-Learning will emerge, one that will better inform the e-Learning process and assist in the development of, for instance, the ingredients for improved guidance to support those faced with implementing e-Learning: academic staff.

Secondary data, in the form of university documents and academic staff teaching and learning material, will also be collected to form part of the analysis. The secondary data will come from a variety of documented sources:

- University Strategic Plan
- IBS Plan for 2002/03–2005/06
- Division X's Strategic Plan
- Learning, Teaching and Assessment Strategy (LTAS) 2000–2004
- APU E-Learning Strategy.

The secondary data, coupled with the interview data, will assist in providing a rich picture of e-Learning in the university by facilitating a comparison of the stated University/Business School/Divisional objectives against staff perceptions, at various levels within the institution.

Appendix A contains the collection of structured questions to be used for the academic staff; Appendix B contains the actual interview transcripts of interviews with academic staff; and Appendix C contains the questions and transcripts of interviews with elite staff.

### Framework for data analysis

To help focus the interviews in terms of reflecting the main objectives of this research and ease the analysis of the qualitative data, the interviews will be structured according to themes. These themes reflect the overall aim and objectives in this research and also echo the main areas arising from the review of literature: *University Drivers for e-Learning, Barriers, Preparation, IT Infrastructure, Academic Staff Motivation* and, to conclude, *Reflections and Future Directions*. It is important not to view these themes as separate topics: they are inter-related. All of the topics could have been placed under the heading 'Preparing for e-Learning'. For example, questions on academic staff motivation relate specifically to what motivates/demotivates staff to become involved in e-Learning; similarly, IT Infrastructure concerns the IT support suitable for an e-Learning environment. The themes are there to help the interviewer and interviewees focus, and as an aid to the analysis of the transcripts. Further, as an indication to the quest for depth as well as focus to this research, academic staff will be asked 4 questions on Drivers, 5 questions on Barriers, 2 questions on IT Infrastructure, 5 questions on Motivation, 3 questions on Reflections and Future Directions, and over 30 questions (including sub-questions) on Preparation. Table J.1 reveals the breakdown of questions (including sub-questions) under each theme, for academic staff and elite staff. An additional theme – e-Learning Strategy – is included for elite staff, to reflect their role in the strategic shaping and delivery of e-Learning.

**Table J.1**  Case study: breakdown of themes and questions

| Theme | Academic staff questions | Elite staff questions |
| --- | --- | --- |
| X. e-Learning Strategy | — | 10 |
| A. Drivers | 5 | 4 |
| B. Barriers | 5 | 6 |
| C. Preparation | 33 | 12 |
| D. IT Infrastructure | 2 | 6 |
| E. Academic Staff Motivation | 6 | 3 |
| F. Reflections and Future Directions | 3 | 4 |

Under each theme, staff will receive a combination of open and closed questions. For example, under the initial theme *University Drivers for e-Learning*, academic staff will be questioned on their knowledge of the University's Strategic Planning Document, the IBS's plan for 2002/03–2005/06, their views on why they think management wish academic staff to become involved in e-Learning, what advantages they think e-Learning will have for students, and on the advantages e-Learning will have for academic staff.

Figure J.3 illustrates graphically the approach that will be adopted to analyse data from the case study, based on the iterative process of *description*, *analysis* and *interpretation* (Wolcott, 1994) of the collected data, particularly with regard to extracting and understanding emerging themes. However, analysis of qualitative data is not a linear activity and requires an iterative approach to capturing and understanding themes and patterns (Miles and Huberman, 1984; Creswell, 1997).

The question of how to record the interviews is one that has been given much consideration in this case study. Taking notes as respondents talk is

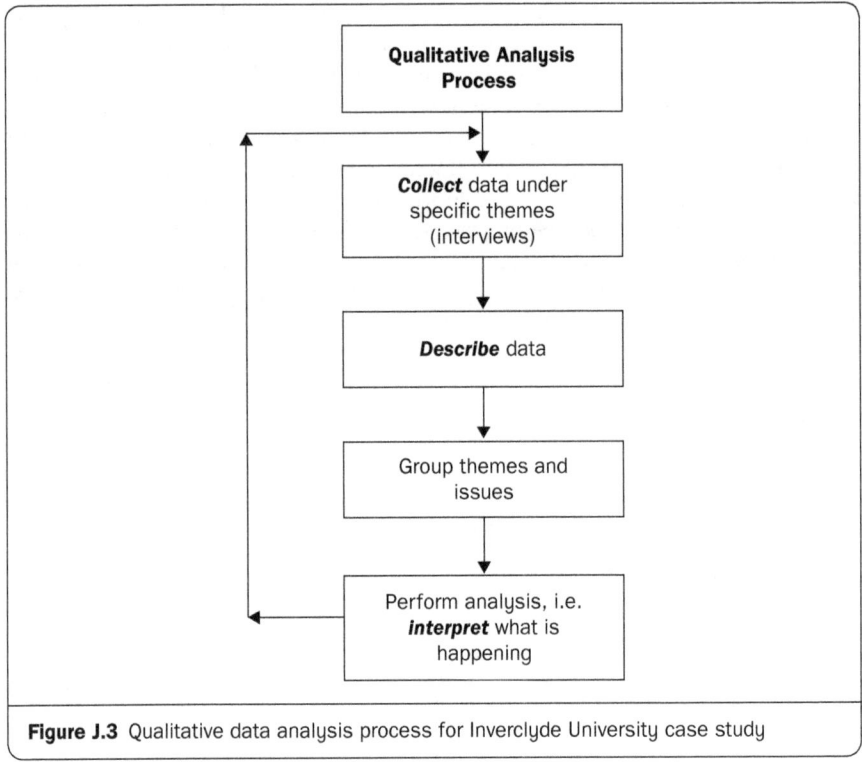

**Figure J.3** Qualitative data analysis process for Inverclyde University case study

one simple alternative. However, the disadvantage of having to write as respondents are talking, and so failing to give respondents your full attention and, in turn, perhaps omitting crucial comments and nuances, together with the problem of having to interpret summary comments some time after the event, in the end made this mode of recording unsuitable. Instead, all interviews will be recorded on tape and transcribed. Such an activity will prove time-consuming, but the resulting data will aid in the researcher's aim of gathering enriching, qualitative data. Overriding advantages include the freedom to concentrate on the interview process and, crucially, the capture of everything said by the respondents. As each interview will be structured under the themes mentioned earlier (Drivers, Barriers, etc.), the transcriptions for each interview will not form one mass of oral text, but rather be categorised under pre-determined topics and sub-topics, in turn aiding the analysis phase. One last point on transcribing: all the interviews will be transcribed. As Strauss and Corbin (1990, p. 31) recommend: 'better more than less'. The researcher has decided to err on the side of caution and have all interviews transcribed.

An important part of this research is to analyse the case study data, comparing and contrasting different stakeholder perspectives (as above), and to reflect on the case study results with respect to the findings in the

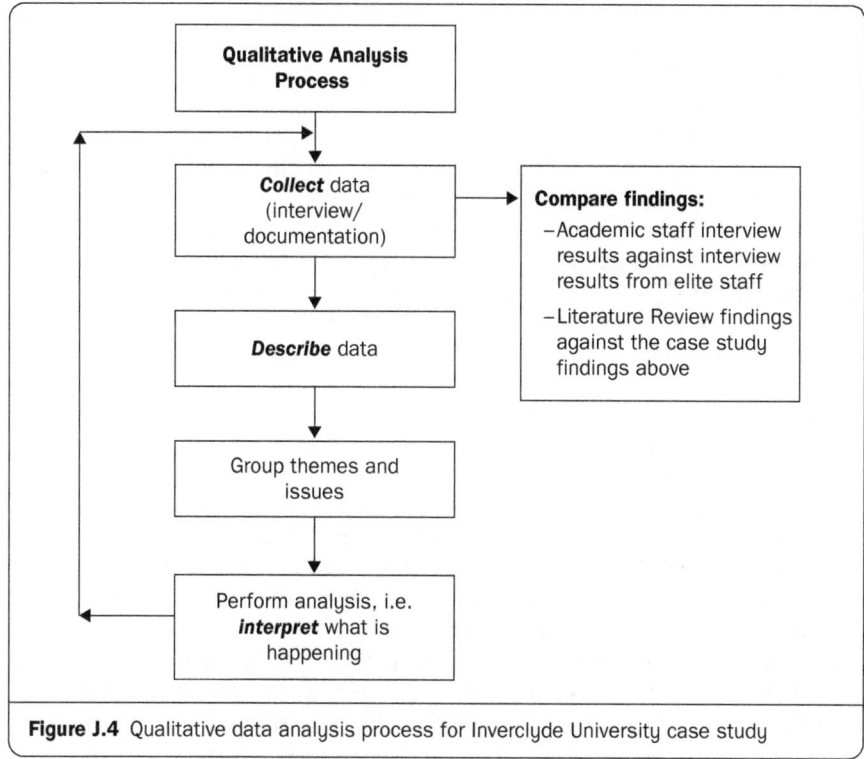

**Figure J.4** Qualitative data analysis process for Inverclyde University case study

Literature Review. Figure J.3 is updated (Figure J.4) to show this over-arching reflective process.

In terms of analysis, there will be a two-pronged approach: first, academic staff case study findings will be described and analysed; second, elite staff case study findings will be described and analysed, not only comparing elite staff findings against each other, but also comparing elite staff findings against academic staff findings. However, it is in the second phase that, as well as comparing elite staff findings against academic staff findings, relevant Literature Review findings will also be compared and contrasted against the case study findings (this is to avoid repetition of comment with reference to the findings in the Literature Review). The essence of this qualitative analysis paradigm reflects accepted practice in dealing with qualitative data, and is perhaps more succinctly described by Bogdan and Biklen (1982, p.145) as 'working with data, organizing it, breaking it into manageable units, synthesizing it, searching for patterns, discovering what is important and what is to be learned, and deciding what you will tell others'.

## Limitations and potential problems

There are limitations to this research, as well as issues related to implementing a case study in an environment where one is both a student and employed.

The results of this study cannot be generalised to the wider research community. Indeed, the results of this research cannot even be generalised to represent the university under study: although key elite staff will be interviewed, and strategic documentation will be referred to, the study of a different programme team in the institution, preparing for e-Learning, may lead to different results. The question of the validity of case study research, in the sense that generalisations cannot normally be made, has already been discussed and addressed. This researcher is using a tried and tested research strategy, appealing to the concept of *relatability* rather than *generalisability*, although it was also argued that generalisation, although not immediate, can take place over a period of time – incremental generalisability – as more empirical research case studies are implemented. This researcher is sacrificing immediate generalisability for depth of study.

Nonetheless, there is also the question of the *reliability* of using such a strategy, particularly when interviews are used as the main means of data collection. In the first place, there is the matter of studying one instance of one phenomenon, the results of which are not open to immediate generalisation. Next, there is the question of depending on a data collection technique – interviews – that relies on personal opinion, and so is open to bias and inaccuracy. Even more problematic, how can the researcher maintain *objectivity* when he interviews colleagues in an environment wherein he works?

In terms of the reliability of case study research, Yin (2003, p. 38) states that the way to deal with reliability in a case study is to 'make as many steps as operational as possible and to conduct the research as if someone were looking over your shoulder'. This research work meets this test of reliability by providing details of the appropriateness of the case study strategy to this research, as well as the data collection techniques to be used, the site selected, the type of staff to be interviewed, their roles, the specific themes that will be addressed, the actual interview questions, and the method of data analysis. In addition, full transcripts are provided. Reliability is sought through a highly structured, transparent, and detailed approach to this study, using a research strategy and data collection techniques that have validity in the research community.

The issue of depending on interviews as the main source of data, when interviewees can exhibit bias or poor memory recall, was dealt with by ensuring that the researcher was not depending on his results from one or two respondents, but on a number of sources. To begin with, a team of academics preparing for a new suite of programmes will be interviewed. A number of views are collected on the same issues from staff working on the same programmes, ensuring that the researcher is not dependent on one or two respondents for key data. Second, staff from outwith this programme will be interviewed, further removing the dependence on opinion that may be factually wrong or skewed and to place academic staff views in a wider context, lessening the opportunity for bias or misinformation. Third, the interview questions are extensive and detailed, where some of the same issues are tackled in different themes (e.g. barriers to e-Learning), which presents an opportunity for staff to consider some topics in different contexts and acts as a check on the consistency of staff views. Fourth, documentation will be used as a means of understanding the university's e-Learning objectives and implementation issues, and also used to compare against interview answers. It must also be accepted that people are not robots and that to err is human, both in terms of expressing occasional bias and making honest errors of recollection; but that for the most part respondents will answer interview questions in a professional, competent manner. Nonetheless, by adopting the aforementioned procedures, it is expected that any bias or misinformation will be minimised.

Interviewing one's colleagues raises the issue of objectivity. Implementing a case study within one's place of employment has the comforting advantage of access to subjects. However, such a scenario brings with it problems that, if not managed properly, may hinder the research and endanger relationships between the researcher and the participants in the research project. There may be the concern expressed that 'how can a colleague, albeit one engaging in research, not be influenced by his prior knowledge of his fellow colleagues' views and bring such knowledge to bear when interpreting transcripts of interviews?' To minimise such an influence, the researcher will adopt the following strategy: until he has secured all staff interviews and completed the transcripts, the researcher will refrain from attending any e-Learning seminars within Division X (to avoid directly or indirectly presenting his views of e-Learning or acquiring the views of his research subjects); after the transcription of interviews, staff names will be replaced by codes (Lecturer A, Lecturer B, Senior Member of Staff A, and so on); and a deliberate and significant time-gap created between the transcriptions and transcription analysis to further minimise the possibility of bias when interpreting staff views. Furthermore, as far as is practical, staff transcriptions will be edited to remove identifying comments. This may help allay any concerns that staff may have concerning their transcriptions, with the added benefit that they may speak more freely.

Another important issue relates to interviewing staff within Division X. These staff are also the researcher's colleagues and, although access to such staff for interview purposes is almost guaranteed, nevertheless access to one's colleagues to facilitate research brings with it responsibilities on the part of the researcher. The researcher now has to view his fellow colleagues, not as colleagues, but as research subjects and this role change needs to be communicated to staff. Linked to this role change is the need for the researcher to gain the trust of his research subjects (in terms of how the research data will be used). It is the intention that interviews be recorded, where allowed, to facilitate accurate analysis. Staff may understandably be nervous about expressing their views openly and so to encourage open and honest discussion, anonymity for academic staff will be guaranteed where requested.

The transcribing of interviews, in particular, is a sensitive matter. To avoid quotations that may embarrass respondents, if identified, or worse, cause concern or internal strife, quotations will not be attributed to specific named individuals, unless prior permission has been sought and given. As stated earlier, when analysing transcriptions, academic staff will be identified as Lecturer A, B, and so on; and elite staff will be identified as Senior Member of Staff A, B, and so on.

Another issue, connected to objectivity, is that it may prove more difficult for colleagues to view the researcher other than a colleague than it may be for the researcher to view current colleagues as research subjects. This is a danger that the researcher is aware of and will attempt to minimise by clarifying the researcher's role and by informing participants of the purpose of the research, the uses of the collected data, and the manner in which participants could assist in the research. The fact that the researcher is recognised within Division X as a researcher with publications in the field may go some way to gaining the respect and trust of colleagues.

This chapter has provided the rationale and operational details of the research strategy used in this research. It has also addressed the limitations of this research and illustrated the approaches used to minimise potential criticisms. The next chapter – Case Study Results – initially places the study within the context of IU, and then discusses and analyses the results of the case study.

# Appendix K: Sample questionnaire

## Data collection technique: Structured interview (Academic Staff)

Interviewer:

Interviewee reference:

Date:

Time:

Place:

*Thank you for agreeing to this meeting. This interview forms part of my dissertation research into e-Learning in universities. The purpose of this interview is to obtain your views on a number of aspects related to e-Learning within Inverclyde University.*

### A. THEME: University Drivers for e-Learning

Question 1A
The university's Strategic Planning Document makes reference to e-Learning targets and objectives.
*Do you know what these are?*

Question 2A
The Inverclyde Business School's (IBS) plan for 2002/3 to 2005/6 also makes reference to e-Learning targets and objectives.
*Do you know what these are?*

Question 3A
*Why do you think university management wish academic staff to become involved in e-Learning?*

Question 4A
*What advantages do you think e-Learning will have for students?*

Question 5A
*What advantages do you think e-Learning will have for academic staff?*

## B. THEME: Barriers

Question 1B
*Which of the following terms best describes your reaction to e-Learning?*

- *Enthusiastic*
- *Interested*
- *Indifferent*
- *Not interested*
- *Concerned*

*Could you elaborate, please?*

Question 2B
*Do you think that e-Learning will have any disadvantages for students? If so, what?*

Question 3B
*Do you think that e-Learning will have any disadvantages for academic staff? If so, what?*

Question 4B
*Overall, do you have any concerns or fears about implementing e-Learning in your department (impact on pass rates, social exclusion, dependence on technology, job security, diminution of power)? If yes, what are your main concerns?*

Question 5B
*Are there any barriers to hinder you becoming involved in e-Learning and, if so, what would you suggest are ways to overcome such barriers (if they exist)?*

## C. THEME: Preparation

Question 1C
*Do you think that you are adequately prepared to cope with e-Learning? If not, why not?*

Question 2C
*Do you think that academic staff need any special skills or aptitude to be able to cope with e-Learning? If so, what?*

Question 3C
*Do you think that students need any special skills or aptitude to be able to cope with e-Learning? If so, what?*

Question 4C
*Do you know how students are being prepared for e-Learning?*

Question 5C
*How do you think IU students will cope/are coping with e-Learning? What impact do you think e-Learning will have for IU on-campus students?*

Question 6C
*The e-Learning environment Blackboard was used as the vehicle to prepare the postgraduate E-Business programme for the China market. Using the suite of post-grad programmes prepared for the China market as a case study of a blended approach to e-Learning:*

(a)   *What will encourage you to place your material on Blackboard?*
(b)   *What will discourage you?*
(c)   *Will you place your material on Blackboard? (and why?)*
       *If yes:*
       *How do you envisage that your material (content and presentation) will differ from that given to traditional IU students for the same module?*

Question 7C
(i)   *Your department invited several guest speakers to talk about e-Learning:*
      (a) *Were these seminars compulsory or optional?*
      (b) *Did you attend these seminars? If not, why not and what would encourage you to attend?*
          *If yes,*
          *– why did you attend?*
          *– how long were the seminars?*
          *– what did you think of the seminars (specifically what did you learn)?*
          *– did the seminars differentiate between on-campus e-Learning and distance learning?*
          *– what models of good practice, if any, were you encouraged to adopt? What did you think of these models?*
(ii)  *The university offers courses in e-Learning:*
      (a) *Are these courses compulsory or optional?*
      (b) *Have you attended any of these courses? If not, why not and what would encourage you to attend?*
          *If yes,*
          *– what courses did you attend (and why)?*
          *– what did you think of them (specifically what did you learn)?*
          *– did these courses differentiate between on-campus e-Learning and distance learning?*
          *– what models of good practice, if any, were you encouraged to adopt? What did you think of these models?*
          *– and do you now feel confident about implementing an e-Learning environment?*

Question 8C
*Is there an e-Learning guidance framework to assist academic staff in preparing for e-Learning?*

## D. THEME: IT Infrastructure

Question 1D
*What do you think of the current system of IT support in IBS? (happy/unhappy with it?)*

Question 2D
*Are you confident that the existing IT support system is good enough to facilitate e-Learning environments? If not, why not?*

## E. THEME: Academic Staff Motivation

Question 1E
*Do you think that academic staff should be rewarded for developing e-Learning environments? If yes:*

– *what sort of rewards do you think would be appropriate?*
– *what incentives are currently on offer to develop e-Learning initiatives, if any?*

Question 2E
*Are you expected to develop e-Learning initiatives in addition to your xisting duties?*

Question 3E
*What would encourage you to become/continue to be involved? What would discourage you?*

Question 4E
*Would you consider the university's approach to involving staff in e-Learning encouraging or discouraging? Why?*

Question 5E
*Do you think academic staff need to be motivated to become involved in e-Learning? If yes:*

– *what should be done to motivate staff to participate in e-Learning?*

## F. THEME: Reflections and Future Directions

Question 1F
*How would you rate the progress of e-Learning initiatives within your department as a whole?*

Question 2F
*What factors do you consider to be crucial to the successful implementation of e-Learning?*

Question 3F
*In what way do you envisage e-Learning changing your role as a university teacher? Is this good or bad (this change)?*

# Appendix L: Sample marking sheet

**MSc. BUSINESS MANAGEMENT**
**(UNIVERSITY OF BARRA)**

**MARKING SCHEME**

**STUDENT NAME:** _____

1st marker: _____

2nd marker: _____     AGREED MARK: _____

| Aspect | Possible mark | Actual mark |
|---|---|---|
| 1. Aims and Objectives | 10 | ___ |
| 2. Literature Review | 15 | ___ |
| 3. Research Methods | 15 | ___ |
| 4. Findings and Discussion | 20 | ___ |
| 5. Conclusion(s) and Recommendation(s) | 15 | ___ |
| 6. Referencing | 5 | ___ |
| 7. Abstract | 10 | ___ |
| 8. Structure and Quality of Written English | 10 | ___ |
| | 100 | **Total Mark:** ___ |

**Comments:**

# Appendix M: Sample completed marking sheet

**MSc. BUSINESS MANAGEMENT
(UNIVERSITY OF BARRA)**

**MARKING SCHEME**

**STUDENT NAME:** Pat Houston

1st marker:      Dr John Biggam

2nd marker:      Dr Alan Hogarth          AGREED MARK:  87%

| Aspect | Possible mark | Actual mark |
|---|---|---|
| 1. Aims and Objectives | 10 | 10 |
| 2. Literature Review | 15 | 11 |
| 3. Research Methods | 15 | 12 |
| 4. Findings and Discussion | 20 | 17 |
| 5. Conclusion(s) and Recommendation(s) | 15 | 12 |
| 6. Referencing | 5 | 5 |
| 7. Abstract | 10 | 10 |
| 8. Structure and Quality of Written English | 10 | 8 |
| | 100 | **Total Mark:** 85% |

**Comments:**

This is an excellent dissertation, showing a clear grasp of both theory and practice. In particular:

- The aims and objectives are crystal clear, as well as being realistic;
- The abstract is faultless, as is the student's use of the Harvard system of referencing;
- The research methods used for his empirical work are appropriate, lucidly explained and justified;
- The discussion follows a clearly mapped-out frame of analysis, eliciting interesting comparisons between theory and practice;

▶

- The concluding chapter admirably summarises the work, revisiting the initial research objectives, and provides logical conclusions, as well as making sensible recommendations on the way forward.

In terms of room for improvement, the Literature Review concentrates too much time and effort on definitions, and he has omitted some recently published surveys that are particularly pertinent to his Literature Review. That said, this is a very impressive effort, for which the student is to be applauded.

# References

Adelman, C., Jenkins, D. and Kemmis, S. (1977) 'Re-thinking case study: notes from the second Cambridge conference', *Cambridge Journal of Education*, 6, pp. 139–50.

Akister, J., Williams, I. and Maynard, A. (2006) 'Innovations in the supervision of social work undergraduate dissertations: group and individual supervision', *Proceedings of the Higher Education Academy Annual Conference*, Harrogate, UK, 5 July. Available at: https://www.heacademy.ac.uk/system/files/web0402_innovations_inthe_supervision_ of_social_work_undergrad_dissertations.pdf (Accessed: 16 April 2017).

Anderson, L. W. and Krathwohl, D. R. (2001) *A taxonomy for learning, teaching and assessment: a revision of Bloom's taxonomy of educational objectives*. New York: Longman.

Azouzi, R., Beauregard, R. and D'Amours, S. (2009) 'Exploratory case studies on manufacturing agility in the furniture industry', *Management Research News*, 32(5), pp. 424–39.

Barrett, E. and Bolt, B. (2010) *Practice as research: approaches to creative arts enquiry*. London: Routledge.

Bassey, M. (1981) 'Pedagogical research: on the relative merits of search for generalization and study in single events', *Oxford Review of Education*, 7(1), pp. 73–93.

Bates, A. (2000) *Managing technological change: strategies for colleges and university leaders*. San Francisco, CA: Jossey-Bass.

Bell, J. (1993) *Doing your research project*. Buckingham: Open University Press.

Bell, J. (2005) *Doing your research project: a guide for first-time researchers in education, health and social science*. 4th edn. Maidenhead: Open University Press.

Bell, J. (2014) *Doing your research project: a guide for first-time researchers*, 6th edn. Maidenhead: Open University Press.

Bettany-Saltikov, J. and McSherry, R. (2016) *How to do a systematic literature review in nursing: a step-by-step guide*. 2nd edn. Maidenhead: Open University Press.

Biggam, J. (2007a) 'Re-thinking dissertation supervision practices: collaborative learning through learner circles', *Proceedings of the International Association for Technology, Education and Development (INTED)*, Valencia, Spain, 7–9 March.

Biggam, J. (2007b) 'Give credit where credit is due: e-plagiarism and universities', *Proceedings of the International Association for Technology, Education and Development (INTED)*, Valencia, Spain, 7–9 March.

Biggam, J. and McCann, M. (2010) 'A study of Turnitin as an educational tool in student dissertations', *Journal of Interactive Technology and Smart Education*, 7(1), pp. 44–54.

Blair, J., Czaja, R. and Blair, E. (2013) *Designing surveys: a guide to decisions and procedures*. London: Sage.

Bloom, B. S. (1956) *Taxonomy of educational objectives: the classification of educational goals handbook I: cognitive domain*. New York: McKay.

Bogdan, R. C. and Biklen, S. K. (1982) *Qualitative research for education: an introduction to theory and methods*. Boston, MA: Allyn & Bacon.

Boland, A., Cherry, M. G. and Dickson, R. (2013) *Doing a systematic review: a student's guide*. London: Sage.

Bone, A. (2003) *Plagiarism: a guide for law lectures*. The UK Centre for Legal Education/ The Higher Education Academy.

Borg, W. R. (1981) *Applying educational research: a practical guide for teachers.* New York: Longman.

Boud, D. and Walker, D. (1998) 'Promoting reflection in professional courses: the challenge of context', *Studies in Higher Education*, 23(2), pp. 191–206.

Britain, S. and Liber, O. (1999) 'A framework for pedagogical evaluation of virtual learning environments', Joint Information Systems Committee (JISC) Technology Applications (JTAP) Report 41. Available at: www.jtap.ac.uk/reports/htm/jtap-041.htm (Accessed: 30 October 2003).

Buglear, J. (2013) *Practical statistics: a handbook for business projects.* London: Kogan Page.

Buzan, T. (1974) *Use your head.* London: BBC Publications.

Buzan, T. (2011) *Buzan's study skills: memory maps, memory techniques, speed reading.* Harlow: Pearson Education.

Chik, V., Plimmer, B. and Hosking, J. (2007) 'Intelligent mind-mapping', *OzCHI 2007 Proceedings*, Adelaide, Australia, 28–30 November.

Cindy, L. (2006) 'Practice-based research: a guide'. Available at: https://www.research-gate.net/publication/257944497_Practice_Based_Research_A_Guide (Accessed: 4 April 2017).

Cohen, L. and Manion, L. (1995) *Research methods in education.* London: Routledge.

Cohen, L., Manion, L. and Morrison, K. (2005) *Research methods in education.* 5th edn. London: Routledge.

Collis, B. and Moonen, J. (2001) *Flexible learning in a digital world: experiences and expectations.* London: Kogan Page.

Commission of the European Communities (2002) *eLearning: designing tomorrow's education*, Interim Report, SEC (2001) 236, Brussels. Available at: http://www.aic.lv/bolona/Bologna/contrib/EU/e-learn_ACPL.pdf (Accessed: 4 February 2017).

Conole, G., Oliver, M., Isroff, K. and Ravenscroft, A. (2004) 'Addressing methodological issues in e-Learning research', *Proceedings of the Networked Learning Conference 2004*, Sheffield. Available at: www.sef.ac.uk/nlc/Proceedings/ Symposa4.htm (Accessed: 2 October 2004).

Coppola, N. W., Hiltz, S. R. and Rotter, N. (2001) 'Becoming a virtual professor: pedagogical roles and ALN', *Proceedings of the 34th Hawaii International Conference on Systems Sciences*, Maui, Hawaii, 3–6 January. Available at: https://www.computer.org/csdl/proceedings/hicss/2001/0981/00/00926183.pdf (Accessed: 28 December 2007).

Cottrell, S. (2011) *Critical thinking skills: developing effective analysis and argument.* 2nd edn. Basingstoke: Palgrave Macmillan.

Cottrell, S. (2013) *The study skills handbook*, 4th edn. Basingstoke: Palgrave Macmillan.

Council of Writing Program Administrators (2003) 'Defining and avoiding plagiarism: the WPA statement on best practices'. Available at: www.ilstu.edu/~ddhesse/wpa/positions/WPAplagiarism.pdf (Accessed: 1 June 2006).

Cowan, J. (2004) 'Education and Learning Wales (ELWa)'. Available at: http://www.elwa.ac.uk/ElwaWeb/portal.aspx.

Creswell, J. (1997) *Qualitative enquiry and research design.* London: Sage.

Creswell, J. (2013) *Research design: qualitative, quantitative and mixed methods approaches*, 4th edn. London: Sage.

Cunningham, J. B. (1995) 'Strategic considerations in using action research for improving personnel practices', *Public Personnel Management*, 24(2), pp. 515–29.

Davies, C. A. (2007) *Reflexive ethnography: a guide to researching selves and others.* 2nd edn. London: Routledge.

Dearing, R. (1997) *Higher education in the learning society* (The Dearing Report). London: HMSO.

Deech, R. (2006) 'Plagiarism and institutional risk management', *Proceedings of the 2nd International Plagiarism Conference*, The Sage, Gateshead, 19–21 June. Available at: http://www.jiscpas.ac.uk/conference2006/ruth_deech.html (Accessed: 3 June 2007).

Denicolo, P. and Becker, L. (2012) *Developing research proposals*. London: Sage.

Denscombe, M. (2012) *Research proposals: a practical guide*. Maidenhead: Open University Press.

Denzin, N. K. and Lincoln, Y. S. (1994) *Handbook of qualitative research*. London: Sage.

Denzin, N. K. and Lincoln, Y. S. (2011) *The Sage handbook of qualitative research*. 4th edn. London: Sage.

Department of Education and Skills (DES) (2003) *Towards a unified e-learning strategy*. London: HMSO.

Dewey, J. (1927) *The public and its problems*. New York: Holt.

Dewey, J. (1933) *How we think: a restatement of reflective thinking to the educative process*. Boston, MA: D. C. Heath.

Dey, I. (1999) *Grounding grounded theory: guidelines for qualitative inquiry*. San Diego, CA: Academic Press.

Dinwoodie, R. (2007) 'Statisticians claim neutrality is compromised by executive pressure', *The Herald*, 1 February, p. 6.

Egger, M., Smith, G. and O'Rourke, K. (2001) 'Rationale, potentials, and promise of systematic reviews', in Egger, M., Smith, G. and Altman, D. (eds), *Systematic Reviews in Health Care*. 2nd edn. London: BMJ Books.

Ekinci, Y. (2015) *Designing research questionnaires for business and management students*. London: Sage.

Emerson, R., Fretz, R. and Shaw, L. (2011) *Writing ethnographic fieldnotes*. 2nd edn. London: University of Chicago Press.

Epic (2002) *Making Scotland a global e-learning player*. Edinburgh: Scottish Enterprise.

Evans, D. (2003) 'Hierarchy of evidence: a framework for ranking evidence evaluating healthcare interventions', *Journal of Clinical Nursing*, 12, pp. 77–84.

Farrell, G. (2001) *The changing faces of virtual education*. Vancouver, BC: The Commonwealth of Learning. Available at: http://www.dlc-ubc.ca/dlc2_wp/wp-content/media/edcp508/farrell.pdf (Accessed: 18 April 2017).

Flick, U. (2014) *An introduction to qualitative research*. 5th edn. London: Sage.

Flood, J. (2002) 'Read all about it: online learning facing 80% attrition rates', *The Turkish Online Journal of Distance Learning*, 3(2), pp. 1–4.

Follett, M. P. (1970) 'The teacher–student relation', *Administrative Science Quarterly*, 15(1), pp. 137–48.

Gash, S. (2000) *Effective literature searching for research*. 2nd edn. Aldershot: Gower.

Gavron, H. (1996) *The captive wife*. London: Routledge.

Geertz, C. (1973) *Thick description: toward an interpretive theory of culture*. New York: Basic Books.

Gherardi, S. (2013) *How to conduct a practice-based study: problems and methods*. Cheltenham: Edward Elgar Publishing.

Gibbs, G. (2008) *Analysing qualitative data*. London: Sage.

Gill, J. and Johnson, P. (1997) *Research methods for managers*. London: Paul Chapman.

Gillham, B. (2008) *Developing a questionnaire*. 2nd edn. London: Continuum.

Girard, J. P. and Allison, M. (2008) 'Information anxiety: fact, fable or fallacy?', *Electronic Journal of Knowledge Management*, 6(2), pp. 125–40.

Glaser, B. and Strauss, A. (1967) *The discovery of grounded theory*. Chicago, IL: Aldine.

Gough, D., Oliver, S. and Thomas, J. (2017) *An introduction to systematic reviews*. 2nd edn. London: Sage.

Guest, G., MacQueen, K. M. and Namey, E. E. (2012) *Applied thematic analysis*. London: Sage.

Harding, J. (2013) *Qualitative data analysis from start to finish*. London: Sage.

Hart, C. (2006) *Doing your master's dissertation*. London: Sage.

Hartley, J. and Fox, C. (2004) 'Assessing the mock viva: the experiences of British doctoral students', *Studies in Higher Education*, 29(6), pp. 727–38.

Haseman, B. (2006) 'A manifesto for performative research'. Available at: http://eprints. qut.edu.au/3999/1/3999_1.pdf (Accessed: 12 January 2017).

Haywood, J., MacLeod, H., Haywood, D., Mogey, N. and Alexander, W. (2004) 'The student view of ICT in education at the University of Edinburgh: skills, attitudes and expectations', *Proceedings of the 11th International Conference of the Association for Learning Technology (ALT)*, University of Exeter, UK, 14–16 September. Available at: http://www.homepages.ed.ac.uk/jhaywood/papers/studentviews.pdf (Accessed: 25 March 2017).

Haywood, P. and Wragg, E. C. (1982) *Evaluating the literature*. Nottingham: University of Nottingham School of Education.

Heisenberg, W. (1958) *Physics and philosophy*. New York: Harper & Row.

Hemingway, P. and Brereton, N. (2009) *What is a systematic review?* Newmarket: Hayward Medical Communications.

Higgins, J. and Green, S. (2008) *Systematic reviews of interventions*. Chichester: Wiley.

Hoaglin, D. C., Light, R. J., McPeak, B., Mosteller, F. and Stotot, M. A. (1982) *Data for decisions: information strategies for policymakers*. Cambridge, MA: Abt Books.

Hodges, C. B. (2004) 'Designing to motivate: motivational techniques to incorporate in e-Learning experiences', *Journal of Interactive Online Learning*, 2(3), pp. 1–7. Available at: www.ncolr.org (Accessed: 20 November 2007).

International Development Research Centre (2010) 'Systematic reviews: frequently asked questions', The RM Knowledge Translation Toolkit: A Resource for Researchers. Available at: http://www.idrc.ca/uploads/user-S/12266049751122265958971Chapter_9%5B1%5D.pdf (Accessed: 3 June 2010).

Jesson, J. K., Matheson, L. and Lacey, F. M. (2011) *Doing your literature review: traditional and systematic techniques*. London: Sage.

JISC (2005) 'Investing in I.T. skills: a strategy for institutional development'. Available at: http://www.jisc.ac.uk/uploaded_documents/JISC-SISS-Investing-v1-09.pdf (Accessed: 8 October 2009).

Jones, M. (2006) 'Plagiarism proceedings in higher education – quality assured?', *Proceedings of the 2nd International Plagiarism Conference*, The Sage, Gateshead, 19–21 June. Available at: http://www.jiscpas.ac.uk/conference2006/proceedings.html (Accessed: 3 June 2007).

Jones, P., Packham, G., Miller, C. and Jones, A. (2004) 'An initial valuation of student withdrawals within e-Learning: the case of e-College Wales', *Electronic Journal on e-Learning*, 2(1), pp. 113–20.

Jung, I. (2000) *Korea's experiments with virtual education*. Washington, DC: World Bank Human Development Network Education Group.

Kershaw, B. and Nicholson, H. (2010) *Research methods in theatre and performance*. Edinburgh: Edinburgh University Press.

King, N. and Horrocks, C. (2010) *Interviews in qualitative research*. London: Sage.

Kolb, D. A. (1984) *Experiential learning: experience as a source of learning and development*. Englewood Cliffs, NJ: Prentice-Hall.

Lafuente-Lafuente, C. and Melero-Bascones, M. (2004) 'Active chest compression–decompression for cardiopulmonary resuscitation', *Cochrane Database of Systematic*

*Reviews*, 3: CD002751. Available at: http://www2.cochrane.org/reviews/en/ab002751.html (Accessed: 3 June 2010).

Laurillard, D. (2001) 'The e-University: what have we learned?', *International Journal of Management Education*, 1(2), pp. 3–7.

Laurillard, D. (2002) *Re-thinking university teaching*. 2nd edn. London: Routledge.

Leavy, P. (2015) *Method meets art: arts-based research practice*. London: Guilford Press.

Lewin, K. (1946) 'Action research and minority problems', *Journal of Social Issues*, 2(4), pp. 34–46.

Machi, L. A. (2016) *The literature review: six steps to success*. Thousand Oaks, CA: Corwin Press.

MacLeod, A. (2007) 'SNP takes a pounding from the Chancellor', *The Times*, 7 April, p. 6.

Macleod, K. and Holdridge, L. (2009) *Thinking through art: reflections on art as research*. London: Routledge.

Markey, K. (2015) *Online searching: a guide to finding quality information efficiently and effectively*. London: Rowman & Littlefield.

Marshall, C. and Rossman, G. B. (1989) *Designing qualitative research*. London: Sage.

Marshall, C. and Rossman, G. B. (2006) *Designing qualitative research*. 4th edn. London: Sage.

Marshall, S. and Garry, M. (2006) 'NESB and ESB students' attitudes and perceptions of plagiarism', *International Journal of Educational Integrity*, 2(1), pp. 26–37.

Massey, J. (2002) 'Quality and eLearning in Europe', Summary Report for Electronic Training Village. Available at: http://www2.trainingvillage.gr/etv/clearing/surveys/sureport.asp (Accessed: 23 June 2003).

McDaid, C., Hartley, S., Bagnal, A. M., Ritchie, G., Light, K. and Riemsma, R. (2005) 'Systematic review of effectiveness of different treatments for childhood retinoblastoma', *HTA Technology Assessment Report*, 9(48), pp. 1–45.

McMillan, K. and Weyers, J. (2013) *How to cite, reference & avoid plagiarism*. Harlow: Pearson Education.

Mertens, D. M. (1998) *Research methods in education and psychology: integrating diversity with quantitative and qualitative approaches*. Thousand Oaks, CA: Sage.

Miles, M. and Huberman, A. (1984) *Qualitative data analysis: an expanded source book*. London: Sage.

Miles, M. B., Huberman, A. M. and Saldana, J. M. (2013) *Qualitative data analysis: a methods sourcebook*. 3rd edn. London: Sage.

Ministry of Education (2004) *Interim tertiary e-learning framework*. Wellington, NZ: MOE.

Moe, M. and Blodget, H. (2000) *The knowledge web*. New York: Merrill Lynch.

Moore, C., Neville, C., Murphy, M. and Connolly, C. (2010) *The ultimate study skills handbook*. Maidenhead: Open University Press.

Morrison, L. and Agnew, J. (2009) 'Oscillating devices for airway in people with cystic fibrosis', *Cochrane Database of Systematic Reviews*, 1: CD006842. Available at: http://www.ncbi.nlm.nih.gov/pubmed/19160305 (Accessed: 16 April 2017).

Mostrous, A. and Kenber, B. (2016) 'Universities face student cheating crisis', *The Times*, 2 January. Available at: https://www.thetimes.co.uk/article/universities-face-student-cheating-crisis-9jt6ncd9vz7 (Accessed: 12 June 2017).

Myers, M. D. (1997) 'Qualitative research in information systems', *MIS Quarterly*, 2(4), pp. 241–42.

Nelson, R. (2013) *Practice as research in the arts: principles, protocols, pedagogies, resistances*. Basingstoke: Palgrave Macmillan.

Neville, C. (2016) *The complete guide to referencing and avoiding plagiarism*. 3rd edn. Maidenhead: Open University Press.

Northwestern University (2017) 'How to avoid plagiarism'. Available at: http://www. northwestern.edu/provost/policies/academic-integrity/how-to-avoid-plagiarism.html (Accessed: 18 March 2017).

Nunes, J. M. B. and McPherson, M. A. (2002) 'Pedagogical and implementation models for e-Learning continuing professional distance education (CPDE) emerging from action research', *International Journal of Management Education*, 2(3), pp. 16–26.

Ó Dochartaigh, N. (2012) *Internet research skills*. 3rd edn. London: Sage.

Ogden, S., McTavish, D. and McKean, L. (2006) 'Clearing the way for gender balance in the management of the UK financial services sector: enablers and barriers', *Women in Management Review*, 21(1), pp. 41–53.

Oliver, P. (2010) *The student's guide to research ethics*. 2nd edn. Maidenhead: Open University Press.

Oliver, P. (2012) *Succeeding with your literature review*. Maidenhead: Open University Press.

Orlikowski, W. J. and Baroudi, J. J. (1991) 'Studying information technology in organisations: research approaches and assumptions', *Information Systems Research*, 2, pp. 1–28.

Orna, L. and Stevens, G. (2009) *Managing information for research*. 2nd edn. Maidenhead: Open University Press.

Pallant, J. (2016) *SPSS survival manual: a step by step guide to data analysis using IBM SPSS*. 6th edn. Maidenhead: Open University Press.

Palmer, R. and Wilson, H. (2009) 'An exploratory case study analysis of contemporary marketing practices', *Journal of Strategic Marketing*, 17(2), pp. 169–87.

Patton, M. Q. (1990) *Qualitative evaluation and research methods*. 2nd edn. Newbury Park, CA: Sage.

Pears, R. and Shields, G. (2016) *Cite them right: the essential referencing guide*. 10th edn. Basingstoke: Palgrave Macmillan.

Pecorari, D. (2013) *Teaching to avoid plagiarism: how to promote good source use*. Maidenhead: Open University Press.

Phillipi, C. A., Remmington, T. and Steiner, R. D. (2008) 'Biophosphonate therapy for osteogenesis imperfecta', *Cochrane Database of Systematic Reviews*, 4: CD005088. Available at: http://www2.cochrane.org/reviews/en/ab005088.html (Accessed: 2 June 2010).

Phillips, E. M. and Pugh, D. S. (2007) *How to get a Ph.D.: a handbook for students and their supervisors*. Maidenhead: Open University Press.

Poustie, V. J. and Wildgoose, J. (2010) 'Dietary interventions for phenylketonuria', *Cochrane Database of Systematic Reviews*, 1: CD001304. Available at: http://www2. cochrane.org/reviews/en/ab001304.html (Accessed: 17 April 2017).

Proudfoot, R., Thompson, A. and Kastan, D. S. (eds) (2001) *The Arden Shakespeare: complete works*. London: Thomson Learning.

Rapley, T. (2008) *Doing conversation, discourse and document analysis*. London: Sage.

Reason, P. and Bradbury-Huang, H. (2013) *The Sage handbook of action research: participative inquiry and practice*. London: Sage.

Remenyi, D., Williams, B., Money, A. and Swartz, E. (1998) *Doing research in business and management: an introduction to process and method*. London: Sage.

Riddell, P. and Webster, P. (2006) 'Support for Labour at lowest level since 1992', *The Times*, 9 May, p. 2.

Ridley, D. (2012) *The literature review: a step-by-step guide for students*. 2nd edn. London: Sage.

Roberts, B. (2007) *Getting the most out of the research experience.* London: Sage.

Rosenberg, M. (2001) *E-learning: strategies for delivering knowledge in the digital age.* New York: McGraw-Hill.

Rumsey, S. (2008) *How to find information: a guide for researchers.* 2nd edn. Maidenhead: Open University Press.

Rust, C., Mottram, J. and Till, J. (2007) 'Practice-led research in art, design and architecture'. Available at: http://arts.brighton.ac.uk/data/assets/pdf_file/0018/43065/Practice-Led_Review_Nov07.pdf (Accessed: 6 November 2016).

Ryan, Y. (2001) 'The provision of learner support services online', in *The changing faces of virtual education.* Vancouver, BC: The Commonwealth of Learning, pp. 71–94.

Saldana, J. (2015) *The coding manual for qualitative researchers.* 3rd edn. London: Sage.

Salmon, G. (1998) 'Developing learning through effective online moderation', *Active Learning,* 9 December, pp. 71–94.

Salmon, G. (2000) *E-Moderating: the key to teaching and learning online.* London: Kogan Page.

Sapsford, R. and Judd, V. (2006) *Data collection and analysis.* 2nd edn. London: Sage.

Saunders, M., Lewis, P. and Thornhill, A. (2000) *Research methods for business students.* London: Pearson Education.

Saunders, M., Lewis, P. and Thornhill, A. (2015) *Research methods for business students.* 7th edn. Harlow: Pearson Education.

Sauve, L., Renaud, L., Kaufman, D. and Marquis, J. S. (2007) 'Distinguishing between games and simulations: a systematic review', *Educational Technology & Society,* 10(3), pp. 247–56.

Scharzbaum, J. A., George, S. L., Pratt, C. B. and Davis, B. (1991) 'An exploratory study of environmental factors potentially related to childhood cancer', *Medical & Pediatric Oncology,* 19(2), pp. 115–21.

Schön, D. A. (1983) *The reflective practitioner: how professionals think in action.* New York: Basic Books.

Shea, B., Grimshaw, J., Boers, M., Andersson, N., Hamel, C., Porter, A., Tugwell, P., Moher, D. and Bouter, L. (2007) 'Development of AMSTAR: a measurement tool to assess the methodological quality of systematic reviews', *BMC Medical Research Methodology,* 7(10). Available at: https://bmcmedresmethodol.biomedcentral.com/articles/10.1186/1471-2288-7-10 (Accessed: 10 March 2017).

SHEFC (2003) Joint SFEFC/SHEFC E-Learning Group: Final Report. Available at: http://www1.hw.ac.uk/committees/ltb/BackgroundPapers/2003-2004/SHEFC_EL/SHEFCe-learnreportJuly2003.pdf.

Silverman, D. (2013) *Doing qualitative research: a practical handbook.* 4th edn. London: Sage.

Silverman, D. (2015) *Interpreting qualitative data.* 5th edn. London: Sage.

Sloman, M. and Rolph, J. (2003) 'E-Learning. The learning curve. The changing agenda'. A report for the Chartered Institute of Personnel and Development (CIPD). Available at: www.cipd.co.uk.

Smith, H. and Dean, R. T. (2009) *Practice-led research, research-led practice in the creative arts.* Edinburgh: Edinburgh University Press.

Straub, R. (2002) 'Hi-tech hope will never blossom amid chaos', *The Times Higher Education Supplement,* 26 July.

Strauss, A. and Corbin, J. (1990) *Basics of qualitative research.* London: Sage.

Stringer, E. (1999) *Action research.* 2nd edn. London: Sage.

Taylor, A. E. (1955) *Aristotle.* New York: Dover.

Tearle, P., Dillon, P. and Davies, N. (1999) 'Use of information technology by English university teachers: developments and trends at the time of the National Inquiry into Higher Education', *Journal of Further and Higher Education*, 23(1), pp. 5–15.

*The Concise Oxford Dictionary* (1998) 9th edn. London: BCA.

*The Herald* (2007) 'Labour leads in new poll but 50% still to decide', 6 April, p. 6.

Thomas, G. (2013) *How to do your research project: a guide for students in education and applied social sciences*. 2nd edn. London: Sage.

Todd, M. J., Smith, K. and Bannister, P. (2006) 'Supervising a social science undergraduate dissertation: staff experiences and perceptions', *Teaching in Higher Education*, 11(2), pp. 161–73.

Tomei, L. A. (2006) 'The impact of online teaching on faculty load: computing the ideal class size for online courses', *Journal of Technology and Teacher Education*, 14(3), pp. 531–41.

UK Council for Postgraduate Education (1999) *The International Postgraduate: Challenges to British Higher Education*. London: UK Council for Postgraduate Education.

UK eUniversities Worldwide (2003) 'Information support for eLearning: principles and practice', UKeU Briefing Paper. Available at: www.sconul.ac.uk/pubsInformation_Support_for_eLearning_Final.pdf (Accessed: 8 April 2004).

Urquhart, C. (2012) *Grounded theory for qualitative research: a practical guide*. London: Sage.

Vaughan, L. (2017) *Practice based design research*. London: Bloomsbury Academic.

Vermeer, R. (2000) 'Review of internet based learning: an introduction and framework for higher education and business', *Computers & Education*, 35(4), pp. 327–33.

Williams, K. and Carroll, J. (2009) *Referencing and understanding plagiarism*. Basingstoke: Palgrave Macmillan.

Wojtas, O. (2006) 'I've had third-year students ask: is it OK to put bullet points in an essay?', *The Times Higher Education Supplement*, 12 May, p. 2.

Wolcott, H. (1994) *Transforming qualitative data: description, analysis, interpretation*. Thousand Oaks, CA: Sage.

Yin, R. K. (2003) *Case study research: design and methods*. 3rd edn. London: Sage.

Yin, R. K. (2014) *Case study research: design and methods*. 5th edn. London: Sage.

Zellweger, F. (2004) 'Institutional EdTech support for faculty at research universities – insights from a case study at the Massachusetts Institute of Technology (MIT)', *Proceedings of Ed-Media 2004*, World Conference on Educational Media, Hypermedia & Telecommunications, Lugano, Switzerland, 21–26 June. Available at: http://citeseerx.ist.psu.edu/viewdoc/download?doi=10.1.1.523.5496&rep=rep1&type=pdf (Accessed: 15 March 2017).

Zukav, G. (1979) *The dancing Wu Li masters*. New York: William Morrow.

# Index